NEW YORK
Property and Casualty Insurance

License Exam Prep
Updated Yearly

Study Guide Includes State Law Supplement and 3 Complete Practice Tests

Leland Chant

This edition contains the most thorough and accurate information available at printing time. Due to the dynamic nature of insurance licensing, examination content outlines constantly change, and this edition may not feature this new or revised content.

This study guide provides complete and reliable information regarding the covered subject matter. The publisher is not engaged in providing accounting, legal, or other professional services. If such assistance is required, seek the services of a competent professional.

If you find errors or incorrect information in this publication or have any questions or comments, please email us at brightideapublishers@gmail.com.

© 2025 Leland Chant All rights reserved.
Published by Bright Idea Publishers.
Printed in the United States of America.
ISBN: 9798372627451

CONTENTS

Introduction			**v**
Chapter 1	**Insurance Regulation**		**1**
	Licensing		2
	State Regulation		6
	Federal Regulation		17
Chapter 2	**General Insurance**		**23**
	Concepts		24
	Insurers		26
	Agents and General Rules of Agency		29
	Contracts		30
Chapter 3	**Property and Casualty Insurance Basics**		**35**
	Principles and Concepts		36
	Policy Structure		42
	Common Policy Provisions		43
	Certificate of Insurance		49
	Terrorism Risk Insurance Act of 2002		49
Chapter 4	**Dwelling Policy**		**53**
	Purpose and Eligibility		54
	General Form Structure		54
	Coverage Forms – Perils Insured Against		55
	Policy Form – Property Coverages		59
	General Exclusions		64
	Conditions		65
	Selected Endorsements		68
	Personal Liability Supplement		70
Chapter 5	**Homeowners Policy**		**73**
	Purpose and Eligibility		74
	General Form Structure		74
	Definitions		75
	Section I – Property Coverages		76
	Section I – Perils Insured Against		82
	Section I – Exclusions		83
	Section I – Conditions		84
	Section II – Liability Coverages		86
	Section II – Exclusions		87
	Section II – Conditions		89
	Sections I and II – Conditions (Property and Liability)		90
	Selected Endorsements		91
	HO-8 Modified Coverage Form		93
Chapter 6	**Auto Policy**		**97**
	Personal Auto Policy		98
	Commercial Auto		107
	Laws		125
Chapter 7	**Commercial Package Policy (CPP)**		**139**
	General Form Structure		140
	Commercial General Liability		142
	Commercial Property		152
	Commercial Inland Marine		169
	Equipment Breakdown Protection Coverage Form		175
	Commercial Crime		178
	Farm Coverage		182
Chapter 8	**Businessowners Policy**		**189**
	Purpose and Eligibility		190
	Section I – Property		191
	Section II – Liability		199
	Section III – Common Policy Conditions		202
	Selected Endorsements		204
Chapter 9	**Workers Compensation**		**209**
	Workers Compensation Laws		210
	Workers Compensation and Employers Liability Insurance		214
	Volunteer Firefighters and Ambulance Workers Endorsements		217
	Premium Computation		218
	Other Sources of Coverage		219
	New York State Disability Benefits Law		219
	Paid Family Leave		221
Chapter 10	**Other Coverages and Options**		**225**
	Umbrella and Excess Liability Policies		226
	Professional Liability		228
	Excess Lines		230
	Surety Bonds		231
	National Flood Insurance Program		232
	Other Policies – Watercraft		235
	New York Property Insurance Underwriting Association		238

Chapter 11	**Accident and Health Insurance**	**243**
	Individual Health Insurance Policy General Provisions	244
	Disability Income and Related Insurance	247
	Individual Disability Income Insurance	248
	Medical Plans	250
	Group Health and Blanket Insurance	256
	New York Mandated Benefits and Offers (Individual and/or Group)	257
	HIPAA Requirements	258
	Medicare Supplements	259
	Federal Patient Protection and Affordable Care Act (PPACA)	263
Key Facts		**271**
Glossary		**291**
Practice Exam	#1	**299**
Exam 1 Answers		**317**
Practice Exam	#2	**331**
Exam 2 Answers		**348**
Final Exam		**361**
Final Exam Answers		**379**
Index		**393**
A Note from Leland		**397**

INTRODUCTION

Thank you for choosing Bright Idea Publishers. You are preparing to pass the New York Property and Casualty Insurance Agent/Broker license exam using the content found in this book. We've developed our state-specific prep books based on the exam content outlines published by testing providers in each state (e.g., Pearson VUE, PSI Exams, Prometric). Leland Chant, who has over two decades of experience in the Insurance field, provides the most up-to-date information that educates test-takers in a streamlined manner. Our number one goal is to prepare you for the actual exam and to help you pass the test on the first attempt.

Study Pointers

- The author presents the information in each chapter based on the exam subject matter outlines provided by the state of New York. This material covers only the information you need to learn for the exam.
- Be sure to take notes. This best practice will help you be proactive and engage in the learning process to solidify these insurance concepts.
- Create an outline or "hint" sheet. This best practice will help you complete a full review at the end of each chapter or the end of the book.
- Review the Exam Index section later in this Introduction to identify how every chapter corresponds to the actual exam. Test questions are associated with each chapter to help focus your study efforts accordingly.
- Every so often, take a break from studying. If you have been hitting it hard, but feel like you're having trouble retaining the information, try taking a few days off to recharge your mind.
- Keep the information fresh by studying until the day of your exam. When you cannot take the exam immediately after finishing the book, you should begin the study and review process again. It is always better to delay taking the exam than to be unprepared while taking it.
- Practice exam answers include the page number to the corresponding section of the book. This feature will help streamline the studying process!

Test Taking Pointers

- Be sure to get a whole night's sleep, and don't study right before you take the exam. This best practice will allow you to be well-rested and alert when arriving at the testing center.
- Carefully read the test tutorial and be sure to follow the instructions. Depending on your state, test providers may divide the exam into multiple parts. In this case, you may not be able to go back to review your answers once you have completed the section.
- Be calm and feel at ease. Breathe deeply and remember it is just an exam. If you prepare, the correct answers will become clear if you put in the time.
- Read every question and all the answer choices carefully, but do so quickly. Try not to linger on any one question.
- If a particular question has you stumped, you can mark it for review and move on to the next question. Sometimes you may answer a question later in the exam, which may jog your memory.
- Answer every question!
- Try to understand what the question is asking. Don't allow unfamiliar terms to throw you off since test builders mostly use them as examples or distracters. Read the question multiple times if necessary.
- Rule out incorrect answers. Each answer you exclude increases your chance of selecting the correct one.
- Trust your first answer. If you studied thoroughly, you know the material. Listen to your gut instinct and try not to overthink the question.
- Keywords such as NEVER, ALWAYS, EVERY, EXCEPT, ALL, or NOT may change the meaning of a question. Be sure to pay extra attention to them.
- Every question is multiple choice, and they are commonly either direct questions, incomplete sentences, or "all of the following EXCEPT."
- Remember that being a little nervous is not a bad thing. Most people perform better when they know the heat is on.
- Most importantly, RELAX! If you put in the work and if you put in the time, the results will be there.

Setting Expectations

Before taking your state exam, you must know the material and be familiar with testing procedures and the testing center environment.

Each state provides a candidate handbook or bulletin containing important information about specific testing procedures:

- Scheduling or rescheduling exams;
- Required identification;
- Arriving at the testing center; and
- Items prohibited in the testing center.

Test-takers should read the Candidate Information Bulletin (CIB) in preparation for their exam. This handbook is on the New York Department of Financial Services website and their state testing provider's (PSI Exams) website.

The Exam	• It will test your knowledge and includes questions about various concepts and laws. • Test questions are designed to evaluate your basic understanding and retention of the material in this book. • Verify specific forms of identification required for your state exam by reviewing the candidate's handbook or bulletin or calling the testing center.
The Testing Center	• Be sure to arrive at least 30 minutes before your scheduled exam. • You are not allowed to take personal items like cell phones or study materials into the testing center. Some testing centers will provide lockers. • Food, drinks, or gum are not allowed inside the testing center. • Have your identification ready when you check in at the front desk. • Adjust the seat height and computer monitor as needed to feel comfortable. • Before beginning a computer-based exam, you will have a chance to take a tutorial to help you learn how to mark and review answers. • Remain focused and do not get distracted by others around you. Other test-takers may enter and leave the room while taking your exam.
Taking the Exam	• Most testing centers will provide scratch paper and a pencil to write down challenging questions during the exam. • When you review marked questions, go over the rest of the questions to ensure you didn't overlook any familiar concepts or terms that change what the question is asking.

Exam Index

The Exam Index will help you focus your studying. According to each chapter, all three practice tests include the number of questions. You will most certainly benefit when taking the actual exam by concentrating your efforts.

New York Property and Casualty Insurance Agent/Broker Examination

150 Questions (plus five to ten non-scored experimental questions)
Time Limit: 2 hours 30 minutes
Passing Score: 70%

Chapter	% of Exam
Insurance Regulation	9%
General Insurance	9%
Property and Casualty Insurance Basics	13%
Dwelling Policy	6%
Homeowners Policy	14%
Auto Insurance	11%
Commercial Package Policy (CPP)	11%
Businessowners Policy	8%
Workers Compensation Insurance	8%
Other Coverages and Options	7%
Accident and Health Insurance	4%
Total	**100%**

ISO

The Insurance Services Office (ISO) is essential in property and casualty or personal lines insurance licensing exams. One of the ISO's many functions is to create standardized property and casualty insurance policies approved by individual states and utilized as a standard policy form for insurers. The basic ISO policy forms are modified to comply with each state's regulations. They may be modified to a degree by each insurance company to create its own policy form.

State insurance licensing exams will test over the standard ISO policies approved by the state to provide equal opportunities for a passing score to prospective licensees from different insurance companies.

CHAPTER 1: Insurance Regulation

This first chapter focuses your attention on insurance licensing, regulations, and definitions that apply to New York insurance laws. You will learn about various topics, such as the New York State Department of Financial Services, its duties to licensing laws, and federal regulations like the Fair Credit Reporting Act. This chapter contains definitions, numbers for time limits, and dollar amounts. Be sure that you know them for the exam.

- Licensing
- State Regulation
- Federal Regulation

Licensing

Insurance professionals must be appropriately licensed for a specific line of authority to transact insurance. The purpose of licensing is to ensure that a producer meets the ethical and educational standards required to fulfill a producer's responsibilities to the insurance company and the public. Licensing regulations establish the requirements, procedures, and fees relating to the qualification, licensure, and appointment of insurance professionals.

Definitions

Producer – *Insurance producer* refers to an insurance agent, insurance broker, title insurance agent, excess lines broker, reinsurance intermediary, or any other person required to be licensed under the laws of this state to solicit, sell, or negotiate insurance.

Home State – *Home state* refers to any district, state, or territory of the United States where a producer maintains their principal place of business or primary residence. It also refers to where a producer is licensed to transact insurance business.

Negotiate – *Negotiate* (or negotiation) refers to directly consulting with or offering advice to a buyer or prospective buyer of a particular insurance contract regarding any of the essential benefits, terms, or conditions of the contract as long as the individual engaged in that action either sells insurance or obtains insurance from licensed insurance providers, fraternal benefit societies, or HMOs.

Sell – *Sell* (or sale) means to exchange an insurance contract by any means, for money or its equivalent, on behalf of a licensed insurance provider, fraternal benefit society, or HMO.

Solicit – *Solicit* (or solicitation) refers to attempting to sell insurance or asking or urging an individual to apply for a particular kind of insurance from a licensed insurer, fraternal benefit society, or HMO.

Process

To qualify for an insurance license, an applicant must submit an application to the Superintendent and declare that all statements are accurate, true, and complete to the best of the applicant's knowledge. Additional requirements for a license applicant include the following:

- Be a resident of New York;
- Be at least 18 years of age;
- Submit a standard licensing application on a form approved by the Superintendent;
- Fulfill the pre-licensing education requirement of classroom work or the equivalent in correspondence work or similar instruction (20 hours for a single line of authority broker or agent, such as Life only broker or agent, 40 hours for a Life, Accident, and Health broker or agent, Personal Lines broker or agent, and Public Adjuster, and 90 hours for a Property and Casualty broker or agent);
- Pay the required fees;
- Pass the required examination for each line of authority.

Licensing Examination Exemptions – A *written examination* is not required of the following individuals applying for an insurance agent's license:

- Ticket-selling representative or agent (train, airline, bus, or sea) for one-time issuance of baggage or accident insurance;
- Any individual whose license has been suspended or revoked (at the discretion of the Superintendent);
- In association with any certificate of appointment for an additional insurer, provided it is under the same line of authority already licensed;
- A nonresident licensee who is presently licensed in another state;
- An applicant who has passed the written exam for an insurance agent's license and was licensed or an applicant who was licensed as an agent but did not pass the exam, provided the applicant applies within two years after the license termination date;
- Any individual previously licensed for the same line of authority in another state (provided that the applicant's home state grants nonresident licenses to residents of New York on the same basis). Such a person will not be required to complete any pre-licensing education. This exemption is only available if the application is received within 90 days of the date of cancelation of the applicant's previous license;
- If applying for a *life, accident and health, or variable life insurance and variable annuity products* license, or any other line of authority considered to be similar by the Superintendent:
    - A person seeking to be a representative of a fraternal benefit society as its agent;
    - An applicant who is a Chartered Life Underwriter (CLU) or a Chartered Life Underwriter Associate (at the Superintendent's discretion);
- If applying for *property, casualty, personal lines,* or any other similar license:
    - An applicant who the American Institute for Property and Casualty Underwriters has granted the Chartered Property Casualty Underwriter (C.P.C.U.) designation.

Refuse to Issue a License – The Superintendent can refuse to issue any insurance agent or broker license if the proposed licensee is found to be incompetent and dishonest or has not complied with any prerequisites.

Exemption from Licensing – An insurance agent license is not required of any officer, director, or employee of an insurance company or organization employed by insurance companies. They cannot be directly or indirectly involved with the actual sale of an insurance policy and do not receive a commission.

Additionally, the following individuals do NOT have to hold an insurance producer license:

- A director or employee of an insurance provider whose activities are limited to clerical, administrative, managerial, or executive;
- The employee or director of a special agent assisting insurance producers by giving technical advice and assistance to licensed insurance agents;
- A person who secures and provides information for group insurance or performs administrative services regarding mass-marketed property and casualty insurance;
- An employer or association involved in the operation or administration of a program of employee benefits for their own employees;
- Employees of insurance providers or organizations involved in the inspection, classification, or rating of risks or in the supervision of the training of insurance agents and who are not personally engaged in the sale of insurance;
- An individual whose activities are limited to advertising without intending to solicit insurance business;
- A nonresident who solicits, negotiates, or sells an insurance contract for commercial property and casualty risks to an applicant with risks located in multiple states insured under that contract; or
- A salaried full-time employee who advises or counsels their employer about the insurance interests of the employer or subsidiaries.

Types of Licensees

The following are the types of licenses that can be issued in the state of New York:

- Insurance agent;
- Insurance broker;
- Business entity;
- Consultant;
- Adjuster;
- Nonresident; and
- Temporary.

Agents – An insurance agent is authorized by an insurance provider, fraternal benefit society, or HMO to solicit, negotiate, and obtain insurance, HMO, or annuity contracts. The agent represents *the insurance provider, not the insured*.

The following are *excluded* from this definition:

- Any regular salaried employee or officer of an insurance provider, fraternal benefit society, or HMO who does not solicit or accept applications and does not receive a commission; and
- Any representative or agent of a fraternal who devotes less than 50% of their time to the solicitation and procurement of insurance contracts and receives no commission.

Brokers – An insurance broker is any individual, firm, corporation, or association who solicits, negotiates, or obtains insurance for an insured (other than themselves) in exchange for a commission. A broker represents *the insured, not the insurance provider*, and acts in the insured's best interest. The following are excluded from this definition:

- Any regular salaried employee of an insured whose duties are to advise or counsel their employer regarding insurance but who does not solicit or sell insurance or receive any commissions.
- Any regular salaried employee of a licensed insurance broker who does not receive any commissions.

Consultants – Insurance consultants advise the public about insurance policies' benefits, advantages, and disadvantages for a fee. The Superintendent can issue an insurance consultant's license to any individual, firm, corporation, or association that has complied with the following requirements:

- Submit a written application and pay a fee;
- Pass a written exam;
- Be competent and trustworthy;
- Must not be an employee or an executive of or own any shares in the insurance company they represent.

Adjusters – An *independent adjuster* is any individual, firm, corporation, or association who, for a commission, acts on behalf of an insurance provider in investigating and adjusting claims. An independent adjuster cannot include any of the following:

- Director, officer, or regular salaried employee of an insurance company;
- Adjustment bureau or association owned by the insurance companies;
- Licensed agent of the insurance company; or
- Attorney at law.

A *public adjuster* is any individual, firm, corporation, or association who, for a commission, acts on behalf of insureds in negotiating a settlement of a claim for loss or damage to property. The following are not considered public adjusters:

- Employee, broker, agent, or other representative of any insurance company who acts as an adjuster; or
- Attorney at law.

Public adjusters must complete *15 credit hours of continuing education* every license renewal period (biennially). Every adjuster must file a surety bond of $1,000 with the Superintendent before a license can be issued or renewed.

Nonresident – A *nonresident* insurance agent or broker is a resident of another state. Nonresidents are authorized or licensed to act as brokers or agents in New York.

Applicants can qualify for a license as a nonresident only if they hold a similar license in another state or foreign country. Licenses issued to nonresidents by the Superintendent grant the same privileges and rights as resident licenses. This allowance is known as *reciprocity*. Nonresidents are not required to take a written exam.

Suppose an individual licensed in another state moves to New York and wants to become a resident broker or agent. In that circumstance, they have to apply for a license within 90 days of the cancellation of the applicant's previous license. Provided the licensee was in good standing at the time of cancellation, they might not have to satisfy the pre-licensing or examination requirements for lines of authority held in the previous state. The Superintendent ultimately makes the final determination.

Business Entities – A *business entity* is a partnership, limited liability company, corporation, association, limited liability partnership, or other legal entity. Before any original insurance broker or agent license is issued, the prospective licensee is required to apply to the Superintendent. The application must include information about the business entity. The licensee is responsible for the business entity's compliance with New York state insurance laws and regulations.

Temporary – A temporary license can only be used to service *existing business*, not to solicit, negotiate, or procure new business. The Superintendent can issue a temporary license to a broker or agent *without* requiring an examination in the following cases:

- To the next of kin, surviving spouse, or court-appointed personal representative of an agent who dies or becomes physically or mentally disabled;
- To a member or employee of a business entity licensed as an insurance agent upon death, disability, or termination of a designated individual in the business entity; or
- To the designee of an agent entering active military service.

The temporary license can be issued for *90 days* unless the Superintendent renews additional 90-day terms, not to exceed an aggregate of *15 months*. In the case of military service, the temporary license can continue up to 60 days after being discharged from service.

Maintenance and Duration

Renewal – Producer licenses will remain in effect unless revoked or suspended, provided they are appropriately renewed. An insurance broker or agent license has to be renewed every *two years*. The license of a broker or agent born in odd-numbered years will expire on their birthday in odd-numbered years. The license of a broker or agent born in even-numbered years will expire on their birthday in even-numbered years.

A broker or agent must apply for renewal of their license with the Superintendent at least 60 days before the license expires. If it is submitted late, the applicant will be subject to a late filing fee.

The current license remains in effect until the Superintendent issues or denies the renewal license. Before a license can be denied, the Superintendent must notify the applicant of intentions to deny or not renew and give the applicant a hearing. If a renewal license is denied, the current license will expire five days after the licensee is notified.

Continuing Education – *Continuing education (CE)* rules are established to protect the public by maintaining high standards of professional competence in the insurance industry. These rules also preserve and improve licensed producers' insurance knowledge and skills.

To renew a license, any resident or nonresident broker or agent must complete *15 hours* of instruction by an approved continuing education provider biennially (every two years). This continuing education requirement applies to brokers and agents licensed in life insurance and annuity contracts, sickness, accident and health insurance, and all lines of property and casualty insurance.

Licensees cannot carry over excess credit hours accumulated during any biennial licensing period to the next period for the same license class.

The course programs of instruction have to be approved by the Superintendent. The providers must file for approval biennially. Each licensee must pay a fee per license for continuing education certificate filing and recording charges.

Assumed Names – Every licensee must notify the Superintendent upon changing an assumed name. Except for an individual licensee's legal name, licensees cannot use any name unless the Superintendent has previously approved it.

Change of Address – The Department of Financial Services needs to be notified *within 30 days* of any change of address, including residence, business, or email address.

Reporting of Actions – A licensee must report *administrative actions* taken against them in another jurisdiction or another state within *30 days* of the final resolution of the matter. The report, filed with the Superintendent, has to include a copy of any relevant legal documents.

Within 30 days of the initial pretrial hearing, a licensee subject to this article must report to the Superintendent any *criminal prosecution* in any jurisdiction. The report has to contain a copy of the initial complaint, the resulting order from the hearing, and any other relevant legal documents.

State Regulation

The Superintendent's General Duties and Powers

The Superintendent of Financial Services (Superintendent) is appointed by the Governor and continues in office until the end of the Governor's term. The Superintendent has extensive powers, expressed and implied by the insurance business, that extend to all financial service providers.

First and foremost, the Superintendent has the power and authority to *recommend, withdraw, or amend regulations* for the following purposes:

- To regulate the internal affairs of the Department of Financial Services (Department), including governing the procedures used in the practice of the Department;
- To prescribe forms and regulations; and
- To interpret state insurance laws and provisions.

The Superintendent has the authority to take action considered appropriate to ensure the following:

- Economic development and financial industry growth in this state;
- Solvency, safety, and prudent conduct of insurance and financial services providers;
- Fair and timely fulfillment of financial obligations;
- High standards of transparency, honesty, and fair business practices;
- Elimination of criminal abuse, financial fraud, and unethical conduct in the insurance industry;
- Education of product users to enable them to make informed decisions concerning financial products and services.

When an individual has been charged with *five separate* civil penalties within *five years*, the Superintendent can assess an additional penalty of up to $50,000. An additional civil penalty of up to $50,000 can be assessed if the individual is charged for every five subsequent violations.

The Superintendent may grant approval, permission, authorization, or any other order affecting an insurance provider, broker, or agent. These orders will only be effective if they are in writing and signed by the Superintendent.

A notice will be considered delivered when it:

- Is given to the individual affected by the order; or
- Has been placed in the United States mail and addressed to either the individual's last-known residence or place of business.

Examination of Books and Records – The Superintendent can examine the records and books of any insurance provider, retirement system, pension fund, or organization authorized in New York. They may do so, as at any time often as necessary during the policy period, to protect the public interest.

The Superintendent will examine insurance carriers as follows:

- All domestic fraternal benefit societies and domestic property/casualty insurers, at least once every *three years*. If the Superintendent concludes that every three years is not necessary for property and casualty, it can be changed to every five years;
- All domestic *life insurers* must be examined at least once every *five years*;
- All other authorized domestic insurers and all rate service organizations that make or file rates at least once every *five years*.

Unless otherwise required by law or regulation, an insurance provider must keep the following for *six years*, or until the filing of a review of the record, whichever is longer:

- A policy record for every insurance policy or contract (the time starts after the policy or contract is no longer in force);
- An application where no contract or policy was issued;
- A claim file (the time starts after the claim is resolved and the file is closed);
- A licensing record for each licensee with which the insurance provider establishes a relationship;

- A complaint record (the time starts after the complaint is resolved and the file is closed);
- A financial record to verify the financial condition of an insurance provider.

When any individual does not submit the requested information within 15 days, the Superintendent can levy a civil penalty of up to $500 per day for each day beyond the specified date. The total penalty cannot exceed $10,000.

Company Regulation

Certificate of Authority – No individual, firm, association, corporation, or joint-stock company can conduct insurance unless authorized by a *Certificate of Authority* issued by the state. When any business is transacted while not authorized, a $1,000 penalty will be assessed on the first violation and $2,500 for each subsequent offense.

To qualify for a certificate of authority, every individual, firm, corporation, association, or joint-stock company is required to meet the following requirements:

- The entity must be fully compliant with all applicable provisions of New York's insurance laws.
- If a stock company, the amount of capital and surplus required by law are either paid in cash or investments.
- If a mutual company, provide statements of at least three incorporators, proof of the required initial surplus in cash or investments, and the required number and amount of bona fide (actual) applications for insurance, with premiums paid for in cash.

Every license must include the following information:

- The name of the licensee;
- Home office address;
- The state or country under whose laws it was organized; and
- The types of insurance business it will provide and the term of the license.

After receiving a notice and hearing, the Superintendent can refuse to issue a license to a company if any of its officers or directors have been: convicted of any crime involving dishonesty, fraud, or moral turpitude (corruption, wickedness) or is considered an untrustworthy individual.

The Division of Criminal Justice Services processes electronic fingerprints statewide for all individuals requiring a criminal background check. Fingerprinting is required for all brokers, adjusters, life settlement providers, bail bond/charitable bail, or intermediary licenses. Fingerprinting is also required for any individual wishing to be a director or officer of an insurance company.

The Superintendent can also refuse to issue or renew a license if the business name is identical or too similar to an existing insurer's name. The Department cannot allow a business name to mislead or deceive the public.

Solvency – An insurance provider is considered solvent if it has the assets to meet its financial obligations. If an insurance provider becomes unable to meet financial obligations at any time, it is considered insolvent.

It is the Superintendent's responsibility to ensure that every insurer, fraternal, retirement system, pension fund, or state fund remains solvent. Each entity transacting insurance in this state must file with the office of the Superintendent an annual statement on or before March 1 of each year demonstrating its financial condition.

An authorized official of the insurer can verify the annual statement of an alien insurer. The statement must provide information on the business conducted and the assets held within the United States for the protection of policy owners and creditors and the liabilities incurred against the assets.

Suppose any authorized entity does not file an annual statement as required or does not reply to a written inquiry within 30 days. In that situation, there may be a penalty of $250 per day, not to exceed a $25,000 aggregate for each failure.

Guaranty Association – *Guaranty Associations* protect insureds, policyholders, beneficiaries, and anyone entitled to payment under an insurance policy from the insolvency and incompetence of insurance providers. The Association will pay for covered claims to a specific limit established by state law. The Association is funded through assessment by its members. Every authorized insurance provider, which must be a member of the Association, contributes to a fund to provide for the payment of claims for insolvent insurance providers.

It is an *unfair trade practice* to make any statement in advertisements that the existence of the Insurance Guaranty Association guarantees an insurance provider's policies.

Unfair Claims Settlement Practices – The following are improper claims practices if committed in blatant disregard for the law or with such frequency as to suggest a general business practice:

- Misrepresenting to insureds pertinent facts or policy provisions regarding coverages at issue.
- Failing to acknowledge and act with justifiable promptness upon communications concerning an insurance claim.
- Failing to adopt and implement proper standards for prompt investigation and processing of an insured's claim.
- Failing to affirm or deny claims coverage within an acceptable period after proof of loss statements are completed and provided by insureds.
- Not attempting in good faith to influence fair, prompt, and equitable settlement of claims on which liability has become reasonably clear.
- Compelling insureds to file lawsuits to recover amounts due under an insurance policy by offering considerably less than the amount recovered in those lawsuits.

Appointment of Agent – Every insurance provider, fraternal benefit society, or HMO conducting business in New York must file a certificate of appointment for its agents with the Superintendent. The certificate specifies that the appointed agent is trustworthy and competent to transact insurance business.

To appoint an agent, the appointing insurance provider must file a notice of appointment within *15 days* from the date the first insurance application is submitted, or the agency contract is signed.

Certificates of appointment are valid until:

- The appointing insurance provider terminates the license following termination according to the provisions of the agency contract;
- The license is revoked or suspended by the Superintendent; or
- The license expires and is not renewed.

Termination of Agent Appointment – When an insurance provider or health maintenance organization terminates an agent's appointment, it must file a statement with the Superintendent within 30 days. This statement must describe the cause of the termination and the facts involved. The insurance provider or health maintenance organization must also give a copy of this notice to the agent within 15 days of the date of filing with the Superintendent.

Licensee Regulation

Controlled Business – *Controlled business* is any insurance written on a producer's property, life, health, or that of the producer's business associates or immediate family. A licensee cannot collect commissions on controlled business above the state-specified limit. Most states will not issue a license to an individual if it is ascertained that the primary purpose of the license is to write controlled business.

The Superintendent can refuse to issue, revoke, or suspend a license if an applicant or licensee receives more than 10% of the aggregate commissions during 12 months from controlled business.

Sharing Commissions – An insurance provider or fraternal benefit society cannot pay commissions to any individual or organization that is not licensed in New York. Commissions can be split among brokers or agents as long as the agents are licensed with the same insurance provider for the designated lines of authority.

Fiduciary Responsibility – Brokers, agents, and reinsurance intermediaries have a *position of financial trust*, a fiduciary relationship, for all funds they receive during their business. Such funds cannot be commingled with personal or other funds without the express written consent of their principals.

Premiums collected by brokers and agents not remitted immediately to insurance providers must be deposited in an identified account in a New York bank. Withdrawals from these accounts can only transfer premiums to the rightful insurance carriers. Failure to properly submit funds could constitute *embezzlement*.

License Display – The establishing broker or agent has to prominently display the license(s) of the supervising individual(s) responsible for that place of business in each satellite office and a headquarters location.

Commissions and Compensation – Insurance providers and agents cannot pay a commission or provide compensation to an individual or organization that is not licensed in New York. In addition, brokers, agents, surplus line brokers, consultants, adjusters, and reinsurance intermediaries cannot pay any commission to or compensate anyone who is not licensed and authorized in the same lines of insurance at the time of the transaction.

No licensed individual can charge directly or indirectly any compensation or additional fees not authorized for reviewing, examining, evaluating, or appraising any insurance policy, annuity, or retirement plan. This stipulation also includes other services in connection with a life insurance policy. If compensation is authorized, it must be made in writing, including the payment amount, and signed by the individual to be charged. A copy of this record needs to be kept for at least three years.

Termination Responsibilities of Producer – After producers receive the notice of termination, they have *30 days* to file written comments relating to the content of the notice with the Superintendent. The producer must send a copy of the comments to the reporting insurance provider at the same time. These comments will become part of the Superintendent's file and accompany each copy of a report distributed or disclosed about the producer.

Without bad faith, fraud, or gross negligence as the cause for the producer's termination, the terminated producer will not be subject to civil liability.

Reporting – Licensees who believe that a fraudulent insurance transaction has occurred or is about to happen have *30 days* from that determination to submit information about that transaction to the Superintendent. The Superintendent will review each report and conduct any further investigation as needed.

Disciplinary Actions

Hearings – Because the Superintendent's role is to enforce insurance laws and to protect the public from unfair trade practices if the Superintendent suspects that an insurance provider or its agent has committed a violation or is engaged in an unfair trade practice, the Superintendent can issue a statement of charges and hold a hearing for any reason deemed necessary (within the scope of the Insurance Code).

The hearing will be held at least *ten days after the notice is served*. At the hearing, the aggrieved party can:

- Appear in person and by counsel;
- Provide evidence why an order should not be made;
- Inspect all documentary evidence and witnesses;
- Obtain witnesses on the individual's behalf.

All hearings will be open to the public unless the Superintendent or the individual authorized by the Superintendent to conduct the hearing believes that a private hearing would be in the public's best interest.

After the hearing, the Superintendent will complete a written report on their findings and send a copy to the individual charged.

Once it has been ascertained that an individual is liable for a civil penalty, that determination can be entered *120 days* later as a judgment and enforced without court proceedings.

Cease and Desist Order – If the Superintendent determines that the licensee violates an unfair claim, unfair method of competition, or unfair act or practice, the Superintendent will issue a *cease and desist order*. Upon receiving the order, the individual must stop doing whatever activities the Superintendent suspects are violating the insurance laws.

An individual who violates a cease and desist order is subject to penalties of up to *$5,000* for each violation. The determination of the amount will take into consideration whether the violation was intentional.

Suspension, Revocation, and Nonrenewal – The Superintendent can revoke, suspend, or refuse to renew a license of any insurance producer, adjuster, or insurance consultant, if, after notice and hearing, the Superintendent finds that the licensee or any sub-licensee has

- Violated any insurance laws or regulations, subpoena, or order of the Superintendent or another state's Commissioner;
- Provided materially incorrect, incomplete, misleading, or untrue information in the license application;
- Obtained or attempted to obtain a license through fraud or misrepresentation;
- Used fraudulent, dishonest, or coercive practices;
- Demonstrated untrustworthiness, incompetence, or financial irresponsibility when conducting business in New York or elsewhere;
- Improperly misappropriated, withheld, or converted any money or property received during business;
- Deliberately misrepresented the terms and conditions of an actual or proposed insurance contract or insurance application;
- Been convicted of a felony;
- Admitted or been found to have committed insurance fraud or any unfair trade practice;
- Had an insurance producer license, or its equivalent, denied, revoked, or suspended in any other state, district, territory, or province;
- Forged another individual's name to an insurance application or any document related to an insurance transaction;

- Improperly used notes or any other reference material to complete an exam for an insurance license;
- Intentionally accepted insurance business from an individual who is not licensed;
- Failed to abide by an administrative or court order that imposes a child support obligation; or
- Failed to pay state income tax or abide by any administrative or court order instructing state income tax payment.

An individual, firm, corporation, or association whose license has been revoked cannot obtain any license for *one year after revocation*. These entities cannot receive any license for one year after the final judgment is judicially reviewed.

Suppose a firm loses its license. In that scenario, a member, director, or officer of the corporation may be able to obtain one if the Superintendent ascertains, after notice and hearing, that the individual was not at fault.

If a nonresident producer's license is revoked, suspended, or nonrenewed in their state, the license will be revoked, suspended, or nonrenewed in New York. Reinstatement in the producer's home state means reinstatement in New York.

When an administrative action has been taken against a licensee, the licensee must report it to the Superintendent within *30 days*.

The Superintendent will give the applicant or licensee a written reason for action. The applicant or licensee has *ten days* to request a hearing.

Penalties – If the licensee violates *insurance licensing laws*, the Superintendent can issue a penalty instead of suspending or revoking the individual's license. The penalty can be up to $500 for each offense and up to $2,500 for all combined violations.

Unless the court orders a stay, the licensee has *20 days* to pay the penalty. When the licensee does not pay the fine within the allotted time, the Superintendent can suspend or revoke the Individual's license.

Any violation of the *Insurance Code provisions* will be deemed a *misdemeanor* unless categorized as a felony.

Suppose, after receiving a notice and hearing, the Superintendent determines that an authorized insurance provider, broker, representative, or adjuster has willfully violated the Insurance Code. In that circumstance, the Superintendent can order the individual to pay a penalty of up to $1,000 for every offense. Failure to pay the penalty within *30 days* of the order will be considered a further violation of the provision of the Code. However, no penalty will be assessed if the New York Insurance Code otherwise provides a monetary fine.

Prohibitions – In addition to criminal liability, the Superintendent can impose a *civil penalty* of up to $5,000 and the claim amount for each violation upon any individual who committed a *fraudulent insurance act*. The Superintendent can also assess civil penalties on anyone who knowingly assists, solicits, or conspires with another to apply for a premium reduction with materially false information. This stipulation also applies to individuals concealing application information regarding any material fact.

Aiding an Unauthorized Insurer – Neither an individual nor a corporation can act as a broker or agent for an insurer that is not licensed to solicit, negotiate, or sell insurance or annuity contracts. The law allows for some exceptions for reinsurance brokers.

Any individual who violates this regulation can be subject to a $500 penalty for each transaction and any other penalties provided by state law.

Unfair and Prohibited Practices

Insurance companies and producers cannot engage in trade practices defined as, or determined to be, unfair or deceptive acts or practices or an unfair method of competition in the insurance business.

It is considered an unfair trade practice to commit an unfair method of competition deliberately. Unfair trade practices also include participating in such actions with enough frequency that engaging in unfair marketing practices indicates a general business practice.

If, after a hearing, the Department of Insurance determines that a producer or an insurance company has committed an unfair trade or competition practice, the Department can issue an order requiring the individual to cease and desist from participating in the method of competition, act, or practice, and impose penalties for violation of insurance laws.

Misrepresentation – It is illegal to publish, issue, or circulate any illustration or sales material that is misleading, false, or deceptive as to policy benefits or terms, benefits, advantages, the payment of dividends, or the financial condition of any insurance provider. This regulation applies to oral statements made by an insurance provider or its producers and representatives.

It is illegal for a broker or agent to show an incomplete comparison of policies to induce an individual to forfeit, lapse, or surrender a policy.

Any broker or agent who willingly commits misrepresentation and knowingly receives any compensation or commission for a sale induced by the misrepresentation is subject to a civil penalty. In addition, the broker or agent is subject to a civil penalty for any compensation or commission lost by any broker, agent, or representative due to misleading or false statements. Any individual so offended can also sue the broker or agent for the amount gained and the penalty paid during the misrepresentation.

It is considered an unfair trade practice in New York to knowingly misrepresent to a claimant the terms, benefits, and advantages of the insurance policy relevant to the claim. Insurance providers cannot deny any element of a claim based on a specific policy provision or exclusion unless reference to such a provision or exclusion is made in writing. Any payment or settlement that does not include all the amounts reasonably expected from the claim will be considered a communication that misrepresents a pertinent policy provision.

The concept of misrepresentation during policy replacement applies specifically to life insurance and annuities. All brokers and agents must be aware of and in compliance with this regulation. Any replacement of individual life policies or individual annuity contracts of an insurance provider by an agent, representative, or different insurance provider must conform to the following standards implemented by the Superintendent:

- Specify what constitutes the replacement of a life insurance policy or annuity contract and the proper disclosure and notification procedures to replace a policy or contract;
- Require notification of the proposed replacement to the insurance provider whose policies or contracts are intended to be replaced;
- Require the timely exchange of illustrative and cost information necessary for the completion of a comparison of the proposed and replaced coverage; and
- Allow a 60-day period following issuance of the replacement policies or contracts during which the insured can return the policies or contracts and reinstate the replaced policies or contracts.

False Advertising – Advertising covers a wide range of communication, from publishing an ad in a magazine or newspaper to broadcasting a commercial on television or the Internet. Advertisements cannot include any deceptive, untrue, or misleading statements that apply to the business of insurance or anyone who conducts it. Violating this rule is called *false advertising*.

It is forbidden to advertise or circulate any materials that are deceptive, untrue, or misleading. Deceptive or false advertising specifically includes *misrepresenting* any of the following:

- Benefits, terms, conditions, or advantages of any insurance policy;
- The financial condition of any individual or the insurance carrier;
- Any dividends to be received from the policy or previously paid out; or
- The true intention of an assignment or loan against a policy.

Representing an insurance policy as a share of stock or utilizing names or titles that could misrepresent the true nature of a policy will be considered false advertising. Also, a person or an entity cannot use a name that deceptively suggests it is an insurance provider.

Rebating – *Rebating* is any inducement offered during the sale of insurance products not stated in the policy. It is illegal to induce an individual to encourage purchasing an insurance policy. Rebates include sharing commissions, money, promises, personal services, and inducements. Both the offer and acceptance involved in any rebate are illegal.

Articles of merchandise with a stamped or printed advertisement of the broker, agent, or insurer are not rebates if they are valued at *$25 or less*.

Defamation of an Insurer – *Defamation* occurs when oral or written statements are intended to injure a person engaged in the insurance business. It also applies to statements that are maliciously critical of the financial condition of any individual or company.

Unfair Discrimination – *Discrimination* in premiums, rates, or policy benefits for individuals within the *same class* or with the same life expectancy is illegal. Insurers cannot discriminate based on a person's race, national origin, marital status, sexual orientation, gender identity, creed, or ancestry unless it is for business purposes or required by law.

Insurance Frauds Prevention Act

The *Insurance Frauds Prevention Act* allows the Superintendent and the Department to use their expertise to investigate and uncover insurance frauds, stop fraudulent activities more effectively, and receive assistance from state and federal law enforcement agencies.

Insurance Frauds Bureau – The Insurance Frauds Bureau in the Department continues its operations under the Superintendent's supervision, who can designate one or more units to investigate and prevent fraud.

Procedures – Suppose the Insurance Frauds Bureau has reason to believe that an individual is engaged or is about to engage in a fraudulent act. In that situation, it has *30 days* to file a report, including any information about the circumstances and the parties involved.

The Superintendent can conduct investigations within New York or outside of the state.

Immunity – As long as the suspected fraudulent transaction was reported in good faith, the Superintendent will place no civil liability against the individual who reported it.

Fraud Prevention Plans and Special Investigations Units – Every insurance provider writing private or commercial insurance must file a fraud prevention plan to detect, prevent, and investigate fraudulent insurance activities within 120 days. The plan needs to include the details necessary for successfully implementing the plan.

The following rules apply to the implementation of the plan:

- If the Superintendent does not return a fraud detection and prevention plan to the insurance provider within 120 days of filing, it is considered approved.
- If the plan is returned, the insurance provider has up to 45 days to make the necessary revisions and return it to the Superintendent.
- If the plan has been returned more than once, the insurance provider is entitled to a hearing.
- If the insurance provider fails to submit a final plan within 30 days after the determination of the hearing, the Superintendent can assess a fine of up to $2,000 per day or impose an appropriate fraud detection and prevention plan.

Instead of a special investigations unit within the insurance company, an insurer can contract an outside company to provide the investigative services. This insurer is also required to file a detailed plan with the Superintendent.

Consumer Privacy Regulation

Treatment of nonpublic personal financial information concerning individuals requires the insurer to:

- Provide notice about its privacy policies and practices *no later than when an insurance policy is delivered*, yearly after that. Suppose information is collected from a source other than public records or the applicant. In that case, notice must be given when the information is collected.
- Describe the conditions under which a licensee can disclose an individual's nonpublic personal financial information to affiliates and nonaffiliated third parties. The insurance provider is exempt from the disclosure requirements *if the insured requests or authorizes* a transaction related to processing, servicing, or maintaining an insurance product.
- Provide methods for individuals to prevent a licensee from disclosing personal information. An *opt-out notice has to be provided* to give the consumer a choice to limit the disclosure of that information.

Producer Compensation Transparency

The regulation on Producer Compensation Transparency was promoted to help regulate the activities and practices of insurance providers and their producers and protect the public by establishing minimum disclosure requirements concerning the role of insurance producers and their compensation.

For this regulation, the term *compensation* refers to anything of value, including money, gifts, prizes, trips, loans, or credits, whether paid as a commission or otherwise. Advertisements or promotional goods with the insurance provider's name or logo are not compensation as long as their aggregate value per insurer per year is less than $100.

This regulation *does not apply* to:

- Placement of reinsurance;
- Placement of insurance with a captive insurer;
- Producers who have no direct solicitation or sales contact with the purchasers;
- Sale of insurance by an individual who is not required to be licensed; or
- Renewals.

Disclosure of Producer Compensation – A disclosure of producer compensation needs to include the following information:

- A description of the producer's role in the transaction;
- Whether or not the producer will receive compensation from the sales;
- An explanation of factors that affect the amount of producer compensation;
- The purchaser's right to request and obtain information regarding the producer's compensation.

Producers must keep copies of all written disclosures provided to the purchasers for at least *three years*.

Cyber Regulation

To combat the rising menace of hackers extracting sensitive data from companies' databases, New York has established a new regulation outlining the minimum standards for a compulsory cybersecurity program (23 NYCRR 500).

All financial services companies are required to implement and maintain a cybersecurity program designed to prevent cyberattacks and recover if one occurs. The organization's senior management has to be responsible for the cybersecurity program and ensure the safety and soundness of the organization and protect its customers. Regulated entities are required to file an *annual certification* confirming compliance with these regulations.

Definitions

Covered Entity – Any individual operating under a license, certificate, registration, or similar authorization under the Insurance Law, the Banking Law, or the Financial Services Law.

Cybersecurity Event – Any effort to obtain unauthorized access to an Information System (or the data stored on it), whether successful or unsuccessful.

Information System – An organized system designed to collect, maintain, and transmit electronic Nonpublic Information.

Nonpublic Information – Any business-related information that is not publicly available which, if misused, could jeopardize a covered entity's security and operations; any personally identifiable information (e.g., social security numbers or credit card numbers); and any information (other than gender and age) related to health care.

Multi-Factor Authentication – A form of authentication through the verification of at least two factors:

1. Knowledge factor, like a password;
2. Possession factors, like a token or text message through a mobile phone; or
3. Inherence factors, like a biometric characteristic.

Penetration Testing – Refers to a test method where assessors try to bypass or defeat an information system's security features in attempting to penetrate databases or controls from outside or inside the information systems.

Chief Information Security Officer (CISO) – Each covered entity must designate a qualified person to administer and institute its cybersecurity program and enforce its policies.

Cybersecurity Program – All nongovernmental individuals operating under the New York Department of Financial Services must design, implement, and maintain a Cybersecurity Program. This plan must be based on its Risk Assessment that ensures the integrity, confidentiality, and availability of Information Systems. The six critical functions of the Cybersecurity Program include:

1. Identifying cybersecurity risks;
2. Using defensive infrastructure and putting policies and procedures in place to prevent cybersecurity risks;
3. Monitoring and recognizing cybersecurity events;
4. Countering any attacks to reduce undesirable outcomes;
5. Recovering from such events; and
6. Reporting the event as obligated.

The *Cybersecurity Policy* is an approved written document that outlines the policies and procedures in place to keep the Information System secure and must incorporate the following:

- Information security, data governance, and classification;
- Access controls and identity management;
- Asset inventory and device management;
- Disaster recovery and business continuity planning and resources;
- Network security and systems monitoring;
- Systems operations and availability concerns;
- Application and systems development and quality assurance;
- Environmental and physical security controls;
- Vendor and third-party service provider management;
- Customer data privacy; and
- Risk assessment and incident response.

Covered Entities need to ensure that the nonpublic information and information systems accessible by *Third-Party Service Providers* (those authorized to access nonpublic information) are kept secure. The established policies and procedures must include the following:

- Identification and risk assessment of third-party service providers with access to nonpublic information;
- Minimum cybersecurity practices that need to be upheld by third-party service providers;
- Processes in place to determine the effectiveness of the third party's cybersecurity practices;
- Annual (at minimum) evaluation of third parties and their cybersecurity practices.

Training and Monitoring – As part of its cybersecurity program, all Covered Entities *must*:

1. Implement risk-based controls, policies, and procedures intended to monitor authorized users' activity and detect unauthorized tampering with, or access or use of, nonpublic information by these authorized users; and
2. Provide consistent cybersecurity awareness training for all personnel updated to reflect risks identified by the covered entity in a risk assessment.

After a cybersecurity event has been identified, an insurance provider or its agents *must report it* to the Department of Financial Services within *72 hours*.

Federal Regulation

Fair Credit Reporting Act

The *Fair Credit Reporting Act (FCRA)* created procedures that consumer-reporting agencies must follow. The FCRA ensures that records are accurate, confidential, relevant, and properly used. This law also protects consumers against obsolete or inaccurate financial or personal information.

Insurance providers determine risk acceptability by checking the individual risk against several factors directly related to the risk's potential for loss. Along with these factors, an underwriter will sometimes ask for additional information about a particular risk from an outside source. These reports usually fall into two categories: Consumer Reports and Investigative Consumer Reports. Someone with a legitimate business purpose can use both reports, including employment screening, underwriting, and credit transactions.

Consumer Reports include written and oral information about a consumer's character, credit, habits, or reputation collected by a reporting agency from credit reports, employment records, and other public sources.

Investigative Consumer Reports are comparable to Consumer Reports. They also provide information on the consumer's reputation, character, and habits. The main *difference* is that insurers obtain the data through an investigation and interviews with the consumer's friends, neighbors, and associates. In contrast to Consumer Reports, insurers cannot get an Investigative Report unless the consumer receives written notification about the report within three days of the date the consumer requested the report. Consumers must receive confirmation that they have a right to ask for additional information regarding the report. The reporting agency or insurance provider has five days to provide the consumer with the additional information.

The reporting agency and information users are subject to a civil action for failure to comply with the FCRA's provisions. Any individual who intentionally and deliberately obtains information on a consumer under pretenses from a consumer reporting agency may be fined or imprisoned for up to two years.

Any person who *unwittingly* violates the FCRA is liable in the amount equal to the loss to the consumer and any reasonable attorney fees incurred during the process.

Any individual who *knowingly* violates the FCRA enough to constitute an overall pattern or business practice will be subject to a penalty of up to $2,500.

Under the FCRA, if an insurance policy is modified or declined because of information in either an investigative or consumer report, the consumer must be notified and provided with the reporting agency's name and address. It is the consumer's right to know what information is in the report. Consumers have a right to know the identity of anyone who has obtained a report during the past year. When the consumer challenges any information in the report, the reporting agency must reinvestigate and amend the report if warranted. Also, when a consumer report is inaccurate and corrected, the agency must send the updated information to all parties who reported the erroneous information within the last two years.

Consumer reports cannot contain specific types of information if the bank or insurer requests a report in connection with a credit transaction of less than $150,000 or a life insurance policy. The *prohibited information* includes arrest records or convictions of crimes and bankruptcies more than ten years old. It also includes civil suits or other negative information over seven years old. The FCRA defines a negative report as providing information about a customer's delinquencies, late payments, insolvency, or defaults.

Fraud and False Statements Including 1033 Waiver

It is fraudulent for anyone engaged in the insurance business to deliberately make any oral or written statement with the intent to deceive. *Unlawful insurance fraud* includes false statements or omissions of material fact, false information and statements made on an insurance application, and malicious statements regarding the financial condition of an insurance company.

Anyone engaged in insurance whose activities affect interstate commerce and who intentionally makes false material statements can be imprisoned for up to ten years, fined, or both. If the activity jeopardized the security of the accompanied insurance provider, the sentence could be extended up to *15 years*. Anyone acting as an agent, officer, director, or another insurance employee caught embezzling funds will be subject to the imprisonment and fines previously described. However, if the embezzlement was in an amount that is *less than $5,000*, prison time could be reduced to one year.

Federal law makes it illegal for anyone convicted of a crime involving breach of trust, dishonesty, or a violation of the *Violent Crime Control and Law Enforcement Act of 1994* to work in the insurance business affecting interstate commerce without written consent from an insurance regulatory official (Commissioner of Insurance, Director of Insurance, etc.) This requirement is known as a 1033 waiver. The consent from the official has to specify that it is granted for the purpose of 18 U.S.C. 1033. Anyone convicted of a felony involving breach of trust or dishonesty, who also transacts insurance, will be imprisoned for up to five years, fined, or both.

Anyone who engages in conduct that violates Section 1033 can be subject to a civil penalty of not more than $50,000 for each violation or the amount of payment received from the prohibited conduct, whichever is greater.

Section 1034: Civil Penalties and Injunctions – According to this section, the *Attorney General* can bring a civil action in the appropriate United States district court against any individual who engages in conduct constituting an offense under section 1033 and, upon evidence of such conduct, the individual will be subject to a civil penalty of not more than $50,000 for each violation, or the amount of payment which the individual offered or received for the prohibited conduct, whichever is greater.

Numbers, Dollars, Days, and Dates – To perform your best on the state regulations portion of the licensing exam, it is essential to memorize the following numbers and their definitions.

Department of Financial Services Regulations	
5 years	Examination of domestic insurers other than property and casualty (three years)
10 days	Notice given for hearing
10 days	For applicant or licensee to demand a hearing after an action
Licensing and Appointment Requirements	
18	Age to apply for a license
2 years	Producer license is valid
60 days	Before license expiration, agent must file an application for renewal
5 days	License expires after renewal license is denied
90 days	Length of one-term temporary license
15 months	Maximum length of a temporary license
15 days	For an insurer to file an agent's appointment with the Superintendent
30 days	For an insurer to notify the Superintendent of the termination of a producer's appointment
15 days	Send a notice of appointment termination to the producer
Miscellaneous Producer Regulations	
20 hours	Pre-licensing education for Life only or Accident and Health only agent or broker
40 hours	Pre-licensing education for a Life, Accident and Health agent or broker, Personal Lines agent or broker and Public Adjuster
90 hours	Pre-licensing education for Property/Casualty agent or broker
15 hours	Continuing Education (CE) required every two years

Miscellaneous Producer Regulations *(Continued)*	
15 days	Provide requested information to the Superintendent
30 days	To inform the Superintendent about change of address
30 days	To notify the Superintendent of administrative action against a producer
20 days	To pay the penalty for licensing law violations without further action
30 days	To pay the penalty for violation provisions of the Insurance Code
30 days	To report any fraudulent insurance transactions to the Superintendent
6 years	Keep records of insurance transactions
10%	Maximum allowed amount of commissions from controlled business in one year
Important Dollar Amounts	
$500	Penalty for each offense in violation of state insurance laws
$2,500	Maximum aggregate penalty for all offenses in violation of state insurance laws
$10	Late fee for license renewal
$25	Maximum value of any merchandise given by an insurer, broker, or agent to avoid rebating
$2,000	Fine per day without an appropriate Fraud Prevention Plan
$2,500	Fine for willful noncompliance with the Fair Credit Reporting Act
$5,000	Fine for violation of a cease and desist order

Chapter Review

This chapter provided an overview of insurance regulations and discussed licensing and education requirements, duties and authorities, and the code of ethics for producers. Let's review the key facts:

LICENSING REQUIREMENTS	
Licensing Process	• Complete the pre-licensing education • Pass the examination • Submit an application and pay the fees
Types of Licenses	• Individuals: resident and nonresident • Business entities • *Temporary license* – valid for 90 days; issued to maintain the existing business

Maintenance and Duration	• Must be renewed every two years
	• *Continuing education* – must be completed every reporting period
	• Disciplinary actions:
	  - License denial, suspension, revocation, or nonrenewal
	  - Cease and desist order
	  - Monetary penalties

STATE AND FEDERAL REGULATIONS	
Superintendent of Financial Services	<ul><li>Appointed by the Governor until the end of the Governor's term</li><li>Regulates the internal affairs of the Department of Financial Services</li><li>Does not write laws</li><li>Examines all authorized insurers</li></ul>
Agent Regulation	<ul><li>Must be licensed in the line of authority for which the agent transacts insurance</li><li>Avoid unfair trade practices</li><li>Controlled business commissions cannot exceed 10% of aggregate commissions in 12 months</li></ul>
Insurer Regulation	<ul><li>Must obtain a Certificate of Authority</li><li>Responsible for agent appointments</li><li>Solvency requirements (must be a member of the Guaranty Association)</li><li>Avoid unfair trade practices or unfair claim settlements</li></ul>
Fair Credit Reporting Act	<ul><li>Protects consumers against circulation of inaccurate or obsolete information</li><li>*Consumer report* – information about a consumer's credit, character, habits, or reputation</li><li>*Investigative consumer report* – similar to a consumer report, only the information is obtained through investigation and interviews</li><li>The consumer has the right to know what was in the report</li></ul>

CHAPTER 2:
General Insurance

Before you learn about specific types of policies and their provisions, you will first need to understand some basic concepts and terms associated with the insurance industry. First, you must know what insurance is and who or what can become insured. You will learn about the most common types of insurers, their classifications, and their specific functions in the insurance industry. Finally, you should understand certain terms that apply to insurance contracts, from their distinct characteristics to legal interpretations. In general, this chapter discusses ideas that make it easier for you to learn the rest of the content in this book, so you need to master these concepts before moving on to the next chapter.

- Concepts
- Insurers
- Agents and General Rules of Agency
- Contracts

Concepts

Insurance is a transfer of loss or risk from a business entity or a person to an insurance provider, which then spreads the costs of unexpected losses to many people. If there were no insurance, the cost of a loss would have to be incurred solely by the person who suffered the loss.

Risk Management Key Terms

Risk – *Risk* is the uncertainty or likelihood that a loss occurs. There are two types of risk – pure risk and speculative risk, only one of which can be insured.

- *Pure risk* applies to circumstances that can only result in no change or a loss. There is no chance for financial gain. Pure risk is the only kind of risk that insurance companies accept.
- *Speculative risk* includes the opportunity for either gain or loss. Gambling is an example of speculative risk, and insurance companies cannot insure these types of risk.

Hazard – *Hazards* are circumstances or settings that increase the likelihood of an insured loss. Conditions such as congested traffic or slippery floors are hazards and may increase the odds of a loss occurring. Insurers categorize hazards according to physical, moral, or morale hazards.

- *Physical* hazards refer to individual characteristics that increase the likelihood of the cause of loss. Physical hazards exist due to a physical condition, prior medical history, or a condition at birth, like blindness.
- *Moral* hazards are tendencies towards increased risk. Moral hazards involve appraising the character and reputation of the proposed insured. Moral hazards involve applicants who may lie on an insurance application or have submitted fraudulent claims against an insurance provider.
- *Morale* hazards are similar to moral hazards, except that they can arise from a state of mind that causes apathy towards loss, such as carelessness. Actions taken without forethought can cause physical injuries.

Peril – In an insurance policy, *perils* are the insured against *causes of loss* that insurance providers will cover.

- *Life insurance* insures against the financial loss caused by the untimely death of an insured;
- *Health insurance* insures against the loss of income or medical expenses caused by the insured's accidental injury or sickness;
- *Property insurance* insures against (covers) the loss of physical property or the loss of its ability to produce income; and
- *Casualty insurance* insures against the resulting liabilities from the loss or damage of property.

Loss – *Loss* is the decrease, reduction, or disappearance of the value of the individual or property insured in a policy caused by a named peril. Insurance provides a way to transfer loss.

Exposure – *Exposure* is a unit of measure used in calculating insurance coverage rates. A large number of units with the same or similar exposure to loss are known as *homogeneous*. Sharing risk between a sizeable homogeneous group with a similar loss exposure constitutes the basis of insurance.

Methods of Handling Risk

Avoidance – *Avoidance* is one of the methods of dealing with risk, which means removing exposure to a loss. For instance, if a person wants to avoid the risk of dying in a motorcycle crash, they may choose never to ride a motorcycle. Risk avoidance can be effective, but it is hardly practical.

Retention – An insured's planned assumption of risk through self-insurance, co-payments, or deductibles is known as risk *retention*. Self-insurance is when the insured accepts responsibility for the loss before the insurance provider pays. The aim of retention is

1. To decrease expenses and improve cash flow;
2. To increase control of claim settlements and claim reserving; and
3. To finance losses that cannot be insured.

Sharing – *Sharing* is a way of dealing with risk for a group of individuals or businesses with the same or similar loss exposure to share the losses within that group. A reciprocal exchange of insurance is a formal arrangement for risk-sharing.

Reduction – Since risk usually cannot be avoided entirely, we often try to reduce the likelihood or severity of a loss. *Reduction* includes having an annual health exam to detect health problems early, installing smoke detectors in a home, or perhaps even changing one's lifestyle.

Transfer – The most effective approach to handling risk is to *transfer* it so that another party bears the loss. Insurance is the most accepted means of transferring risk from a person or group to an insurance company. Though buying insurance will not remove the risk of illness or death, it relieves the insured of the financial losses accompanying these risks.

There are numerous ways to transfer risk, including holding harmless agreements and other contractual agreements. Still, the most common and safest method is to buy insurance coverage.

Elements of Insurable Risks

Not all risks are insurable. As previously stated, insurance companies will insure only pure risks or those that involve only the chance of loss without a chance of gain. Additionally, even pure risks must possess specific characteristics to be insurable. Insurable risks involve the following elements:

- **Due to chance** – A loss outside the insured's control.
- **Definite and measurable** – A specific loss regarding the time, place, cause, and amount. An insurance company must be able to determine how much the benefit will be and when it becomes payable.
- **Statistically predictable** – Insurance companies must be able to estimate the severity and average frequency of future losses and to set appropriate premiums. Using morbidity and mortality tables in life and health insurance allows the insurance provider to project losses based on statistics.
- **Not catastrophic** – Insurance companies must ensure their losses will not exceed specific limits. Insurance policies generally exclude coverage for loss caused by war or nuclear events. No statistical data provides for the development of rates that would be necessary to cover losses from events of this nature.
- **Randomly selected and large loss exposure** – A sufficiently large pool of insureds must represent a random selection of risks in terms of gender, age, occupation, health and economic status, and geographic location.

Adverse Selection

Insurers strive to protect themselves from *adverse selection*, which refers to insuring risks more prone to losses than the average risk. Poorer risks seek insurance or file claims to a greater extent than better risks.

Insurance companies can refuse to accept a risk, restrict coverage for bad risks, or charge them a higher rate for insurance coverage to protect themselves from adverse selection.

Law of Large Numbers

The foundation of insurance is sharing risk between a large pool of people (a homogenous group) with a similar exposure to loss. The *law of large numbers* states that the actual losses will be more predictable among a *larger* group of people having a similar loss exposure. This law forms the basis for the statistical prediction of loss which insurers use to calculate insurance rates.

Example 2.1 – When an insurance company issues a policy on a 35-year-old male, the company cannot know or accurately predict when he will die. However, the law of large numbers examines a large group of similar risks, which in this case are 35-year-old males of similar lifestyles and health conditions. It makes conclusions based on the statistics of past losses. The law of large numbers gives the insurer a general idea about the predicted time of death for these insureds and sets the premiums accordingly. It is important to note that as the number of individuals in a risk pool increases, future losses become more predictable.

Insurers

Insurance is available to consumers from both private insurers and the government. The primary difference between government and private insurance is that government programs are funded with taxpayer dollars and serve national and state social purposes. Premiums, on the other hand, fund private insurance policies.

Private insurers can be classified in a variety of ways:

- Ownership;
- Domicile (location);
- Authority to transact business;
- Marketing and distribution systems; or
- Financial strength (rating).

As you read about different classifications of insurance companies, remember that these categories are not mutually exclusive. The same company can be described based on who owns it, where it is located and allowed to transact insurance, and what type of agents it appoints.

Types of Insurers

The most common types of ownership include the following:

Stock Companies – *Stock companies* are owned by the stockholders who supply the capital necessary to establish and operate the insurance company and share any profits or losses. Officers manage stock insurance companies and are elected by the stockholders. Stock companies generally issue *nonparticipating policies*, where policy owners do not share in losses or profits.

Policy owners of nonparticipating policies do not receive dividends; however, stockholders are paid taxable dividends.

Mutual Companies – *Mutual companies* are owned by the policy owners and issue *participating policies*. Policy owners are entitled to dividends, which are a return of excess premiums that are *not taxable*. Dividends are generated when the combined earnings and premiums create a surplus that exceeds the coverage costs. Dividends are not guaranteed.

Fraternal Benefit Societies – A *fraternal benefit society* is an organization formed to offer insurance for members of a religious organization, affiliated lodge, or fraternal organization with a representative form of government. Fraternals only sell insurance to their members and are considered charitable institutions, *not insurers*. They are not subject to all the regulations that apply to the insurance providers offering coverage to the public at large.

Lloyd's Associations – *Lloyd's* is not an insurance provider. Lloyd's provides a meeting place and support facilities for underwriters or groups that accept insurance risk to conduct business.

Lloyd's associations are a group of individuals who operate an insurance mechanism using the same principles of individual liability of insurers that Lloyd's of London uses. Each underwriter assumes a part of every risk and promises to pay a specified amount if the insured against contingency occurs. Members are liable only for their portion of the risk and are not bound to assume any portion of a defaulting member.

While Lloyd's formed in this country operate in essentially the same manner as Lloyd's of London, they are not subject to the strict regulation that Lloyd's of London imposes upon its members. Most states have laws prohibiting the organization or licensing of American Lloyd's. Those Lloyd's operate almost exclusively in the property insurance field.

Private vs. Government Insurers

Private insurance providers offer many lines of insurance. Federal and state governments offer insurance in the areas where private insurance is unavailable, called *social insurance programs*. Government insurance programs include Medicaid, Medicare, Social Security, Federal Crop Insurance, and National Flood Insurance.

The primary difference between government and private insurance programs is that government programs are funded with tax dollars. They serve national and state social purposes, while premiums fund private policies.

Admitted vs. Non-Admitted Insurers

Before insurers can transact business in a state, they must be granted a license or *certificate of authority* from the Department of Insurance and meet the state's financial capital and surplus requirements. Insurance providers who meet the state's financial requirements and are approved to do business in the state are considered *authorized or admitted* into the state as legal insurance companies. Insurance providers not approved to do business in New York are deemed *unauthorized or non-admitted*. Many states do not allow unauthorized insurance companies to do business in the state, except through excess and surplus lines brokers.

Surplus lines coverage is not readily available on the admitted market. Under each state's surplus lines laws, such coverages are marketed through non-admitted insurers who specialize in providing insurance to the high-risk market on an unregulated basis. While surplus lines insurers are not admitted, most states require that they be on that state's "approved" list.

It is contrary to state law for a broker or an agent to represent a non-admitted carrier unless the transaction occurs through a surplus lines broker as the intermediary.

Domestic, Foreign, and Alien Insurers

Insurance companies are classified according to where they are incorporated. An insurance company must obtain a certificate of authority before transacting insurance within the state, regardless of the location of incorporation.

A *domestic insurer* is an insurance company that is incorporated in this state. In most cases, the company's home office is in the state where it was formed (the company's domicile). For instance, a company chartered in Colorado would be considered a Colorado domestic company.

Insurance companies incorporated in another state, the District of Columbia, or a territorial possession are known as *foreign insurers*. Presently, the United States has five major U.S. territories, including Puerto Rico, the Northern Mariana Islands, Guam, American Samoa, and the U.S. Virgin Islands.

For example, a company chartered in Virginia would be a foreign company within New York. A company chartered in Puerto Rico will be foreign in any state.

An *alien insurer* is an insurance company incorporated outside the United States.

Financial Status (Independent Rating Services)

An insurer's financial strength and stability are critically important factors to potential insureds. Its financial strength is based on investment earnings, prior claims experience, level of reserves, and management, to name a few. Reserves are an amount of money held in a separate account to cover debts to policyholders. Guides to the financial integrity of insurers are published regularly by the following independent rating services:

- Fitch
- AM Best
- Moody's
- Standard and Poor's
- Weiss

Marketing (Distribution) Systems

Insurance companies market their products in different ways – through agents or direct solicitation to the customers through mail, Internet, television, or other mass marketing. The following table shows the various marketing arrangements and their characteristics:

MARKETING ARRANGEMENTS	CHARACTERISTICS
Independent Agency System/ American Agency System	• One independent agent represents several insurers • Nonexclusive and commissions are paid on personal sales • Business renewal with any insurer
Exclusive Agency System/ Captive Agents	• One agent represents one insurance company • Exclusive and commissions are paid on personal sales • Renewals can only be placed with the appointing insurer
General Agency System	• General agent-entrepreneur represents one insurance company • Exclusive and includes both compensation and commissions • Appoints subagents
Managerial System	• Branch manager (supervises agents) • Salaried • Agents can be an insurer's employees or independent contractors
Direct Response Marketing System	• No agents • Company advertises directly to consumers • Consumers apply directly to the company

Reinsurance – Insurance for Insurers

Reinsurance is a contract under which one insurance provider (the reinsurer) indemnifies another insurance provider for part or all of its liabilities. The purpose of reinsurance is to protect insurance providers against catastrophic losses. The originating insurer that procures insurance on itself from another insurer is called the *ceding insurer* (because it cedes, or gives, the risk to the reinsurer). The other insurance provider is called the *assuming insurer* or reinsurer.

Anytime reinsurance is obtained on a specific policy, it is classified as *facultative reinsurance*. When an insurer has an automatic reinsurance agreement between itself and the reinsurer in which the reinsurer is bound to accept all risks ceded to it, it is classified as a *reinsurance treaty*. Treaties are typically negotiated for one year or longer.

Risk Retention and Risk Purchasing Groups

A *risk retention group* (RRG) is a liability insurer owned by its members. The members are exposed to similar liability risks by being in the same business or industry. The purpose of a risk retention group is to assume and spread all or part of its group members' liability. A risk retention group can reinsure another risk retention group's liability as long as the members of the second group are engaged in the same or similar business or industry.

A *risk purchasing group* is an entity that offers insurance to groups of similar businesses with similar risk exposures. The policy is based on the insured's loss and expense experience. It is not provided to other policyholders concerning coverages, policy forms, or rates. Such programs and the groups that offer them are exempt from most state regulations, rules, and laws, except for the state where the group is domiciled.

Agents and General Rules of Agency

An agent or producer is licensed to solicit, negotiate, or sell insurance contracts on behalf of the *principal (insurer)*. The *law of agency* defines the relationship between the principal and the agent or producer. The acts of the agent or producer within the scope of authority are considered acts of the insurance provider.

In this relationship between the principal and the agent or producer, it is a given that:

- An agent represents the insurance provider, not the insured;
- Any knowledge of the agent is assumed to be knowledge of the insurance provider;
- If the agent is working within the boundaries of their contract, the insurance provider is fully responsible; and
- When the insured provides payment to the agent, it is the same as submitting a payment to the insurance provider.

The agent or producer is responsible for accurately completing an insurance application, submitting the application to the insurance provider for underwriting, and delivering the policy to the policyholder.

Authority and Powers of Agents

The agency contract specifies a producer's authority within their insurance company. Contractually, only those actions for which the producer is authorized can bind the principal (insurance provider). In reality, an agent's authority is a lot broader. There are three agent authority types: express, implied, and apparent.

Express – *Express authority* is the authority that is written into the contract. It is the authority a principal intends to grant to a producer through the agent's contract.

Implied – *Implied authority* is the authority that is not expressed or written into the contract but which the producer is assumed to have to conduct insurance business for the principal. Implied authority is incidental to and derives from express authority because not every single authority of a producer can be listed in the written contract.

Example 2.2 – Suppose the agency contract does not explicitly authorize the producer to collect premiums and remit them to the insurance provider. However, the agent routinely does so during the solicitation and delivery of policies. In that situation, the producer has the implied authority to collect and remit premiums.

Apparent – *Apparent authority*, also called perceived authority, is the assumption or appearance of authority based on the principal's words, actions, or deeds or due to circumstances the principal created. For example, suppose a producer uses the insurance provider's stationery when soliciting coverage. In that case, an applicant could believe the producer is authorized to transact insurance on behalf of that insurer.

Responsibilities to the Applicant and Insured

Even though producers act on behalf of the insurance company, they are legally required to treat insureds and applicants ethically. Since an agent handles the funds of the insured and the insurance provider, they have a *fiduciary responsibility*. An individual in a position of trust is called a *fiduciary*. More specifically, it is illegal for insurance agents to commingle premiums collected from the applicants with their own personal funds.

Market conduct describes the way insurers and producers should conduct their business. It is considered a *Code of Ethics* for producers. Producers must comply with specific established procedures, and failure to adhere will result in penalties. Several market conduct regulations include, but are not limited to, the following:

- A request for a loan or gift as a condition to complete business;
- Conflict of interest; and
- Providing confidential information.

Producers are required to perform professionally at all times. *Professionalism* means that a person is engaged in an occupation requiring advanced knowledge, training, or skill. Being a professional means placing the public's interest above one's own interest in all situations. Any deviation may result in a penalty.

Contracts

A *contract* is a legally enforceable agreement between two or more parties. Because of the unique aspects of insurance transactions, the general law of contracts had to be amended to fit the needs of insurance.

Elements of a Legal Contract

For contracts of insurance to be legally binding, they must include four essential elements:

1. Agreement – offer and acceptance;
2. Consideration;
3. Competent parties; and
4. Legal purpose.

Agreement (Offer and Acceptance) – There has to be a definite offer by one party. The other party must accept this offer in its exact terms. Concerning insurance, the applicant usually makes the *offer* when applying. *Acceptance* occurs when an insurance provider's underwriter approves the application and issues a policy.

Consideration – The binding force in any contract is known as *consideration*. Consideration is when each party gives something of value to the other. The consideration on the insured's part is the premium payment and the representations provided in the application. The consideration on the insurance provider's part is the promise to pay if a loss occurs.

Competent Parties – In the eyes of the law, the *parties to a contract* must be able to enter into a contract willfully. Usually, this requires that both parties be mentally competent to comprehend the contract, of legal age (14 ½ in New York), and not under the influence of alcohol or drugs.

Legal Purpose – The contract must have a *legal* purpose and not be against public policy.

Characteristics of Insurance Contracts

In addition to the required elements, insurance contracts possess unique characteristics that distinguish them from other legal contracts. Knowing these features and how they affect the parties to an insurance contract is essential.

Contract of Adhesion – One of the parties to the agreement (the insurer) drafts a *contract of adhesion*. It is either accepted or rejected by the other party (the insured). Insurance companies do not write policies through contract negotiations, and an insured has no input regarding its provisions. Insurers also offer contracts on a "take it or leave it" basis by an insurance provider. Any contract ambiguities will be settled in the insured's favor.

Conditional Contract – Before each party fulfills its obligations, a *conditional contract* requires that the policy owner and insurance company meet certain conditions to execute the agreement. The insured must pay the premium and provide proof of loss for the insurer to cover a claim.

Aleatory Contract – Insurance contracts are *aleatory*. In other words, the parties to the agreement are involved in an unequal exchange of amounts or values. Premiums paid by the insured are small compared to the amount the insurance provider will pay in a loss.

Example of Property and Casualty Insurance – Chad purchases a homeowner's insurance policy for $50,000. His monthly premium is $50. If Chad only had the policy for two months, he only paid $100 in insurance premiums. If a covered peril unexpectedly destroyed the home, Chad would receive $50,000. A $100 contribution on the insured's part in exchange for a $50,000 benefit from the insurance provider demonstrates an aleatory contract.

Example of Life and Health Insurance – Chad purchases a life insurance policy for $50,000. His monthly premium is $50. If Chad only had the policy for two months, he only paid $100 in insurance premiums. If he unexpectedly dies, his beneficiary will receive $50,000. A $100 contribution on the insured's part in exchange for a $50,000 benefit from the insurance provider illustrates an aleatory contract.

Personal Contract – In general, insurance contracts are *personal* contracts because they are between individuals and insurers. Insurance companies have a right to decide with whom they will not do business. The insured cannot be changed to another person without the insurer's written consent, nor can the policy owner transfer the contract to anyone else without approval from the insurance provider. Life insurance is an exception to this rule. A policy owner can assign or transfer policy ownership to another person; however, the policy owner must still notify the insurance provider in writing.

Unilateral Contract – In a *unilateral contract*, only one of the parties to the agreement must do anything according to the law. The insured makes no lawfully binding promises. Regardless, an insurance carrier must legally pay for losses covered by an in-force policy.

Conditional Contract – Before each party fulfills its obligations, a *conditional contract* requires that the policy owner and insurance company meet certain conditions to execute the agreement. The insured must pay the premium and provide proof of loss for the insurer to cover a claim.

Legal Concepts and Interpretations Affecting Contracts

Indemnity – Sometimes referred to as reimbursement, *indemnity* is a provision in an insurance contract that states that in the event of loss, a beneficiary or an insured is allowed to collect only to the extent of the financial loss. The insured cannot be entitled to gain financially because of an insurance contract. Insurance aims to restore an insured following a loss but not let a beneficiary or insured profit from the loss.

Example of Property and Casualty Insurance – Karen has a $200,000 homeowners insurance policy. After the destruction of her house, her cost to rebuild the home totaled $150,000. The insurance policy will only reimburse Karen for the amount of the loss ($150,000) and not for the total amount of insurance ($200,000).

Example of Life and Health Insurance – Karen has a $20,000 health insurance policy. After being hospitalized, her medical expenses totaled $15,000. The insurance policy only will reimburse Karen for the amount of the loss ($15,000) and not for the total amount of insurance ($20,000).

Utmost Good Faith – The principle of *utmost good faith* implies that there will be no concealment, misrepresentation, or fraud between the parties. As it pertains to insurance policies, both the insurance company and the insured must be able to rely on the other for relevant information. The insured is expected to provide accurate information on the insurance application. The insurance company must clearly and truthfully describe policy features and benefits and not conceal or mislead the insured.

Representations and Misrepresentations – *Representations* are statements believed to be true to the best of one's knowledge; however, they are not guaranteed to be true. For insurance purposes, representations are the answers an insured provides to the questions on an insurance application.

Untrue statements on an insurance application are considered *misrepresentations* and can void the contract. A *material misrepresentation* is a statement that would alter the insurer's underwriting decision if discovered. Additionally, if material misrepresentations are *intentional*, they are considered fraudulent.

Warranties – A *warranty* is a true statement upon which the validity of the insurance contract depends. Breach of warranties can be grounds for voiding the policy or a return of premium. Because of such a strict definition, statements made by applicants for life and health insurance policies, for example, are typically not considered warranties, except in cases of fraud.

Concealment – *Concealment* is the legal term for deliberately withholding information about a material fact that is crucial in decision-making. In insurance, concealment refers to the act of withholding information by the applicant that will cause an imprecise underwriting decision. Concealment can void a policy.

Rescission – Suppose an insurance applicant intentionally fails to communicate information that the insurer needs. In that circumstance, the insurer can cancel the policy even if the failure to communicate is disclosed after the policy is issued. This act is known as *rescission*, and the insurance provider is said to have rescinded the policy.

Upon rescission, the insured loses any right to file a claim on the policy, and the insurance provider refunds all money paid.

Fraud – *Fraud* is the intentional concealment or misrepresentation of a material fact used to induce another party to make or refrain from making a contract or cheating or deceiving a party. Fraud is considered grounds for voiding an insurance contract.

Waiver and Estoppel – *Waiver* is the voluntary act of surrendering a legal right, claim, or privilege.

Estoppel is a legal process that can be used to prevent a party to a contract from re-asserting a privilege or right after that privilege or right has been waived. Estoppel is a legal consequence of a waiver.

Chapter Review

This chapter was all about giving you the basics of insurance. Let's review some of the major points:

	GENERAL CONCEPTS
Insurance	• Transfers the risk of loss from an individual to an insurer • Based on the principle of indemnity • Based on the spreading of risk (risk pooling) and the law of large numbers

Hazards	• Conditions that increase the likelihood of a loss
	• The three kinds of hazards include:
	  o *Physical* – physical condition;
	  o *Moral* – a tendency toward increased risk;
	  o *Morale* – an indifference to loss

Risk	• Uncertainty regarding financial loss
	• Two types of risks:
	  - *Pure* – insurable because it involves a chance of loss only;
	  - *Speculative* – not insurable if it involves a chance of gain (e.g., gambling)
	• Methods of handling risk:
	  - Avoidance
	  - Retention
	  - Sharing
	  - Reduction
	  - Transfer

Elements of Insurance Risk	• All of the following elements apply to an insurable risk:
	  o *Due to chance* – chance of loss beyond insured's control
	  o *Definite and measurable* – the loss must have a definite time, place, and amount
	  o *Predictable* – number of losses must be statistically predictable through the use of mortality tables and morbidity tables
	  o *Not catastrophic* – there must be specific limits that the loss cannot exceed
	  o *Large exposure* – the insurer must be able to predict losses based on the law of large numbers
	  o *Randomly selected exposure* – the insurer must have a fair proportion of both good and poor risks

	INSURERS
Stock	• Owned by stockholders • Issue nonparticipating policies (nonpar)
Mutual	• Owned by policyowners (policyholders) • Issue participating policies (par) • Pay dividends to policyholders which are a refund of excess premiums

	INSURERS *(Continued)*
Fraternal Benefit Society	- Not for profit organization - Benevolent and charitable brotherhood - Membership based on religious, national or ethnic lines - Must be a member to receive benefits
	AGENT'S AUTHORITY
Express	- Powers specifically stated in the contract
Implied	- Not specifically stated in the contract, but is assumed necessary to conduct insurance business
Apparent	- The appearance of a relationship between the agent and principal based on words or actions
	COMPANY DOMICILE AND AUTHORIZATION
Domicile	- *Domestic* – incorporated in this state - *Foreign* – incorporated in another state of territory - *Alien* – incorporated in another country
Authorized/ Admitted	- Approved by the Department of Insurance - Has a Certificate of Authority
Unauthorized/ Nonadmitted	- No Certificate of Authority - Cannot transact business in this state
	INSURANCE CONTRACTS

Elements of a Legal Contract	- All of the following requirements apply:
	  - *Agreement* – offer and acceptance
	  - *Consideration* – premiums and representations on the part of the insured; payment of claims on the part of the insurer
	  - *Competent parties* – of legal age, sound mental capacity, and not under the influence of drugs or alcohol
	  - *Legal purpose* – not against public policy

Contract Characteristics	- *Adhesion* – one party prepares the contract; the other party must accept the contract as is - *Aleatory* – exchange of unequal amounts - *Conditional* – certain conditions must be met - *Personal* – between the policyowner and the insurance company - *Unilateral* – only one of the parties to the contract is legally bound to do anything
Legal Interpretations	- *Ambiguities* in the contract are always resolved in favor of the insured - The insured can *reasonably expect coverage* based on the agent's words and actions - *Utmost good faith* – parties rely on each other for information - *Material misrepresentations* (if intentional), *breach of warranties, concealment, fraud* – all can void the contract - *Waiver* – voluntary act of relinquishing a legal right; *estoppel* - consequence of a waiver

CHAPTER 3:
Property and Casualty Insurance Basics

Now that you have learned some basic concepts in the insurance industry, you will focus on the specific terms of property and casualty or liability insurance. You will learn about a property and casualty policy's structure and common provisions. Finally, you will learn some of the New York state laws regarding this type of insurance. This chapter includes essential information that will help you comprehend the rest of the material in this book.

- Principles and Concepts
- Policy Structure
- Common Policy Provisions
- Certificate of Insurance
- Terrorism Risk Insurance Act of 2002

Principles and Concepts

Insurable Interest

To buy insurance, the policyholder must face the possibility of losing money or something of value in the event of a loss. This potential for loss is known as *insurable interest*. At the time of application, in life insurance, an insurable interest exists between the policy owner and the insured. However, once the insurance provider has issued a life insurance policy, they must pay the policy benefit whether or not an insurable interest exists.

A valid insurable interest exists between the policy owner and the insured when the policy insures:

1. The policy owner's own life;
2. The life of a family member such as a close blood relative or a spouse; or
3. A key employee's life, a business partner's life, or someone who has a financial responsibility to the policyholder, such as the debtor to a creditor.

It is important to note that beneficiaries do not require an insurable interest. Since the beneficiary's well-being depends on the policy owner, and the beneficiary's life is not insured, the beneficiary does not have to show an insurable interest when purchasing a policy.

Underwriting

Underwriting is the process of reviewing insurance applications and the information on them. Specifically, it is a risk selection process.

Function – The underwriter's *function* refers to an insurer's operations where an employee, called an *underwriter*, classifies risks and evaluates applications submitted to the insurer. Underwriters determine whether or not to issue a policy and, if so, the policy's rates, terms, and conditions.

Loss Ratio – The *loss ratio* is a formula used by insurers to compare premium income to losses, including paid claims and expenses related to claims. The formula is as follows:

$$\text{Loss ratio} = (\text{Loss adjusting expense} + \text{Incurred losses}) \div \text{Earned premium}$$

Prohibition of Geographical Redlining – *Geographic redlining* is refusing to serve a specific area solely because of its location or because a volunteer fire department serves it. In New York, *redlining is illegal*. Insurance companies cannot terminate or refuse to issue or renew a homeowners policy that includes the following:

- Fire insurance or fire and extended coverage insurance;
- Stand-alone fire insurance or fire and extended coverage insurance; or
- Auto insurance based solely on the risk or property's geographical location or the agent's or broker's location.

New York Insurance Regulation requires insurance providers to report information relevant to property and casualty policies annually. Insurance companies must maintain records, by postal ZIP code, of their agents and those agents whose contracts were terminated. Insurers must also keep records, by postal ZIP code, of all policies issued, renewed, canceled (for a reason besides nonpayment of premium), or nonrenewed.

Insureds, applicants, agents, and brokers can file geographical redlining complaints with the Superintendent when the action taken by an insurance provider or its representative is believed to violate this provision. Insurers who violate this provision will be considered engaged in unfair methods of competition and deceptive or unfair acts or practices. These insurers will be subject to the appropriate provisions of the Insurance Law.

Insurance Risk Score (Credit Scoring) – An *insurance risk score*, or *insurance credit score*, is a point system used by underwriters to predict risk and the possibility of claims and determine charges for premiums. Insurance credit scoring is used mainly in homeowners and personal auto insurance.

Rates

In simple terms, an *insurance rate* is a dollar amount charged for a particular coverage amount. The actuarially concluded unit of cost is applied against the rating basis from which a policy premium is developed or the charge per unit of exposure.

Example 3.1 – The policy owner wants to insure a 1,000-square-foot building. The insurance provider has established a rate of $1.00 per square foot. The required premium will be $1,000 ($1.00 x 1,000 sq. ft).

Rates can be developed by property values (e.g., property or fire insurance), revenues receipts (e.g., casualty or liability insurance), or payroll (e.g., workers compensation insurance).

The method of setting rates is very similar in most cases. However, it is possible to distinguish between two different types of rates, including *class* and *individual*.

Class rating – *Class rating* (or *manual rating*) refers to calculating a price per unit of insurance that applies to every applicant possessing a given set of characteristics. For example, a class rate may apply to all drivers of a particular gender and age driving in the same geographic area or all types of dwellings of a given kind of construction in a specific city.

The advantage of the class-rating system is that it allows the insurance provider to apply a single rate to many insureds, simplifying the process of calculating their premiums. In creating the classes to which class rates apply, the rate maker has to compromise between a large class. This large class will include more exposures that increase the credibility of predictions and one sufficiently narrow to allow homogeneity.

Class rating is the most common approach used by the insurance industry. It is used in life insurance and most property and casualty fields.

In some areas of risk, the characteristics of the insured units are widely varied. It is considered desirable to depart from the class approach and calculate rates based on the attempt to measure an individual's loss-producing characteristics more precisely. There are five basic individual rate-making approaches:

1. Judgment rating
2. Schedule rating
3. Experience rating
4. Retrospective rating
5. Merit rating

Judgment rating – *Judgment rating* is used when credible actuarial data is lacking or when the exposure units are so diverse that it is impossible to build a class. Underwriters must use their skills and experience to develop judgment rates. This approach is used in Ocean Marine insurance, and it is also used in other lines where permitted by a state's rate laws. Risks that have been judgment-rated can also be referred to as "A" rated.

Schedule rating – In *schedule rating*, the rates are calculated by applying a schedule of credits and charges to some base rate to determine the appropriate rate for an individual exposure. Today, schedule rating is used less frequently due to the introduction of ISO's *class-rating program* for various types of commercial buildings previously schedule-rated. This reduction in use leaves only the largest and most complex risks to schedule-rated.

Experience rating – In *experience rating*, the insured's past loss experience becomes a factor in determining the final premium. Experience rating is overlaid on a class-rating system. It adjusts the insured's premium up or down, depending on whether the insured's experience deviates from the average experience of the class.

Retrospective rating – *Retrospective rating* is a *self-rating* plan under which the policy term's actual losses determine the final premium, subject to a minimum and maximum premium. A deposit premium is mandatory at the inception of the policy. That premium is adjusted at the end of the policy period based on the actual loss experience.

Merit rating – Another type of rating is *merit rating*, commonly used in personal auto insurance. In this rating method, the insured's premium is *not* based on the actual loss record but on other factors that signify the *probability* that a loss will occur. An example would be a bad driving record that does not include any at-fault accidents.

Loss Costs – The ISO developed a rating method known as *loss costs*. This method provides insurers with a portion of a rate that does not include expense or profit provisions. It is based on actual cumulative loss and loss adjustment expenses projected through a future point in time. The insurer must add the expense and profit components to develop the final rate.

Components – *Components* determine rates, including loss reserves, operating expenses, loss adjusting expenses, and profits.

Negligence

Negligence is failing to use the care that a prudent, reasonable person would have taken under the same or similar circumstances to prevent injury to another individual or damage to their property.

Elements of Negligence – Most people behave in a manner that is prudent and reasonable – with exceptions for incompetent individuals and minors. Failure to act in this manner constitutes *negligence*. When this negligence causes damage to property belonging to another or injury to another, the negligent party may be held legally responsible for the damage. Generally, the burden of proof is on the injured party to prove that the other party was negligent. However, certain doctrines also shift the burden of evidence from the injured party to the defendant or impose liability by statute. There are four primary elements to be considered when negligence is established, and all four must be present to prove that another party is negligent:

1. Legal duty;
2. Standard of care;
3. Unbroken chain of events; and
4. Actual loss or damage.

Legal Duty – It must be proven whether the defendant had a legal duty to act.

Standard of Care – The defendant must have used a standard of care that breached their legal duty. Standard of care infers acting as a reasonable person would act.

Proximate Cause – *Proximate cause* is an event or act considered reasonably foreseeable and a natural cause of the event that occurs and damages property or injures a plaintiff. The negligence must have been the proximate cause of the damage if the injured party is to be compensated for the damage. This correlation signifies an unbroken chain of events, starting with negligence and leading to damage or injury. Also referred to as *direct liability*, this negligence must be the cause without which the accident would not have occurred.

Actual Loss or Damage – The mere fact that carelessness existed is not adequate cause for legal liability. Actual damage or injury must have been suffered by the party seeking recovery.

Defenses Against Negligence – An individual's negligent behavior does not necessarily result in that person being held legally liable. Certain defenses may be interceded by the negligent party to defeat a claim.

Assumption of Risk – This defense of an action for compensation for injuries affirms that if a person understands and recognizes the danger involved in an activity and willingly chooses to encounter it, the *assumption of risk* may bar compensation for injury caused by negligence. Courts have held that in seeking admission to a PGA event, a spectator has chosen to undergo the risk of being struck by a golf ball. Another common example is a passenger in a car. In many jurisdictions, a passenger is considered to have assumed the risk of injury while riding in an automobile. Even if the vehicle is driven in a grossly negligent way, the passenger may be considered to have assumed the risk of injury if the passenger fails to protest the dangerous driving.

Comparative Negligence – Due to the harshness of contributory negligence, most states have adopted a somewhat more lenient doctrine, known as *comparative negligence*. Here, the other party's negligence or fault will not necessarily defeat the claim but will be used to mitigate the damages payable to the other party. Under this statutory defense, the fault is shared between the parties involved. The awards for damages are decreased by the percentage of negligence of each party.

Some states have adopted the rule of *pure comparative negligence*, which allows the party who brings the lawsuit (the plaintiff) to recover the damages, as long as they are not 100% negligent. In contrast, under the rule of *modified comparative negligence*, the injured party can only recover damages if their fault is less than that of the party being sued (the defendant). This rule is also known as the "equal to or greater than" rule.

Contributory Negligence – Under *contributory negligence*, the injured party must be completely free of fault to collect. Any negligence that contributed to the injury on the part of the injured party, however slight, will usually defeat the claim. A variation of contributory negligence is called the last clear chance rule. It may be used as a defense by a negligent party who can prove the injured party had the last clear chance to avoid the loss but did not.

Intervening Cause – The *intervening cause* bars or reduces recovery for an injured person if an intervening cause interrupts the chain of events and sets a new chain of events in motion. For example, a person clears their sidewalk of snow and ice after a storm, but it begins to snow again shortly after. Before the person can shovel again, an individual walks by, slips, and is injured.

Statute of Limitations – By law, some states have set a time limit for an injured party to bring legal action against another party for specific injuries.

Damages

A tort can result in two forms of injury to another, including property damage and bodily injury. In the case of *property damage*, the loss is typically easy to determine. Insurers measure the monetary loss the injured party suffered by calculating the destroyed or damaged property's value and the loss of use of that asset.

In the case of *bodily injury*, it is harder to determine the loss monetarily. Bodily injury can lead to claims by the injured party not only for lost wages and medical expenses but also for loss of consortium, mental anguish, pain and suffering, and disfigurement. The two classes of *compensatory damages* insurers can award are special and general damages. *Special damages* are specific out-of-pocket expenses for lost wages, miscellaneous expenses, and medical coverage. *General damages* compensate the injured person for disfigurement, mental anguish, pain and suffering, and other similar losses. Determining the general damages amount is highly subjective and can amount to whatever a judge or jury decides is suitable. *Punitive damages* are another class of damages; it is a form of punishment for gross negligence, outrageous extreme behavior, or willful intent.

Absolute Liability

Absolute liability is imposed upon a company or person engaged in a dangerous or potentially hazardous business that results in injury or harm to another person or property by negligence or omission. Examples of absolute liability include harboring wild animals, owning a swimming pool, or selling explosives. The injured party does not have to prove negligence.

Strict Liability

Strict liability is usually applied in product liability cases. A business or person that manufactures or sells a product makes an implied warranty that the product is safe. The business is responsible for defective products, regardless of negligence or fault. Suppose the product causes injury, and the claimant can prove the defect. The defendant will be held strictly liable for the damage in that case.

Vicarious Liability

The doctrine of *vicarious liability* comes from the old English law "respondeat superior," in which the master was liable for their servants' negligent acts. This doctrine aims to transfer the liability from one person to another who would probably have a greater ability to pay. In some jurisdictions, employers may be held vicariously liable for negligent acts of their employees and parents liable for their children's actions.

Causes of Loss (Perils)

A *peril* is a specific cause of loss. Perils insured against in a standard property policy include fire, hail, wind, and explosions.

Named Perils vs. Special (Open) Perils – *Named peril* is a term used in property insurance to describe the extent of coverage provided under an insurance policy form that lists covered perils. Insurance providers do not cover unlisted perils.

Open peril is a term in property insurance to describe the extent of coverage provided under an insurance policy form that insures against any risk of loss not explicitly excluded. The term open peril has replaced the term "all risks."

Direct Loss

Direct and *indirect* losses are the two types of property losses a business or individual could experience. Property insurance only covers direct losses. However, indirect losses are related to the direct loss, and coverage to protect against these indirect losses is often added to property insurance policies. Direct losses mean direct physical damage to personal property (e.g., vehicle, furniture, or equipment) or real property, like a building.

Direct loss also involves other damage where the covered peril was the *proximate cause of loss*. For example, an insured building catches fire. When the local fire department uses water to put out the fire, the floor and wall coverings suffer water damage. While water damage is not an insured peril, the damage is covered under the peril of fire because the fire was the proximate cause.

Consequential or Indirect Loss

Indirect losses, also called *consequential losses*, are losses resulting from a direct loss. Such losses typically result from the time it takes to replace or repair damaged property. The most prevalent indirect loss for individual homeowners is the extra living expense they may incur while the home is under repair. The primary type of indirect or consequential loss for commercial risks is the loss of profits a business may suffer because of having to close down until the repairs are complete.

Blanket vs. Specific Insurance

Blanket insurance is a single property policy that offers coverage for more than one class of property at one location or multiple classes of property at more than one location. Every insured property is issued one total amount of coverage, and no single insured item is assigned a specific amount of coverage. However, different amounts may be listed for buildings, equipment, and other items.

Specific insurance is a property policy that insures a particular kind or unit of property for an exact amount of coverage.

Basic Types of Construction

An essential element in the underwriting and rating of property insurance is the type of construction of the building to be insured. A building with materials less prone to fire damage would be more favorably rated than a building more prone to fire damage. The following are the basic classes of construction used for underwriting:

- **Fire-resistive** — Buildings constructed with masonry or other materials with a fire-resistance rating of two or more hours. Fire-resistive usually receives the most favorable rating.
- **Modified fire-resistive** — Buildings constructed with masonry or other materials with a fire-resistance rating between one and two hours.
- **Masonry noncombustible** — Buildings with masonry or fire-resistive walls and noncombustible or slow-burning floors and roof.
- **Noncombustible** — Buildings with noncombustible materials (materials that will not ignite and burn when subjected to fire).
- **Joisted-masonry** — Buildings constructed with masonry or fire-resistive walls and combustible floors and roofs.
- **Frame** — Buildings with combustible materials or noncombustible or slow-burning walls and combustible floors and roofs. The frame usually receives the least favorable rating.

Loss Valuation

When a property insurance policy is written, the policy owner has several options as to how the insurer will value a loss to the insured property at the time of a loss. *Loss valuation* is a factor in calculating the premium charged and the coverage amount required.

Actual Cash Value — The *actual cash value (ACV)* method of valuation reinforces the principle of indemnity because it recognizes the decline in value of a property as it ages and becomes subject to obsolescence and wear and tear. Generally, insurers calculate actual cash value as follows:

Actual Cash Value (ACV) = Current Replacement Cost − Depreciation

Replacement Cost — *Replacement cost* refers to replacing the damaged property with like kind and quality at today's price, without deducting depreciation. This loss valuation method opposes the basic concept of indemnity because it could give the insured a settlement that exceeds the property's actual cash value after a loss.

Functional Replacement Cost – Another loss valuation method allows the insurance company to adjust the loss based on the *functional replacement cost* at the time of a loss. This cost is for replacing the damaged property with less expensive and more modern equipment or construction. For example, the insurer may replace a building with lath and plaster walls with drywall at a lower cost to repair but just as functional.

Market Value – *Market value* is a rarely used method of loss valuation based upon the amount a willing buyer would pay to a willing seller for the property before the loss occurs. This method considers the value of land and location rather than just the cost of rebuilding the structure itself.

Agreed Value – *Agreed value* is a property policy that includes a provision agreed upon by the insured and the insurance provider. Both parties agree to the amount of coverage that signifies a fair valuation for the property when the policy is written and suspends any other contribution clauses or coinsurance. Insurers use this valuation method for items whose value does not fluctuate much. When a loss occurs, the policy pays the agreed value as stated on the policy schedule, irrespective of the insured item's depreciation or appreciation.

Stated Amount – A *stated amount* is an amount of coverage scheduled in a property policy that is not subject to any coinsurance requirements if a covered loss occurs. This scheduled amount is the maximum amount the insurance provider will pay in the event of a loss.

Policy Structure

Each property or casualty policy includes the following major components:

- Declarations;
- Definitions;
- Insuring agreement;
- Additional coverage;
- Conditions;
- Endorsements; and
- Exclusions and policy limits.

Declarations

Declarations are the mandatory part of an insurance policy containing the basic underwriting information, such as the name and address of the insured, amount of coverage and premiums, and a description of insured locations. It also contains any additional representations by the insured. This section is generally the first page of the policy.

Definitions

The *definitions* section of an insurance policy clarifies the terms used in the policy. Usually, words printed in bold, italics, or quotations have a definition of their meaning in that contract.

Insuring Agreement or Clause

An *insuring agreement* (sometimes labeled Agreement) is the part of an insurance policy that establishes the obligation of the insurer to provide the insurance coverages stated in the policy. Among other things, the insuring agreement lists the perils, the description of the coverage delivered, effective and renewal dates, and the parties to the contract. It is generally placed after the policy Declarations but may come after the Definitions.

Additional or Supplementary Coverage

Additional (or supplementary) coverage is an insurance policy provision that provides additional coverage for specific loss expense at no additional premium. Examples include claim-related expenses, reasonable expenses incurred by an insured to protect damaged property from further loss, and defense expenses.

Conditions

Conditions (also called common policy conditions) are the portion of an insurance policy that specifies the general procedures or rules that the insured and insurance provider agree to follow under the terms of the policy.

The following illustrates examples of conditions:

- *Inspections* can be made as needed by the insurer. The insurer maintains the right to examine or inspect the insured's books or location to determine the exact exposure for rating and underwriting purposes.
- *Changes to the policy* have to be made by the insurance provider and be in writing.
- The *liberalization clause* guarantees that if the insurer introduces new or free coverage, the insured will immediately receive these benefits and will not have to wait until policy renewal.
- *Return of premium* determines the method that the insurer will use to compute the return of premium when the policy is canceled before the expiration date.

Exclusions

The exclusions section of an insurance policy describes the perils that are not insured against and the individuals who are not covered. Exclusions limit some of the broad terms used in the insuring agreement. This section can exclude perils, property, and people (except a spouse).

The following examples of exclusions are from coverage in a property policy, including *earth movement* and *water damage*.

- Earth movement is excluded if it resulted from an earthquake, volcanic eruption, or a mudflow; and
- The water damage exclusion does not cover the following perils: flood and subsurface water, water that backs up through drains and sewers, water that overflows from a sump pump, or water below ground that leaks through a basement's walls.

Endorsements

Endorsements are printed supplements to a contract that modify the policy's original coverages, conditions, or terms. Policy owners can include endorsements when the policy is issued or during the policy's term. Endorsements must be in writing, attached to the policy, and signed by an executive officer of the insurance provider to have any effect on the contract. They may be used to delete or add coverage or to correct items such as the insured's name, address, etc.

Common Policy Provisions

Insureds – Named, First, Additional

In property and casualty insurance policies, an *insured* is any person covered under the policy, whether named or not. An example of an insured would include any resident relative that is a member of the named insured's household or an unnamed spouse.

A *named insured* refers to the individual(s) whose name appears on the policy's declarations page.

The *first named insured* refers to the person whose name appears first on the policy's declarations page. In a commercial insurance policy, the first named insured controls the policy. Only the first named insured can request changes to the policy or cancel the policy, and also is the one responsible for paying the premiums and reporting losses.

Additional insureds are businesses or individuals not named as insureds on the declarations page. Still, they are protected by the policy, typically regarding a specific interest. Additional insureds generally are added to the policy by an endorsement.

Policy Period

The *policy period* is the period, stated on the declarations page, during which the policy provides coverage.

Policy Territory

The *policy territory* defines the location where the insurance company will provide coverage.

Cancellation and Nonrenewal

Cancellation is terminating an insurance policy that is in force, by either the policy owner or the insurance provider, before the expiration date shown in the policy. Termination can be involuntary, voluntary, or in mutual accordance with provisions found in the policy.

Nonrenewal is the termination of an insurance policy at its expiration date by not providing a replacement or a continuation of the existing policy.

Earned Premium Calculation

An *earned premium* is the portion of a premium that belongs to the insurer for providing coverage for a specified period. The paid-in-advance premiums belong to the insurance provider.

To calculate the earned premium of a policy, one must know its original amount, its total term of effectiveness, and how long the policy has been in effect at the time of calculation.

Calculation Period X (Amount of Policy ÷ Term of Policy) = Earned Premium

This accounting method is the more prevalent of the two ways to calculate earned premiums. In the second exposure method, earned premiums are based on the portion of the total premium exposed to loss during the calculation period.

Example 3.2 – A professor has a 3-year policy with a value of $1,500. The policy has been effective for one year. In this case, the earned premium is $500.

($1,500 ÷ 3 years) X 1 year = Earned Premium
$500 a year X 1 year = $500

When a policy is canceled upon its effective date, it is called a *flat-rate cancellation*, and there is usually no premium penalty.

When the insurer cancels a policy mid-term, the insured will receive a *pro-rata refund*. This refund is determined by calculating how many days of coverage were paid minus how many days the policy was in force. The unearned (or unused) premium is fully returned to the insured.

Example 3.3 (pro rata) – Chad has a homeowner's policy with ABC Insurers. His policy runs from Jan 1 through Dec 31 and pays the $730 premium annually. Chad receives notice that ABC Insurers is canceling his policy effective June 1. Because Chad's policy was in effect for 151 days, he will receive a refund of $428.

- 365 days/year - 151 days used = 214 days to refund.
- $730 annual premium / 365 days = $2/day cost of insurance.
- 214 days to refund × $2/day = $428 refunded to Chad.

Short-rate cancellation is applied when the insured cancels the policy before its renewal date. A short rate allows the insurer to impose a penalty (usually 10%) on the refund of unearned premiums.

Example 3.4 (short rate) – Chad has a homeowner's policy with ABC Insurers. His policy runs from Jan 1 through Dec 31 and pays the $730 premium annually. Chad notifies ABC Insurers he is canceling the policy effective June 1. ABC Insurers will refund Chad $385.20.

- 365 days/year - 151 days used = 214 days to refund.
- $730 annual premium / 365 days = $2/day cost of insurance.
- 214 days to refund × $2

Deductibles

In property and casualty insurance, a *deductible* is a dollar amount an insured must pay on a claim before the insurer provides coverage. Higher deductibles usually mean lower premiums.

Coinsurance

The *coinsurance* clause states that the insured agrees to maintain a minimum amount of insurance on the insured property in consideration of a reduced rate. This clause encourages the policy owner to insure the property closer to its total value. In cases of partial loss, the insurer will pay for the partial loss in full, provided that the insured has maintained the minimum amount of insurance in relation to the property's value. Suppose the amount of insurance carried is less than the requirement in the coinsurance clause. In that case, the insurer will only cover the percent of the loss the insurance bears in relation to the needed insurance. In the event of a total loss, the coinsurance clause is not activated, and the insurer pays the face amount of the policy.

The formula for calculating *coinsurance penalties* is the amount of insurance carried over the amount the policy owner should have had, multiplied by the loss, which equals the reduced payment for the loss.

Loss Payment – Loss Amount X (Insurance Carried ÷ Insurance Required)

For a $100,000 building insured with an 80% coinsurance percentage, the policy owner must carry at least $80,000 of coverage ($100,000 x .80) to meet the coinsurance requirement. If the insured only maintained $40,000 of coverage and had a $10,000 loss, they would have to bear 50% of the loss due to the deficiency, or $5,000, plus any deductible.

Self-Insured Retention (SIR)

The *self-insured retention (SIR)* provision (typically in liability insurance policies) sets an amount the insured must pay before the insurance company pays.

Other Insurance

Other insurance is a policy provision that defines how an insurance policy responds if other valid insurance is written on the same risk.

Primary and Excess – A *primary* policy is a policy that pays first if a covered loss occurs. In a layered program of insurance, it is the policy that pays for the first layer of loss.

An *excess* policy is a policy that only pays for a loss after the primary policy has paid up to its limit. All other insurance has to be exhausted before the excess policy will apply.

Pro Rata Share – *Pro rata* is a provision included in some property insurance policies that allows losses to be shared with other insurance. This other insurance can be written on the same risk and in the same proportion as their limits of insurance bear to the total coverage of all policies covering the risk, whether collectible or not.

Limits of Liability

Limits of liability are the insurance carrier's liability for payment as stated in an insurance policy's Declarations. They are the maximum amount the insurer will pay for a particular loss or loss during a period.

Per Occurrence (Accident) – *Per occurrence* is a liability policy sublimit that puts a ceiling on the payment for all claims that result from a single occurrence or accident. The occurrence form is triggered by the date when damage or injury occurs. It covers claims made at any time for injuries arising during the policy period.

Per Person – *Per person* is the maximum payment amount available for bodily injury to a single person in an accident, regardless of the stated policy limit for bodily injury claims.

Per Project, Per Location – Umbrella or excess insurance providers may apply the aggregate general liability insurance limit on a per-location or project basis. A *per-project* limit means the insurer will pay up to that limit for claims from a specific project. A *per-location* limit sets separate liability limits for each location.

Aggregate – The *aggregate limit* is the maximum limit of available coverage provided under a liability policy during a policy year, regardless of the number of accidents that occur or how many claims are made. Losses paid under coverages subject to aggregate limits lower the available amount for future losses. Aggregate limits are restored on the policy's anniversary date.

Sublimit – *Sublimits* are coverage limits for a specific exposure that are less than the overall policy limits. For example, property insurance providers may set sublimits for direct damages and business interruptions caused by equipment breakdown, flood, earth movement, or transit.

Split – *Split limits* are separate limits of liability for different coverages. The limits can be stated per occurrence, per person, per policy period, or split between property damage and bodily injury. Insurers issue many auto liability policies with split limits. For example, 25/50/25 indicates the following: the policy will pay up to $25,000 for the injury of a single individual; up to $50,000 for bodily injury to two or more individuals (but not more than $25,000 to any one individual); and up to $25,000 for damage to the property of others.

Combined Single – *Combined single* is a single dollar limit of liability that applies to the total damages for property damage and bodily injury resulting from one occurrence or accident. Insurers can use the limit in any combination of amounts, but it may not exceed the single limit.

Ordinance or Law

Policy owners can add the *ordinance or law endorsement* to a property coverage form. It covers a building if the enforcement of any zoning, building, or land use law causes loss or damage, higher repair or reconstruction costs, or demolition and removal costs.

The endorsement is split into three coverages, which must be activated by obtaining each coverage. The insured can obtain all or some of the coverages included. Policy owners can add the ordinance or law coverage endorsement only to a property policy issued on a replacement cost basis. Coinsurance will not apply.

The building shown in the endorsement must sustain covered direct damage to at least a portion of the structure. Only the section of the structure covered by a policy peril and subject to the ordinance or law can benefit from this endorsement.

Coverage is for completing minimum requirements as mandated by the ordinance or law. No coverage will apply for ordinances or laws the policyholder was required to comply with before the loss.

This endorsement provides the following coverages when selected:

- **Coverage A** — loss to the undamaged part of the building-loss in value to the undamaged section of the building;
- **Coverage B** — the demolition cost of the undamaged portion of the covered building; and
- **Coverage C** — any increased construction cost for the damaged and undamaged sections of the building.

Vacancy and Unoccupancy

Vacancy refers to a covered structure in which no one has been working or living. Also, no property has been stored for the required period stated in the policy (generally 60 days).

Unoccupancy (non-occupancy) refers to a covered structure in which no one has been working or residing within the required period, but some property is stored there.

For instance, if the policy owner moves, the house is considered *vacant*. The house is considered *unoccupied* if the policy owner travels for two weeks.

First Named Insured Provisions

The *first named insured* is the person whose name appears first in the policy's Declarations. Under the terms of a policy, the first named insured must perform specific duties, including paying the premium and giving prompt notice of a claim to the insurer in the event of a loss.

Duties After Loss – When a loss covered by the policy occurs, the named insured must:

- Protect the damaged property from further damage;
- Prepare an inventory of damaged property;
- Cooperate with the insurer in settling the loss;
- Notify the police in the case of a theft loss; and
- Submit to the insurance provider a signed sworn proof of loss within an allotted amount of time after being requested to do so.

Assignment – *Assignment* means transferring a legal right or interest in an insurance policy. In property and casualty insurance, assignments of policies are valid only with the insurer's prior written consent.

Abandonment – *Abandonment* is the relinquishing of insured property into the hands of another or the possession of no one in particular. Most property insurance policies prohibit an insured from abandoning insured property following a loss and require that the insured protect the property from additional loss.

Insurer Provisions

Insurer provisions are used in the event of loss to replace or repair damaged property with property of like kind and quality or to adjust the loss and make payment to the insured or individual legally entitled to receive compensation within 60 days of receiving proof of loss.

Liberalization – *Liberalization* is a property insurance clause that extends broader regulated or legislated coverage to current policies, provided it does not result in a higher premium. For instance, if the insurer introduces a new coverage or improves coverage, the insured will immediately acquire the benefit of that coverage. It won't have to wait for their policy to renew.

Subrogation – *Subrogation* is the legal right of an insurer to seek compensation for damages from third parties after it has reimbursed the insured for the loss. Subrogation is based on the *indemnity* principle, which prevents insureds from collecting twice on the loss – once from the insurance company and a second time from the party that caused the damage.

Salvage – Salvage is the amount of money realized from the sale of damaged merchandise. An insurance provider may have a right to salvage the damaged property in an insured loss to recover a portion of the paid loss.

Loss Settlement Options – At the time of loss, the insurance provider's loss payment options or claim settlement options, including paying the least of the following:

- The value of the damaged or lost property;
- The cost of replacing or repairing the lost or damaged property;
- The cost of taking all or part of the property at an appraised or agreed value; or
- The cost of repairing, rebuilding, or replacing the property with other property of similar kind and quality.

Duty to Defend – Liability coverage includes a promise to defend the insured in any lawsuit involving the type of liability insured under the coverage. It also promises to pay all sums that the insurance provider becomes legally obligated to pay. Once the limit of the liability has been paid, the insurance company has no further obligation to defend the insured.

Third-Party Provisions

Third-party provisions address the rights of a third party that could have a secured financial interest in the insured property.

Standard Mortgage Clause – The *standard mortgage clause*, also called the loss payable clause, is a keystone provision of all property policies for real property. In insurance, non-movable property like a house and other structures is considered real property. Movable property like an auto, mobile home, furniture, and equipment is considered personal property. If a loss to real property occurs, insurers will pay the policy owner and the mortgagee as their insurable interest appears. In other words, the mortgagee's right to recover is limited to the amount of the outstanding debt. At no time will the mortgagee receive more than the insurable interest in the property. If an insurance policy is to be canceled, a mortgagee must receive prior written notice of such cancellation.

When a person is named in a mortgagee clause attached to a fire or other direct damage policy, the compensation for the loss will be paid to the mortgagee as their interest may appear. The mortgagee's rights of recovery will not be defeated by any act or neglect of the policy owner. The mortgagee is also given other rights, such as bringing a lawsuit in their own name to recover damages, paying policy premiums, and submitting proof of loss. There is nothing that *either the insured or the insurer* can do to defeat the mortgagee's position.

Loss Payable Clause – The *loss payable clause* is the clause used to cover the interest of a secured lender in personal property. An insurer must notify the loss payee in writing if the it decides to cancel or not renew a policy.

No Benefit to the Bailee – The *no benefit to the bailee* provision excludes assignment or granting any policy provision to an individual or organization storing, holding, repairing, or moving insured property for a fee. A bailee is a business with temporary possession of the property of another. It will do something with this property for the mutual benefit of both parties.

Certificate of Insurance

A *certificate of insurance* is any document that verifies insurance is effective. It is used as evidence of property or casualty insurance coverage. A certificate of insurance does not include a policy of insurance or an insurance binder.

A certificate of insurance cannot extend, amend, or alter the coverage provided by the policy to which it refers. It also does not grant any person rights beyond those expressly provided by the insurance policy referenced.

Terrorism Risk Insurance Act of 2002

The *Terrorism Risk Insurance Act of 2002 (TRIA)* established a temporary federal program to share the risk of loss from future terrorist attacks with the insurance industry. The act mandates that all commercial insurers offer coverage for acts of terrorism. The federal government will reimburse the insurance carriers for a portion of paid losses resulting from terrorism.

TRIA defines *terrorism* as an act certified by the Secretary of the Treasury, in agreement with the United States Attorney General and the Secretary of State, with the following attributes:

- The act must be violent or dangerous to infrastructure, property, or human life;
- The act must have caused damage within the U.S., to a United States air carrier, to a U.S. flag vessel or another vessel that is based primarily in the United States and insured under U.S. regulation, or on the premises of any mission conducted by the United States;
- An individual must have carried out the act as part of a coordinated effort to intimidate the civilian population of the U.S., influence U.S. policy, or affect the conduct of the United States government by coercion; or
- The act must cause property and casualty insurance losses exceeding $5,000,000.

Insurance providers will have specific deductibles and retentions to meet before the federal government reimburses their expenses. The federal government will not reimburse an insurer for the first dollars of its insured losses (the deductible amount). The deductibles apply on a calendar year basis. Under the Act, the deductible amount for each insurance provider is set to a *percentage of its direct earned premiums* for the previous year. Since the Act's enforcement, the deductible amount has been rising annually.

The federal government will recover a portion of the payments it makes under the program in two phases. The first recovery phase is the premium surcharge on property and casualty insurance policies. These surcharges may be at most 3% of the policy premium.

The mandatory recovery of federal payments is based on the difference between the total paid out by insurers in certified terrorism losses (percentage-of-earned-premium deductibles plus the percentage participation) and the *insurance marketplace aggregate retention amount*. The aggregate retention amount is the maximum dollar amount that all insurance companies participating in the programs will be liable to pay for certified terrorism losses in a program year. If the total of insurer deductibles and percentage participation does not equal the aggregate retention, insurers must pay the difference back to the federal government. When the insurance provider deductibles and percentage participation total amounts equal or exceed the aggregate retention, there will be no mandatory federal recovery.

Terrorism Risk Insurance Program Reauthorization Act of 2015

The Terrorism Risk Insurance Act of 2002 has been revised several times. The final amendment is the Terrorism Risk Insurance Program Reauthorization Act of 2015, which has further amended and extended the Terrorism Insurance Program and revised several provisions as follows:

- The insurer deductible was set at 20% of an insurer's direct earned premium from the previous calendar year. The federal share of compensation was set at 85% of insured losses that exceed insurer deductibles. After that, the federal share will be reduced by one percentage point per calendar year until it reaches 80%;
- The certification process was amended to require the Secretary of the Treasury to authenticate terrorist acts with the Secretary of Homeland Security rather than the Secretary of State;
- The aggregate of industry insured losses caused by certified acts of terrorism will activate the federal share of compensation under the Program, which is now $200 million;
- The required indemnification of the federal share through policy owner surcharges increased to 140% (from 133%);
- Revised requirements for mandatory recoupment from insurers of federal financial assistance provided in connection with all acts of terrorism.

National Association of Registered Agents and Brokers (NARAB) Reform Act — This Act amends the Gramm-Leach-Bliley Act to revoke the incidental conditions under which the NARAB may not be established. NARAB is also prohibited from merging with or into any other public or private entity.

In addition, without affecting state regulatory authority, the NARAB must provide a mechanism for the adoption and multi-state application of conditions and requirements concerning:

- Licensing, continuing education, and other credentials of non-NARAB insurance producers;
- Appointments of resident or nonresident insurance producers;
- The supervision and disciplining of such producers; and
- Assessing licensing fees for insurance producers.

Also, the Property and Casualty Insurance Committee of the NAIC and its Terrorism Insurance Implementation Working Group (TIIWG) recently implemented a *Model Bulletin*. This enforcement measure includes an expedited filing form to help state regulators advise insurance companies about regulatory requirements related to terrorism coverage under the modified program.

Chapter Review

This chapter explained the general structure and common provisions of property and casualty policies. Let's review them:

	BASIC PRINCIPLES AND CONCEPTS
Insurable Interest	• Must exist at the time of loss • Financial interest in preserving the property to be insured • Destruction or property damage will cause a direct economic loss
Underwriting	• Consists of risk selection and the evaluation process • Establishes terms, rates, and conditions

Rates	• The amount charged for coverage
	• A class/manual rating applies to applicants with particular characteristics (e.g., gender, geographic location, etc.)
	• Includes individual rate-making approaches:
	   o Judgement rating
	   o Schedule rating
	   o Experience rating
	   o Merit rating

Negligence	• Failure to use reasonable and prudent care
	• Includes four elements:
	   o Legal duty
	   o Standard of care
	   o Unbroken chain of events
	   o Actual loss or damage

Damages	• Comprised of bodily injury or property damage • *Special damages* – out-of-pocket expenses for medical, miscellaneous expenses, or loss of wages • *General damages* – compensate for pain and suffering, mental anguish, or disfigurement • *Punitive damage* – punishment for extreme behavior, gross negligence, or willful intent
Liability	• *Strict liability* – often applied to product liability cases • *Vicarious liability* – liability imposed on one party as a result of another
	POLICY STRUCTURE
Policy Components	• *Declarations* – contains underwriting information such as the insured's name, address, amount of coverage, premiums, and a description of insured locations • *Definitions* – clarifies the terms used in the policy • *Insuring agreement* – establishes the obligation of the insurer to provide the insurance coverages as stated in the policy • *Additional coverage* – provides an additional amount of coverage for specific loss expenses at no additional premium • *Conditions* – indicates the general procedures or rules that the insured and insurer agree to follow under the terms of the policy • *Exclusions* – perils that are not insured against and individuals who are not insured • *Endorsements* – addendums that modify a contract

COMMON POLICY PROVISIONS	
Insureds	• *Named Insured* – the individual whose name appears in the Declarations • *First named insured* – first appears in the Declarations; has control of policy • *Additional insureds* – individuals protected under a policy but not named
Policy Period and Territory	• *Policy period* – the period in which the policy provides coverage • *Policy territory* – the location where coverage is provided
Cancellation and Nonrenewal	• *Cancellation* – the termination of an in-force policy before its expiration date • *Nonrenewal* – the termination of a policy at its expiration date
Deductibles	• A dollar amount that must be made before the policy provides coverage • The higher the deductible, the lower the premium amount
Other Insurance	• A provision defining how a policy will pay in response to other valid insurance on the same risk • *Primary policy* – pays first for covered loss • *Excess policy* – pays for covered loss after primary policies pays up to limit • *Pro rata* – the sharing of a loss written on the same risk in proportion to their limits • *Contribution by equal shares* – each insurer contributes an equal amount
Limits of Liability	• The maximum amount of money an insurer will pay for a particular loss • *Per occurrence* – sets the amount for all claims arising from a single accident or occurrence • *Per person* – the maximum amount payable for bodily injury of a single person • *Aggregate* – the maximum limit of coverage available during a policy year • *Split* – separately stated limits of liability for different coverages • *Combined single* – a single dollar limit that applies to combined damages for bodily injury or property damage as a result of one accident or occurrence
Insurer Provisions	• *Liberalization* – broader legislated or regulated coverage is extended to current policies at no additional premium • *Subrogation* – *an insurer's right to seek damages from third party, after reimbursing insured* • *Duty to defend* – an insurer's requirement to defend insured in lawsuit arising out of covered liability
Binders	• A temporary agreement offering temporary coverage before issuing a policy • Binders can be written or oral • Expiration occurs when a policy is issued
FEDERAL LAWS	
Terrorism Risk Insurance Act (TRIA)	• A temporary federal program • Intended to share the risk of loss from terrorist attacks with other insurers • The insured must meet deductibles and retentions before receiving government reimbursement

CHAPTER 4:
Dwelling Policy

This chapter will teach you about the dwelling property policy, its purpose, coverage forms, provisions, and endorsements. By the end of the section, you should be able to explain what is covered and excluded under the three dwelling property forms: basic, broad, and special.

- Purpose and Eligibility
- General Form Structure
- Coverage Forms – Perils Insured Against
- Policy Form – Property Coverages
- General Exclusions
- Conditions
- Selected Endorsements
- Personal Liability Supplement

Purpose and Eligibility

The ISO created the dwelling property policy to be used mainly as a property coverage form. Property owners can use the policy to insure the dwelling, its contents, or both. There are three separate coverage forms available under the dwelling program, which include *basic*, *broad*, and *special* form coverage. Endorsements exist to alter the coverage to tailor it to the applicant's particular needs. The policy does not include liability coverage, but it can be added. This form is a commonly used policy form to insure rental dwellings.

It is critical to note that the ISO classifies dwelling property policies as DP with a corresponding form number to indicate the policy type (DP-1, DP-2, or DP-3).

Property owners can purchase a dwelling property policy to cover properties used exclusively for residential purposes in the following situations:

- Up to four residential units;
- Up to five roomers or boarders;
- Properties in the course of construction;
- Owner-occupied, tenant-occupied, or both;
- Mobile homes on the basic form only, if they contain no more than one apartment and are located at a permanent site listed in the policy;
- Seasonal dwellings vacant for three or more months during a 12-month period; or
- Not intended as farm property.

Under the dwelling property program, business occupancies may impact eligibility. Insurers can accommodate business occupancies if they are incidental, conducted by the policy owner on the dwelling premises, and as long as no more than two workers are employed. Allowable incidental occupancies include small service operations where the sale of merchandise is not the primary function. Examples include tailors, beauty and barber shops, or shoe repair operations that use handwork only. Insurers may also consider studios such as music or photography, private schools, or professional offices.

General Form Structure

The three coverage forms that apply to the dwelling property policy define the perils or causes of loss insured against, coverages, other coverages, exclusions, and conditions. All ISO forms have a specific flow to the information. The DP form structure is as follows:

1. **Agreement** — Insuring agreement (states that the insurer will provide coverage described in the policy in return for the premium paid and compliance with all applicable policy provisions);
2. **Definitions** — Limited in nature;
3. **Deductible** — Applies to every covered loss unless otherwise noted in the policy form;
4. **Coverages, including Other Coverages** — Defines direct and indirect property coverages and other coverages that are included with the premium;
5. **Perils Insured Against** — Perils vary by form and are a key differentiator in selecting a form;
6. **General Exclusions** — Perils that are not covered in all forms; and
7. **Conditions** — Specify when coverage applies.

The forms available in the dwelling program include:

Form Name	Form Number	Peril Type(s)
Basic	DP 00 01 or DP-1	Named Peril
Broad	DP 00 02 or DP-2	Named Peril
Special	DP 00 03 or DP-3	Open and Named Peril

Coverage Forms – Perils Insured Against

Basic

Dwelling Property 1 – Basic Form (DP-1)		
Included in Base Form	**Option 1 (Additional Charge)**	**Option 2 (Additional Charge)**
Fire Lightning Internal Explosion	Basic Perils + Extended Coverage Perils Windstorm or Hail Explosion Smoke Aircraft Vehicles Riot or Civil Commotion Volcanic Eruption	Basic Perils + Extended Coverage Perils + Vandalism or Malicious Mischief (must be purchased)

The *basic* dwelling form DP-1 is a named peril coverage form that provides the most limited coverage of the three forms. Understanding the conditions in which a particular peril does not apply is essential. Unlike the broad and special forms, no minimum coverage is required for the basic form. The basic form covers the following perils or causes of loss:

Fire or Lightning and Internal Explosion – An explosion that occurs in a dwelling, other structure, or a structure containing insured personal property will be covered. Coverage does not include damage or loss caused by electric arcing, breakage or operation of pressure relief devices, breakage of water pipes, or explosion of steam pipes or steam boilers leased, owned, or operated by the policyholder. An explosion of a gas stove is an example of a covered loss.

For the peril of fire to be covered, the loss must result from a hostile fire. This type of fire is not intentional and not contained within its intended boundaries, unlike a friendly fire (e.g., a fireplace or firepit). If a friendly fire escapes these boundaries and causes damage to other property, the fire would then be considered a hostile fire and will be covered by the policy. However, a fire does not have to originate from a friendly fire to be considered hostile.

In addition to these causes of loss, the policy owner can add the *extended coverage perils* to the basic policy for an *added premium*. This coverage is included in the basic form. Still, it is only activated if it appears in the Declarations and with payment of the added premium.

Windstorm or hail – Damage to the covered property from windstorm or hail is insured subject to the following limitations:

- Antennas, signs, and awnings outside the dwelling are not covered.
- Damage by rain, sleet, snow, dust, or sand to the interior of a building or personal property located in the dwelling. Insurers will only cover this damage if the wind or hail damages a wall or the roof of the building first, which creates an opening to the interior of the building. For example, if interior damage resulted from wind or hail entering through an open window, there would be no coverage.
- No coverage applies to canoes and rowboats (outside of the building); and
- No coverage for lawns, plants, shrubs, or trees.

Explosion – The peril of *internal explosion* is broadened in the extended coverage perils. The explosion does not have to take place *inside* the dwelling. The same coverage limitations apply to explosions as in the internal explosion peril.

Riot or civil commotion;

Aircraft – Includes spacecraft and self-propelled missiles.

Vehicles – Coverage does not apply to damage resulting from vehicles operated or owned by a policyholder or a resident of the location listed in the policy. There is also no coverage for damage or loss to walks, driveways, or fences caused by a vehicle.

Smoke – Sudden and accidental damage caused by smoke is covered (including the puff back or emission of vapors, fumes, soot, or smoke from a boiler or furnace). Coverage does not include smoke from a fireplace (friendly fires), industrial operations, or agricultural smudging.

Volcanic eruption – There is no coverage for loss caused by earthquakes, tremors, or land shock waves.

It may be helpful to use the following acronyms to help remember the extended coverage perils:

WHARVES	W.C. SHAVER
• **W**indstorm;	• **W**indstorm;
• **H**ail;	• **C**ivil commotion;
• **A**ircraft/vehicles;	• **S**moke;
• **R**iot/civil commotion;	• **H**ail;
• **V**olcanic eruption;	• **A**ircraft;
• **E**xplosion;	• **V**ehicle and volcano;
• **S**moke.	• **E**xplosion;
	• **R**iots.

The policy owner could also add protection against vandalism and malicious mischief if the policy insures against extended coverage perils.

Vandalism or malicious mischief (VMM) – Covers damage or loss to property resulting from malicious and willful destruction of the insured property. Exceptions to coverage include:

- Glass breakage or safety glazing material that is part of the building (except glass building blocks) is not covered by this peril. For example, insurers would not cover a vandalized window, but they would cover decorative glass building blocks.
- Damage to the building resulting from burglary or theft is covered; however, the stolen property is not covered.
- There is no coverage if, immediately before the loss, the insured's location has been vacant for *more than 60 consecutive days (30 consecutive days in New York)*.

Broad

The *broad form* (DP-2) coverage expands the causes of loss insured under the basic form with extended coverage perils, and protection against vandalism or malicious mischief (must be purchased). The broad form further broadens coverage for the following perils:

- Breakage of glass and safety glazing material that is part of the building would be protected against vandalism or malicious mischief. Remember, under the DP-1 form, only glass building blocks are covered for this type of loss;
- The explosion peril no longer has the exceptions listed under the basic form.

Described below are the *seven additional broad form perils*:

Damage by burglars – The dwelling broad form includes burglary damage as a separate peril. The DP-1 form has this protection under vandalism or malicious mischief. Coverage is now provided for damage to any covered property (not just the building) if it resulted from burglary. There is no coverage for property theft if the dwelling has been unoccupied for *more than 60 consecutive days* immediately before the loss occurs.

Falling objects – Coverage for loss or damage caused by falling objects, except damage to towers, masts, outdoor radio and television antennas or aerials, outdoor equipment, fences, or awnings. Damage to a building's interior is covered only if an exterior wall or the roof was damaged first. There is no protection against the falling object itself.

Weight of snow, sleet, or ice – Loss or damage to the building or contents caused by the weight of snow, sleet, or ice is covered. There is no coverage for damage to patios, pavement, retaining walls, foundations, fences, awnings, swimming pools, docks, wharves, or piers.

Accidental discharge or overflow of water or steam – Damage from accidental discharge or leakage of water or steam from an automatic sprinkler system, heating, air conditioning, or plumbing is covered. The cost of tearing out and replacing part of the building is also covered if necessary to replace or repair the appliance. Tear-out coverage will apply to other structures only if actual damage occurs to these structures.

However, the policy will not pay for damage or loss resulting from repeated or continuous seepage over weeks, months, or years. It will also not cover the cost of replacing or repairing the appliance itself. Nor will it consider a downspout, gutter, roof drain, or sump pump as an appliance that triggers coverage. Damage caused by discharge from an off-premises storm drain, sewer, or steam pipe is not covered. When a dwelling is unoccupied for more than 60 consecutive days (*30 days in New York*) before the loss, this peril will be excluded from coverage.

Sudden and accidental bulging, burning, cracking, or tearing apart – The sudden and accidental bulging, burning, cracking, or tearing apart of appliances from an automatic fire protection sprinkler system, an air-conditioning system, steam or hot water heating system, or an appliance for heating water is covered. Loss resulting from freezing is not covered, but it is covered in the freezing peril noted below.

Freezing – The freezing of automatic sprinkler systems, heating, air conditioning, or plumbing is covered only if the policy owner has shut off the water and drained the pipes and appliances or has taken appropriate steps to maintain heat in the building. Items that are not considered appliances will not be covered for freezing.

Sudden and accidental damage from artificially generated electrical current – There is no coverage for damage to transistors, tubes, circuitry, or electronic components of computers, appliances, fixtures, and home entertainment units.

The acronym **B.B. BICE-GOLF** can be utilized to memorize the broad form coverage perils:

- **B**ursting of heating systems;
- **B**urglary damage;
- **B**reaking of water heaters;
- **I**ce, snow, or sleet weight;
- **C**ollapse of a building;
- **E**lectrical damage (artificially generated);
- **G**lass breakage;
- **O**bjects falling from outside;
- **L**eakage of water or steam damage;
- **F**reezing of plumbing.

In addition, the following other coverages are included in the broad form:

Lawns, trees, shrubs, and plants – Plants, shrubs, trees, and lawns are covered if the damage or loss was caused by the following: lightning, fire, explosion, riot or civil commotion, vandalism, malicious mischief (excluding theft), non-owned or operated vehicles, or aircraft. This additional insurance is limited to $500 per plant, shrub, or tree and a maximum per loss of 5% of the dwelling's coverage.

Breakage of glass – Glass or safety glazing material that is a part of the insured building, including storm windows and storm doors, is covered. Also covered is damage or loss to other covered property resulting from the glass breakage. There is no protection for glass breakage if the building or structure has been unoccupied for a certain number of days (more than 60 consecutive days).

Collapse – The broad and special forms protect against the collapse of a building or a part of a building if the loss is caused by the following: the use of defective methods or materials in construction (if the collapse occurs during construction), the weight of personal property, or rain that collects on the roof, insect, vermin (only if the existence of such was unknown to the policyholder) or hidden decay, or one of the broad form perils. Collapse does not include expansion, bulging, shrinkage, cracking, or settling; it is not considered an additional amount of insurance.

Special

The special form (DP-3) is an open peril form, unlike the basic and broad forms, which are named peril forms. In other words, every peril is covered except those that are excluded. The special form only insures the dwelling and other structures on an *open peril basis*. The policy owner's personal property is covered for the *broad named perils* found in the DP-2 form, with a few exceptions that will be discussed.

The main differences between the special form DP-3 and broad form DP-2 coverages include the following:

- Theft of property that is a part of the dwelling or other structure is insured against in the special form.
- Coverage for *accidental discharge or overflow of water and steam* is broadened to cover loss caused by accidental discharge or overflow from steam or water pipes that occurs *off* the insured premises.

- Awnings, fences, outdoor equipment, or antennas are not excluded from the peril of *falling objects* in the special form.
- The special form policy will provide coverage for damage to a roof resulting from freezing or thawing of water under roof shingles (an ice dam).

BASIC FORM	BROAD FORM	SPECIAL FORM
Fire **Lightning** **Internal explosion** **Extended Coverage Perils:** Windstorm or hail Explosion Riot or civil commotion Aircraft Vehicles Smoke Volcanic eruption **Added coverage:** Vandalism and malicious mischief	**Basic perils + Extended coverage perils + VMM** Damage by burglars Falling objects Weight of ice, snow, or sleet Accidental discharge or overflow of water or steam Sudden and accidental damage from artificially generated electrical current Sudden and accidental tearing apart, cracking, burning, or bulging Freezing	All risks except those specifically excluded

Policy Form – Property Coverages

The dwelling policy has four core property coverages for policy owners. The broad and special forms add additional coverage, totaling five property coverages. The table on the following page breaks down these coverages:

	Damage Type	DP-1	DP-2	DP-3
A – Dwelling	Direct	x	x	x
B – Other Structures	Direct	x	x	x
C – Personal Property	Direct	x	x	x
D – Fair Rental Value	Indirect	x	x	x
E – Additional Living Expense	Indirect	Added by Endorsement	x	x

Coverage letters A through D are included in the basic, broad, or special policy forms. Additional living expense (Coverage E) is not included in the basic form but can be added by endorsement. Fair rental value (Coverage D) and additional living expense (Coverage E) are indirect coverages that can only be added to direct property coverage.

Coverage is indicated by showing a premium and limit of liability on the declarations page. A standard deductible will apply to all property coverages except for fair rental value (Coverage D) and additional living expense (Coverage E).

Coverage A – Dwelling

Coverage A – Dwelling defines what is covered as a dwelling. The owner must use the dwelling primarily for dwelling or residential purposes. The description of coverage is divided into two parts, including property covered and not covered.

PROPERTY COVERED

1. Dwelling on the listed premises described in the Declarations and all attached structures;
2. Any supplies or materials located on or next to the described premises used to repair, alter, or construct the dwelling or other structures on the premises;
3. Outdoor equipment and building equipment located on the premises and used to service the location unless insured elsewhere.

PROPERTY NOT COVERED

1. Land, including land on which the dwelling described on the declarations page is located.

Coverage B – Other Structures

Coverage B – Other Structures insures separate structures at the same location, such as a detached garage and other *outbuildings* (e.g., fences or sheds). The policy allows other structures to be used for business purposes within defined parameters.

PROPERTY COVERED

1. Other buildings or structures on the described premises that are separate from the dwelling by a clear space or connected only by a utility line, fence, or similar connection;
2. Other buildings or structures rented to anyone besides a tenant of the dwelling, but only when used as a private garage; and
3. Buildings or structures used in business (farming, manufacturing, and commercial) when storing property owned solely by a tenant of the dwelling or the policy owner. Property owners must store liquid or gaseous fuel in a tank that is part of a craft or vehicle in the building or structure.

PROPERTY NOT COVERED

1. Land, including the land where the other buildings or structures are located;
2. Buildings or structures rented or held for rental to anyone besides a tenant of the dwelling when not used as a private garage;
3. Other buildings or structures that are used in business (farming, manufacturing, and commercial), whether in part or whole, unless used as noted above;
4. Mausoleums and grave markers.

Coverage C – Personal Property

Coverage C – Personal Property can be purchased to cover personal property found in a residence. When no premium is charged, and no limit is shown, the coverage does not apply even though it may be referenced in the policy. Personal property coverage provided by the dwelling policy is primarily designed to protect private property located on the described premises. In actuality, personal property coverage is defined more by the property that is not covered. Be sure to carefully review the list of property covered and not covered below.

PROPERTY COVERED

1. Personal property found in a dwelling, located on the described premises for the policy owner and resident family members, as well as property of residence employees or guests (may be insured at the discretion of the policy owner);

2. Hobby or model aircraft (not designed or used to carry cargo or people), including any parts whether or not they are attached to the aircraft;
3. Motor vehicles and other conveyances but only while used to assist the disabled or designed to service the premises;
4. Canoes and rowboats;
5. Prepackaged computer software and blank storage media;
6. Property relocated to a newly acquired residence for 30 days. The limit shown on the declarations page will be applied proportionally to each residence. Insurers will not extend coverage beyond the expiration date of the policy.

PROPERTY NOT COVERED
1. Currency, coins, securities, accounts, bills, deeds, banknotes, passports, manuscripts, and evidence of debt;
2. Birds, fish, animals, and property that was damaged by domestic animals;
3. Aircraft designed or used for flight, including any parts, whether they are attached or not, other than hobby aircraft noted above;
4. Watercraft other than noted above;
5. Hovercraft and parts;
6. Motor vehicles and other motorized land conveyances, including electronic equipment powered by the vehicle, other than noted above. Also included are accessories, parts to the vehicle, and electronic equipment, but only while in or upon the vehicle;
7. The cost to recover data stored in various mediums;
8. Debit cards, credit cards, or any device used to transfer, withdraw or deposit funds;
9. Water or steam (e.g., a broken water pipe significantly increases an insured's water bill);
10. Mausoleums and grave markers.

Coverage D – Fair Rental Value

Coverage D – Fair Rental Value is applied if the property under Coverage A, B, or C is destroyed or damaged by a covered peril in the policy.

For example, Don owns a 2-family home that he rents to tenants. A fire damages the downstairs unit, rendering the property uninhabitable. Don cannot collect his standard rent while the property is under renovation. Insurers will cover this type of loss. However, when a flood damages Don's rental property, insurers will not cover this loss because the dwelling property form does not cover the flood.

Key points of this coverage include the following:

- The policy will pay the fair rental value of the described premises. It will deduct any expenses that discontinue while the premises are unfit for use (such as electricity and heat).
- Coverage continues until all repairs are complete, but only for the shortest time required. The insurance provider will pay only a proportional share of the total rental amount for every month the rented area of the insured location is unfit for its regular use.
- Policy expiration will not end the payment of an existing covered claim.
- If a civil authority prohibits the use of the insured property due to direct damage to a neighboring property, insurers will cover payment for the loss for up to two weeks.
- Coverage does not apply to any expense or loss associated with the cancellation of a lease.

Coverage E – Additional Living Expense

Coverage E – Additional Living Expense is only available if broad or special form dwelling coverage is issued. It can be added to the basic form by endorsement. It pays for the increase in the insured's usual living expenses while the described premises are unfit for regular use. This coverage is indirect, like fair rental value, so the policy is triggered only when the policy covers a direct damage claim (A, B, C). These increased expenses include things such as rent for alternative housing. The intention is to allow the family to maintain their usual standard of living.

The following are essential points for this type of coverage:

- Coverage will continue until all repairs are complete, but only for the shortest time required;
- Policy expiration will not end the payment of an existing covered claim;
- If a civil authority prohibits the use of the insured property due to direct damage to a neighboring property, payment for the loss will be covered for up to two weeks; and
- Coverage is not applied to any expense or loss associated with the cancellation of a lease.

Other Coverages

The DP-1, DP-2, and DP-3 coverage forms include other coverages that extend the major coverages (A, B, C, D, and E). These other coverages are included in the premium and are subject to the property deductible unless noted in the form. Every coverage form contains the following eight other coverages:

Other structures – The policy owner may elect to apply up to 10% of the dwelling insurance amount (Coverage A) to protect other structures on the insured premises. In the basic form, this is not an additional amount of insurance and will lower the available amount under Coverage A by 10% in the event of a concurrent loss. In the broad and special forms, coverage is automatically provided and considered an additional amount of insurance.

Debris removal – Debris removal coverage pays reasonable costs to remove debris after a covered loss occurs. Coverage includes the cost of removing dust or ash caused by a volcanic eruption. This coverage is not considered an additional amount of insurance.

Improvements, alterations, and additions – If the policy owner is a tenant, up to 10% of the personal property limit (Coverage C) will apply to damage or loss to additions, alterations, or improvements by the tenant. In the DP-1 form, this is not considered an additional amount of insurance and will not increase the total amount of insurance payable in the event of a loss. In the DP-2 and DP-3 forms, this is considered an additional amount of insurance and will not lower the Coverage C limit for the same loss.

Worldwide coverage – The policy owner may apply up to 10% of the personal property limit (Coverage C) to pay for losses to personal property away from the premises anywhere in the world. Coverage is not applied to canoes or rowboats in any dwelling form. Property of servants and guests is not covered away from the insured premises in the DP-1 form; however, the broad and special forms allow for servant or guest property coverage. This coverage is not regarded as an additional amount of insurance.

Rental value and additional living expense – Up to 20% of the limit of liability (Coverage A) may be used for loss of both fair rental value (Coverage D) and additional living expense (Coverage E). The DP-1 form will only apply this coverage to fair rental value because additional living expense is not included. The 20% coverage extension is not considered additional insurance in the DP-1 form; it is additional insurance in the DP-2 (broad) and DP-3 (special) forms.

Reasonable repairs – Reasonable expenses incurred by the policy owner for repairs necessary to protect property from further damage at the time of a covered loss are also covered. This coverage is not considered an additional amount of insurance.

Property removed – The policy will protect against loss or damage to property removed from the insured premises when threatened by a covered peril. Perils insured against are converted to *open peril coverage* during the removal process. The basic form provides five days of coverage, while the broad and special forms provide coverage for 30 days.

Fire department service charge – Insurers will cover up to $500 for expenses incurred by the policy owner because of an agreement to pay the fire department if they respond to a fire at the described premises. This coverage is considered additional insurance, and no deductible applies to this coverage.

Other coverages that are only included in the *broad and special forms* are as follows:

Plants, shrubs, trees, and lawns – Loss or damage to plants, shrubs, trees, and lawns are covered on a named peril basis if the loss or damage resulted from the following: lightning, fire, explosion, riot or civil commotion, vehicles (if not owned or operated by a policy owner), aircraft, or vandalism and malicious mischief (excluding theft). This coverage is considered an additional amount of insurance and is limited to a maximum of:

- 5% of the amount of coverage on the dwelling per loss; or
- $500 per plant, shrub, or tree.

Breakage of glass – Glass or safety glazing material that is a part of the insured building or structure, including storm windows and storm doors, is covered in the policy from perils, including earth movement. Loss or damage to other covered property resulting from the breakage of glass is also covered. There is no coverage for the breakage of glass if the building or structure has been unoccupied for a stated number of days. This limitation does not apply to damage resulting from earth movement. If safety glazing materials are required by law or ordinance, the insurer will settle the loss on a replacement basis.

Collapse – Collapse refers to an abrupt falling down of the building or part of the building in which the building can no longer be used for its intended purpose. Suppose the building is in danger of collapse or shows signs of settling, leaning, bending, sagging, bulging, cracking, shrinkage, or expansion. In that case, it will not be considered in a state of collapse.

The covered perils include:

- Damage from vermin or insects hidden from sight;
- Decay that is hidden from sight;
- The use of defective methods or materials in construction (if the collapse happens during construction);
- The weight of rain that collects on the roof or personal property; and
- Broad form perils for both the broad and special forms.

Ordinance or Law – This coverage provides a policy owner additional insurance for expenses associated with changes to building codes and ordinances after a covered loss. The broad and special form policies allow up to 10% of Coverage A (or B if there is no coverage limit for A) if the policy owner owns the premises. If the insured is a tenant, then 10% of the limit of liability associated with additions, alterations, and improvements will apply. Coverage is provided for the undamaged and damaged portions of the dwelling with limitations for cleanup of pollutants and loss of value.

General Exclusions

Several general exclusions in the dwelling policy forms define the extent of coverage provided. The exclusions contained in all three dwelling forms are explained below.

Ordinance or law – Coverage does not apply to costs incurred from any ordinance or law that regulates the use, construction, or repair of any property. Also, costs incurred from the required tear-down of any property are not covered. This general exclusion conveys the intent of the form. It narrows the focus of covered claims to only what is described in the Other Coverage section. Coverage is also excluded for requirements to test, monitor, clean up, or remove pollutants and a resulting loss in value of the structure.

Earth movement – Earthquakes and land shock waves associated with volcanic activity are not covered. Sinkholes, mudslides, rising, sinking, mudflow, shifting, and landslides (caused by or resulting from any act of nature or human or animal forces) also are not covered. However, any resulting damages caused by the ensuing fire or explosion are covered.

Water damage – Damage resulting from the following is not covered: surface water, flood, waves (including tsunami and tidal wave, tidal water, tides, the overflow of any body of water or spray from any of these), whether driven by wind or not, including storm surge. Water or waterborne material that backs up through drains or sewers or overflows from a sump or sump pump is also not covered. Below-surface water that seeps or exerts pressure on a building and other structures would be excluded from coverage.

Power failure – A failure of power or other utility services that occurs off the location listed in the policy. When a power failure occurring off-premises triggers a peril covered in the policy, the insurer will cover damage to property by that peril.

Neglect – If further damage occurs at the time of loss because the policy owner neglected to try to preserve or save the property, there is no coverage for the additional damage or loss.

War – Damage resulting from war, revolution, rebellion, or insurrection is not covered.

Nuclear hazard – This exclusion refers to a policy condition we will discuss later in the chapter. The policy will not respond to losses caused by nuclear reaction, radiation, or radioactive contamination.

Intentional loss – Coverage is not provided for an individual who commits or directs another to commit an act with the intent to cause a loss.

Governmental action – This refers to the seizure, confiscation, or destruction of property (Coverages A, B, and C) by order of governmental authority. This exclusion is not applied to action taken to prevent the spread of a fire if the policy covers fire losses.

Special Form (DP-3) Exclusions – Other than the general exclusions found in all dwelling forms, the special form contains the following additional exclusions that only apply to Coverages A and B. There is no coverage for damage or loss that results from:

- Weather conditions contributing to an excluded cause of loss;
- Decisions, acts, or the failure to act; and
- Faulty design, planning, or materials.

Conditions

All dwelling policy forms include the following conditions:

- Policy period;
- The limit of insurance and insurable interest;
- Fraud or concealment;
- Loss settlement;
- Duties after a loss;
- Appraisal;
- Pair or sets;
- Subrogation;
- Other insurance;
- Insurer's option to repair or replace;
- Suit against the insurer;
- Abandonment;
- Loss payment;
- No benefit to bailee;
- Mortgage holders;
- Liberalization;
- Cancellation and nonrenewal;
- Death;
- Assignment;
- Recovered property;
- Nuclear hazard;
- Volcanic eruption; and
- Loss payable clause.

Because some of these conditions are explained elsewhere in the book, the following only describes parts of any condition specific to the dwelling property forms.

Insurable Interest and Limit of Insurance

Suppose more than one individual has an insurable interest in the property. In that situation, the insurance provider will not be liable for more than the insured's interest under the policy at the time of loss or more than the applicable limit of liability.

Deductible

Unless otherwise noted, in regards to any one loss:

- The insurer will pay only the part of the total of all loss payable that exceeds the deductible shown in the Declarations; and
- Only the high deductible will apply if two or more deductibles apply to the loss.

Concealment or Fraud

Insurers will not provide coverage to any insured if one or more individuals have:

- Intentionally *concealed or misrepresented a material fact* regarding to the insurance;
- Has made false statements relating to the insurance; or
- Has engaged in fraudulent conduct.

Duties After Loss

In the event of a loss to covered property, the insurer has no obligation to provide coverage under the policy unless the policy owner complies with the following duties:

1. Give prompt notice to the insurance provider or its agent;
2. Protect the property from additional damage; if repairs are needed, the policy owner must make necessary and reasonable repairs to protect the property and keep an accurate record of repair costs;

3. Cooperate with the insurance provider in the investigation of the claim;
4. Prepare an inventory of the damaged personal property, showing the amount, actual cash value, description, and quantity of the loss;
5. Show the damaged property, provide documents and records, and agree to an examination under oath while not in the presence of another policy owner; and
6. Send the insurance provider a signed, sworn proof of loss within 60 days.

Loss Settlement

The *loss settlement* condition will vary depending on the dwelling policy form used.

Under the *basic form*, property losses are settled on an actual cash value (ACV) basis, subject to the limit of insurance and the cost to replace or repair the damaged property.

Under the *broad and special forms*, the following loss settlement conditions apply:

Personal property, structures that are not buildings, awnings, carpeting, household appliances, and outdoor equipment are all covered on an ACV basis at the time of the loss.

Dwellings and other structures insured to at least 80% of the *replacement cost* at the time of the loss are covered on a replacement cost basis with the insured receiving no more than the limit of insurance, the cost to replace or repair with like kind and quality, or the actual amount spent. If the structure is rebuilt at a new location, the cost to rebuild will be no more than what it would have cost to rebuild at the premises described in the policy. Claims covered under Coverage A (dwelling) or Coverage B (other structures) are settled at replacement cost without deducting depreciation. At the time of the loss, the insurance amount on the damaged building must be 80% or more of the total replacement cost immediately before the loss but not more than the limit of liability that applies to the building.

When the property is insured for less than 80% of the replacement cost at the time of the loss, the policy will pay the ACV or the amount calculated by the coinsurance formula, whichever is greater. The coinsurance formula determines the reimbursement a property owner or homeowner will receive from a claim.

Replacement cost losses are first paid on an actual cash value basis. When the insured confirms that repairs have been made, the insurance provider pays the balance to the insured. However, small claims (less than 5% of the insurance and less than $2,500) will be settled whether or not the repair or replacement is complete. The 80% coinsurance requirement still applies.

The policy does describe what items are not included in determining the 80% value previously noted.

The insured may disregard the replacement cost provisions and make a claim only for the actual cash value of the buildings. This election must be completed within 180 days of the loss.

Loss to a Pair or Set

The insurance provider may elect how to insure losses to the property that was part of a pair or set. The insurance provider can elect to replace or repair the missing piece to restore the set to the value before the loss. The second option is to compare the actual cash value of the pair or set before the loss to the value after the loss and then pay the difference.

Appraisal

Suppose there is a disagreement between the insurance provider and the insured regarding the value of any *property loss*. In that situation, either party can make a written request for an *appraisal*. Each party will choose an impartial and competent appraiser within 20 days of receiving a written request from the other party. The two appraisers will select an umpire. If they cannot agree on an umpire within 15 days, the insurance company and the insured can request the selection to be made by a judge in the state where the property is located.

Each party must pay their own appraiser and bear any other expenses of the appraisal and umpire equally.

Suit Against the Insurer

No one may bring a lawsuit against the insurer unless the policy owner has complied with all policy conditions. Policy owners must bring legal action within *two tears* of the date of loss.

Insurer's Option to Repair or Replace

The insurance company can repair or replace any part of the damaged property with like property. It must provide written notice to the policy owner within *30 days* of receiving a signed, sworn proof of loss.

Liberalization

There will be times when the insurance provider makes changes that broaden coverage in the policy during the policy period or 60 days before the effective date. In these cases, the revisions will apply automatically without needing to be endorsed by the policy. There are restrictions to this condition in case of general program changes from a form change or amendatory endorsement.

Death

In the event of a policy owner's death, the legal representatives of the deceased policy owner will be considered insured but only concerning the covered property at the time of death.

Nuclear Hazard

Nuclear hazard refers to any nuclear reaction or radioactive or radiation contamination. Losses from nuclear hazards will not be considered caused by smoke, explosion, or fire. This condition also states that direct or indirect losses are not insured if related to a nuclear hazard unless a fire ensues. The insurer will cover the fire damage in this case.

Recovered Property

There may be cases when the property is recovered, and the insurer has already made a loss payment. The policyholder can take the property and return the amount paid or give the property to the insurer.

Volcanic Eruptions

All volcanic eruptions within 72 hours of the initial eruption will be regarded as a single occurrence, with only one deductible.

Specific Conditions – New York

In New York, the following conditions can apply to dwelling policies:

- **Loss Payment** — Insurance providers must pay losses *within 60 days* of receiving proof of loss and agreeing with the insured on the amount payable. When a fire loss must be paid on any 3- or 4-family dwelling, the insurance provider will pay the claim of any tax district with a certificate of lien as required by New York Insurance Law. The insurer will not be obligated to pay the insured the amount necessary to pay the lien.

- **Cancellation** — The cancellation notice must be mailed to the insured at the address listed on the declarations page. Proof of mailing will be sufficient proof of notice. The insurance provider can cancel the entire policy only for the following reasons stated in this condition:
    - At any time for nonpayment of premium, by mailing the insured at least a *15-day notice* of cancellation;
    - When the policy has been effective for *no more than 60 days* and is not renewed with the insurer, it can cancel the policy for any reason with *30 days' notice* before the cancellation;
- When the policy has been effective *for 60 days or more*, or at any time if it is a renewal with the same insurer, the insurer may cancel the entire policy only for one or more of the following reasons with a *30-day notice* prior to the proposed cancellation date:
    - Conviction of a crime arising from acts increasing the hazard insured against;
    - Material misrepresentation or fraud in obtaining the policy or in presenting a claim;
    - Reckless or willful acts or omissions that increase the hazard insured against;
    - Physical changes in the property taking place after issuance or the last anniversary date of the policy if those changes make the property uninsurable or not in compliance with the insurance provider's underwriting standards;
    - A judgment by the Superintendent of Financial Services that the continuation of the policy would violate New York Insurance Law; or
    - When the policy is subject to an anti-arson application provision, an insurance provider can cancel the policy with timely notice.
    - When the insurance provider has the right to cancel, it can, instead of canceling the policy, amend the limits of liability or reduce coverage not required by law. If the insurance provider takes this action, the insured must be notified by mail *at least 20 days* before the date of such change.
- **Nonrenewal** — An insurer may only refuse or create conditions for renewing a dwelling policy if the action complies with New York regulations. The conditions can include but are not limited to, amending the limits of liability or reducing coverage not required by law. If an insurance provider takes this action, it must notify the insured *by mail at least 45 days, but no more than 60 days,* before the expiration date of this policy. Proof of mailing will serve as sufficient proof of notice. Delivery of such written notice by the insurer to the insured at the mailing address listed on the declarations page or at a forwarding address is equivalent to mailing;
- **Estimation of Claims** — Upon request, the insurance provider will furnish the insured or a representative with a written estimate of damages to real property, specifying all deductions. Such an estimate must be prepared by the insurance provider or on its behalf. The insurer will provide this estimate *within 30 days* after its request or preparation, whichever is later.

Selected Endorsements

Several optional endorsements are available to the policy owner to broaden their coverage. Listed below are the most commonly added optional dwelling policy endorsements.

Special Provisions – New York

This endorsement modifies policy language to comply with New York law. The changes have been incorporated into the text where appropriate to facilitate your study.

Dwelling Under Construction

Dwellings under construction are eligible for insurance. However, due to the distinctive nature of these risks, an endorsement is required to change the policy provisions. The limit of liability for a structure under construction is provisional and based on the finished value of the dwelling. When a loss occurs, the applicable limit is a percentage of the provisional limit, based on the proportion of the property's actual cash value at the time of loss. The premium is based on an average amount of coverage during construction.

Broad Theft Coverage

The only theft coverage provided in any dwelling policy forms is theft of property that is a part of the building listed under the special form.

There are no policy forms that insure the theft of personal property. However, policy owners can add broad theft coverage by endorsement to a dwelling policy if the insured is the owner-occupant of the dwelling.

The endorsement will cover loss or damage to personal property owned by the policy owner or a resident of the policy owner's household caused by the following: theft, attempted theft, malicious mischief, or vandalism. There is no coverage if the premises are unoccupied for more than *60 consecutive days* before the loss.

The broad theft endorsement can provide both on-premises and off-premises insurance coverage. Insurers can only insure off-premises coverage if on-premises coverage is written first. The Declarations will show a separate limit of liability for both coverages.

On-premises coverage insures loss of property used or owned by the policy owner or a resident employee at the premises listed in the policy. It also extends to property placed for safekeeping in a public warehouse, a bank, trust, or safe-deposit company, or a vacant dwelling not occupied, owned, or rented by the insured.

Off-premises coverage protects property either used or owned by the policy owner when it is away from the described premises. This coverage also protects a resident employee's property while in a dwelling occupied by a policy owner or employed by the policy owner.

No off-premises coverage for the property at a newly acquired primary residence exists. However, the on-premises limit will automatically apply for 30 days while the property is transported to the new location.

Insurers can cover certain types of property for specific amounts. Policy owners can purchase additional insurance if they require higher limits for these particular items. Listed below are the categories of property with these special sub-limits.

For a Dwelling Policy, the following coverage limits apply:

- $200 for banknotes, money, coins, bullion, gold, silver, platinum, and other metals;
- $1,500 for securities, deeds, accounts, letters of credit, evidence of debt, notes other than banknotes, passports, manuscripts, stamps, and tickets;
- $1,500 for watercraft and their outboard motors, equipment, furnishings, and trailers;
- $1,500 for other trailers;
- $1,500 for jewelry, furs, watches, and precious and semiprecious stones;
- $2,500 for firearms and related equipment; and
- $2,500 for gold and gold-plated ware, silver and silver-plated ware, and pewterware, including hollowware, flatware, trays, tea sets, and trophies.

In addition to the special limits of coverage, certain property types are *excluded*. The following are the types of property not insured by the broad theft endorsement:

- Fish, birds, or animals;
- Fund transfer cards and credit cards;

- Aircraft, hovercraft, and their parts (except hobby or model aircraft);
- Property while in the mail;
- Property held for sale or as a sample;
- Property specifically described and covered by any other insurance;
- Property of roomers, boarders, and tenants (other than relatives);
- Business property of the policy owner or resident employee;
- Property in the custody of a cleaner, laundry, tailor, dryer, or presser, except loss by burglary or robbery;
- Property at any other location occupied, rented, or owned by the policy owner, except if the policy owner is temporarily residing there;
- Motor vehicles (except motorized vehicles used to service the premises that are not subject to motor vehicle registration and vehicles designed to assist the disabled); and
- Motor vehicle accessories and equipment, including sound recording, transmitting, or receiving devices, while in the vehicle.

In New York, vandalism and malicious mischief coverage will not apply if a covered property has been *vacant* for *more than 30 consecutive days* (not the 60 days specified in generic ISO forms).

Personal Liability Supplement

Unlike homeowners policies, dwelling policies do not include *personal liability* coverage. Policy owners can add the personal liability supplement to the dwelling policy, or it can be written as a separate stand-alone policy. Endorsements are added for comprehensive on-premises or off-premises personal liability or premises-only liability, provided the dwelling is rented to other individuals. The coverage form includes three coverage types:

1. Coverage L – Personal Liability;
2. Coverage M – Medical Payments to Others; and
3. Additional Coverages.

The additional coverages include:

- Claims expenses;
- First aid to other individuals; and
- Damage to the property of others.

Liability insurance excludes a list of perils for Coverage L or Coverage M. Instead, coverage is subject to the definitions, conditions, and exclusions present in the policy.

A basic limit of $100,000 per occurrence applies to the personal liability coverage, and a limit of $1,000 per person is applied for medical payments to others. Policy owners can increase these limits for an additional premium.

Personal liability provides coverage for property damage or bodily injury to third parties that resulted from the policy owner's negligence or a condition of the policy owner's premises. Medical payments coverage pays for necessary medical expenses incurred by individuals other than an insured injured on the insured's premises or because of an insured's off-premises activities.

Chapter 4: Dwelling Policy

Chapter Review

This chapter explained the dwelling property policy, its purpose, coverage forms, and general provisions and exclusions. Let's review them:

\<td colspan=2\>	
DWELLING POLICY OVERVIEW	
Purpose and Eligibility	<ul><li>Property coverage for dwelling, contents, or both</li><li>Solely for properties used for residential purposes, including the following:<ul><li>Owner-occupied, tenant-occupied, or both;</li><li>Properties in the course of construction;</li><li>Properties with up to five roomers or boarders;</li><li>Properties with up to four residential units;</li><li>Mobile homes (Basic form only) if they contain no more than one apartment;</li><li>Seasonal dwellings unoccupied for three or more months during 12 months;</li><li>Properties not intended as farm properties</li></ul></li></ul>
Form Structure	<ul><li>Agreement</li><li>Definitions</li><li>Deductible</li><li>Coverages, including Other Coverages</li><li>Perils Insured Against</li><li>General Exclusions</li><li>Conditions</li></ul>
Coverage Forms	<ul><li>*Basic (DP1):*<ul><li>Named peril</li><li>Basic perils</li></ul></li><li>*Broad (DP2):*<ul><li>Named peril</li><li>Basic perils + extended coverage perils + VMM + broad form perils</li></ul></li><li>*Special (DP3):*<ul><li>Open Peril</li></ul></li><li>Basic perils + extended coverage perils + VMM</li></ul>
PROPERTY COVERAGES	
Property Coverages	<ul><li>*Coverage A - Dwelling* defines what is included for coverage as a dwelling and must be used primarily for residential or dwelling purposes</li><li>*Coverage B - Other Structures* covers other separate structures at the same location, like detached garages and other outbuildings (e.g., fences or sheds)</li><li>*Coverage C - Personal Property* can be purchased to insure personal property common to a residence</li><li>*Coverage D - Fair Rental Value* applies if property under Coverage A, B, or C becomes destroyed or damaged by a peril covered in the policy</li><li>*Coverage E - Additional Living Expenses* is only available if broad or special form dwelling coverage is written and pays for the increase in normal living expenses the policy owner sustains while the described premises are unfit for use</li></ul>

	PROPERTY COVERAGES *(Continued)*
Conditions	- Policy period - Insurable interest and limit of insurance - Concealment or fraud - Duties after a loss - Loss settlement - Pair or sets - Appraisal - Other insurance - Subrogation - Suit against the insurer - Insurer's option to repair or replace - Loss payment - Abandonment - Mortgage holders - No benefit to bailee - Cancellation and nonrenewal - Liberalization - Assignment - Death - Nuclear hazard - Recovered property - Volcanic eruption - Loss payable clause
General Exclusions	- Ordinance or law - Earth movement - Water damage - Power failure - Neglect - War - Nuclear hazard - Intentional loss - Government action

CHAPTER 5:
Homeowners Policy

This chapter explains the purpose and types of coverage of homeowners policies, which protects dwellings, other structures, personal property, and personal liability. You will read about covered perils, policy conditions, and exclusions. Finally, you will learn about selected endorsements available in a homeowners policy.

- Purpose and Eligibility
- General Form Structure
- Definitions
- Section I – Property Coverages
- Section I – Perils Insured Against
- Section I – Exclusions
- Section I – Conditions (Property)
- Section II – Liability Coverages
- Section II – Exclusions
- Section II – Conditions (Liability)
- Sections I and II – Conditions (Property and Liability)
- Selected Endorsements
- HO-8 Modified Coverage Form

Purpose and Eligibility

A *homeowners* insurance policy is a comprehensive coverage form used to insure residential risks. The homeowners and dwelling property forms are very similar; however, the homeowners form includes coverage for personal liability protection and personal property of the insured.

The ISO specifies homeowners policies as HO with a corresponding form number to signify the policy type (HO-2, HO-3, HO-4, HO-5, HO-6, and HO-8).

Homeowners policies can be used in the following situations or for the following types of properties:

- Owner-occupied residences with *one to four families*;
- No more than two roomers or boarders or two families per unit;
- Various ownership types to include duplexes, townhomes, dwellings under construction, life estates, and sales installment contracts;
- Insuring a tenant of a non-owned dwelling (under a renter's form);
- A residential cooperative unit or condominium (under a condominium form); and
- Secondary residences and seasonal dwellings.

Business occupancies can have an impact on eligibility under the HO program. An insurer may accommodate business occupancies provided they are incidental and conducted by the policyholder on the dwelling's premises. Acceptable incidental occupancies include studios, schools, or offices.

Coverage for businesses is very limited in the property section of the homeowners policy. These limitations affect the coverage of personal property and other structures. Liability associated with a business is omitted from the policy; however, business owners can use endorsements to offer coverage.

General Form Structure

The currently used six coverage forms applicable to HO policies define the coverages, perils, exclusions, conditions, and additional coverages. The homeowners form includes personal liability coverage. The form is separated into two sections. Section I explains the property coverage, and Section II describes the liability coverage. The insuring agreement, definitions, and common conditions unify the form.

1. Agreement;
2. Definitions;
3. Section I – Property Coverage;
4. Section I – Perils Insurance Against;
5. Section I – Exclusions;
6. Section I – Conditions;
7. Section II – Liability Coverages;
8. Section II – Exclusions;
9. Section II – Additional Coverages;
10. Section II – Conditions; and
11. Sections I and II – Conditions.

Unlike the dwelling property (DP) coverage form, the use of a homeowners form is first determined by the type of residential exposure. For example, a single-family residence owned and occupied by the policyholder will be eligible for certain HO forms. If the policyholder rents an apartment or a home, they will use a different form. After the appropriate form is selected, the ISO homeowners program offers other cause of loss forms based on the needs and budget of the insured.

Form Name and Number	Peril Type	Residential Dwelling Use
Broad Form HO 00 02 or HO-2	Named Peril	1-4 Unit Owner Occupied
Special Form HO 00 03 or HO-3	Open Peril and Named Peril	1-4 Unit Owner Occupied
Renters or Tenants Form HO 00 04 or HO-4	Named Peril	Occupied by Tenant
Comprehensive Form HO 00 05 or HO-5	Open Peril	1-4 Unit Owner Occupied
Condominium Form HO 00 06 or HO-6	Named Peril	Condominium Unit Owner Occupied
Modified Form HO 00 08 or HO-8	Named Peril	1-4 Unit Owner Occupied, Historic or Older Home

Definitions

Homeowners policy forms include a Definitions section that defines several important terms. Understanding the terms used throughout the policy is vital to comprehend the extent of coverage provided. Some of the essential terms described in the policy include the following:

Bodily Injury – *Bodily injury* includes bodily harm, sickness, or disease, including loss of services, required care, and death caused by the bodily injury.

Insured – The policy defines *an insured* as any of the following:

- The named insured;
- Family members of the named insured who reside with the named insured;
- Resident relatives under age 21 or nonrelative residents in the care of the named insured;
- Full-time students under the age of 24 who are relatives of the named insured and who were residents before attending school (the coverage is provided only until the age of 21 if the full-time student is a nonrelative); and
- In addition, for Section II – Liability, any individual who is legally liable for the insured's animals, watercraft, or certain motorized vehicles.

Insured Location – An *insured location* can be any of the following:

- The residence premises;
- Part of other premises used by the named insured as a residence and listed in the Declarations or newly acquired during the policy period;
- A location not owned by the insured but where the policy owner is living temporarily (a hotel room);
- Vacant land rented or owned by the insured, excluding farmland;

- Land owned or rented by the insured where a 1- to 4-family residential dwelling is being constructed;
- Individual or family burial vaults or cemetery plots of the insured; and
- Any part of the premises occasionally rented by an insured, except for business purposes (e.g., an insured rents a hall for a daughter's birthday party).

Residence Premises – *Residence premises* refers to:

- The single-family dwelling where the policy owner resides;
- The 2-, 3- or 4-family dwelling where the policy owner resides in at least one of the family units; or
- The part of any other building where the policy owner resides listed as the residence premises in the Declarations. Residence premises also include other grounds and structures at that location.

Property Damage – *Property damage* is the destruction of, the physical injury to, or the loss of use of any tangible property.

Residence Employee – *Residence employee* includes employees of the policy owner whose duties are related to the use or maintenance of the home, including performing similar responsibilities elsewhere.

"You," "Your," and "We" – The words *"you"* and *"your"* refer to the named insured listed on the declarations page and the spouse if they reside in the same household.

The word *we*, *us*, and *our* refers to the insurance company providing the coverage for the policy owner.

Business – According to the HO ISO forms, "business" means a trade, occupation, or profession engaged in on a full-time, part-time, or occasional basis.

Section I – Property Coverages

The homeowners policy form includes property coverage for the insured residence (Coverage A – Dwelling), other structures (Coverage B), and personal property (Coverage C – Contents), similar to the dwelling policy forms. The fourth coverage, loss of use (Coverage D), is similar to the additional living expense and fair rental value coverage described in the broad and special dwelling forms.

Every coverage form includes a basic deductible, which applies to all coverages unless noted in the policy.

Coverage Name	Damage Type	HO-2	HO-3	HO-4	HO-5	HO-6	HO-8
A Dwelling	Direct	x	x	None	x	x	x
B Other Structures	Direct	x	x	None	x	In A	x
C Personal Property	Direct	x	x	x	x	x	x
D Loss of Use	Indirect	x	x	x	x	x	x

Coverage A – Dwelling

Dwelling coverage is provided in every form except the HO-4. The coverage is defined similarly to the dwelling property form, except that outdoor equipment or building equipment used for servicing the residence is no longer in Coverage A. Because contents coverage is in every HO form, these items will be insured in Coverage C. The HO-6 condominium form combines Coverage A and Coverage B in this policy section.

PROPERTY COVERED

1. A dwelling on the described premises shown on the declarations page and all attached structures;
2. Supplies or materials located on or next to the residence used to construct, repair, or alter the dwelling or other structures on the premises;
3. HO-6 policies also include the following: appliances, alterations, items of real property, fixtures that are part of the building, property which is the policy owner's duty to insure as part of an agreement, and structures owned solely by the policy owner other than the residence.

PROPERTY NOT COVERED

1. Land, including land on which the residence or other tangible property is located;
2. The HO-6 form also includes items that typically are not insured under Coverage B. Such items include:
    - Other structures for renting to an individual who is not a tenant of the dwelling unless it is a private garage;
    - Structures used to conduct business operations; and
    - Structures used to store business property unless the policy owner or a tenant of the dwelling owns the property.

Coverage B – Other Structures

Under *Coverage B – Other Structures*, a basic amount of insurance equal to 10% of the limit found in Coverage A is included for other structures. Still, a policy can be issued with higher limits. The definition of other structures is similar to that of the dwelling policy program, with several notable exceptions. The HO form substitutes the definition of a business with the coverage description. The homeowners forms add coverage for mausoleums and grave markers as they are no longer included in the list of property not covered.

PROPERTY COVERED

1. Other structures on the residence premises that are separated by a clear space from the dwelling or connected only by a utility line, fence, or similar connection;
2. Other structures rented to another person besides the dwelling's tenant, but only when used as a private garage;
3. Structures used to store the dwelling tenant's business property, as long as liquid or gaseous fuel is stored in a fuel tank of a craft or vehicle stored in the structure.

PROPERTY NOT COVERED

1. Land, including land on which the other structures are located;
2. Structures held for rental or rented to another person besides the dwelling's tenant when not being used as a private garage;
3. Other structures used to transact any business.

Coverage C – Personal Property

Personal property coverage is the most notable change from the dwelling property policy. Coverage C was optional in the dwelling policy but is now mandatory coverage in every homeowners form. The HO-2, HO-3, HO-

5, and HO-8 will automatically include a limit of insurance equal to 50% of the Coverage A limit. This limit may be increased or decreased, but not below 40% for 1- and 2-family residences. Because the HO-3 policy form covers structures on an open peril basis, the insurance provider would pay $1,000 minus any deductible the policy owner must pay. In the HO-4 and HO-6 policy forms, the amount of insurance is chosen by the policy owner, with coverage minimums varying by state.

Special limits of liability in a homeowners policy are as follows:

- $200 for money, banknotes, coins, bullion, gold, silver (except goldware and silverware), platinum, and other metals;
- $1,500 for securities, accounts, notes other than bank notes, deeds, letters of credit, evidence of debt, tickets, passports, manuscripts, and stamps;
- $1,500 for watercraft and their outboard motors, equipment, furnishings, and trailers;
- $1,500 for other trailers;
- $1,500 for theft of jewelry, furs, watches, precious, and semiprecious stones;
- $2,500 for theft of firearms;
- $2,500 for theft of goldware and gold-plated ware, silverware and silver-plated ware, and pewterware, including hollowware, flatware, trays, tea sets, and trophies;
- $2,500 for the business personal property on the premises;
- $1,500 for property away from the premises used to conduct business;
- $1,500 for loss of portable electronic equipment that produces, transmits, or receives audio, visual, or data signals while in a motor vehicle; and
- $250 for loss of wires, antennas, or any media used with the electronic equipment in a motor vehicle.

The limit of property at *other residences* includes the following:

- Personal property usually located at another residence of the policy owner is covered for 10% of the Coverage C limit, or $1,000, whichever is larger. This limitation does not apply if the property is moved because the residence premises is being rebuilt, renovated, or repaired.
- When the property is moved to a newly obtained residence for 30 days, the limit shown in the Declarations will apply proportionally to each residence. Coverage will not extend beyond the policy's expiration date.

PROPERTY COVERED

1. Personal property used or owned by the policyholder while it is anywhere in the world. At the named insured's discretion, guests, property of others, or residence employees may also be covered while on the residence premises. Residence employees may also have their personal belongings covered while in any residence a policyholder is occupying;
2. Property of roomers and boarders related to a policyholder;
3. Hobby aircraft and parts not used or designed to transport people;
4. Motor vehicles and other conveyances but only while in use to service the premises or designed to assist disabled individuals;
5. Prepackaged computer software and blank storage media.

PROPERTY NOT COVERED

1. Any items that are separately described and insured irrespective of the limit of insurance;
2. Fish, birds, and animals;
3. Aircraft and parts, whether attached or not, except hobby aircraft noted above;
4. Hovercraft and parts;
5. Motor vehicles and other motorized land conveyances, except those noted above. Included in this is

electronic equipment powered exclusively by the vehicle. Also included are vehicle accessories and parts and electronic apparatus, but only while in or upon the vehicle;
6. Business data contained in paper records or books of accounts in computer equipment;
7. Property of tenants, roomers, and boarders (when not a relative of the policy owner);
8. Property in an apartment usually held for rental or rented by a policy owner;
9. Property held for rental or rented by the policy owner to others while off the residence premises;
10. Debit cards, credit cards, or any device used to withdraw, deposit, or transfer funds;
11. Water or steam (e.g., a broken water pipe considerably increases a policy owner's water bill).

Coverage C in homeowners forms is divided into four categories. Some of the notable *differences* between HO and DP property policy forms include

1. **Covered property** — HO policies extend coverage to anywhere in the world. The DP policy is predominantly used for personal property in the described location.
2. **Limit for the property at other residences** — Similar to the worldwide property coverage included in the DP policies. The sublimit only applies to other owned residences.
3. **Special limits of liability** — Sublimit amounts and property types are similar to those found in the Broad Theft Endorsement for DP forms; however, in HO forms, it is essential to note the categories that are only limited by the peril of theft.
4. **Property not covered** — Limitations are added to the HO policy for the property of tenants, roomers, and boarders.

Coverage D – Loss of Use

Every homeowners policy contains the *Loss of Use* coverage, which is a combination of Coverage D (Fair Rental Value) and Coverage E (Additional Living Expense) found in the dwelling property policy. When a covered loss makes part of the residence premises unfit to live in, the insurer will cover the loss of rent and additional living expenses for the shortest time required to replace or repair the damage. If the policy owner permanently relocates, the insurer will pay additional living expenses for the shortest time necessary to settle elsewhere.

Additional living expenses include any necessary increase in the cost of living the policy owner incurs for their household to maintain its usual living standard. Suppose loss of use results from the order of a civil authority. In that instance, the fair rental value payments and additional living expenses are limited to *two weeks*.

The policy expiration will not impact the payment of this indirect coverage.

Additional Coverages

The following additional coverages are available under HO policy forms:

1. Debris removal will cover reasonable expenses for the debris removal of covered property for a covered cause of loss.

This coverage is not an additional amount of insurance. The HO policy will allow for additional debris removal expense coverage if the amount for the removal, plus the property damage amount, exceeds the limit of liability. This limit is an extra 5% of the applicable limit. Debris removal expenses can apply to Coverage A, B, or C.

A homeowners policy also will pay a policy owner's reasonable expense for the removal of trees from the residence premises:

- The policy owner's tree(s) felled by the peril of hail or windstorm or weight of snow, sleet, or ice; or
- A neighbor's tree(s) felled by a Coverage C peril (broad form perils), provided the tree:
  o Damages a covered structure;
  o Does not damage a covered structure but blocks a driveway that prevents a motor vehicle registered for use on public roads from leaving or entering the residence premises; or
  o Blocks a ramp or other fixture designed to assist a disabled individual in entering or leaving the dwelling.

The total amount of coverage included for tree removal is $1,000, with a $500 sublimit for the removal of any one tree.

2. Reasonable repairs coverage is provided to pay for the expenses incurred by the policy owner to make reasonable repairs to protect property from additional damage following a loss caused by a covered peril.

3. Trees, shrubs, and other plants are covered if damage or loss is caused by the following: lightning, fire, explosion, riot or civil commotion, a vehicle not operated or owned by a resident of the residence premises, aircraft, malicious mischief or vandalism, or theft. This additional insurance has a maximum limit of $500 per tree, shrub, or plant and a maximum per loss limit of 5% of the amount of coverage on the dwelling. In both the HO-4 and HO-6 forms, the maximum limit per loss is 10% of the Coverage C limit.

4. Fire department service charge will cover up to $500 for liability assumed by agreement for fire department service charges to protect covered property. The deductible is not applied, and the limit is considered an additional amount of insurance.

5. Property removed coverage is provided for any cause of loss (up to 30 days) while the covered property is removed due to endangerment by a covered peril.

6. Credit card, electronic funds transfer card or access device, counterfeit money, and forgery will cover up to $500 to insure the legal obligation of a policy owner to pay due to the unauthorized use or theft of a credit card or electronic funds transfer card. Loss resulting from the forgery of a check or loss through acceptance of counterfeit money replicating currency from the U.S. or Canada are also covered. No deductible applies, and the limit is an additional amount of insurance.

7. Loss assessment will cover up to $1,000 for the policy owner's share of a loss assessment during the policy period against the policyholder as a tenant or owner of the residence premises by an association of property owners or corporation. The assessment must be made due to direct loss to property owned collectively by all members. It must be of the type of property the insured's policy would cover if it were owned by the named insured. Damage to association property must result from a peril insured against and does not include land shock waves after a volcanic eruption or earthquake.

8. Collapse applies to covered property under Coverages A and B concerning this additional coverage. This additional coverage does not increase the limit of liability.

Collapse refers to the abrupt caving in or falling over of a building or any part of a building. The collapse must result in the building or part of the building being unable to be occupied for its current intended purpose. A building or any part of a building not at risk of caving in or falling over is not in a state of collapse.

Direct physical loss to covered property that involves the collapse of a building or any part of a building is insured if the collapse resulted from one or more of the following:

- The perils insured against;
- Decay that is hidden from view unless the presence of this decay is known to a policy owner before the collapse occurs;
- Vermin or insect damage that is hidden from view unless the presence of this damage is known to a policy owner before the collapse occurs;
- Weight of people, animals, equipment, or contents;
- Weight of any rain or snow that collected on a roof; or
- The use of defective methods or materials in construction, renovation, or remodeling if the collapse occurs during the course of the work.

Unless the loss directly results from the collapse of a building or any part of a building, the following items are not included under the definition of collapse: loss to retaining walls, foundations, pavement, septic tanks, cesspools, underground pipes, drains, flues, swimming pools, decks, patios, fences, or awnings.

9. Glass or safety glazing material will cover breakage of glass or safety glazing material that is part of a covered building, storm window, or storm door. Coverage is provided for the same property if the loss results from earth movement. Covered property is protected from splinters or fragments of broken glass or safety glazing material. Insurers will not provide coverage if the dwelling has been unoccupied for more than 60 consecutive days immediately before the loss. This limitation does not apply to loss resulting from earth movement.

10a. (Except in the HO-4 form) Landlord's furnishings will cover up to $2,500 for a policy owner's carpeting, appliances, and other household furnishings in each apartment on the residence premises typically rented or held for rental to others. Covered causes of loss are limited to Coverage C perils, except theft. This coverage is not regarded as an additional amount of insurance.

10b. (In the HO-4 form only) Building additions and alterations — If the policyholder acquires or makes improvements to the residence premises at their expense, the policy will provide an additional limit of insurance equal to 10% of Coverage C.

11. Law or ordinance allows policy owners to use up to 10% of the limit of liability that applies to Coverage A (or the limit for buildings, additions, and alterations in the HO-4 form) for the additional cost incurred due to the enforcement of any ordinance or law that requires one of the following:

- The demolition, construction, or renovation of part of a covered building damaged by a covered peril; or
- The demolition and reconstruction of a covered building's undamaged part if it must be demolished because of damage to another part of the covered building resulting from a covered peril.

Law or ordinance *does not cover*:

- The loss in value to a covered building or structure because of the requirements of any law or ordinance. For example, although the Americans with Disabilities Act (ADA) establishes specific requirements for minimum clear floor space dimensions in restrooms, law or ordinance coverage does not include any costs necessary to ensure the restroom's compliance with the ADA; or
- The costs to comply with any law or ordinance that requires any policy owner to clean up, test for, or respond to pollutants on any covered building.

12. Grave markers will cover up to $5,000 for grave markers, including mausoleums, for loss resulting from a peril insured against, on, or off the residence premises. This coverage does not increase the limits of liability that apply to the damaged covered property.

13. New York Credit Card Coverage – In New York, the *credit card endorsement* will cover up to $1,000 following the theft or unauthorized use of an insured's credit card.

Section I – Perils Insured Against

In the HO-2, HO-4, and HO-6 forms, the *broad form perils insured against* in the event of property damage, include:

- Windstorm or hail;
- Fire or lightning;
- Explosion;
- Riot or civil commotion;
- Vehicles or aircraft;
- Smoke;
- Theft, vandalism, or malicious mischief;
- Falling objects;
- Sudden and accidental burning, cracking, tearing apart, or bulging;
- Weight of snow, ice, or sleet;
- Freezing;
- Accidental discharge or overflow of water or steam;
- Electrical damage; and
- Volcanic action.

The perils mentioned above were covered in depth in the dwelling policy section and have the same characteristics in the homeowners form. Broad form perils will apply to all applicable coverages (A, B, C, and D). These are the covered perils insured against under Coverage C in the HO-3, HO-4, and HO-6 forms.

The HO-3 form provides open or special coverage on Coverages A and B. Damage to the dwelling, and other structures will be covered unless excluded. The major exclusions are also listed in the section on dwelling policies. Losses under Coverage C in the HO-3 form are covered for broad form perils.

The HO-5 (Comprehensive) form is unique among the homeowners forms in that the entire policy is an open peril or special form. As a result, Coverage A, B, and C and the resulting indirect losses in coverage D will be covered unless excluded.

	COVERED PERILS
HO-2 (Broad)	Broad form perils on Coverages A, B, and C
HO-3 (Special)	Coverages A and B – open peril Coverage C – same perils as Form HO-2
HO-4 (Contents Broad)	Coverage C same perils as Form HO-2 (broad)
HO-5 (Comprehensive)	Building, other structures, and contents – open peril or special
HO-6 (Condominium)	Coverage A, B*, and C for the same perils as Form HO-2 (broad) *In this form, Coverage B is merged with Coverage A
HO-8 (Modified Homeowners)	Fire or lightning; windstorm or hail; explosion; riot or civil commotion; aircraft; vehicles; smoke; vandalism; theft; volcanic eruption

Section I – Exclusions

The exclusions in the homeowners forms are similar to the dwelling property form. The property section has a list of general exclusions. The HO-3 and HO-5 forms will have additional exclusions for any open peril or special form coverage.

General property exclusions in HO policies are as follows:

- Ordinance or law;
- Earth movement (e.g., earthquake, landslide, mudslide or mudflow, sinkhole, and any earth movement that includes earth sinking, rising, or shifting);
- Water damage (e.g., flood, tidal waves, overflow of any body of water, sewer backup, overflow from a sump pump or related equipment, or water below the surface of the ground);
- Power failure;
- Neglect;
- War;
- Nuclear hazard;
- Intentional loss; and
- Government action.

The *HO-3 form* will also have these additional exclusions:

- Freezing of plumbing, heating, air conditioning, or sprinkler system unless the heat is maintained or the water is shut off, and the systems are drained. However, if an automatic fire protective sprinkler system protects the building, the insured must use reasonable care to continue the water supply and maintain heat in the building for coverage to apply;
- Freezing, thawing, weight or pressure of water or ice, whether wind driven or not, applies to fences, pavement, patios, swimming pools, footings and foundations, retaining walls, piers, wharves or docks;
- Theft in or to a dwelling under construction;
- Damage by wind, hail, ice, snow, or sleet to antennas, masts, towers, lawns, trees, shrubs, and plants;
- Vandalism and malicious mischief if the dwelling has been vacant for more than 60 consecutive days before the loss;
- Mold, fungus, or wet rot unless the loss is hidden from view and caused by the accidental overflow or discharge of steam or water from within a heating, air conditioning, plumbing, sprinkler system, storm drain or water, steam, or sewer pipe off the residence premises;
- Repeated or constant seepage or leakage of water or steam over weeks, months, or years;
- Wear and tear, mechanical breakdown, smog, rust, mold, wet or dry rot;
- Smoke from agricultural smudging or industrial operations;
- Discharge, dispersal, seepage, migration, release or escape of pollutants unless caused by a Coverage C peril (broad form peril);
- Settling, shrinking, bulging, or expansion to include cracking that results to pavement, patios, footings, foundations, walls, floors, roofs, or ceilings;
- Damage done by birds, vermin, rodents, insects, or animals owned by the insured;
- Weather conditions to the extent they contribute to an excluded cause of loss Acts, decisions, or the failure to act; or
- Faulty planning, design, or materials (applies only to Coverage A and B).

The HO-5 form will have all of the same exclusions as HO-3 and some additional exclusions for Coverage C because coverage is offered on an open peril basis:

- Breakage of eyeglasses, glassware, statues, bric-a-brac, porcelains, and similar fragile articles unless breakage occurs as a result of named perils listed in the HO-5 exclusion section;
- Dampness, extreme temperature changes unless the direct loss is caused by rain, snow, sleet, or hail;
- Refinishing, renovating, or repairing property other than watches, jewelry, and furs;
- Collision (other than with a land vehicle), sinking, swamping, or stranding of watercraft, including trailers, furnishings, equipment, and outboard engines;
- Governmental seizure, confiscation, or destruction; and
- Acts or decisions, or the failure to act or decide of any individual, organization, group, or governmental body.

Section I – Conditions

The homeowners policy divides the conditions of the insured and insurer by section. The conditions that apply to *Section I – Property* are listed below. Since we have previously explained many of these conditions in the dwelling policy and property/casualty basics sections, we will only discuss the additions or differences.

Insured duties after a loss – If a loss occurs, the insured must do the following:

- Provide an agent or the insurer with prompt written notice of the loss;
- Notify law enforcement if a loss resulted from theft;
- Notify the fund transfer card or credit card company if the loss is covered under the fund transfer card and credit card coverage;
- Protect the property from additional damage, make necessary and reasonable repairs, and keep records of any repair expenses;
- Cooperate with the insurance provider during their investigation of a claim;
- Allow the insurance provider to inspect the property as often as reasonably necessary;
- If requested, agree to a medical examination under oath; and
- Send a signed, sworn proof of loss within 60 days of the insurer's request. This document must include an inventory, the time and events leading to the loss, any changes in occupancy or title, bills, receipts, other coverage on the property, interests of all insureds, and repair estimates.

Loss settlement – Insured property losses for the HO-2, HO-3, HO-4, and HO-5 policy forms will be settled as follows:

Actual cash value (ACV)

- Personal property;
- Carpeting, awnings, household appliances, outdoor antennas, and equipment;
- Structures that are not buildings;
- Mausoleums and grave markers; or
- If applicable, buildings or other structures at the time of loss are not covered to 80% of replacement value. The insurance provider can pay the greater of the ACV or the applied coinsurance formula.

Suppose the policy owner chooses not to file a claim on a replacement cost basis (e.g., the insured decides not to rebuild). In that situation, the policy owner may notify the insurer within 180 days after the date of loss.

Replacement cost

- Buildings and other structures if insured for at least 80% of their replacement cost. The insurer has the option of paying the *least* of the limit of liability, replacement with like kind and quality, or the amount necessary to replace or repair the damaged building;
- If the building is rebuilt at another location, the insurer will pay no more than the cost associated with building at the original premises; or
- The insurer will pay no more than ACV until actual replacement or repairs are complete. Suppose the cost to replace or repair the damaged property is less than 5% of the total amount of coverage, or less than $2,500. In that circumstance, the insurer will settle the loss without requiring the property to be replaced or repaired.

Appraisal – When handling claims, if the insurance company and the policy owner cannot agree on the value of the damaged property, either party may make a written request for appraisal.

Other insurance and service agreement – When other insurance applies to the same loss, the insurer is liable only for the portion of the loss that the coverage limit bears to the total amount of all insurance on the property. This condition is also known as proportionate share or pro rata. If a service agreement is in place for insured property (e.g., a home warranty), the policy will pay on an excess basis.

Loss payment – All losses will be covered within 60 days of receiving a signed, sworn proof of loss or after one of the following:

- An agreement as to the amount of loss has been reached;
- There is a final judgment; or
- An appraisal award has been filed with the insurance company.

Mortgage holders clause – When an insurer denies a claim, the denial will not apply to the mortgagee if they notify the insurer of any change in occupancy or ownership, pay any premiums due, and submit a signed proof of loss within 60 days. In addition, if the insurance provider decides to cancel or nonrenew coverage, it will provide the mortgage holder with *ten days'* advance written notice.

Volcanic eruption period – All volcanic eruptions that occur within *72 hours* will be considered *one event*.

Loss payable clause – If the Declarations show a loss payee for specific covered personal property, the loss payee will be considered an insured under the policy. If the policy is canceled or not renewed, the insurer must notify the loss payee in writing.

Other conditions that we previously discussed include:

- Insurable interest and limits of liability;
- Suit against the insurance provider;
- Pair or set clause;
- Insurer option to replace or repair;
- Recovered property;
- Nuclear hazard clause;
- The policy period; and
- Fraud or concealment.

Estimation of Claims (NY) – Upon request by the insured or a legal representative, the insurer must provide an estimate of damages if one has been prepared. It must furnish the estimate within 30 days of the insured's request or completion of the report, whichever is later.

Section II – Liability Coverages

Unlike the dwelling policy, liability coverage is included in every HO policy form. The liability section of all HO policies includes two liability coverages:

1. Coverage E – Personal Liability; and
2. Coverage F – Medical Payments to Others.

Coverage E – Personal Liability

Personal Liability (Coverage E) will respond if a claim is made or a lawsuit is brought against a policy owner for damages resulting from property damage (PD) or bodily injury (BI). Damages must have resulted from an occurrence to which the coverage applies. This coverage will do the following:

- Pay up to the policy's limit of liability for the damages for which a policyholder is legally liable. Damages include prejudgment interest awarded against a policyholder.
- Provide a defense at the insurance carrier's expense by counsel of the insurer's choice, even if the lawsuit is false, groundless, or fraudulent. The insurance company may investigate and settle any claim or suit that it decides is appropriate. The insurer's responsibility to defend and settle ends when the policy's limit of liability for the occurrence has been exhausted by payment of a settlement or judgment.

Under Coverage E, a $100,000 basic limit of liability is standard. However, the policy owner can purchase higher limits for an additional premium.

Coverage F – Medical Payments to Others

Medical Payments to Others (Coverage F) is automatically included in Section II of all unendorsed HO policies. It will cover necessary medical expenses incurred within *three years* of an accident causing bodily injury. Necessary medical expenses include medical, surgical, ambulance x-ray, dental, and funeral services.

Coverage applies if an individual is injured on the residence premises with the policy owner's permission to be there (e.g., a guest or visitor). Coverage will also apply if a policy owner injures a person off the residence premises, and the injury:

- Arises from the residence premises or ways adjoining the premises;
- Is caused by the activities of a policy owner;
- Is caused by a residence employee of a policy owner during their employment; or
- Is caused by an animal in the care of or owned by the policy owner.

This coverage *does not apply* to the policy owner or residents of the policy owner's household, except for residence employees.

Additional Coverages

As with the personal liability supplement, the liability section of the HO policy includes several additional coverages that are *paid in addition* to the limit of liability:

- **Claims expense** — The policy will cover the following: expenses incurred and costs taxed against the policy owner in any lawsuit the insurer defends, premiums on bonds required in a suit, valid expenses incurred by the policy owner, including up to $250 per day for loss of income, and interest on the entire judgment that accumulates after judgment has been entered and before the insurance company pays it.

- **First aid to others** — The policy will cover expenses the policy owner incurs to render first aid for bodily injury to third parties. The insurer, however, will not pay for first aid to a policy owner.
- **Damage to the property of others** — The policy will cover up to $1,000 per occurrence on a replacement cost basis for damage the policy owner causes to the property of others. This coverage does not apply to the extent a loss is covered for intentional damage under Section I. Coverage will apply if the damage results from a minor under age 13 to property owned by a policy owner or resident of the household, to property rented to or owned by the insured's tenant, or arising out of the policy owner's business.
- **Loss assessment coverage** — The policy will cover up to $1,000 per occurrence for the policy owner's share of loss assessment charged against them as tenant or owner of the residence premises, during the policy period, by an association of property owners or corporation.

Section II – Exclusions

The exclusions section of the HO policy contains exclusions specific to both Coverage E and Coverage F, as well as exclusions that apply to both coverages.

Exclusions that apply to *both Coverages E and F* include:

Motor Vehicle Liability – Coverages E and F do not apply to motor vehicle liability arising from the following:

- Unregistered motor vehicles that should have been registered;
- Vehicles registered for public roads;
- Motor vehicles used in a competition or race;
- Vehicles rented to others;
- Motor vehicles used to carry individuals or cargo for a fee; or
- Vehicles used in a business unless it is a motorized golf cart.

The exclusion further clarifies coverage by stating that if the above situations are not applicable, the motor vehicle is still not covered unless it meets the following conditions:

- Is on an insured location in dead storage;
- Solely used to service the residence premises;
- Designed to assist the disabled and parked at the insured location;
- Designed for use off public roads and not owned by the policyholder or owned by the policyholder, but at the time of the occurrence, the vehicle is located on the insured premises that meet specific criteria; or
- A motorized golf cart not altered from factory specifications meeting specific speed criteria and used for golf and leisure activities in a private residential community.

Watercraft Liability – Liability arising from the use of watercraft is not insured in the following instances:

- While the watercraft is operated in a speed contest or race. Coverage is allowed for a sailboat and if a vessel is used in a predicted log race;
- Rented to others;
- Used to carry cargo or individuals for a fee; or
- Used for any business purposes.

However, this exclusion does not apply to watercraft meeting the following criteria:

- Is stored;
- Is a sailing vessel under 26 feet long, or 26 feet or longer if not rented to or owned by an insured;
- Is a watercraft powered by an inboard-outboard engine, including those that power a water jet pump, and if it is 50 horsepower (hp) or less but only when borrowed or rented by an insured. If the watercraft is over 50 hp, coverage applies if borrowed by the policy owner; or
- If one or more outboard engines or motors are 25 hp or less, but if more than 25 hp, coverage is applied if borrowed or rented by the policy owner. Coverage for over 25 hp will also apply when newly acquired by the policy owner within specific timeframes and if the insurance carrier is notified.

Expected or Intended injury – Property damage or bodily injury expected or intended by the policyholder, even if it is of a different kind or degree than initially expected or is sustained by a separate entity, individual, or property than initially expected or intended.

Business liability – Coverage does not apply to business exposures of a policy owner. Coverage is arranged for the occasional rental of an insured location, but only if it is used as a residence. The policy also provides coverage for the partial rental of the home, but only if the portion rented is intended to house no more than two roomers or boarders. Coverage is also provided for specific business exposures such as schools, offices, private garages, or studios.

Other *exclusions that apply to both coverages*:

- Hovercraft liability;
- Aircraft liability;
- War;
- Professional Services;
- Controlled substances;
- Corporal punishment, sexual molestation, or physical or mental abuse; and
- Communicable disease.

The following exclusions only apply to *Coverage E – Personal Liability*:

- Damage to property owned by the policy owner;
- Damage to property of others in the control, custody, or care of the policy owner (damage caused by an explosion, smoke, or fire is covered);
- Bodily injury to any individual eligible for workers compensation or similar benefits;
- Bodily injury to the named insured or any minor or relative living in the household;
- Liability for any assessment charged against the policy owner as a member of a corporation, association, or community of property owners; and
- Contractual liability (excluding contracts related to the use, maintenance, or ownership of the insured premises).

The following exclusions only apply to *Coverage F – Medical Payments*:

- Bodily injury caused by any nuclear hazard;
- Bodily injury to a residence employee if it does not occur during employment;
- Bodily injury to anyone, not including a resident employee, who regularly lives on the premises; and
- Bodily injury to anyone eligible to receive workers compensation or benefits under another similar law.

Section II – Conditions (Liability)

The following common policy conditions apply to *Section II – Liability*:

Bankruptcy of an insured — Bankruptcy of the policyholder will not free the insurance provider of its obligations under the policy.

Limit of liability — The total limit shown on the declaration page is the insurer's total liability for any occurrence, regardless of the number of claimants involved or lawsuits filed. The insurer's responsibility to settle or defend a lawsuit ends when the limit of liability for the occurrence is exhausted by payment of a settlement or judgment.

Severability of insurance — The insurance applies separately to each policy owner. This condition does not increase the insurance company's liability for any occurrence.

Duties after an occurrence — In the event of a covered occurrence, when applicable, the policy owner is required to perform the following duties:

- Provide written notice to the agent or insurance provider as soon as possible that identifies the following:
    - The identity of the policy and named insured;
    - Reasonably available information on the place, time, and circumstances of the offense; and
    - Names and addresses of any claimants and witnesses;
- Cooperate with the insurer during the investigation, defense, or settlement of any claim or lawsuit;
- Promptly forward to the insurer every summons, demand, notice, or other process relating to the offense;
- At the request of the insurer, assistance with:
    - Making settlement;
    - Enforcing indemnity or any right of contribution against any individual who may be liable to an insured;
    - Conducting suits and attending trials and hearings;
    - Securing and presenting evidence and obtaining the attendance of witnesses;
- Except at their own cost, insureds may not voluntarily assume the obligation, make payment, or incur expenses other than for first aid to others at the time of the personal injury;
- Assist the insurance provider in any subrogation rights; or
- If the loss involves property damage to others, submit to the insurance provider a signed, sworn proof of loss within 60 days of their request.

When the insured does not comply with these requirements, the insurance provider has no obligation to provide coverage under the policy.

Duties of an injured person – Coverage F (Medical Payments to Others) — Injured parties or someone representing the injured party must provide the insurance company (or its agent) written authorization to obtain any medical records and proof of claim. The injured person also must agree to a physical examination by a doctor of the insurer's choosing, as often as requested.

Payment of claim – Coverage F (Medical Payments to Others) — Payment of any claim under this section is not considered an admission of liability by the policy owner or the insurer.

Suit against the insurer — No legal action can be brought against the insurance provider until all policy provisions have been satisfied. No one has a right to join the insurer in legal action against the insured.

Other insurance – Coverage E (Personal Liability) — The insurance will be considered excess over any other valid and collectible coverage unless the other insurance is intended to be excess coverage (e.g., umbrella liability policies).

Policy period — Coverage only applies to losses during the policy period.

Sections I and II – Conditions (Property and Liability)

The following conditions apply to both *property* and *liability* coverages:

Liberalization clause — Suppose the insurer adopts any revisions that broaden coverage in the policy. In that case, those revisions will automatically apply to the policy at no additional premium as of the date the insurer administers the revisions in the insured's state. This date must fall 60 days before or during the policy period listed in the Declarations.

Waiver or Change of Policy Provisions — Any waiver or change of policy provisions must be in writing by the insurance company.

Cancellation and Nonrenewal — The policy owner can cancel the policy at any time by returning it to the insurer or providing the insurer with a written notice. If the insurer cancels coverage, it must give the policy owner a *10-day* advanced written notice for cancellation due to nonpayment of premium. Insurers can also cancel a policy with a 10-day advanced notice if the policy has been effective for no more than 60 days. The insurer must provide the policy owner with at least a *30-day* advanced written notice for all other cancellations or nonrenewals. The insurer can only cancel a policy after it has been effective for 60 days for two reasons:

1. Material misrepresentation, which would have precluded the insurer from issuing the policy; or
2. Substantial change in the risk after the policy was issued.

Assignment — The insured may not assign the policy to any other individual without the insurance company's written consent.

Subrogation — The policy owner may waive all rights of recovery against any other person; however, that has to be done in writing and before a loss. If the rights are not waived, the insurer may require an assignment of the rights of recovery for a loss to the extent that the insurance provider makes payment. If an assignment is sought, an insured must sign and deliver all related papers and cooperate with the insurer. This condition does not apply to additional coverage damage to the property of others and *Coverage F – Medical Payments*.

Death — If a named insured or spouse dies, the deceased's legal representative will be considered an insured under the policy, but only regarding the deceased's property covered at the time of death. The definition of an insured is broadened to cover an insured who is a member of the deceased's household but only while residing at the residence location. It also extends to a person in the care of the insured's property, but only until a legal representative is appointed.

Selected Endorsements

Many endorsements available under the homeowners policy program broaden the coverage provided by the basic policy forms. The following optional endorsements are available on the homeowners policy. (Some also are available for the dwelling policy.)

Special Provisions – New York

This endorsement modifies policy language to comply with New York law. The changes have been incorporated into the text where appropriate to facilitate your study.

Earthquake

Earth movement (earthquake) is excluded from all property policies but can usually be purchased separately for an additional premium. The coverage can be purchased to cover the dwelling, other structures, and personal property. Rates generally are determined by the type of construction that determines the dwelling's vulnerability to earthquake losses. Frame buildings are less susceptible to severe damage than masonry veneer buildings. Therefore, they have lower rates for this coverage.

Earthquake coverage provided by endorsement in a homeowners form considers one or more earthquake shocks occurring within *72 hours* as a single earthquake.

The *deductible* under earthquake coverage is stated as a percentage of loss. However, it cannot be less than a specified minimum dollar amount (e.g., $500 in the ISO HO form). The deductible applies separately to buildings, other structures, personal property, and loss of use.

Masonry veneer structures are not covered by an endorsement issued for a frame dwelling. A separate endorsement can be added for this type of construction.

Identity Fraud Expense

The *identity theft/fraud expense coverage endorsement* offers up to $15,000 in coverage for expenses incurred by an insured as a direct result of identity fraud if discovered during the policy period. Any series of acts committed by one or more individuals against an insured is considered *one identity fraud occurrence*. This coverage excludes loss arising out of or in connection with a business, expenses because of a fraudulent, dishonest, or criminal act by an insured, or loss that does not meet the endorsement's definition of expenses. The insured will be responsible for the $500 deductible.

Scheduled Personal Property

Suppose the policy owner requires higher limits for certain types of property. In that circumstance, the *scheduled personal property endorsement* can be used to schedule specifically described items or classes of items on a blanket basis. This endorsement usually provides open peril or special form coverage on listed items. This endorsement allows for the scheduling of nine different classes of property:

1. Furs;
2. Jewelry;
3. Musical instruments;
4. Cameras;
5. Golfer's equipment;

6. Silverware;
7. Fine arts (including glassware and porcelains);
8. Rare and current coins; and
9. Postage stamps.

Newly acquired furs, jewelry, musical instruments, and cameras are insured up to the lesser of the following limits:

- $10,000; or
- 25% of the amount of coverage for that class of property.

The new property must be reported within 30 days of being acquired, and the policy owner may have to pay the additional premium from that date. For coverage to apply to fine arts, a policy owner must submit the acquisition report within 90 days.

Insured Perils – The *insured perils endorsement* covers direct physical loss to property caused by any of the following perils:

- Nuclear hazard;
- War;
- Insects or vermin;
- Wear and tear;
- **If fine arts are covered** – breakage resulting from malicious damage or theft, explosions, earthquake or flood, windstorm, and fire or lightning; or
- **If postage stamps are covered** – disappearance, transfer of colors, denting or scratching, creasing, and fading.

The following are additional features and benefits of the scheduled personal property endorsement:

- The Coverage C limits do not apply to the scheduled property on this endorsement;
- Insured locations – scheduled personal property endorsement insures eligible property worldwide;
- Antiques and fine arts can be covered on a basis other than ACV;
- The special limits of liability do not apply to items or classes of scheduled property; and
- No deductible will be applied to a covered property loss.

Personal Property – Replacement Cost

The *personal property replacement cost endorsement* adjusts the actual cash value settlement on personal property, carpeting, household appliances, awnings, and outdoor equipment to a replacement cost basis. Specific property types will not benefit from this coverage, including items that are stored and have become obsolete, items that are not in good working order, memorabilia, antiques, and fine arts.

No personal property is required to be insured to 80% of replacement cost at the time of loss. However, some insurance companies require that Coverage C be raised to 70% of the Coverage A amount when purchasing this endorsement.

Home Business

Certain incidental businesses, like studios or offices, are eligible. A *permitted incidental occupancies endorsement* can be attached to cover other structures used for business activities, remove the special limit of liability for business property, and the personal liability and medical payments coverage. The limitations are eliminated only for the business listed in the endorsement.

Personal Injury – New York

Coverage for personal injury may be added by endorsement for an additional premium. *Personal injury* refers to an injury arising from one or more offenses. Such offenses include the following:

- False arrest or detention;
- Malicious prosecution;
- Wrongful eviction;
- Oral or written libel or slander; and
- Oral or written publications that violate another person's right to privacy.

Workers Compensation – Residence Employees – New York

This endorsement provides workers compensation coverage for residence employees. A *residence employee* is engaged in regular employment for fewer than 40 hours per week or in casual employment (e.g., household chores, yard work, making repairs, or painting). Work must be performed in a 1- to 4-unit residence only. No coverage is provided for rental properties. This endorsement offers coverages required by workers compensation law for the items noted above. It does not provide voluntary or statutory coverage for the insured. The insured must purchase a workers compensation policy to cover these exposures.

This endorsement is automatically applied to the policy, and there is no separate premium charge.

Water Back-Up and Sump Discharge or Overflow – New York

The *water backup and sump discharge or overflow endorsement* will provide up to $5,000 coverage for direct physical loss to property resulting from water or water-borne material which overflows through drains or sewers. Coverage also applies to discharge from a sump, sump pump, or other equipment. The coverage is only for the property damage from the water or water-borne materials, not damage to the equipment that caused the overflow or discharge. A special deductible, usually $250, applies to this coverage except for *Coverage D – Loss of Use*.

The loss cannot be due to the insured's negligence. In addition, coverage is not provided if a flood causes the backup.

HO-8 Modified Coverage Form

The *HO-8 (modified coverage form)* is a homeowners form used when replacement cost coverage is not practical. This form may be useful when the replacement cost is considerably higher than the structure's market value, such as in some older homes, elaborate homes, and those with detailed designs or decorative architecture. Some of the differences that apply to this form are listed below:

- **Theft coverage** — A $1,000 basic limit applies to theft losses, and coverage is not provided for theft of personal property off the premises.
- **Worldwide coverage** — Coverage for personal property away from the insured premises is limited to the larger of $1,000 or 10% of the personal property limit.
- **Debris removal** — This is not considered an additional coverage and is included in the total policy limit.
- **Shrubs, plants, or trees** — The maximum limit for any one shrub, plant, or tree is only $250.
- **Property of residence employees or guests** — Property may be covered only while on the insured premises.

- **Coverages A and B** — These coverages are written on a functional replacement cost basis.
- **Glass or safety glazing material** — These losses will have a limit of $100.

Chapter Review

This chapter explained the purpose and types of coverage in a homeowners policy, which protects dwellings, other structures, personal property, and personal liability. Let's review some of the key points:

HOMEOWNERS POLICY OVERVIEW	
Coverage Forms	• HO-2 (Broad Form) • HO-3 (Special Form) • HO-4 (Contents) • HO-5 (Comprehensive Form) • HO-6 (Condominium Owners) • HO-8 (Modified Coverage)
Types of Properties Covered	• 1-to-4 family-owner-occupied residences • No more than two families or two roomers/boarders per unit • Tenants in non-owned dwellings (HO-4) • Residential condominiums (HO-6) • Seasonal dwellings and secondary residences • Other types of ownership (e.g., dwellings under construction)
COVERAGE FORMS	
General Form Structure	• Agreement • Definitions • Section I - Property Coverage • Section I - Perils Insurance Against • Section I - Exclusions • Section I - Conditions • Section II - Liability Coverages • Section II - Exclusions • Section II - Additional Coverages • Section II - Conditions • Sections I and II - Conditions
Coverage Forms	• *HO-2 (broad form)* – named peril basis • *HO-3 (special form)* – dwelling and other structures on an open peril basis; personal property only for broad perils • *HO-4 (contents broad form)* – tenant broad form; insures personal property for broad perils • *HO-5 (comprehensive form)* – covers both dwelling and other structures on an open peril basis • *HO-6 (condominium owners)* – broadens coverage to include parts of the building • *HO-8 (modified coverage)* – used when replacement cost coverage is not practical (e.g., older homes)

	SECTION I – PROPERTY COVERAGE
Coverage A – Dwelling	• Dwelling coverage is provided in every form except the HO-4 • The coverage is defined similarly to the dwelling property form, except that outdoor equipment or building equipment used for servicing the residence is no longer in Coverage A • The HO-6 condo form combines Coverage A and Coverage B in this section
Coverage B – Other Structures	• A basic amount of insurance equal to 10% of the limit found in Coverage A is included for other structures • The HO form substitutes the definition of a business with the coverage description
Coverage C – Personal Property	• Coverage C was optional in the dwelling policy but is now mandatory coverage in every homeowners form • The HO-2, HO-3, HO-5, and HO-8 will automatically include a limit of insurance equal to 50% of the Coverage A limit
Coverage D – Loss of Use	• A combination of Coverage D (Fair Rental Value) and Coverage E (Additional Living Expense) found in the dwelling property policy
	SECTION II – LIABILITY COVERAGE
Coverage E – Personal Liability	• Will respond if a claim is made or a lawsuit is brought against a policy owner for damages resulting from property damage (PD) or bodily injury (BI) • Pay up to the limit of liability for the damages for which a policyholder is liable • Provide a defense at the insurance carrier's expense by counsel of the insurer's choice, even if the lawsuit is false, groundless, or fraudulent
Coverage F – Medical Payments to Others	• Will cover necessary medical expenses incurred within three years of an accident causing bodily injury • Necessary medical expenses include medical, surgical, ambulance x-ray, dental, and funeral services • Coverage applies if an individual is injured on the residence premises with the policy owner's permission to be there (e.g., a guest)
Additional Coverages	• Claims expense • First aid to others • Damage to the property of others • Loss assessment coverage
Exclusions	• The exclusions section of the HO policy contains exclusions specific to both Coverage E and Coverage F, as well as exclusions that apply to both coverages
	CONDITIONS
Section I - Property	• Insured's duties after a loss • Loss settlement • Appraisal • Other insurance and service agreement • Loss payment • Mortgage holders clause • Volcanic eruption period • Loss payable

	CONDITIONS *(Continued)*
Section II - Liability	<ul><li>Bankruptcy</li><li>Limit of liability</li><li>Severability of insurance</li><li>Duties after an occurrence</li><li>Duties of an injured person</li><li>Payment of claim</li><li>Suit against the insurer</li><li>Other insurance</li><li>Policy period</li></ul>
Property and Liability	<ul><li>Liberalization</li><li>Waiver or change of policy</li><li>Cancellation and nonrenewal</li><li>Assignment</li><li>Subrogation</li><li>Death</li></ul>

CHAPTER 6:
Auto Policy

In this chapter, we will discuss personal and commercial auto policies, their purpose, types of coverage, and general provisions. By the end of this chapter, you will know the similarities and differences between personal auto and commercial auto insurance. You will also learn about your state's requirements for auto insurance coverage.

- Personal Auto Policy
- Commercial Auto
- Laws

Personal Auto Policy

Purpose and Eligibility

The *personal auto policy (PAP)* is insurance for anyone who owns a private passenger vehicle. The policy combines insurance for physical damage to the automobile with liability insurance for claims from operating the auto. The PAP includes several parts, each describing a specific area of coverage:

- Part A – Liability Coverage;
- Part B – Medical Payments Coverage;
- Part C – Uninsured Motorist Coverage;
- Part D – Coverage for Damage to Your Auto;
- Part E – Duties After an Accident or Loss; and
- Part F – General Provisions.

Most of the PAP parts include the insuring agreement, exclusions, and limits of liability sections.

The operation or ownership of an auto involves three types of potential loss, and the PAP is required to protect these losses under diverse circumstances:

1. Legal liability (for property damage or injuries to others);
2. Injury to the policyholder or family members of the policyholder; and
3. Loss of or damage to the auto.

Definitions

The Definitions section of the personal auto policy is on the first page of the policy. It defines various terms used throughout the policy. Several of the more important terms are listed below.

Bodily Injury – *Bodily injury* refers to sickness or disease, bodily harm, and death resulting from the injury.

Property Damage – *Property damage* refers to destruction, physical injury, or the loss of use of tangible property.

You and Your – The terms *"you"* and *"your"* used throughout the PAP refer to:

- The named insured listed on the declarations page; and
- The named insured's spouse, if they are a resident of the same household. Suppose the spouse ceases to be a resident of the same household before the policy's inception or during the policy period. In that case, the spouse falls under the terms *you* and *your* until the earlier of:
    - The end of 90 days after the spouse changes residency;
    - The effective date of another insurance policy listing the spouse as a named insured; or
    - The end of the policy period.

Family Member – A *family member* is an individual who is related by blood, adoption, or marriage and who is a resident of the household. This term also includes a ward or foster children.

Your Covered Auto – The term *"your covered auto"* includes:

- Any vehicle listed in the Declarations;
- A newly acquired auto;

- Any owned trailer; or
- Any auto or trailer not owned by the policyholder but used as a temporary substitute for a vehicle listed above which is out of regular use because of its destruction, loss, service, repair, or breakdown.

Trailer – A *trailer* refers to a vehicle designed to be pulled by a private passenger auto, van, pickup, or farm wagons and implements while towed by any of the above vehicle types.

Newly Acquired Auto – A *newly acquired auto* refers to any of the following vehicle types that the policy owner acquires during the policy period:

- A private passenger auto;
- A van or pickup, for which no other insurance policy provides coverage, that:
    - Has a gross vehicle weight (GVW) of less than 10,000 lbs. (GVW is the maximum recommended weight including the vehicle, passengers, fuel and fluids, and all cargo);
    - Is not used for the transportation or delivery of goods and materials unless such use is incidental to a business of maintaining, installing, or repairing equipment or furnishings; or
    - Is not used for ranching or farming.

Insurers will provide coverage for a newly acquired auto with several notification requirements. The requirements will depend on the new vehicle's coverage type and if the vehicle is replacing an existing auto listed in the Declarations or is in addition to the listed vehicles.

Uninsured motorist coverage, medical payments, and liability will be extended to a newly acquired auto for replacement vehicles as follows:

- The coverage will be the broadest offered on any existing vehicle on the declarations page, and there is no stipulation that the insurance carrier be notified; and
- If the vehicle is in addition to the listed vehicles, the policy will offer coverage but only if the insurance provider is notified within *14 days* of the policyholder becoming the owner.

Collision – *Collision* refers to the upset or impact of a covered vehicle or non-owned auto with an object or another vehicle.

Other-than-collision – *Other-than-collision* (previously called comprehensive) includes losses that result from the following:

- Fire;
- Falling objects or missiles;
- Explosion or earthquake;
- Theft or larceny;
- Windstorm;
- Water, flood, or hail;
- Malicious mischief or vandalism;
- Civil commotion or riot;
- Contact with animals or birds; and
- Breakage of glass.

Collision Coverage and Other Than Collision Coverage – This coverage for a newly acquired auto starts on the date the policyholder becomes the owner:

- The policy owner must ask the company to insure the vehicle within 14 days of taking ownership when the Declarations section indicates that this coverage applies to at least one vehicle.
- In this case, the newly acquired auto will have the broadest coverage currently provided for any auto listed in the Declarations.
- If no such indication is made and the policy owner incurs a loss within the first *four days* of ownership, coverage can still be requested (within the first four days). A $500 deductible will apply.

Occupying – *Occupying* means in, upon, getting in, out of, on, or off a vehicle.

Part A – Liability Coverage

Insuring Agreement – Liability coverage protects the policy owner against loss arising from legal liability when an automobile that the policy owner operates, owns, or maintains is involved in an accident. Under liability coverage, the policy pays for the following:

- Property damage and bodily injury because of an accident for which the policy owner is legally responsible;
- Defense expenses as long as the policy covers a particular loss (these expenses are paid over and above the policy limits); and
- Expenses for defending or settling the policy owner as deemed appropriate (these expenses end when the limits of insurance are expended).

Who is an Insured – An *insured* is the individual named in an insurance policy protected under the contract and to whom the insurance carrier provides services or pays benefits.

Under *Part A – Liability*, an insured is defined as:

- The policy owner or any family member for the use, ownership, or maintenance of any auto or trailer;
- Any individual using an insured's covered auto with permission;
- For a policy owner's covered auto, any individual, or organization (this is only concerning legal responsibility for acts or omissions of an individual for whom coverage is afforded under liability); and
- For any auto or trailer other than the policy owner's covered auto, any other individual, or organization, but only concerning legal liability for acts or omissions of the policy owner or a family member for whom coverage is afforded under liability. This provision will apply if the individual or organization does not own or hire the auto or trailer.

Supplementary Payments – Under the supplementary payments provision, the insurance carrier promises to pay certain costs on behalf of a policy owner:

- Bail bonds required of the policy owner due to a covered loss are paid up to $250;
- Premiums on appeal bonds and bonds to release attachments in lawsuits covered under the policy are paid in full;
- Insurers pay interest on a judgment after it has been entered; and
- Other reasonable expenses incurred at the request of the insurance provider are covered, including up to $200 per day for loss of earnings to assist in legal proceedings.

Amounts payable under the supplementary payments provision are paid *in addition to the liability limit*.

Exclusions – The following *exclusions* apply to the liability coverage provided for specific vehicles and individuals in the personal auto policy:

- Intentional damage or injury;
- Damage to property being transported or owned by a covered person;
- Damage to property used, rented, or in the care of a covered person, except a home or private garage;
- Bodily injury to an employee during employment, except for domestic employees who are not required to be covered by workers compensation;
- Use of a vehicle as a livery or public conveyance, except carpools;
- Damage caused by any person while engaged in the business of parking, storing, repairing, servicing, or selling vehicles designed for use mainly on public highways (this exclusion does not apply to the use, maintenance, or ownership of your covered auto by the policy owner, any family member, or any employee, agent or partner of the policy owner or any family member);
- Use of commercial-type vehicles in any business operation;
- Individuals using a covered auto without permission;
- Individuals covered under a nuclear energy policy, including individuals that would have been covered except for the exhaustion of the policy limits;
- The use, maintenance, or ownership of:
    - A motorized vehicle with fewer than four wheels;
    - A vehicle designed mainly for use off public roads;
    - A vehicle owned or available for everyday use by the policyholder, other than a covered auto;
    - A vehicle owned by or furnished for regular use by a family member, other than a covered auto; the named insured is covered while occupying or maintaining such a vehicle; and
    - A vehicle located inside a racing facility for racing.

Limits of Liability – Under a personal auto policy, the insured can pick between two liability limits: split and combined single.

Split limit coverage uses three specific dollar amounts. If an automobile accident occurs, these numbers specify the maximum amount the policy will pay:

- Bodily injury for each person involved;
- Bodily injury for the entire accident (irrespective of the total number of individuals involved); and
- Property damage.

Split limits are always expressed in this order.

For example, policy limits expressed as 25/50/25 provide $25,000 coverage for the bodily injury per individual, $50,000 for all bodily injury, and $25,000 for property damage coverage per accident.

By contrast, *combined single* coverage uses a single dollar amount, indicating the maximum coverage for all losses irrespective of the number of individuals involved or the amount of property damaged.

When the policy is used to satisfy any *financial responsibility* requirements, the policy will comply with the law to the extent required.

Out of State Coverage – Suppose a covered auto is involved in an auto accident in any state or Canadian province besides the one where the vehicle is principally garaged. In that circumstance, the *out-of-state coverage* will apply, and the insurer will interpret the policy for that accident as follows:

- If the state or province has a financial responsibility law requiring limits of liability higher than those shown on the declarations page, the insured's policy will provide the *higher specified limits*; or

- Suppose the state or province has compulsory insurance specifying a nonresident to maintain insurance whenever the vehicle is used in that state. In that scenario, the insured's policy will provide *at least the required minimum* amounts and types of coverage.

It is worth noting, however, that no one is entitled to duplicate payments for the same loss.

Each state establishes the minimum liability limits for its policies. The limits *will not change* when a vehicle travels from state to state and remain the same regardless of where the auto is located. However, suppose the insured is in an accident, to be insured at the required minimum limits for the state the accident occurs in. In that case, the limits *adjust* to the minimum limits for that state and, where necessary, add other coverage.

Other Insurance – The liability section also includes the *other insurance* clause. It states that the insurance provider will only pay its share of the loss if other insurance is available to pay for a covered loss. The insurance provider's share is the proportion that the limit of insurance bears to the total of all available limits. For non-owned vehicles, the insurance will be considered excess over any other collectible insurance.

Part B – Medical Payments

Insuring Agreement – *Medical payments* coverage pays reasonable expenses associated with necessary medical and funeral expenses resulting from an accident sustained by a policyholder regardless of fault. They must use these services and costs within *three years* of the accident.

Who is an Insured – An insured is defined under *Part B – Medical Payments* as:

- The named insured *"you"* or a family member while occupying a motor vehicle designed for use on public roads or any trailer;
- The named insured or family member as a pedestrian if struck by a motor vehicle or trailer intended for use on public roads; and
- Any other individual while occupying a covered auto.

Exclusions – The following *exclusions* apply to the medical payments coverage. The insurance company will not provide coverage for any policy owner for bodily injury sustained in the following situations:

- While occupying any vehicle that meets the following characteristics:
    - With fewer than four wheels;
    - Used as a residence or premises;
    - Used as a public livery (excluding carpools);
    - Used without permission;
    - A commercial-type vehicle when it is being used for an insured's business; or
    - Located inside a racing facility and to prepare for or compete in any organized or prearranged speed or racing contest.
- While occupying or when struck by a vehicle that is
    - Owned or regularly used by the policy owner; or
    - Owned or used by a policy owner's family, other than a covered vehicle (this exclusion does not apply to the named insured).
- During employment, if workers compensation benefits are required; and
- While occupying a vehicle inside a racing facility when used for competition or practicing for a prearranged or organized speed contest.

In addition, insurers will exclude losses caused by war, a nuclear weapon, rebellion, insurrection or revolution, nuclear radiation, reaction, or radioactive contamination.

Limits of Liability and Other Insurance – The coverage amount depends on the policy. It will apply on a per-person basis for bodily injury sustained in an accident covered by the policy, irrespective of fault. Medical payments coverage is similar to personal injury protection (PIP) coverage. For example, the policy has a medical payment coverage limit of $10,000. The policy owner and the passenger were injured in an accident; one person had $12,000 in injuries, and the other had $10,000. Part B will pay each person $10,000, up to the coverage limit.

Any payments available under uninsured motorist or liability coverage will reduce the amount payable under this coverage.

The *other insurance* clause is explained in the medical payments section of the policy, which is the same as the provision found in the liability coverage section.

Part C – Uninsured and Underinsured Motorists

Bodily injury resulting from an accident with an uninsured driver is included in the ISO personal auto policy. Some states amend this section as a requirement of state law. States that do not have laws requiring this coverage can make it optional or include it as outlined below.

We will discuss the New York-specific requirements for uninsured motorists in this chapter's *Laws* section.

Insuring Agreement – *Uninsured Motorist (UM)* coverage provides the policy owner with money for bodily injuries that they would be legally entitled to recover from the operator or owner of a vehicle without the required liability coverage. A vehicle not carrying the required insurance is defined as an *uninsured vehicle* in this section of the personal auto policy. The limits for uninsured motorist coverage are established when the auto policy is purchased.

Although some definitions can vary by state law, uninsured motorist coverage usually defines four categories of uninsured motor vehicles, including a land motor vehicle or trailer. At the time of the accident:

1. There is no insurance or liability bond for the vehicle;
2. The insurance or bond is less than that required by the financial responsibility laws of the state in which the accident occurred;
3. The accident was a hit-and-run accident, and the driver is unable to be identified; and
4. The insurance provider or bonding company denies coverage or is insolvent.

Uninsured motor vehicle coverage does not include any vehicle or equipment:

- Owned or available for regular use by the policy owner or a family member;
- Owned by a government agency;
- Owned by a self-insurer unless it becomes insolvent;
- Designed primarily for use off public roads;
- Operated on crawler treads or rails; or
- Used as a residence or premises.

Who is an Insured – Insured is defined under *Part C – Uninsured/Underinsured Motorist* as:

- The named insured and any family members;
- Any other individual while occupying a covered vehicle; and
- Any person eligible to recover damages because of injuries to one of the above.

Part D – Coverage for Damage to Your Auto

Coverage for Damage to Your Auto, also called physical damage coverage, includes both Collision and Other Than Collision coverage (previously known as comprehensive). Coverage only applies when a premium is listed in the Declarations next to these coverages.

Insuring Agreement – The insuring agreement states that the insurer will pay for direct and accidental loss to a non-owned or covered auto minus any deductible listed on the declarations page. Only the highest deductible will apply when a loss to more than one non-owned or covered auto results from the same accident.

The PAP defines *non-owned autos* as any private passenger auto, van, pickup, or trailer in the custody of or operated by but is not owned or furnished for the regular use of the named insured or a relative.

Transportation Expenses – *Transportation expenses* will be covered if the loss results from collision or other-than-collision, provided that the corresponding coverage is indicated on the declarations page. Coverage will apply to a non-owned auto and a covered auto.

The policy will typically pay up to $20 per day up to a maximum of $600 (can vary by state) for transportation costs incurred by the policy owner due to a covered loss.

Expense payments will begin after a 24-hour waiting period for causes other than theft. Expenses are covered 48 hours after the theft if a covered vehicle is stolen.

Transportation expenses are not subject to a deductible. They are limited to the period reasonably required to replace or repair the covered auto.

Exclusions – The *exclusions* shown below apply to the physical damage coverage section of a personal auto policy for losses or damages caused by any of the following:

- While the vehicle is used as a public livery, except for car pools;
- Mechanical or electrical breakdown, wear and tear, freezing, and road damage to tires (*excluding* damage resulting from vandalism or the total theft of the covered vehicle);
- War, nuclear weapons, radioactive contamination, insurrection, revolution, or rebellion;
- Electronic equipment intended for reproduction of sound, including stereos, radios, compact disc players, and tape decks and accessories (unless permanently installed in the vehicle by the manufacturer);
- Any other electronic equipment that transmits or receives audio, visual, or data signals, including telephones, two-way mobile radios, citizen band radios, radar detection equipment, scanning monitor receivers, audio cassette recorders, video cassette recorders, television monitor receivers, and personal computers and accessories (does not include permanently installed equipment in the vehicle);
- Destruction or confiscation by civil or governmental authorities;
- To a trailer or camper body not listed in the Declarations (does not apply to newly acquired camper bodies or trailers obtained during the policy period or insured within 14 days of ownership);
- Cabanas, awnings, or equipment designed to create additional living space;
- Radar detection equipment;
- Any custom equipment or furnishings in or on any van or pickup exceeding coverage of $1,500, including special carpeting and insulation, bars, furniture, facilities for sleeping or cooking, height-extending roofs, grilles, winches, side pipes, louvers, hood scoops or spoilers, tires, wheels, spinners, covers, caps, bedliners, paintings, custom murals, or other decals;
- Any auto located in a racing facility to practice, prepare for, or compete in any organized speed or racing contest;

- Any non-owned vehicles under the following situations:
  - Used without permission or a reasonable belief that any insured can do so;
  - Being used or maintained by any individual while engaged in the business of parking, storing, servicing, repairing, or selling vehicles;
  - Rented by any policyholder if the rental company is prevented from recovering loss or loss of use from the policyholder because of the rental agreement or state law;
  - Being used by any insured in connection with a personal vehicle sharing program if a program provision or state law prevents the recovery of loss or loss of use from the insured; and
- Any loss to a vehicle that can be used for flight.

Limits of Liability – The limit of liability is the *lesser* of:

- The vehicle's ACV at the time of the loss (including an adjustment for depreciation and physical condition); or
- The amount necessary to replace or repair the vehicle.

Losses to non-owned autos are covered the same as the coverage available for any covered auto, except non-owned trailers, which have a limit of $1,500. Permanently installed electronic equipment in a location not usually used by the auto manufacturer is covered up to $1,000.

Other Provisions – The physical damage section of the personal auto policy also includes four other provisions. These provisions are similar to the conditions discussed for other property coverages and include:

1. **Payment of Loss** — The insurance carrier can pay money, replace, or repair the damaged or stolen property. In addition, if the stolen property is recovered, the insurance provider can return the property to the policy owner, paying for any damage. The insurer can also take all or part of the property at an appraised or agreed-upon amount.
2. **No Benefit to Bailee** — The insurance will not directly or indirectly benefit any bailee or carrier. For example, suppose a vehicle is in the care of a service station for repairs or a garage, and it is damaged. In that case, the policy owner will need to seek recovery for the damages from the service station or garage.
3. **Other Sources of Recovery** — If other insurance can be applied, the insurer will pay proportionally. Coverage for any covered non-owned auto is over and above any other collectible source, including insurance and any other source of recovery available to the non-owned auto's owner.
4. **Appraisal** — If the policy owner and the insurance carrier cannot agree on a settlement, either party can request an appraisal. Each party will then choose and pay for its own appraiser. The appraiser will jointly select a third appraiser, known as an umpire. The decision reached by at least two appraisers will bind both parties.

Part E – Duties after an Accident or Loss

Part E – Duties after an Accident or Loss outlines the required duties of anyone seeking damages under the policy after a loss or accident. This part of the personal auto policy's coverage does not include subsections.

When the policy owner does not comply with this policy section, harming the insurance company, the insurer is relieved of its duty to provide coverage. These duties are similar to those previously discussed for other types of insurance and include:

- Prompt notification of loss;
- Cooperating with the insurance company;
- Forwarding any received legal papers;
- When requested, agreeing to a physical exam or an examination under oath;

- Providing the insurance company access to medical records;
- Submitting proof of loss;
- Notifying the police if a vehicle is stolen or when a hit-and-run accident occurs;
- Preventing the property from incurring additional loss; and
- Allowing the insurance company to appraise and inspect the damaged property.

Part F – General Provisions

Part F – General Provisions in the personal auto policy form describe the conditions applied to all coverage parts and the conditions applied to the individual coverages. These conditions, which are similar to some previously discussed, are as follows:

- **Bankruptcy** —A policy owner's bankruptcy does not relieve insurers of their obligations under the policy.
- **Policy changes** — The terms and conditions may not be waived or changed except by endorsement.
- **Fraud** — The insurance company will not provide coverage for any policy owner who has made a fraudulent statement or engaged in fraudulent conduct regarding any accident or loss.
- **Legal action against the insurer** — No individual can bring any legal action against the insurance provider until they comply with all policy provisions.
- **Subrogation (insurer right to recover payment)** — Subrogation rights apply to all coverages except physical damage coverage if it resulted from a person using the auto with a reasonable belief they were allowed to do so.
- **Policy period and territory** — The policy territory consists of the United States, its territories and possessions, Puerto Rico, or Canada.
- **Termination** — This provision specifies the duties and rights of the policy owner and insurance provider not to renew or cancel coverage. If a law where the policy was issued mandates a different notice period or any special procedures other than those listed below, the policy will comply with the state provisions. In most states, the insurance company must provide ten days' notice for nonpayment of premium or if the policy is canceled within the first 60 days of initial coverage. Insurers must provide 20 days' notice for any other reason. When the policy has been in force for more than 60 days, the insurer can only cancel due to nonpayment of premium. It can also cancel a policy for a revoked or suspended driver's license or if the policy was obtained through material misrepresentation. If the insurer decides not to renew coverage, they must provide at least 20 days' notice before the renewal date. When the policy owner obtains other insurance on a covered auto, the policy will terminate on the new policy's effective date.
- **Assignment (transfer of the insured's interest in the policy)** — The policyholder may not transfer their rights or interest in the policy without the *written consent* of the insurance carrier. If the named insured dies, coverage will be provided for the surviving spouse or legal representative of the policyholder, but only until the end of the policy period.
- **Two or more auto policies** — If the insurance provider has issued two or more policies that will respond to the same loss, the insurance provider's liability will be the highest applicable limit of insurance under one policy.

Selected Endorsements

Optional endorsements can be used to amend the PAP to fit the needs of individual policy owners. We will discuss some of the more commonly used endorsements next.

Amendment of Policy Provisions - New York – The Amendment of Policy Provisions modifies policy language to comply with New York law. The state-specific requirements have been incorporated into the text where appropriate to facilitate your study.

Towing and Labor Costs – The *towing and labor costs* endorsement includes a basic limit of $25 for towing and labor costs incurred at the location where a vehicle is disabled. Higher limits of coverage are available for an additional premium. Coverage will apply to a covered auto or a non-owned auto but only applies to costs incurred at the location of disablement.

Miscellaneous Type Vehicles – The *miscellaneous type vehicle* endorsement is used to broaden the definition of covered autos to include motorized vehicles such as motor homes, motorcycles, dune buggies, golf carts, and other recreational vehicles. The liability and medical payments exclusions on vehicles with less than four wheels do not apply when this endorsement is attached to the policy. Coverage is not provided for vehicles rented or borrowed unless it is a temporary substitute for a miscellaneous vehicle listed in the endorsement.

Named Nonowner – The *named nonowner* endorsement provides coverage for individuals who do not own a car but rent or borrow vehicles as needed. Coverage is considered excess over and above any other valid and collectible insurance on the rented or borrowed vehicle and is only for the person named on the endorsement. Spouses and their family members are not provided automatic coverage and must also be listed on the endorsement. The exclusion for vehicles furnished and available for regular use of the policyholder will apply unless deleted in the Declarations. Physical damage coverage is typically not provided.

Rental Vehicle Coverage - New York – Policy owners must add a rental vehicle coverage endorsement in New York under *Part A – Liability*. This endorsement covers a *rental vehicle* defined as a private passenger motor vehicle, station wagon, pickup truck, delivery sedan, or panel truck. This coverage is not extended to autos owned by someone engaged in business renting or leasing vehicles.

Coverage is provided for a rental vehicle rented in the U.S., its territories or possessions, and Canada as long as the rental agreement has a term no longer than 30 continuous days. Coverage applies if the vehicle is rented or operated for business or pleasure and is provided regardless of fault. This coverage does not apply to transporting individuals for a fee. The policy will pay for a loss to the vehicle and the loss of use of the auto. An insured under this endorsement is the named insured and a *relative*, which is very similar to the *family member* definition found in the personal auto policy.

This endorsement will pay for damages to a rental vehicle and loss of use even if no physical damage coverage applies to the policy. Insurers will still afford liability-only policies protection if a covered auto is rented in the coverage territory as outlined in the endorsement.

Joint Ownership Coverage – The *joint ownership coverage* endorsement is used when multiple individuals own a vehicle together (insurable interest), but do not fit the traditional definition of an insured in the PAP. Coverage applies to individuals other than a husband and wife who reside in the same household and are nonresident family members. The vehicle owned must be shown in the endorsement, and coverage will not extend to any vehicle owned by a party not listed or included in the definition of a covered auto.

Commercial Auto

General Form Structure

The *business auto coverage form* includes the following sections:

1. Section I – Covered Auto;
2. Section II – Liability Coverage;
3. Section III – Physical Damage Coverage;

4. Section IV – Business Auto Conditions; and
5. Section V – Definitions.

Each section is broken down to describe specific perils that are covered and excluded from coverages and limits of insurance as they apply to different types of coverage.

Covered Autos – The *covered auto* section of a commercial auto policy (Section I) describes the designation symbols used in that coverage form. It also specifies whether newly acquired, and temporary vehicles are covered.

Liability Coverage – *Liability coverage* (Section II), or third-party insurance, covers the insured's legal responsibilities in a negligent act or accident. Liability coverage pays for bodily injury or property damage to others and any legal fees incurred by defending the insured in a lawsuit brought against the insured.

Liability coverage is different for each commercial auto coverage form but is included in every policy. Minimum limits for liability coverage are established by state law.

Physical Damage Coverage – *Physical damage* coverage (Section III) explains the coverage for damage done to the insured's property, including any covered autos. Physical damage coverage is customized to each commercial auto coverage form. For example, Garage Coverage Physical Damage can pay for damage to autos in the custody or care of the insured business or even autos being held for sale. However, Truckers Coverage Physical Damage only covers the autos owned by the insured or used for business purposes.

Conditions – A commercial auto policy's conditions section (Section IV) defines the coverage in greater detail. The conditions determine the coverage territory, policy period, and how coverage applies in certain situations.

Definitions

The *definitions* section (Section V) of a commercial auto policy defines terms and phrases that appear throughout the policy.

The Commercial Auto (CA) coverage form includes some essential definitions at the end of the policy. The following are key terms and definitions used in explaining the coverages provided by commercial auto insurance.

Auto — A land motor vehicle, trailer, or semitrailer intended for use on public roads and any other land vehicle must adhere to compulsory financial responsibility laws where it is licensed or principally garaged. However, *auto* does not include mobile equipment.

The term *trailer* also includes a semitrailer.

Mobile equipment – Includes any of the following types of land vehicles, including any equipment or attached machinery:

- Forklifts, farm machinery, bulldozers, and other vehicles primarily used off public roads;
- Vehicles that travel on crawler treads;
- Vehicles that provide mobility to road construction equipment, loaders, shovels, or cranes; and
- Vehicles that are not self-propelled that provide mobility to spraying or welding equipment, pumps, compressors, cherry pickers, and similar devices used to raise and lower workers.

This definition does not include self-propelled vehicles used in street cleaning, road construction, snow removal, or cherry pickers mounted on vehicles or autos subject to compulsory financial responsibility laws. Those will be considered autos.

Insured Contract — Coverage for contracts is excluded unless the contract falls within the following parameters:

- A contract for a lease of premises;
- A sidetrack agreement (made with a railroad when a policy owner uses a track);
- License or easement agreement (except within 50 feet of a railroad);
- Indemnification of a municipality unless work is being performed for a municipality;
- Part of a contract, including work for a municipality, in which the tort liability of another is assumed (would be imposed in the absence of a contract); or
- Rental agreements for "autos" but not for any damage to the auto.

An insured contract does not include agreements for autos rented with a driver, demolition near railroads, or certain agreements made by carriers for hire.

Commercial Auto Coverage Forms

Several coverage forms used with the commercial auto coverage part protect business owners that have an auto-related exposure to loss. These coverage forms include the following:

- The *business auto coverage form*, which covers most commercial auto exposures, *except* garages, truckers, and motor carriers;
- The *business auto physical damage coverage form* provides physical damage protection only for the insured's owned or hired business autos;
- The *garage coverage form* is used for businesses that regularly have the autos of others in their custody, care, or control. These types of businesses would include auto dealerships, auto repair and service garages, and businesses that park vehicles for others; and
- The *motor carrier coverage form* is an alternative to the truckers coverage form. It insures businesses that transport either owned or non-owned property.

The commercial auto coverage part can be written as part of a commercial package policy or as a monoline policy. The coverage protects the business owner against liability and physical damage losses arising from owning or using autos.

Similar to commercial coverage parts, a specific declarations page must be attached to the policy. Each of the five commercial auto coverage forms uses a different declarations page. The policy declarations page includes information about the named insured, premium, limits of insurance, coverage provided, and a list of all applicable endorsements. The nuclear energy liability exclusion (broad form) must also be attached to the commercial auto coverage part.

Under the commercial auto coverage part, the types of vehicles that can be covered include:

- Commercial vehicles, including trucks of all shapes and sizes, semi-trailers, truck-tractor units, and service and commercial trailers;
- Public vehicles, like cabs or livery vehicles (transporting people) and rental cars;
- Private passenger type vehicles, including pickup trucks, jeeps, station wagons, panel vans, and utility trailers intended to be pulled by private passenger autos; and
- Other types of vehicles, like antique autos, ambulances, fire trucks, and police cars, farm machinery intended for use on public roads (e.g., combines and tractors), construction equipment used on public roads (e.g., snow removal equipment, cherry pickers), and special or mobile equipment towed or carried by a covered auto.

Business Auto

Section I – Covered Autos

Section I of the *business auto coverage form* explains the auto designation symbols that define the vehicle types insured for specific coverages. The symbols are listed next to the appropriate coverage on the declarations page.

The business auto coverage form uses the following auto symbols:

AUTO SYMBOLS USED WITH BUSINESS AUTO COVERAGE FORM	
1=	Any auto, including owned, leased, hired, or borrowed autos (used only for liability coverage)
2=	Owned autos only
3=	Owned private passenger autos only
4=	Owned autos, other than private passenger autos only
5=	Owned autos subject to no-fault
6=	Owned autos subject to a compulsory uninsured motorists law
7=	Specifically described autos only
8=	Hired autos only (rented, leased, hired or borrowed other than from partners, employees or members of an LLC)
9=	Non-owned autos only (autos that are not rented, leased, hired or borrowed. Coverage is included for autos owned by partners, employees and members, if an LLC, if used in the policyholder's business or personal affairs)
10=	Mobile equipment subject to financial responsibility, compulsory, or other motor vehicle insurance laws only

It is worth noting that the commercial auto policy does not use the definition of *your covered auto* like the personal auto policy. The covered auto symbols are a vital component of the form as they describe the vehicles granted coverage.

Example 6.1 – The commercial auto policy will cover liability for autos that fall into categories 7, 8, or 9. However, the policy will cover auto medical payments only for vehicles that fall into category 7. An attached Vehicle Schedule will list the year, make, model, and other specifics about a particular auto.

Newly Acquired Autos – If symbols 1, 2, 3, 4, 5, or 6 are listed for any of the coverages, the policy will apply to any additional autos of the same type that the policy owner acquires during the policy period.

However, if Symbol 7 is used, newly acquired auto coverage applies if the insurer already covers all vehicles owned by the policy owner or if the newly acquired vehicle is replacing a previously owned auto. The insured must notify the insurer that coverage is requested within 30 days of obtaining the vehicle.

Certain Mobile Equipment, Trailers, and Temporary Substitutes – If liability coverage is provided, specific types of other vehicles are also covered for liability. These other vehicles include

- Mobile equipment that is being carried or towed by a covered vehicle;
- Trailers possessing a load capacity of 2,000 pounds or less; and
- Temporary substitute vehicles used while a covered auto is out of service because of loss, destruction, breakdown, servicing, or repair.

Section II – Liability Coverage

Section II – Liability Coverage states that the policy will pay for property damage or bodily injury to third parties resulting from an accident caused by the insured's use, maintenance, or ownership of any covered auto. The liability section also covers pollution expenses caused by an accident resulting from the use, maintenance, or ownership of a covered auto that results in property damage or bodily injury.

Who is an Insured – Under Section II of the business auto coverage form, an insured is any of the following:

- The organization or person named in the Declarations for any covered auto;
- Anyone else while using a covered auto with the policy owner's permission, *except* the following:
    - Owners of the auto (from whom a policy owner hires or borrows an auto other than a trailer);
    - Someone using a covered auto in the business of storing, parking, servicing, repairing, or selling autos unless the business is owned by the insured;
    - Anyone, other than partners, employees, lessees, or borrowers, while moving property from a covered auto;
    - Partners and employees for autos they own; and
- Anyone liable for a policy owner's conduct is an insured, but only to the extent of their liability.

Coverage Extensions – In addition, the liability section provides certain coverage extensions. The insurance company will pay the following *supplementary payments* in addition to the limit of insurance for property damage or bodily injury:

- All expenses the insurance provider incurs;
- The cost of bonds to release attachments;
- Up to $2,000 for bail bonds;
- Reasonable expenses sustained by the policy owner at the insurer's request, including up to $250 per day for time off work;
- Expenses taxed against the policy owner in any suit; and
- Accrued interest on any judgment.

A second coverage extension offers *out-of-state coverage* when a vehicle is driven in a state in which it is not registered. This extension provides increased liability protection to meet another state's financial responsibility requirements. It does not apply to carriers of property or people. If required, this extension also provides minimum amounts of other coverage, such as no-fault.

Exclusions – The liability coverage exclusions are shown in this section of the policy form. The coverage does not apply to:

- Intended or expected injury or damage;
- Contractual liability besides an insured contract;
- Duties under any disability benefits, workers compensation, unemployment, or similar law;
- Employer's liability and employee indemnification;
- Bodily injury to any fellow employee of the policy owner caused by a fellow employee's employment;
- Covered pollution expense or cost of property damage involving property that is transported or owned by an insured or in the insured's control, custody, or care;
- Property damage or bodily injury resulting from the operation of machinery or mobile equipment or equipment attached to or part of a vehicle that would be defined as mobile equipment if it were not subject to financial responsibility laws or other compulsory laws;

- Property moved by mechanical device unless the device is a hand truck or is attached to the covered vehicle;
- Losses resulting from work after it has been completed and is no longer in the hands of the policyholder (completed operations);
- Property damage or bodily injury caused by the handling of the property before or after it was moved;
- Losses because of pollution from operating a covered auto while pollutants are being loaded, unloaded, or transported from a covered auto. There is coverage when the pollution is from an object other than a covered auto, where the loss is caused by a covered auto;
- Stunts, demolition, or racing, including preparing for such activities; and
- War.

Limits of Insurance – The last section under *Section II – Liability Coverage* describes the limits of insurance. The limit of liability for property damage and bodily injury can be expressed as a single limit or split limit. A single limit defines the total amount the insurer will pay for all property damage or bodily injury, including any covered pollution expenses caused by a single accident.

Section III – Physical Damage Coverage

Coverage – Physical damage coverages available to the policy owner include the following:

- *Comprehensive coverage* pays for loss or damage to a covered auto by any cause other than overturn or collision;
- *Specified causes of loss coverage* will pay for loss to a covered auto if it resulted from lightning, fire, explosion, mischief or vandalism, theft, hail, windstorm, earthquake, or the burning, sinking, derailment, or collision of any conveyance transporting the covered auto;
- *Collision coverage* pays for losses to a covered auto caused by a collision with another object or overturn;
- *Towing coverage*, where the insurance provider will pay for labor costs incurred due to a disabled auto at the place of the disablement up to the towing limit of insurance listed in the Declarations. Coverage is provided only for passenger-type autos; and
- *Glass breakage (hitting an animal or bird, falling objects, or missiles)* is coverage for glass breakage, a loss caused by hitting an animal or bird or falling objects or missiles. Policy owners can collect for glass damage if the loss results from overturning the vehicle or a collision with an object.

The physical damage section provides *coverage extensions* for the following:

- *Transportation expenses* that would pay for substitute transportation, up to $20 per day for a maximum of $600, after the theft of a covered auto (private passenger type). The covered auto must be insured for comprehensive or specified causes of loss for this extension to be applied. This coverage included a 48-hour waiting period that lasts until the vehicle is returned or the insurance provider pays for the loss; and
- *Loss of use expenses* the insurer will pay for which a policy owner becomes legally liable for the loss of use of a vehicle hired or rented without a driver under a written rental contract. When coverage is purchased, this coverage extension pays for the damaged auto's loss of use up to $20 per day to a maximum of $600.

Exclusions – The exclusions found in the physical damage section of the business auto coverage form are as follows:

- War and military action;
- Nuclear hazard;
- Stunt, demolition, or racing activities;
- Freezing, wear and tear, mechanical breakdown, or tire damage (unless another covered loss caused it); and

- Loss to sound devices, such as audio-visual equipment, radar detection equipment, and other electronic equipment and accessories. However, permanently installed equipment intended solely for the reproduction of sound (e.g., a tape deck) is covered.

Limits of Insurance – The physical damage limit of insurance is the *lesser* of:

- The actual cash value of the covered vehicle at the time of the loss; or
- The cost of replacing or repairing the stolen or damaged property with other similar property.

The maximum paid for loss of electronic, audio, and video equipment is $1,000 for equipment permanently installed in the vehicle or removable from a permanently installed housing unit.

The *deductible* provision states that any loss will be decreased by the amount of the deductible listed in the Declarations. Any comprehensive deductible shown will not apply to losses caused by lightning or fire.

Comprehensive and Specified Causes of Loss coverage deductibles apply to losses caused by theft, mischief, vandalism, or all perils. Regardless of the number of covered autos damaged or stolen, the deductible for losses incurred in any event cannot exceed five times the highest deductible applicable to any vehicle.

Section IV – Conditions

The following *conditions* apply:

- **Appraisal for physical damage coverage**;
- **Duties in the event of a loss, accident claim, or lawsuit**;
- **Legal action against the insurance company**;
- **Loss payment – physical damage coverage** — The insurance provider has the option to:
    o Pay for the replacement or repair of damaged property;
    o Return the stolen property and pay for any essential repairs; or
    o Take all or any part of the damaged property at an appraised or agreed value.
- **Subrogation** — The transfer of rights of recovery against others to the insurance company;
- **Fraud, misrepresentation, or concealment**;
- **Bankruptcy**;
- **No benefit to bailee – physical damage coverage**;
- **Liberalization**;
- **Other insurance** — If more than one policy applies to a loss, the policy will respond in the following ways:
    o **Primary insurance** — Owned auto, a trailer attached to an owned auto, when Hired Auto Physical Damage is selected and if liability is assumed in an insured contract;
    o **Excess insurance** — For the use of non-owned autos and when an owned trailer is attached to a non-owned auto;
- **Premium audit**;
- **Policy period, coverage territory** — The United States, its territories and possessions, Puerto Rico and Canada, or anywhere in the world if the covered auto is a private passenger auto rented, leased, hired, or borrowed without a driver for no more than 30 days. Any lawsuit must be based on the merits of the legal system within the United States and its territories and possessions, Puerto Rico, and Canada. Coverage also exists when a covered auto is in transit between locations); and
- **Two or more coverage forms or policies** — If more than one policy applies to a loss and is issued by the same insurer or affiliate, only the highest limit of liability will apply unless the policy is excess coverage.

Garage

Businesses that store, park, repair, service, or sell vehicles do not qualify for coverage under the other Insurance Services Office forms. Therefore, specialized coverage is required. Similar to the Business Auto Coverage Form, the *Garage Coverage Form* provides the same basic coverage, and special coverages developed to meet these unique needs. Types of risks that qualify for coverage under the Garage Coverage Form include the following:

- Franchised and nonfranchised auto dealers;
- Commercial trailer, truck, and truck-tractor dealers;
- Mobile home, recreational vehicle, and motorcycle dealers;
- Service stations;
- Automotive repair shops;
- Car washes; and
- Public parking facilities and storage garages.

General Form Structure – The Garage Coverage form is split into six sections. Pay special attention to Section II – Liability, as it is divided into two categories for Garage Operations. Garage operations will either be for covered autos or other than covered autos. The garage policy, as it pertains to covered autos, is similar to the business auto coverage form. The part of the policy that relates to other than covered autos protects the garage operation from liability exposures not arising from the ownership, use, and maintenance of vehicles.

The following are sections in the garage form:

1. Section I – Covered Autos;
2. Section II – Liability;
3. Section III – Garagekeepers Liability;
4. Section IV – Physical Damage Coverage;
5. Section V – Garage Conditions; and
6. Section VI – Definitions.

Definitions – The Definitions section is technically the last section of the Garage Coverage form. Still, it is helpful to know these terms before reviewing each section below.

Most of the definitions used in the garage form are similar to the business auto coverage form, so make sure to review these definitions as needed. Some of the definitions unique to the garage form include the following:

Garage operations are the ownership, maintenance, or use of locations for garage businesses, including adjoining roads and other accesses. It also includes the ownership, maintenance, or use of covered autos and all necessary or incidental operations.

Products include goods or products made or sold by the insured in the garage business. It also includes the failure to provide warnings or instructions.

Work performed by the insured includes work that someone performed on the insured's behalf and providing or failing to provide warnings or instructions.

Section I – Covered Autos

This section of the Garage Coverage Form defines the covered auto designation symbols. Although some descriptions are similar to the Business Auto Coverage Form, the numerical symbols vary. Some additional descriptions are added that apply specifically to garage operations.

AUTO DESIGNATION SYMBOLS FOUND IN THE GARAGE COVERAGE FORM	
21=	Any auto
22=	Owned autos only
23=	Owned private passenger autos only
24=	Owned autos other than private passenger autos only
25=	Owned autos subject to no-fault
26=	Owned autos subject to a compulsory uninsured motorists law
27=	Specifically described autos
28=	Hired autos only (rented, leased, borrowed, or hired by the policy owner, but not autos owned by partners, employees, or members of an LLC)
29=	Non-owned autos used in your garage business (for vehicles not owned, rented, leased, borrowed, or hired by the policy owner also applies to vehicles owned by partners, employees, and members of an LLC)
30=	Autos left for safekeeping, storage, repair, or service (used to provide garagekeepers coverage for employees or customers and members of their household who pay for services)
31=	Dealer's autos (physical damage coverage)

Newly Acquired Autos – When symbols *21, 22, 23, 24, 25, or 26* are listed for any of the coverages on the declarations page, the coverage applies to any additional vehicles of the same type the insured acquires for the rest of the policy period.

However, if *Symbol 27* appears in the Declarations, coverage for newly acquired vehicles will be limited to 30 days if every owned auto is covered unless the vehicle is a replacement.

Certain Trailers and Temporary Substitutes – If liability coverage is provided, insurers will also cover certain types of other autos for liability. These other vehicles include:

- Trailers possessing a load capacity of 2,000 pounds or less; and
- Substitute vehicles used temporarily while a covered auto is out of service due to destruction, loss, servicing, repair, or breakdown.

Section II – Liability Coverage

Section II — Liability Coverage is split into two parts:

1. Garage Operations — Other than Covered Autos; and
2. Garage Operations — Covered Autos.

As with other liability coverages, an accident must result from property damage or bodily injury. The policy owner must be legally liable for the loss of coverage to apply. Also, the *Garage Operations — Other than Covered Autos* form requires that the damage or loss directly results from the policy owner's garage operations. The *Garage Operations — Covered Autos* form protects the policy owner from losses resulting from the use, maintenance, or ownership of covered autos. Pollution costs or expenses are also covered under the liability coverage section.

Who is an insured – The definition of an insured is also in the liability section of the Garage Coverage Form. The insured individuals differ according to whether the loss results from garage operations or covered auto exposure. For covered auto exposures, insured means:

- The organization or individual named on the declarations page;
- Individuals operating a covered auto with the policy owner's permission, except:
    - Owners of the auto (from whom an insured hires or borrows a vehicle other than a trailer);
    - Someone using a covered auto who is in the business of selling, servicing, repairing, parking, or storing autos unless the business is owned by the insured;
    - The insured's customers unless they do not have insurance or less than the compulsory amount of insurance. Coverage applies only up to the mandatory limits; or
    - Employees and partners for autos they own;
- Any individual liable for the conduct of the policy owner, but only to the extent of their liability; and
- The insured's employee using a non-owned covered auto in the insured's personal or business affairs.

For garage operations (excluding covered autos), an insured refers to:

- The organization or individual named in the Declarations; or
- Partners, employees, officers, directors, and shareholders while acting within the scope of their duties.

Coverage Extensions – The coverage extensions provide the same supplemental payments and out-of-state coverage extension included in the Business Auto Coverage Form.

Exclusions – Garage liability coverage excludes the following:

- **Expected or Intended Injury** — There is an exception to this exclusion when the property damage or bodily injury results from using reasonable force to protect property or individuals;
- **Contractual Liability** — The liability assumed under any agreement or contract; coverage only applies to liability assumed in an insured contract or if the insured would be liable in the absence of a contract;
- **Workers Compensation**;
- **Employee Indemnification and Employer's Liability** – This exclusion is broader in that it excludes bodily injury resulting from employment-related practices, such as harassment, discrimination, or termination;
- **Fellow Employee**, including the fellow employee's spouses, children, parents, or siblings;
- **Care, Custody, or Control** — This exclusion is broadened to exclude property occupied, rented, loaned, or held for sale by the policy owner;
- **Leased Autos** — This exclusion is not in the Business Auto Coverage Form. It excludes autos rented or leased to others. However, autos rented to customers while their vehicles are serviced will be covered;
- **Pollution Exclusion Applicable to Garage Operations (Other than Covered Autos)** — There is no coverage for loss or expenses incurred because of dispersal, discharge, seepage, or escape of pollutants at locations used or owned by the insured or for contaminants handled, transported, stored, disposed of, or processed as waste by the insured or the insured's contractor. However, there is coverage for fumes, smoke, or heat that result from a hostile fire;
- **Pollution Exclusion Applicable to Garage Operations (Covered Autos)** — The pollution exclusion found in the Garage Coverage Form is similar to the one in the Business Auto Coverage Form
- **Racing**;
- **Aircraft or Watercraft** — There is no liability coverage for aircraft or watercraft, except watercraft ashore on the policy owner's garage premises;
- **Defective Products** — There is no liability coverage for property damage to the policy owner's products resulting from an existing defect in the product;

- **Work Performed** — No liability coverage is provided for property damage to work performed by the policy owner if the damage results from the work or the materials or parts used. Work performed is defined as work that someone performs for the policy owner, including providing or failing to provide instructions or warnings;
- **Loss of Use** — Property damage under the Garage Coverage Form includes loss of use. However, there are situations in which loss of use is not covered. Loss of use does not cover property that is not physically damaged because of delays or failure to perform according to the terms of an agreement or contract. It also does not cover any deficiency, defect, inadequacy, or dangerous condition in the product or work performed. Loss of use from sudden and accidental damage from a deficiency or defect is covered.
- **Products Recall** — Insurers will not cover any loss or expense incurred due to a recall or withdrawal of the policy owner's product;
- **War**, including rebellion, insurrection, revolution, or actions taken by a governmental authority in hindering or defending against any of these perils; and
- **Distribution of Material in Violation of Statutes** — Bodily injury or property damage resulting from The Telephone Consumer Protection Act, CAN-SPAM Act of 2003, or any other statute that prohibits the transmission, distribution, or communication of any material or information. (This exclusion applies to Garage Operations – Other than Covered Autos.)

Limits of Insurance and Deductibles – The liability coverage limit includes an aggregate insurance limit that applies to Garage Operations – Other than Covered Autos. This coverage is the total amount the insurer will pay for all covered losses during the policy term. Also, there is a per accident limit that is the most the insurer will pay for a single loss. There is no distinction between property damage or bodily injury losses. The limit of liability insurance that applies to Garage Operations – Covered Autos is also stated as a per accident limit; it is not subject to an annual aggregate.

Garage Liability Coverage has a deductible provision that is not included in the Business Auto Coverage Form. This deductible applies to completed operations. A $100 deductible applies for property damage to vehicles resulting from work performed by the insured business.

Section III – Garagekeepers

Garagekeepers coverage insures against damage for which the policy owner is liable to a customer's auto left in the policy owner's control, custody, and care for storage, parking, repairs, or service. This coverage is typically excluded unless this coverage is purchased). This section is triggered by the auto designation *Symbol 30*.

A *customer's auto* refers to a land motor vehicle, trailer, or semi-trailer lawfully in the policy owner's possession with or without the owner's consent. The vehicle must be held in the policy owner's custody for safekeeping, storage, repair, or service. It also includes autos owned by the policy owner's employees, or their family members, if they are paying for services performed.

The causes of loss that insurers may cover include:

- **Comprehensive** — All loss to a customer's auto except overturn or collision;
- **Specified Causes of Loss** — Loss to a customer's auto due to lightning, fire, explosion, theft, vandalism, or mischief; and
- **Collision** — A customer's auto loss caused by overturning or hitting an object.

The insurance provider has a right and duty to defend the policy owner against those seeking damages unless the insurance does not apply. The insurer can investigate and settle any claims as they deem appropriate. The duty to defend ceases when the limits of insurance are exhausted.

Unless noted otherwise in the Declarations, the garagekeepers coverage is triggered only when the policy owner is legally liable for the damages. This option is known as the *Legal Liability (or Standard) Coverage* option. Suppose the policy owner would prefer the coverage to be triggered without regard to liability. In that case, a *Direct Coverage* option must be activated on the declarations page and the additional premium paid.

Who is an insured – The following are considered insureds under the garagekeepers coverage form:

- The named insured; and
- Partners, directors, shareholders, or employees of the named insured while acting within the scope of their duties.

Coverage Extensions – *Coverage Extensions* for garagekeepers insurance are identical to those in the Business Auto Policy:

- All expenses incurred by the insurance provider;
- Cost of bonds to release attachments in lawsuits against the policy owner defended by the insurer;
- Reasonable expenses sustained by the insured at the insurance provider's request, including $250 per day for time off from work;
- Costs taxed against the insured in lawsuits against the insured defended by the insurance provider; and
- Interest on the total amount of a judgment accrued after entry of a judgment in lawsuits against the policy owner defended by the insurer.

Garagekeepers insurance has the following *exclusions*:

- **Contractual obligations** — Liability resulting from an agreement in which the policy owner accepted responsibility for loss;
- **Theft** — Theft or conversion by the policy owner, shareholders, or employees;
- **Defective parts** — Defective materials or parts;
- **Faulty work** — Faulty work done by or for the policy owner; and
- **Loss to any of the following**:
    - Tape decks or other sound reproducing devices unless permanently installed;
    - Records, tapes, or other sound reproducing equipment;
    - Telephone, sound receiving equipment, 2-way mobile radios, citizens' band radios, scanning monitor receivers, and accessories for such equipment, including antennas, unless permanently installed where the manufacturer would typically install a radio; and
    - Equipment used for radar detection.

Limits of Insurance and Deductibles – A limit of insurance must be listed in the Declarations and applies irrespective of the number of customers' autos. The deductibles chosen on the declarations page will apply to all collision, other than collision, and specified causes of loss coverages.

Section IV – Physical Damage

Section IV – Physical Damage Coverage is similar to the Business Auto coverage form. (Be sure to review those coverages).

The garage form has some *additional exclusions*:

- The insurance provider will not cover a loss of expected profits, including loss of market or resale value;
- Loss to a covered auto stored or displayed at a location not listed in the declarations for more than 45 days;

- No collision coverage exists for covered autos while driven or transported if the point of purchase and destination are more than 50 miles apart; and
- If specified causes of loss are selected, no coverage exists if the covered auto is being transported and a collision occurs to the vehicle transporting the covered auto.

Limits of Insurance and Deductibles – This section is similar to the Business Auto coverage form. However, it includes additional explanations applicable to an operation selling autos or trailers.

When a limit of insurance is listed on the declarations page for an insured location, this is the most the insurance provider will pay for any loss.

Quarterly or Monthly Reporting Premium Basis – If on the date of the last report, the actual value of the covered autos exceeds the value reported, the insurance provider will only cover a percentage of the loss based on what the insured reported and the actual value. If the first report is late, the insurer will only pay 75% of the limit shown on the declarations page.

Nonreporting Premium Basis – If the insured does not carry adequate limits of insurance, the insurance provider can invoke a penalty and pay only the percentage of the loss. This percentage is calculated by comparing the insured value to the property's actual value at the time of the loss.

A *deductible* will apply for each covered auto for collision losses. The comprehensive or specified causes of loss option will apply per loss when a maximum deductible is listed in the Declarations. This deductible will apply regardless of the number of vehicles damaged or stolen.

Section V – Garage Conditions

The *Garage Conditions* are the same as those found in the Business Auto Coverage Form, except for the policy period and the coverage territory condition. The Business Auto Coverage Form states that accidents and losses occurring during the policy period and within the coverage territory are covered. However, in the Garage Coverage Form, the wording is slightly different. It refers to property damage and bodily injury within the coverage territory. This distinction is to clarify liability associated with *Garage Operations – Other Than Covered Autos* coverage. The garage form refers to covered pollution costs or expenses resulting from accidents.

Because the garage form offers product liability coverage, the language is revised to afford the policy owner coverage for losses associated with their products sold in the coverage territory. Policy owners must also file the original lawsuit in one of the places located in the coverage territory.

Truckers

Businesses that use their vehicles to transport goods for others require specialized insurance coverage that is not available through the business auto or garage coverage forms. Some of these additional coverages are required due to the very nature of the job. Others are necessary because of governmental regulations. The *truckers coverage form* was created to address the unique insurance needs of these businesses.

Businesses that haul goods for others are called *truckers* or *carriers for hire*. There are two classes of carriers for hire, both of which qualify for coverage under the truckers coverage form:

1. Common carriers who haul goods for anyone; and
2. Contract carriers who have written contracts with other companies to transport their merchandise

Businesses that use their vehicles to carry their own goods are known as *private carriers* and cannot be issued coverage under the truckers coverage form. Private carriers can be insured under the motor carrier coverage form or the business auto coverage form.

The truckers coverage form is identical to the business auto coverage and garage coverage forms. This coverage requires a separate declarations page and the nuclear energy liability exclusion (broad form). The truckers coverage form has one expanded definition and two new definitions not contained in the business auto coverage form:

Private passenger type — Includes a private passenger or station wagon type of auto, including a van or pickup if not used for business.

Trailer — This expanded definition from the business auto coverage form includes a semi-trailer or a dolly used to convert a semi-trailer into a trailer. The trailer also includes a container regarding trailer interchange coverage.

The difference between a semi-trailer and a trailer is that a semi-trailer must be attached to a fifth-wheel coupling device (dolly) that becomes the semi-trailer's front wheels. In contrast, a trailer has both front and rear wheels. A service or utility trailer can be either a trailer or a semi-trailer but is limited to a load capacity of 2,000 pounds or less.

Section I

Section I – Covered Autos of the truckers form includes specific auto designation symbols that define the type of vehicles that insurers can cover under the policy. These symbols' descriptions are similar to those in the business auto coverage form. However, the designation numbers are different. The designation for owned private passenger vehicles is not included in the truckers coverage form.

Section II

Section II — Liability Coverage includes the same coverage, exclusions, extensions, and limit of insurance as the business auto coverage form. However, the definition of an insured is slightly different. The truckers coverage form includes liability coverage for partners and employees if they lend the insured a vehicle, *other than a private passenger vehicle*. Under the business auto coverage form, there is no liability coverage for any vehicle borrowed from partners or employees.

As in the business auto coverage form, any borrowed or hired trailers do not have to be attached to a covered auto owned for the owner of the trailer to be considered an insured for liability. The trailer can be attached to any vehicle considered a power unit, including hired and non-owned vehicles, if designated in the Declarations.

Section III

Section III – Trailer Interchange Coverage is unique to truckers and motor carrier insurance. These businesses commonly hire or borrow trailers from others through a written trailer interchange agreement. The insurance provider will pay all sums the insured must legally pay as damages under three types of coverage:

1. Comprehensive (resulting from any cause except for the trailer's overturn or collision with another object);
2. Specified Causes of Loss; or
3. Collision Coverage (resulting from the trailer's overturn or collision with another object).

Exclusions – The trailer interchange coverage provides identical supplemental payments as the business auto policy, except for *costs related to bail bonds*.

The following *exclusions* apply to the trailer interchange coverage:

1. War or military action;
2. Nuclear hazard;

3. Loss of use; and
4. Freezing, wear and tear, mechanical breakdown, or road damage to tires.

Limits of Insurance – The most the insurance provider will pay for any one trailer is the *least* of the following, minus any deductible that applies:

- The actual cash value;
- The cost to repair the damage or replace with like kind and quality; or
- The limit of insurance listed on the declarations page.

Section IV

Section IV — Physical Damage includes the same coverage as discussed for the business auto coverage form. However, one additional exclusion in the truckers physical damage coverage is not included in the business auto physical damage coverage section. This additional exclusion states that there will not be any coverage for a covered auto while in the possession of anyone else under a trailer interchange contract. This coverage has to be selected explicitly by the policy owner.

Designation Symbols

The following provisions in Section I are the same as those in the business auto coverage form (except the numerical symbols). If symbol 41, 42, 43, 44, 45, or 59 is listed for any coverages in the Declarations, coverage applies to any additional vehicles of the same type the insured acquires throughout the policy period. However, when symbol 46 is used, coverage for newly acquired vehicles will be limited to 30 days. Coverage only applies if all owned autos are covered, or the auto is a replacement vehicle. When symbol 42 or 43 is used to cover liability, coverage will also be provided for non-owned trailers, including semitrailers attached to an owned power unit.

	DESIGNATION SYMBOLS FOUND IN THE TRUCKERS COVERAGE FORM
41=	Any auto (used only for liability coverage)
42=	Owned autos only
43=	Owned commercial autos only
44=	Owned autos subject to no-fault
45=	Owned autos subject to a compulsory uninsured motorists law
46=	Specifically described autos
47=	Hired autos only
48=	Trailers in your possession under a written trailer or equipment interchange agreement
49=	Your trailers in the possession of anyone else under a written trailer interchange agreement
50=	Non-owned autos only
59=	Mobile equipment subject to compulsory, financial responsibility, or other motor vehicle insurance laws only

Liability Coverage

If liability coverage is provided, certain types of other vehicles are covered automatically for liability. This coverage includes mobile equipment while being transported by a covered auto and trailers possessing a load capacity of 2,000 pounds or less. Temporary substitute non-owned vehicles used in place of an out-of-service auto are also covered.

This form also provides liability coverage to the owner of a borrowed vehicle (other than a trailer). It also covers a non-owned trailer not attached to a power unit if used exclusively in the policy owner's business or according to the operating rights awarded by a public authority.

The truckers coverage form's *conditions* are identical to those in the business auto coverage form. However, the truckers form includes an additional condition. The *Other Insurance – Primary and Excess Insurance Provision* specifies that the truckers liability coverage will be considered primary insurance when:

- A covered auto is an owned auto, not hired or loaned out to another;
- A covered auto is hired or borrowed by the policy owner for use in business as a trucker and used according to operating rights awarded by a public authority;
- A covered trailer is attached to a covered auto for which this coverage is primary;
- A non-owned trailer is not connected to a power unit and is being used by the policy owner in the business as a trucker; or
- If liability for damage has been assumed under an insured contract or agreement.

The truckers liability coverage will be considered *excess* when

- A covered auto (not borrowed or hired) is not owned by the named insured;
- An owned covered auto is borrowed or hired by the policy owner from another trucker;
- A covered trailer is attached to a covered auto for which this coverage is excess; or
- A covered trailer is attached to an auto that is not covered.

Under the liability coverage section of the truckers coverage form, the following are *not* defined explicitly as an insured:

- Other truckers subject to motor carrier insurance laws that meet these requirements through other than auto insurance;
- Other truckers whose coverage is not considered primary insurance for owners of borrowed vehicles; or
- Any water, rail, or air carrier for a detached trailer loaded, unloaded, or transported by the carrier.

Motor Carrier

As defined by the ISO form, a *motor carrier* is an individual or organization providing transportation by auto on behalf of a commercial enterprise. The motor carrier coverage form can cover *any carriers* that transport goods, including private carriers (those who transport their own goods). This policy is a relatively recent development. It has the same coverage, provisions, conditions, and definitions as the Business Auto coverage form with minor differences.

This form uses the covered auto designation symbols 61 through 69 for various types of autos.

General Form Structure – The Motor Carrier Coverage form consists of the following sections:

1. Section I – Covered Autos;
2. Section II – Liability Coverage;
3. Section III – Trailer Interchange Coverage;
4. Section IV – Physical Damage Coverage;
5. Section V – Motor Carrier Conditions; and
6. Section VI – Definitions.

Most of this form's sections are similar or identical to the Business Auto Coverage form. We will discuss only Trailer Interchange coverage in this section.

Trailer Interchange Coverage

Trailer interchange coverage has no equivalent in either the business auto coverage form or the garage coverage form. Motor carriers regularly borrow or hire trailers from others with a written trailer interchange agreement. They require coverage for the trailer in their possession to cover the liability imposed upon them due to the contract. Coverage for loss or damage to property in the policyholder's control, custody, or care is usually excluded under liability coverage forms, including the business auto form. The trailer interchange coverage will cover loss or damage to a non-owned trailer in the policyholder's control, custody, or care if the insured is legally liable for the damage. Coverage can be provided for comprehensive or specified causes of loss and collision.

Exclusions – The trailer interchange coverage provides identical supplemental payments as the business auto policy, except for *costs related to bail bonds*. In addition, three types of exclusions apply to the trailer interchange coverage:

1. War or military action;
2. Nuclear hazard; and
3. Freezing, wear and tear, mechanical breakdown, or road damage to tires.

Limits of Insurance – The most the insurance provider will pay for any one trailer is the *least* of the following, minus any deductible that applies:

- The actual cash value;
- The cost to repair the damage or replace with like kind and quality; or
- The limit of insurance listed on the declarations page.

Selected Endorsements

Several optional endorsements are available to revise the coverage in the commercial auto coverage part.

Lessor - Additional Insured and Loss Payee – If an insured has leased autos, they can use this endorsement to provide liability and physical damage coverage for the lessor's interests as an additional insured.

Mobile Equipment – In the Business Auto Coverage Form, mobile equipment is insured for liability when being carried or towed by a covered auto. Suppose a land vehicle meets the mobile equipment definition. However, because of where or how it is used, it becomes subject to compulsory insurance like it were an auto. In that scenario, a policy owner could have a coverage problem. For example, an excavator must have mandatory insurance. It must be driven on a public road to get from one part of a work site to another. When the policy owner has a Symbol 7 (Specified Auto) listed in the Declarations, that excavator would need to be included on the policy owner's vehicle schedule to be covered for liability. If it is not listed on the declarations page, a solution would be to use this endorsement for an added premium. The excavator would be described explicitly in the endorsement and granted coverage.

Covered autos liability coverage does not apply to property damage, bodily injury, or covered pollution expense or cost from operating equipment or machinery that is on, attached to, or part of any of the covered autos.

Auto Medical Payments Coverage – Commercial auto coverage forms do not automatically include coverage for medical payments. Typically, any individual who occupies the vehicle would be covered under workers compensation. Policy owners can add this coverage to a commercial auto policy through the *auto medical payments coverage* endorsement.

Personal Use of Non-owned Auto Endorsements – A potential coverage gap exists for the personal use of non-owned automobiles for individuals who have a vehicle insured on a commercial auto policy and do not have a personal auto policy in their household. The Business Auto coverage form offers two endorsements to fill this coverage gap. The purpose of both endorsements is the same, but they are used to insure different corporate structures.

Drive Other Car - Broadened Coverage for Named Individuals – This endorsement extends coverage from Business Auto, Business Auto Physical Damage, Motor Carrier, and Garage coverage forms to vehicles not owned, borrowed, or hired by the named insured and puts no stipulation that use must take place during the course of business. Because a corporate entity could have many people, only those listed (and their spouses while a resident of the same household) are provided coverage.

Individual Named Insured – The *Individual Named Insured* endorsement is used with the Business Auto and Motor Carrier coverage forms to insure a sole proprietor. Any owned private passenger vehicle (auto, van, or pickup not used in business) covered by the policy will include family members as insureds by adding this endorsement. Coverage is also granted to the policy owner and family members for the use of a non-owned auto subject to the similar exclusions found in the personal auto policy.

Physical damage coverage is also provided to the policy owner's family members for owned private passenger vehicles and non-owned autos. However, physical damage coverage for non-owned trailers will have a limit of up to $500. The endorsement also eliminates the fellow employee exclusion from the liability section of the Commercial Auto Coverage Form.

Employees as Insureds – The *employees as insureds* endorsement will provide the policy owner's employees additional protection while using a vehicle not owned, borrowed, or hired for the insured business. For instance, an employee uses a personal auto to run an errand on behalf of the insured business owner. Employees are not covered under the commercial auto coverage section while using their own vehicles during the course of business because of one of the exceptions listed in the permission clause in the Who is an Insured portion of the policy.

Hired Auto and Non-owned Auto Liability – *Hired* autos include leased, hired, rented, or borrowed vehicles from someone other than an employee or partner.

The classes *hired automobiles*, and *non-owned automobiles* are mutually exclusive. We must better understand the distinction between the two. Hired automobiles include leased, hired, rented, or borrowed vehicles, *excluding* autos that employees own. Autos leased, hired, rented, or borrowed *from employees* are considered non-owned automobiles. The distinction between a hired and non-owned auto does not depend on whether or not payment is made for the auto's use but rather on whether or not an employee owns it. This artificial distinction exists primarily for rating and premium determination purposes.

Non-owned autos are vehicles that are not owned, leased, hired, rented, or borrowed in connection with the insured business. This endorsement includes autos owned by employees, partners, and members only while being used in the affairs of the insured business.

The *Hired Autos Specified as Covered Autos You Own* endorsement may be added to Commercial Auto policies to add coverage for specified hired automobiles. Any hired auto scheduled in the endorsement will be treated as if they were covered autos owned by the insured.

Commercial Carrier Regulations

The state and the federal government have implemented regulations specific to trucking risks for truckers who travel within the boundaries of a single state and across state lines. The *Federal Motor Carrier Safety Administration (FMCSA)* is the federal body that regulates interstate truckers. Federal regulation also applies to interstate or intrastate truckers that transport hazardous materials.

The Motor Carrier Act of 1980 – The *Motor Carrier Act of 1980* established the federal regulations that apply to common carriers hauling goods for a fee, contract carriers transporting goods of others under contract, and freight forwarders. The act establishes the minimum financial responsibility requirements for carriers of hazardous property and all for-hire interstate carriers.

These minimum requirements for haulers of property are:

- $1 million for the transportation of oil and specific categories of hazardous material or waste by private (haul their own goods) or for-hire carriers in interstate commerce;
- $750,000 for the transportation of nonhazardous property by for-hire carriers in interstate commerce; and
- $5 million for transporting other specifically defined hazardous materials and waste, gas, explosives, or radioactive material hauled by private or for-hire carriers. This amount applies to both interstate and intrastate carriers.

Endorsement for Motor Carrier Policies of Insurance for Public Liability – The FMCSA has developed an endorsement, MCS-90, that has to be attached to every motor carrier's policy under its jurisdiction. This endorsement ensures that motor carriers comply with the federally mandated public liability coverage, including property damage, bodily injury, and environmental restoration. This endorsement allows the insurance provider to seek reimbursement from the policyholder to pay a claim for public liability if the insurer would not cover the claim under the policy without the MCS-90 endorsement.

Environmental restoration is not usually covered in commercial auto policies unless it meets specific parameters defined in the policy. The environmental restoration definition in the MCS-90 endorsement is broad and includes coverage for damage done by commodities transported by a motor carrier. The endorsement uses the word commodity instead of pollutants, so the mitigation and cleanup expenses could be incurred for any commodity hauled by a carrier that is introduced into the environment.

Laws

New York Motor Vehicle Financial Responsibility Law

Required Limits of Liability – The required limits of liability include the following:

- $25,000 for bodily injury or $50,000 for the death of one person due to any one accident;
- $50,000 for bodily injury or $100,000 for the death of two or more individuals as the result of any one accident; and
- $10,000 for the destruction of property damage due to any one accident.

Payments made to settle any claims because of death, bodily injury, or property damage from a motor vehicle accident must be credited in reducing the above amounts.

Required Proof of Insurance – Required *proof of insurance* or *proof of financial security* means proof of ability to respond with damages for liability arising from the use, maintenance, or ownership of a motor vehicle. Evidence of such financial security may include any of the following:

- A policy of liability insurance;
- A financial security bond;
- A financial security deposit; or

- Qualification as a self-insurer (the Superintendent, at their discretion, can, upon the application of an individual having registered in their name more than 25 motor vehicles, issue a certificate of self-insurance when they are satisfied that such an individual possesses the financial ability to respond to judgments).

Auto ID Cards – New York requires all auto policy owners to have an encrypted, two-dimensional barcoded auto ID card. Policy owners can issue cards using the New York State Department of Financial Services software. They can manually enter the card information or export it to the NY State Insurance ID Card software.

Transportation Network Companies (Ride-sharing) – With the upward trend in ride-sharing services like Uber and Lyft, most states have passed legislation mandating insurance protection for transportation network company drivers. A *transportation network company (TNC)* is any company that uses a digital network to connect riders to drivers to provide transportation.

The National Association of Insurance Commissioners (NAIC) divides TNC services into three exposure periods:

1. Waiting for a match (or pre-match);
2. Match accepted (driver is on the way to pick up the passenger); and
3. The passenger inside the vehicle and until they exit the vehicle.

Because drivers who contract with TNCs are using their personal vehicles, many do not have a livery driver's license, nor are their vehicles registered or insured as commercial vehicles. This difference is opposed to limousine or taxi drivers who drive commercial vehicles and have commercial insurance coverage. Personal auto policies do not typically provide coverage for ride-sharing.

In New York, *transportation network companies* (TNCs) cannot operate without obtaining a license from the Department of Financial Services. TNCs must also adhere to the automobile financial responsibility insurance requirements established by state statutes.

For TNC drivers logged into a TNC digital network but *not engaged in a prearranged trip*:

- $75,000 for bodily injury/death to any one individual per accident;
- $150,000 for bodily injury/death to two or more individuals per accident; and
- $25,000 for property damage per accident.

For TNC drivers logged into a TNC digital network *while engaged in a prearranged trip*: $1,250,000 for bodily injury/death of one or multiple individuals or property damage per accident.

Within *15 days* of filing a claim, a TNC and respective insurance company must provide relevant information to the involved parties. This information includes times when the TNC driver was logged into the TNC digital network, occurring *12 hours* before or after the accident, description of coverage, exclusions, and motor vehicle insurance limits. Also, TNC drivers must maintain all TNC trip records for at least *six years*.

New York law requires that TNCs do not hire applicants if the applicant:

- Is younger than 19 years of age;
- Does not have a valid NY driver's license;
- Does not have proof of auto liability insurance used for TNC prearranged trips;
- Is a match in the U.S. Department of Justice National Sex Offender Public Website; or
- Is on the sex offender registry.

Insurance Information and Enforcement System (IIES) Notification to DMV – The Insurance Information Enforcement System (IIES) is a database that monitors the insurance status of vehicles registered in New York. It identifies, sanctions, and eventually removes uninsured drivers and vehicles from the road.

An insurance provider must alert the Commissioner of the state department of motor vehicles within *30 days* of an insurance policy termination, whether by cancellation or nonrenewal.

This notice is not required if the policy was replaced by another insurance contract that took effect when or before the original contract ended. This notice is also not required if the insured surrendered the registration certificate and number plates when or before the contract ended.

New York Automobile Insurance Plan (Assigned Risk)

Purpose – The Automobile Insurance Plan (the Plan) aims to provide insurance for applicants who cannot obtain it through ordinary methods. These applicants are distributed fairly among the various insurers in New York. All insurance providers licensed to write motor vehicle insurance in New York must participate in the Automobile Insurance Plan.

Eligibility – For an applicant to be eligible for coverage in the Automobile Insurance Plan, the applicant must have a valid driver's license and be unable to purchase insurance in the standard market.

Coverage – The assigned risk plan must provide the following coverages:

- Up to $50,000 for bodily injury or the death of one individual in any single accident, up to $100,000 for bodily injury or the death of two or more individuals in any single accident, and up to $10,000 for injury or the destruction of the property of others in any single accident;
- Up to $10,000 actual cash value for loss or damage to an automobile insured under the policy, with a deductible of less than $100;
- Medical payments of up to $1,000 because of bodily injury or the death of any individual insured; and
- Supplementary Uninsured Motorists insurance. Any supplementary plan must provide twice the dollar level of first-party benefits and equal first-party benefits for personal injury arising from the use or operation of a motor vehicle in any state or Canada.

Binding Authority – Upon receiving a Notice of Designation and the premium or deposit from the NY Automobile Insurance Plan, the designated insurance company must, within the time allowed in the performance standards established by the Governing Committee:

- Issue a binder or policy if all information necessary for the insurance provider to fix the proper rate is contained in the application form. All policies will specify the territory and classifications used for each vehicle, any rating credits allowed, the specific accidents, and a description of each particular conviction used for point surcharges.
- Bind the risk if all information necessary for the insurance provider to fix the proper rate is not included in the application form.
- Bind the risk if the insurance provider does not have on file policy forms applicable to the risk assigned to it or the Plan does not have rates approved for such risk. The insurer will immediately apply to the Plan for the rate applicable to the assigned risk.

Comprehensive Motor Vehicle Insurance Reparations Act (PIP)

According to the New York Comprehensive Motor Vehicle Insurance Reparations Act (the Act), Personal Injury Protection requires motorists to carry first-party coverage for *basic economic loss with an aggregate limit of $50,000 per person* for the following combined benefits.

Medical – The medical portion of the Comprehensive Motor Vehicle Insurance Reparations Act includes all necessary expenses incurred for the following:

- Medical, hospital, nursing, surgical, dental, x-ray, ambulance, prescription drug, and prosthetic services;
- Physical, psychiatric, and occupational therapy and rehabilitation;
- Any non-medical, corrective care and treatment provided according to a religious method of healing recognized by New York State laws; and
- Any other professional health services.

All of these benefits are offered without a limitation to time. However, within *one year* of the accident causing the injury, it must be ascertained that additional expenses will be incurred due to the injury.

Rehabilitation – All rehabilitative expenses incurred due to an economic loss are covered under the Comprehensive Motor Vehicle Insurance Reparation Act. There is no time limitation for filing a claim on losses that occur for rehabilitative expenses.

Loss of Earnings – The Act also covers loss of earnings of up to $2,000 per month for work the individual would have performed had they not been injured. This coverage includes reasonable and necessary expenses incurred when obtaining services instead of those they would have performed for income. The insured can receive benefits for up to *three years* from the date of the accident causing the injury.

An employee entitled to receive benefits or who receives voluntary employer-paid benefits because of their inability to work due to personal injury arising from the operation or use of a vehicle is not entitled to receive first-party benefits for a loss of earnings from work. Such employer benefits or payments do not result in the employee experiencing a reduced income. They will not suffer a reduction in the employee's future benefits from a subsequent injury or illness.

Other Expenses – A basic economic loss also includes all other reasonable and necessary expenses incurred, *up to $25 per day* for no more than one year from the accident causing the injury.

Funeral – The Act provides $2,000 of death benefits paid to the estate of any covered individual. The death benefit does not apply to the occupant of another auto or motorcycle. This benefit is in addition to any first-party benefits for basic economic loss.

Substitution Services – Any authorized health insurance carrier can provide, either individually or jointly, substitution service coverage with the approval of the Superintendent. Such an insurer must demonstrate it is qualified to provide medical services related to economic loss. Suppose a policy owner chooses to be covered for a suffered financial loss under a Life and Health insurer rather than the coverage provided by the Auto insurer. In that circumstance, the Life and Health insurer will give the Auto insurer the names of all individuals it covers. These individuals cannot be entitled to benefits under the Auto policy. The Auto insurer must appropriately reduce the premiums for the Auto policy to reflect the elimination of coverage for economic loss. Coverage by the Auto insurer of the eliminated services will be affected or restored upon request by the insured's payment of the premium for such coverage.

Tort Limitation and Verbal Threshold – In any action by a covered individual against *another covered* individual for personal injuries arising from negligence in the use of a motor vehicle, there is no right of recovery for *non-economic loss* except in the case of a serious injury.

In any action of a covered individual against a *non-covered* individual, where damages for personal injuries may be recovered, an insurance provider that paid for first-party benefits has a *lien* against recovery to the extent of any benefits paid to the covered individual. Any legal action must commence within *two years* of the accident.

Notice of Claim – Insurers must pay first-party benefits within *30 days* after the claimant supplies proof of loss. After 30 days, the payment will be considered overdue and will begin accruing an interest rate of 2% per month.

When there is reason to believe that more than one insurer would be the source of first-party benefits, the insurers can agree that one will accept and pay the claim initially. Lacking that agreement, the first insurer to whom notice of claims is given will be responsible for payment.

Other insurers will reimburse any insurer paying first-party benefits for their proportionate share of the costs of the claim and the allocated expenses of processing the claim.

Optional Coverages

OBEL – OBEL (Optional Basic Economic Loss) coverage is offered to residents of New York in addition to the coverage mandated by the state. The OBEL supplement provides an additional $25,000 in coverage for injuries or lost wages due to a severe accident. In addition to protecting the policy owner, the OBEL supplement covers any passengers and pedestrians injured during an accident associated with the policy owner or their immediate family.

When coverage is put in place, the OBEL policy owner chooses which out-of-pocket expenses would be covered.

Additional PIP – Policy owners in New York also have the option of obtaining Additional Personal Injury Protection of $50,000, raising the total PIP coverage to $100,000. Additional PIP coverage extends to the policy owner, their family, and all out-of-state guest occupants.

There are six levels of APIP coverage that supplement the PIP coverage required by New York State:

1. **No APIP, no work loss** — Maintains state-mandated PIP coverage with no extra coverage.
2. **No APIP, work loss only** — Supplements state-mandated PIP coverage with work loss coverage that helps recover lost wages up to $2,000 per month.
3. **Out-of-state, no work loss** — Extends state-mandated PIP coverage to guest occupants. Lost wages are not covered if the policy owner or passengers cannot work.
4. **Out-of-state + work loss** — Extends state-mandated PIP coverage to guest occupants, including work loss coverage that helps recover lost wages, up to $2,000 per month.
5. **Full APIP, no work loss** — Extends state-mandated PIP coverage to guest occupants and increases PIP coverage to a $100,000 limit. It does not cover lost wages.
6. **Full APIP + work loss** — Extends state-mandated PIP coverage to guest occupants and increases PIP coverage to a $100,000 limit. Additionally, it supplements basic PIP coverage with work loss coverage that helps recover lost wages up to $4,000 per month.

Motor Vehicle Accident Indemnification Corporation Act

Purpose – The *Motor Vehicle Accident Indemnification Corporation Act* fills in the coverage gaps left by the motor vehicle financial security act in the vehicle and traffic law. It provides more comprehensive coverage for victims of motor vehicle accidents caused by uninsured or underinsured motor vehicles, stolen motor vehicles, unregistered motor vehicles, or those operated without the owner's permission.

Membership – Every insurance company authorized to write motor vehicle liability insurance in New York must join the non-profit Motor Vehicle Accident Indemnification Corporation. The corporation is bound to provide the protection required by this Act to a qualified person on account of a motor vehicle accident caused by operators or owners of motor vehicles occurring within the state.

Board of Directors – The board of directors will consist of nine members, seven of whom are representatives of motor vehicle liability insurers. These individuals will not be compensated for serving on this board and are elected by the Corporation's members. Each member shall have one vote.

In addition, the Superintendent will appoint two directors representing broad segments of the public, one as a licensed insurance broker or agent and one with no affiliation to insurance providers or insurance agents.

Each director serves for a term of two years. When the initial term expires, their successors in office will serve for terms as fixed in the by-laws of the Corporation.

Powers of the Corporation – The powers of the Corporation include the following:

- Use a corporate seal, contract, sue, adopt and amend by-laws, and exercise all powers necessary and convenient to accomplish the purposes of the Act;
- Prescribe, subject to the Superintendent's approval, the policy or endorsement form to be issued by the members embodying the required coverage;
- Provide for the investigation of any claim asserted by a qualified individual against a financially irresponsible motorist;
- Settle and pay any judgment or claim asserted by a qualified individual against a financially irresponsible motorist;
- Appear and defend, through attorneys representing the Corporation, on behalf of the financially irresponsible motorist or behalf of the Corporation in any action brought against them;
- Levy and collect assessments against its members for any operating deficits of the Corporation and any funds needed for its operation and to enforce payment by legal proceedings;
- Borrow for its corporate purposes, with or without security, and pledge its assets as security for the loan; and
- Pay expenses reasonably incurred by the Corporation in exercising any of its powers.

Assessment Against Members – Suppose the board decides that the Corporation requires funds to continue operating. In that situation, the board can levy an assessment against the members of the Corporation. Each member will be liable to pay a portion of the assessment based on the total number of policies written in New York in the last calendar year, as indicated by the Superintendent's records.

Notice of Claim – The protection provided by the Corporation on account of motor vehicle accidents caused by *financially irresponsible motorists* is available to any qualified individual who has a cause of action due to death or bodily injury following a motor vehicle accident as follows:

- **For action against the owner/operator of an uninsured motor vehicle** – A claim is filed with the Corporation within 180 days of the cause of action;
- **For action against an individual whose identity is unascertainable** – The accident is reported within 24 hours following the occurrence to police, peace, or judicial officers in the vicinity of the Superintendent, and a claim is filed with the Corporation within 90 days of the cause of action;
- **For action against an individual whose insurer has disclaimed liability or denied coverage due to some act or omission of the individual** – A claim must be filed with the Corporation within 180 days of the victim's receipt of notice of the disclaimer or denial of coverage.

Application for Payment of Judgment – Suppose a victim has not recovered losses from a financially irresponsible motorist, even after a judgment has been made and the time for appeals has expired. In that circumstance, the victim can petition the court to direct the corporation to pay the unpaid amount. However, a covered individual cannot recover funds from the corporation for non-economic loss unless such an individual has incurred a serious injury. A *serious injury* is an injury resulting in the following:

- A fracture;
- Significant disfigurement;
- Dismemberment;
- Death;
- Loss of a fetus;
- A significant limitation of the use of a body function or system;
- Permanent loss of use of a body member, organ, function, or system; or
- A medically determined impairment or injury that prevents the injured individual from performing daily activities for no less than 90 days during the 180 days immediately after the injury or impairment.

The judgment cannot exceed the following amounts:

- $25,000 on account of an injury to one individual in any single accident;
- $50,000 on account of death to one individual in any one accident;
- $50,000 on account of an injury to more than one individual in any single accident subject to the limit of $25,000 for any one person; or
- $100,000 on account of death to more than one individual in any single accident subject to the limit of $50,000 for any one person.

Orders for Payment of Judgment – The court can order the Corporation to pay the sum it finds payable on the claim according to the provisions and limitations. However, it must be satisfied that the petitioner has fully pursued and exhausted all remedies for recovering such judgments.

Penalties for False Statements – Any entity who knowingly files any false document or one containing any material misstatement of fact with the Corporation will be guilty of a misdemeanor. It will be subject to a fine of at least $500 but no more than $2,500 or imprisonment for a maximum of 30 days.

Uninsured and Underinsured Motorist

Definitions – By definition, an *uninsured* motorist is one of the following:

- Anyone driving a car with no auto liability insurance;
- Anyone with an auto liability policy issued by an insurance provider who has become insolvent;
- An unidentified hit-and-run driver; or
- Anyone with an auto liability policy with limits lower than those required by law.

If any of these are the at-fault driver in an auto crash, the harmed party's *Uninsured Motorist* coverage applies.

A hit-and-run driver does not need to physically contact the insured's vehicle to be considered a hit-and-run claim. Suppose a policy requires that the insured report a hit-and-run accident to a police officer or the Department of Motor Vehicles within 24 hours. In that scenario, the policy language must be amended to read: within 24 hours or as soon as reasonably practicable.

Uninsured motorist policies cannot contain a mandatory arbitration clause. Also, policies cannot forbid the insured from taking legal action against an uninsured motorist without the insurer's written consent. The insurance provider is entitled to a copy of the lawsuit if an insured files one.

By definition, an *underinsured* motorist is a motorist with auto liability coverage at least at legally required minimums but too low to pay for all the damage done to another. Once the at-fault driver's limits have been reached, the harmed party's *underinsured motorist* coverage will begin to pay.

Bodily Injury Only – In New York, Uninsured Motorists protection covers the cost of bodily injuries to the insured and their family. Uninsured Motorists protection does not cover property damage caused by an uninsured motorist.

Uninsured motorist bodily injury coverage pays for lost wages, medical expenses, and other general damages when the insured or their passengers are injured in an accident caused by an uninsured motorist. The limits for uninsured motorist coverage are established at the auto policy's purchase.

Underinsured motorist bodily injury coverage pays for lost wages, medical expenses, and other damages when the insured or their passengers are injured in an accident caused by a driver with insufficient auto insurance coverage. This bodily injury coverage usually pays the difference between the insured's underinsured motorist bodily injury limit and the other driver's bodily injury coverage limit. The limits for underinsured motorist coverage are established at the purchase of the auto policy.

Required Limits – The required liability insurance limits for the state of New York are:

- $25,000 for injury and $50,000 for the death of one individual in one accident; and
- $50,000 for injury and $100,000 for the death of more than one individual in one accident.

These limits apply to those accidents that occur within the state of New York.

Mandatory Coverage – Uninsured Motorists coverage is a statutory requirement in New York. The required minimum mandatory limits are $25,000/$50,000 split limits to cover the insured for injuries sustained by the insured and their passengers caused by an uninsured motorist.

Supplementary Uninsured and Underinsured Motorist Coverage

Definitions – Supplementary Uninsured/Underinsured Motorists insurance provides coverage in any state or Canadian province. The limits of liability under all insurance policies and bodily injury liability bonds of another motor vehicle liable for damages must be less than the bodily injury liability insurance limit of coverage provided by such policy.

Optional – Supplementary Uninsured/Underinsured Motorist coverage provides protection to cover injuries to the insured and any passengers caused by an uninsured/underinsured motorist outside of New York State.

Nonstacking – By definition, the stacking of limits means the application of two or more policies (coverages) to the same loss or occurrence, resulting in higher combined limits of liability. A typical situation involves a claimant injured as a passenger in a collision with an uninsured vehicle.

Suppose several injured individuals sustain losses in the same accident exceeding the statutory minimum Uninsured Motorist limit. In that case, some states allow combining (or stacking) the passenger-claimant's and insured driver's policies. However, stacking such policies is not permitted in New York.

Coverage Limits – Any Personal Auto Policy, at the insured's option, can also provide Supplementary Uninsured/Underinsured Motorists insurance for bodily injury up to the bodily injury liability insurance limits under the auto policy, subject to the following limits:

- $250,000 due to bodily injury or the death of one individual in any single accident; and
- $500,000 due to bodily injury or the death of two or more individuals in any single accident.

Mandatory Inspection Requirements for Private Passenger Automobiles

Insurance companies must inspect vehicles before issuing a new policy or endorsement to cover a private passenger vehicle for automobile physical damage. Automobile physical damage coverage will not be effective on an additional or replacement private passenger vehicle until the insurance provider has inspected the automobile.

The inspection includes two color photos of the vehicle and one close-up shot of the Environmental Protection Agency (EPA) sticker on the driver's side door jamb. The sticker, also known as the Federal Safety Certification Label, ensures the vehicle conforms to safety standards in effect at the time of production and includes the Vehicle Identification Number.

Vehicle models seven years or older are waived from the inspection requirement.

Cancellation and Nonrenewal

Grounds – While an Auto policy is in effect, the insurance provider cannot issue a notice of nonrenewal or conditional renewal *unless* the action is based on a reason that could have resulted in the policy's cancellation or one or more of the offenses listed below. The offense must occur during the 36 months ending on the last day of the month, four months before the effective nonrenewal or conditional renewal date.

- A named insured or any other individual operates a motor vehicle under any of the following conditions:
    - While impaired or intoxicated by alcohol or drugs;
    - While committing a felony (either directly or indirectly);
    - Exceeding the speed limit or driving in a reckless way that leads to an injury or death;
    - Speed testing or racing;
    - Driving without a valid license or registration in effect, or during a period of license suspension or revocation, or intentionally allowing an unlicensed driver to operate an insured motor vehicle under the policy;
    - Avoiding arrest or apprehension by a law enforcement officer;
    - Leaving an incident without reporting it;
    - Criminal negligence in the operation or use of a motor vehicle, or assault or homicide arising out of the operation or use of a motor vehicle, causing the injury or death of another individual;
    - Filing a fraudulent or falsified Auto Insurance claim or intentionally aiding or abetting in filing or attempting to file any such claim; or
    - Filing a falsified document with the Department of Motor Vehicles or using a license or registration acquired through a false document filed with the Department of Motor Vehicles.
- A named insured, or any other individual who operates a covered auto, is individually or collectively involved in three or more auto accidents while using a covered auto. Such accidents must result in personal injury or property damage exceeding $200. Insurers will not consider any of the following events involving a motor vehicle operated by a named insured or another individual an accident:
    - The covered auto was struck in the rear (rear-ended);
    - The covered auto was struck while parked legally;
    - Only the operator of a different motor vehicle involved in the accident was convicted of a crime, violation, or offense contributing to the accident; or
    - The named insured or another operator of the covered auto was reimbursed by an individual responsible for the accident.

Notice – During the first *60 days* a covered policy is in effect, an insurer cannot issue a notice of cancellation unless it is accompanied by a statement confirming the specific reason(s) for such cancellation.

After a covered policy has been effective for 60 days, an insurer can cancel the policy only for one or more of the following reasons:

- Nonpayment of premium;
- Revocation or suspension, during the required policy period, of the driver's license of the named insured or any other individual who customarily operates a covered auto; or
- Discovery of fraud or material misrepresentation in acquiring the policy or in presenting a claim.

An insurer must give policy owners a cancellation notice at least *20 days* before it takes action. If a policy is nonrenewed by the insurer, the required notice is at least 45 days but no more than 60 days from the nonrenewal date. Insurers must include the reason for nonrenewal in the notice. If this is not done, the named insured will be entitled to renew the policy by paying the premium for the renewal on time.

Proof of mailing for a notice of cancellation, reduction of limits, the substitution of policy form, elimination of coverages, conditioned renewal, intention not to renew, or of the reasons for any such action to the named insured at the address listed in the policy, will be sufficient proof of notice and the giving of reasons required.

An insurance provider cannot refuse to issue or renew a covered policy exclusively on the grounds of the advanced age of the insured or applicant.

Choice of Repair Shop

Suppose a motor vehicle collision or comprehensive loss is suffered by an insured. In that situation, the insurance company providing that type of coverage to the insured *cannot require* repairs to be performed at a particular business or shop. In processing any such claim, the insurance provider cannot recommend or suggest repairs to the vehicle at a specific business or shop unless expressly requested by the insured. This requirement does not apply to a claim exclusively involving window glass.

Supplemental Spousal Liability

Policy owners should not assume that their insurance policies or contracts insure them against any liability due to death or injuries to their spouses or because of injuries or the destruction of their spouses' property unless a provision expressly relating to that is included in the policy. This exclusion applies only where the injured spouse must prove the culpable conduct of the insured spouse to be entitled to recover.

After a motor vehicle liability policy is issued, the insurance provider should notify the insured of supplemental spousal liability insurance availability. This notification, which should be provided at least once a year, must include the following:

- A concise statement that supplementary spousal coverage is available;
- An explanation of such coverage; and
- The insurer's premium for such coverage.

Chapter Review

This chapter explained the key concepts and major types of personal and commercial auto policies. Let's review the main features:

PERSONAL AUTO	
Policy Parts	• Part A – Liability • Part B – Medical Payments • Part C – Uninsured Motorist • Part D – Coverage for Damage to Your Auto • Part E – Duties after an Accident or Loss • Part F – General Provisions
Types of Auto	• *Owned* - a vehicle titled to the policyholder or acquired during the policy period • *Non-owned* - private vehicles operated or in the custody of the named insured, not titled to the policyholder • *Hired* - leased, borrowed, or rented autos • *Temporary substitute* - an auto or trailer not owned by the policyholder used while the insured vehicle is out of service due to repair, loss, or destruction

Part A – Liability Coverage	• Pays for property damage and bodily injury, defense costs, and costs resulting from settlement or defense of the policy owner
	• *Limits of liability* - the maximum amount the policy will pay:
	   o *Split limit* - broken into bodily injury for each person involved, bodily injury for the entire accident, and property damage
	   o *Combined single limit* - A dollar amount indicating the maximum coverage for all losses
	• Common exclusions:
	   o Intentional injury or damage
	   o Use of an auto without permission
	   o Use of commercial-type vehicles in the business
	   o Damage to property in transit

Part B – Medical Payments	• Pays for necessary medical and funeral expenses resulting from an accident • Payments available from liability or uninsured motorist coverage reduce the amount of medical payments coverage
Part C – UM and UIM Motorist Coverage	• *Uninsured motorist (UM)* - for bodily injuries caused by another motorist who does not have the required liability insurance coverage • *Underinsured motorists (UIM)* - for bodily injuries caused by another motorist with insufficient insurance coverage • UIM coverage = the insured's UIM limits minus the driver's BI limits

Part D – Coverage for Damage to Your Auto	• Includes Collision and Other Than Collision coverages
	• Pays for direct and accidental loss to a covered or non-owned auto
	• Transportation expenses:
	   o Paid if the loss is a result of a collision or caused by something other-than-collision
	   o Applies to owned autos
	   o A 24-hour waiting period applies for losses other than theft
	   o A 48-hour waiting period applies for expense payments from theft

	PERSONAL AUTO *(Continued)*
Part E – Duties After an Accident or Loss	• Prompt notification of loss • Cooperation with the insurance provider • Forwarding legal papers • Submitting to a physical or other examination under oath • Allowing the insurance provider to access medical records • Notification of a hit-and-run or theft • Protection of property from an additional loss • Allowing the insurance provider to inspect and appraise the damaged property
Part F – General Provisions	• *Bankruptcy* - does not relieve the insurer of their obligation to pay • *Policy changes* - terms and conditions cannot be waived except by endorsement • *Fraud* - coverage is not provided to an insured making fraudulent statements • *Legal action against the insurer* - legal action cannot be made against the insurer until there is full compliance with all policy provisions • *Subrogation rights* - the insurer has the right to recover payments • *Policy period and territory* - the United States, U.S. territories, and Canada • *Termination* - includes the rights and duties of the insured and the insurer to cancel or not renew coverage • *Assignment* - the insured cannot transfer their right or interest in the policy without the written consent of the insurer • *Two or more policies* - the insurer's liability is the highest limit of insurance if multiple policies cover the same loss
Common Endorsements	• *Towing and labor costs* - includes a basic limit of $25 • *Extended non-owned coverage for named individual* - provides coverage for non-owned autos, autos carrying individuals or property for a fee, or covered vehicles in other businesses • *Miscellaneous types of vehicles* - expands the definition of a covered auto to include motorized vehicles (e.g., golf carts, motorcycles, motor homes) • *Joint ownership coverage* - coverage for individuals who jointly own a vehicle together
	COMMERCIAL AUTO
Commercial Auto Coverage Form	• Covers commercial auto exposures except for garages, truckers, and motor carriers • *Section I – Covered Autos* - auto designation symbols that define the types of vehicles insured • *Section II – Liability Coverage* - designates how much a policy will pay for property damage or bodily injury to third parties • *Section III – Physical Damage Coverage* - includes comprehensive coverage, specific causes of loss, collisions coverage, towing coverage, and glass breakage • *Section IV – Conditions* • *Section V – Definitions*

Garage Coverage Form	- Covers businesses that regularly have autos of others in their care, custody, or control
- *Section I – Covered Autos* - auto designation symbols that define the types of vehicles insured
- *Section II – Liability:*
- Garage Operations – Other than Covered Autos
- Garage Operations – Covered Autos
- *Section III – Garagekeepers* - covers damage to a customer's auto left in the insured's care:
- Comprehensive
- Specified cause of loss
- Collision
- *Section IV – Physical Damage* - similar to the Business Auto Coverage Form with additional exclusions
- *Section V – Garage Conditions* - similar to the Business Auto Coverage Form
- *Section VI – Definitions*
Truckers Coverage	- Covers truckers or carriers for hire
- Carriers for hire include:
- Common carriers who haul goods for anyone; and
- Contract carriers who have written contracts with other companies to transport their merchandise
- *Section I – Covered Autos* - auto designation symbols that define the types of vehicles insured under the policy
- *Section II – Liability*
- *Section III – Physical Damage* - covers damage to a customer's auto left in the insured's care
Motor Carrier Coverage Form	- Covers businesses that transport owned or non-owned property
- *Trailer interchange coverage* – cover loss or damage to a non-owned trailer in the insured's care, custody, or control if the insured is legally liable for the damage

CHAPTER 7:
Commercial Package Policy (CPP)

This chapter will teach you about the commercial package policy or CPP. It is a pre-designed type of policy that includes multiple coverage parts. You will learn about the CPP components, coverage forms for different property types, and exclusions and limitations. By the end of this chapter, you will be able to explain the advantages and disadvantages of monoline and package policies.

- General Form Structure
- Commercial General Liability
- Commercial Property
- Commercial Inland Marine
- Equipment Breakdown Protection Coverage Form
- Commercial Crime
- Farm Coverage

General Form Structure

The coverages available under the *commercial package policy (CPP)* can all be *written together in a single contract (package)* or *written separately as a single line of coverage (monoline)*. A package policy does not necessarily include all the available policies; it can be personalized to meet the insured's needs.

The following scenario illustrates the commercial package policy's flexibility and how the insured may use it in pieces based on their needs:

Marty and his wife, Sandra, decided to open a food manufacturing business. After years of planning and fine-tuning their fudge brownie recipe, they locate a commercial kitchen to begin processing their brownies. Using a commercial kitchen makes sense to Marty and Sandra because they can rent space and equipment instead of spending the money on a building and equipment during the early stages of the business.

The commercial kitchen uses a standard contract for every tenant. It requires at least liability insurance to be in place before the tenant can begin using the space. Marty and Sandra start their business with a monoline Commercial General Liability policy. This policy will provide the necessary coverage to meet the commercial kitchen's requirements. It will also protect them in case of a lawsuit for their business's operation and their product's consumption.

As the business grows, so does the need for additional space that the commercial kitchen cannot provide. Marty and Sandra find a small commercial building for sale in another part of town. They decide to buy the space and purchase equipment to run their business. Since they already have a General Liability policy, they add a Building and Business Personal Property form to their program. Both policies have a common policy number but cover different hazards associated with the business.

Because Marty and Sandra both work full-time in the business, they become concerned with the ramifications of their business being unable to operate because of a loss to the building. They purchase Business Income and Extra Expense coverage to protect against indirect losses associated with a covered direct damage loss.

The business continues to grow, and they later add Inland Marine, Equipment Breakdown, and Crime coverage to their package policy.

The following are *seven coverage components* that can be included in the commercial package policy:

1. General Liability;
2. Commercial Property (direct and indirect coverages);
3. Inland Marine;
4. Commercial Auto;
5. Equipment Breakdown (also called Boiler and Machinery);
6. Crime; and
7. Farm.

In every case, the policy contains *modular parts* combined to create the contract. A commercial policy written in this format includes the following parts:

- Policy cover;
- Common policy declarations;

- Interline endorsements applying to more than one component to eliminate redundancy);
- Line(s) of insurance declaration page(s);
- Line(s) of insurance coverage form(s);
- Common policy conditions;
- Line(s) of insurance conditions;
- Causes of loss forms; and
- Endorsements.

Common Policy Declarations

The *Declarations* page includes information about who, what, where, when, and how much. This information is consistent in every policy. It is important to note that *when* (when the policy takes effect) is 12:01 AM at the mailing address of the *who* (first named insured).

The Declarations page also lists the seven coverage components that can be made a part of the policy. When a premium amount is listed for these coverage parts, the insurer will include that coverage in the policy. If no premium amount is listed, that component has no coverage (shown in the sample Declarations below).

COMMON POLICY DECLARATIONS	
Named Insured(s): Marty and Sandra Jones.	
Policy Period: 01/01/08 to 01/01/09 Time: 12:01a.m.	
The policy consists of the following coverage parts for which a premium is indicated:	
Commercial General Liability	$ 10,000
Commercial Property	$ 10,000
Inland Marine	$ _____
Commercial Auto	$ _____
Equipment Breakdown	$ 10,000
Crime	$ _____
Farm	$ _____

Common Policy Conditions

This interline form contains provisions applicable to each line of coverage that can be included in the policy. The conditions are as follows:

- **Cancellation** — The first named insured can cancel the policy at any time by providing written notice to the insurance company. The insurer can cancel for an allowable reason by giving the proper notice to the first named insured, based on state regulations.
- **Changes** — Changes in the terms can be made only by endorsement issued by the insurance company. Request for change in the policy must be made by the first named insured.
- **Examination of books and records** — The insurer has the right to audit the insured's records and books relating to the policy for up to three years after the end of the policy.
- **Inspections and surveys** — The insurer is given the right but is not responsible for making inspections, surveys, reports, and recommendations relating to the insurance. An insurance company does not warrant that conditions are safe and comply with laws, regulations, standards, or codes.
- **Premiums** — Responsibility for payment of the premium rests solely with the first named insured. All refunds will also be returned to the first named insured.

- **Transfer of rights and duties** — The insured's rights and duties under the policy can be transferred to another only with the written consent of the insurance carrier. However, in the event of the insured's death, rights and duties are automatically transferred to the insured's legal representative.

Commercial General Liability

Commercial General Liability (CGL) Coverage Forms

General liability encompasses any business liability hazards not covered by specialized coverages, such as professional liability, automobile, or marine.

General liability loss exposures include any claims associated with damage to property of third parties or injuries to individuals arising out of the course of doing business. The most common general liability exposures are the following types of liability: premises, operations, products, independent contractors, completed operations, and personal and advertising injury.

Businesses require general liability insurance to cover their exposure to liability losses that may occur from their business operations. *Commercial General Liability (CGL)* policies come in two forms: *occurrence* and *claims-made*. The essential difference between these two forms is how the coverage is triggered, which will be explained later in this chapter.

The latest ISO CGL Coverage Form is split into six sections as follows:

1. Section I coverages:
    - Coverage A – Bodily Injury and Property Damage;
    - Coverage B – Personal Injury and Advertising Injury; and
    - Coverage C – Medical Payments;
2. Section II – Who is an Insured;
3. Section III – Limits of Insurance;
4. Section IV – Commercial General Liability Conditions;
5. Section V – Extended Reporting Periods; and
6. Section VI – Definitions.

The earlier iterations of the ISO forms distinguish between occurrence and claims-made forms. The Extended Reporting Period section is available only in claims-made forms.

Definitions

The *definitions* section appears last in the CGL form. However, you must understand these terms as you are learning about CGL coverages, so the definitions are presented next. The following are terms and definitions that apply to commercial general liability insurance:

Occurrence – An *occurrence* refers to an accident, including repeated or continuous exposure to the same dangerous conditions. Coverage exists for covered occurrences *during and after* the policy period if they are due to the same circumstances that took place during the policy period. An occurrence must also occur *within the coverage territory*, as defined in the policy.

Bodily Injury – *Bodily injury* refers to any bodily injury, disease, or sickness sustained by an individual, including death from any of these at any time.

Property Damage – *Property damage* is any physical injury to and the loss of use of tangible property. Also included is the loss of use of property that is not physically injured. Electronic data is not considered tangible property.

Personal and advertising injury refers to an injury, including bodily injury, arising from these offenses:

- Trade secret, copyright, or slogan infringement used in a policy owner's advertisement;
- Imprisonment, detention, or false arrest;
- Unlawful or wrongful eviction, entry, or invasion of privacy by an owner, landlord, lessor, or someone on their behalf;
- Malicious prosecution;
- Use of another's advertising idea;
- Slander or libel in oral or written publication; or
- Oral or written publication that invades or violates the privacy of another.

Coverage Territory – The coverage territory in which the policy applies includes the following:

- The U.S. and its territories/possessions, Puerto Rico, and Canada;
- International airspace and waters if the damage or injury occurs during travel to or from the defined coverage territories; and
- Anywhere in the world if damage or injury results from products or goods manufactured or sold in a coverage territory.

Premises and Operations – *Premises and operations* include the use, maintenance, or ownership of the insured's premises and all business operations.

Products and Completed Operations – This term refers to property damage or bodily injury away from the policy owner's premise and arising out of their work (your work) or product (your product). This definition includes several exceptions. Products still in the policy owner's physical possession do not meet the meaning of products and completed operations. Work not yet completed and products while being transported by the policy owner are also exceptions:

- **Your Work** — Work or operations performed by the policy owner or on their behalf. This term includes materials, equipment, or parts furnished in connection with the work;
- **Your Product** — Any products or goods, other than real property, manufactured, handled, sold, distributed, or disposed of by the policy owner, others trading in the policy owner's name, and acquired business assets. This term includes materials, containers, equipment, or parts used in connection with the products.

Employee – The term *employee* includes a leased worker but not a temporary worker. A *leased worker* in the policy refers to an individual who performs duties for the policy owner related to their business and is leased from a labor leasing firm. A *temporary worker* refers to a person who is a substitute for a permanent employee on leave or to meet short-term or seasonal workload conditions.

Mobile equipment – The following are included in the definition of mobile equipment:

- Farm machinery, bulldozers, forklifts, and other vehicles, including attached equipment, intended for use off public roads;
- Vehicles provided for use solely on or next to the insured premises;
- Vehicles used mainly to provide mobility to drills, diggers, loaders, shovels, and power cranes;

- Vehicles that travel on crawler treads; and
- Any other road resurfacing or construction equipment.

Vehicles falling under a compulsory financial responsibility law, insurance law, or motor vehicle insurance law will not be considered mobile equipment, even if it fits the definition.

Auto – A land motor vehicle, trailer, or semi-trailer used for traveling on public roads, including attached equipment or machinery. It also includes any other land vehicle that requires compulsory financial responsibility or insurance other than where it is licensed or primarily garaged.

Fire legal liability – Also known as *fire damage liability*, this coverage protects the insured against liability for fire losses associated with premises they rent or temporarily occupy. The policy only grants coverage for premises occupied or rented for no more than seven days. When the insured leases the space for longer periods, the policy extends coverage only for fire losses by eliminating the damage to property exclusion for these situations. A separate limit of insurance will apply to this coverage.

Section I – Coverages

Coverage A — Bodily Injury and Property Damage Liability – This coverage protects bodily injury and property damage sustained by third parties because of the negligence of the policy owner. The bodily injury or property damage must emanate from the policy owner's premises, operations, products, or completed operations within the coverage territory and a time frame described by the policy.

The *insuring agreement* is summarized as follows: The insurer will pay those sums the insured is legally required to pay as damages from bodily injury or property damage under the policy. The insurer also has the right and responsibility to defend the insured in a lawsuit against them. This right and responsibility do not apply if the policy does not cover the nature of the suit. The insurer, at their discretion, can investigate any occurrence or lawsuit but will pay no more than the policy limits, and the right and duty to defend ends when the limits of insurance have been exhausted.

Exclusions – Causes of loss or perils do not determine coverage in liability policies; coverage is subject to exclusion. The policy cannot respond to settlements or pay for defense costs if one or more exclusions are applicable.

The *Coverage A – Bodily Injury and Property Damage* exclusions are as follows:

- **Expected or intentional injury** — Intentional losses caused by the insured are excluded, except if they result from using reasonable force to protect the property or individuals.
- **Contractual liability** — Assumptions of liability due to contractual agreements are excluded. This exclusion will not apply unless, in the absence of the agreement, the policy owner would be liable or it was assumed in an insured contract as noted below:
    - Sidetrack agreement;
    - Contracts for the leasing of premises;
    - License or easement agreements, except in connection with demolition or construction within 50 feet of a railroad;
    - Obligation to indemnify a municipality, except concerning work performed for a municipality;
    - Elevator maintenance agreements; and
    - Liability the policy owner assumes under any contract that would have been imposed by law even if no contract exists.
- **Liquor liability** — This exclusion applies to liability arising from contributing to or causing the intoxication of any individual, furnishing alcoholic beverages to individuals under the legal drinking age

or individuals under the influence of alcohol, and any regulation, ordinance, or statute. However, this exclusion only applies to policyholders in the business of manufacturing, selling, or serving alcohol, in which case, there is no liability for alcohol-related injuries.

- **Workers compensation and employers liability** — The policy excludes coverage for bodily injury, disease, sickness, or death of any employee while employed by the policy owner. Insurers cover these types of losses more appropriately under workers compensation and employers liability policies.
- **Pollution** — A catastrophic exposure and one that is excluded for almost any cause under the general liability policy.
- **Aircraft, auto, or watercraft** — Insurers will not cover property damage or bodily injury caused by the use or ownership of any auto, aircraft, or watercraft under the general liability policy. The exclusion, however, does not apply to:
    - Non-owned watercraft less than 26 feet in length and not being used to transport property or individuals for a fee;
    - Watercraft while ashore on premises the policy owner rents or owns;
    - Parking a non-owned auto on or next to property rented or owned by an insured;
    - Liability assumed in an insured contract for the use, maintenance, or ownership of watercraft or aircraft; or
    - Operation of mobile equipment.
- **Mobile equipment** — There is no coverage for the transportation of mobile equipment by an auto operated or owned by the insured or while in a contest or race.
- **War** — Whether or not war is declared, it is excluded.
- **Damage to property** — Insurers will not cover damage to property rented by, owned, or loaned to the insured or property in the insured's control, custody, or care.
- **The insured's product** — Damage to the insured's products is not covered.
- **The insured's work** — Damage to the insured's work is not covered. This exclusion is not applicable if a subcontractor did the job for the insured.
- **Impaired property or property not physically injured** — Property damage to impaired property or property that has not sustained damage resulting from a deficiency or defect in the insured's product or work is not covered. There is no coverage for any damage caused by a delay or failure of the policy owner to perform under an agreement or contract.
- **Recall of products, work, or impaired property** — The policy excludes any loss sustained by the insured or others for withdrawal, loss of use, or recall of the insured's work or product.
- **Personal and advertising injury** — Bodily injury due to personal and advertising injury is not covered.
- **Electronic data** — There is no coverage for damages arising from the loss of, damage to, loss of use, inability to access, corruption of, or inability to manipulate electronic data.
- **Recording and distribution of material in violation of communications laws** — Property damage and bodily injuries are excluded if arising directly or indirectly out of any omission or action that violates the following: CAN-SPAM Act, the Telephone Consumer Protection Act, the Fair Credit Reporting Act, or any other local, state, or federal statute or regulation.

Coverage B — Personal Injury and Advertising Injury – This coverage insures against specific acts resulting in a non-physical injury to a third party due to offenses defined as personal and advertising injuries.

The *insuring agreement* for this coverage is similar to the bodily injury and property damage insuring agreement. However, third-party injuries must result from personal and advertising injury. The offense must be committed within the policy period and the coverage territory described on the declarations page.

Exclusions – The *Coverage B – Personal and Advertising Injury* exclusions are as follows:

- **Knowing violation of rights of another** — Personal or advertising injury if it is intentional and with the knowledge that the act would violate another's rights is not covered.
- **Material published with knowledge of falsity** — There is no coverage for personal and advertising injury resulting from the publication of oral or written material known to be false.
- **Material published prior to the policy period** — Injuries arising from oral or written material published before the policy's inception are not covered.
- **Criminal acts** — If the policy owner or someone at the policy owner's direction commits a criminal act, there is no coverage for any resulting damage.
- **Contractual liability** — There is no coverage for any liability the policy owner assumes through an agreement or contract. This exclusion will be the case unless, if no agreement exists, the insured would have been liable for the damages.
- **Breach of contract** — Breach of contract is not covered unless it is an implied contract to use another's advertising idea.
- **Quality or performance of goods – failure to conform to statements** — If the goods, product, or services fail to conform to the advertised performance or quality, there is no coverage.
- **Wrong description of prices** — There is no coverage for the resulting damage if the advertising material states the wrong price.
- **Infringement of copyright, patent, trademark, or trade secret** — There is no coverage for damage arising from the infringement of trademark, copyright, patent, trade secret, or other such intellectual property rights (excluding the use of another's advertising idea).
- **Insureds in media and Internet-type businesses** — There is no coverage for the business of broadcasting, telecasting, or advertising. Determining or designing the content of websites for others or an Internet search, content, access, or service provider is also not covered.
- **Electronic chatrooms or bulletin boards** — There is no coverage for damage caused by electronic chat rooms or bulletin boards controlled, owned, or hosted by the insured.
- **Unauthorized use of another person's name or product** — Insurers will not cover personal and advertising injury arising from the unauthorized use of another individual's or entity's name or product to mislead their potential customers.
- **Recording and distribution of material in violation of law** — Property damage and bodily injuries are excluded if arising directly or indirectly out of any omission or action that violates the CAN-SPAM Act, the Telephone Consumer Protection Act, the FCRA, or any other local, state, or federal statute or regulation;
- **Pollution or pollution-related losses**; and
- **War**.

Coverage C — Medical Payments – This coverage provides medical, hospital, surgical, ambulance, professional nursing, or funeral expenses for injuries to third parties. This coverage is viewed as goodwill coverage because insurers will make payments without regard to the negligence or fault of the insured. Medical expenses must be incurred and reported within *12 months* of the date of the accident to be covered.

A bodily injury must result from an accident and occur on premises rented or owned by the insured, on ways next to the rented or owned premises, or due to the insured's operations. The injury must occur within the coverage territory and during the policy period.

The table below summarizes all three coverages included in Section I of the Commercial General Liability policy:

COVERAGE	DESCRIPTION
Coverage A Bodily Injury (BI) and Property Damage (PD)	**BI** provides coverage for any injury, sickness, disease, or death third parties suffer because of the insured's business activities. **PD** provides coverage for injury to, destruction of, or loss of use of the property of others due to the insured's business activities.
Coverage B Personal Injury (PI) and Advertising Injury (AI)	**PI** covers injuries caused to third parties that result from mental anguish, false arrest or imprisonment, wrongful eviction or detention, malicious prosecution, defamation of character, slander or libel, and invasion of privacy. **AI** covers injuries that occur if, in the course of advertising, the policy owner inadvertently slanders, libels, defames, or violates the privacy of another.
Coverage C Medical Payments	Medical payments coverage provides for necessary medical, surgical, ambulance, hospital, professional nursing, or funeral expenses for third parties injured because of the insured's business operations, without regard to fault.

Exclusions – *Coverage C – Medical Payments* will not pay for bodily injury to or resulting from:

- Any policy owner except volunteer workers;
- Employees or anyone hired by the policy owner;
- The insured's tenants;
- If benefits have to be provided under workers compensation or similar law;
- Individuals injured while instructing, practicing, or participating in sports, physical games or exercises, or athletic contests;
- War, revolution, rebelling, or insurrection; or
- If excluded under Coverage A.

Supplementary Payments – Supplementary payments are provided for *Coverage A – Bodily Injury and Property Damage*, and *Coverage B – Personal and Advertising Injury*. These are the amounts the insurance provider will pay in addition to the stated policy limits. However, the insurer's duty to defend ends when the total of all claims paid reaches the aggregate limit. The following are similar to the supplementary payments provided in other liability insurance policies:

- Any expenses incurred by the insurance provider;
- Up to $250 for the cost of bonds to release attachments and bail bonds;
- Reasonable costs incurred by the policy owner, including up to $250 a day for loss of income;
- Court costs taxed against the policy owner (except attorney's fees or expenses);
- Prejudgment interest; and
- Interest that accrues on any judgment.

Section II – Who is an Insured

The ISO form describes *who is an insured* based on the following designations found in the Declarations:

Individual (sole proprietor) – An individual insured and their spouse, but only regarding the conduct of a business in which the insured is the sole owner.

Partnership or joint venture – A partnership, including joint ventures, is a legal entity in which two or more individuals agree to share the profits and losses of the business. Under this arrangement, the policy owners are the named insured, partners, members, and their spouses, but only regarding the business.

Limited Liability Company (LLC) — Named insured and members for business activities. Managers are considered insureds for their roles and duties as managers.

An organization other than a partnership, joint venture, or LLC — Named insured, directors, executive officers, and stockholders but only for their duties or liabilities as such.

Trust — The named insured and trustees but only concerning their duties as trustees.

Each of the following is also considered an insured under the policy, regardless of legal entity:

- The policy owner's volunteers and employees for acts within the scope of their employment;
- Any person or agent while acting as the insured's real estate agent (except volunteers and employees);
- Any person or legal representatives, or organization, having temporary custody of the insured's property if the insured dies; and
- Newly formed or acquired organizations (other than a limited liability company, joint venture, or partnership) for which no other insurance applies for up to 90 days after the policy expiration or ownership is acquired, whichever is earlier.

Section III – Limits of Liability

This section describes how each limit shown in the Declarations works in case of a covered claim. Before this is explained, it will be helpful to visualize the components of a typical CGL policy declarations page.

CGL POLICY DECLARATIONS	
Occurrence Limit	$1,000,000
Damage to Property Rented to You	$100,000
Medical Expense Limit	$10,000
Personal and Advertising Injury Limit	$1,000,000
General Aggregate	$2,000,000
Products and Completed Operations Aggregate	$2,000,000

It is vital to understand the concepts of the aggregate limits to know how the limits of liability work together. Each of these limits is the maximum available during the policy period. Once these aggregates are drawn down, the policy's limits are depleted, and any supplementary payments will cease.

There is a limit per occurrence for property damage and bodily injury and per occurrence for personal and advertising injury. Depending on the type of claim, each limit will be the maximum the policy will pay. Products and completed operations claims are also subject to the occurrence limit but exhaust a different aggregate. Medical expense payments are subject to a limit per person but have an occurrence limit for one event.

The general liability policy also includes a specific amount of coverage for fire damage legal liability, which can be increased.

Section IV – Conditions

A commercial general liability policy commonly includes the following conditions:

- **Bankruptcy** — Bankruptcy of the policy owner will not relieve the insurance provider of its obligation under the policy.

- **Insured duties in the event of an offense, occurrence, claim, or lawsuit** — The following duties are required of the insured in the event of a loss:
    o   Inform the insurer as soon as possible of an occurrence or the possibility of a claim;
    o   Immediately record the specifics of any claim or lawsuit brought, and notify the insurer;
    o   Immediately provide the insurer any notices, demands, or summons relating to a suit or claim;
    o   Authorize the insurance provider to obtain any records or other pertinent information, and assist the insurer in its investigation;
    o   Don't assume any obligations, make any voluntary payments, or incur any costs without the insurer's consent, or it will be at the policyholder's own expense.
- **Legal action against the insurance provider** — No party can join the insurer as a party in any lawsuit asking for damages against the policy owner. In addition, no party may sue the insurance company until all policy provisions have been met.
- **Other insurance** — If other valid and collectible insurance is available to cover a loss under Coverages A and B, the general liability policy will pay as follows:
    o   **Primary basis** — Except as noted in the excess section below, if other insurance is the primary coverage, the policy will share liability depending on how the other insurance shares liability. It will be shared pro rata up to the policy limit or in equal shares.
    o   **Excess basis** — Certain insurance contracts regardless of the other insurance clause in those policies; any other primary insurance in which the policy owner has been added as an additional insured.
- **Premium audits** — The insurer is permitted to audit the policy owner's records or books at the end of the policy term to ensure sufficient premium has been collected for the exposure.
- **Representations** — By accepting the policy, the insured agrees that the statements listed on the declarations page are true and complete and that the policy was issued based on the representations made by the policy owner.
- **Separation of insureds** — This condition demonstrates how the coverage will apply to each individual insured. The insurance will apply as if the policy owner named in the lawsuit were the only named insured and separately to each policy owner against whom a claim or suit is brought. This clause, however, does not increase the limit of insurance listed in the Declarations.
- **Subrogation (transferring the rights of recovery against others to the insurer)** — The policy owner must transfer any rights they possess to recover damages from a negligent third party. The insured may not do anything to obstruct these rights after the loss.
- **Nonrenewal** — The minimum number of days' notice the insurance company will provide to the insured if the insurer decides not to renew the coverage is usually 30 days. This period can differ according to each state's regulations.
- **Insured's right to claim and occurrence information** — The insurer will provide the first named insured with information about the claim and occurrence. It will also give the insured information regarding any previous general liability claims-made coverage issued in the past three years.

Occurrence vs. Claims Made

As you have previously learned, general liability policies come in two forms. The most common is the *occurrence* form. The other form is called the *claims-made* form. It is used for special situations such as product, professional, employment, and environmental liability.

The claims-made policy is often used when the occurrence could take a long time to manifest itself or spread over several years. The ISO developed this form because of how the legal system interpreted an occurrence. The ISO also developed the claims-made form because of how complex claims triggered occurrence forms.

The claims-made form has several unique features that include the following:

Retroactive Date — A date is entered on the declarations page to inform the policy owner that the policy will not cover any claim before this date.

Extended Reporting Period (ERP) — The policy allows the insured a period to report a claim and provide coverage even though the policy was canceled by the insurance provider or the insured. For example, an attorney decides to retire and no longer wants the insurance policy. It would provide the policy owner time to report any claim they become aware of even though the policy is no longer in force.

The combination of these two timeframes allows the insurer to predict better when the policy will respond. The insured's ability to report a claim, and the amount of time the policy responds to an occurrence, are now contingent upon defined periods.

Insurers do not include an extended reporting period in the occurrence form that pays for property damage and bodily injury *during the policy period*. Even if the loss is not identified or reported until months or years after the policy expiration, an occurrence form will pay for property damage and bodily injury.

Trigger – The *coverage trigger* causes a policy to respond to a claim. The policy in force when the claim is initially made will respond to a claims-made trigger, and the policy in force when the event took place responds to an occurrence trigger.

Example 7.1 – To help you better understand the concept, let's go back to Marty and Sandra Jones and apply the idea to their brownie operation.

First, let's assume that Marty and Sandra have an occurrence form CGL policy. The coverage trigger is, therefore, the occurrence of property damage or bodily injury. If a person were to claim an injury that occurred in 2008 but did not bring a lawsuit until 2010, the policy Marty and Sandra had in 2008 would pay any settlement and defend them. The limits that Marty and Sandra had at the time would also apply.

What if Marty and Sandra had a claims-made policy in the same situation? We need to know more information about the policy before we can decide. The policy in effect in 2010 has a retroactive date of 1/1/2006. Since the injury occurred after that date, the policy in force in 2010 would cover the defense costs and any settlement with the carried limits. If the injury had occurred in 2005, the claims-made policy would not respond.

Extended Reporting Period - Claims-Made Form – The claims-made form also has another distinctive feature. Since the form defines the period in which an insured can report a claim, it lets the insured file a claim after policy expiration or if an insurer renews a policy with a later retroactive date.

It is important to remember that these extended reporting periods do not extend the policy period. Any claim filed during the extended reporting period must have occurred *on or after the retroactive date*. Extended reporting periods are called *tail coverage*, so think of the last policy period as the head and these extended reporting periods as the tail. They allow the insured to use the previous policy in force to cover claims reported during the extended period.

The reporting periods are broken into two categories:

Basic Extended Reporting Period – This period is extended to the insured without an additional premium charge. It is broken down into two timeframes and two different situations:

- **Known claim** — if the insured reports a claim not later than 60 days after the policy expiration, the claim is covered for up to 5 years (*Midi Tail*);
- **Unknown claim** — coverage is only extended for 60 days after policy expiration. No coverage will apply if an insured receives notice of a previously unknown claim on day 70 after policy expiration. If it became known on day 45, coverage would apply up to five years after policy expiration (*Mini Tail*).

Supplemental Reporting Period – This period must be purchased by the insured and added by endorsement. It allows an unlimited period to file a claim against the expired policy. This additional coverage has the following characteristics:

- The insured must make their election to purchase coverage within 60 days of policy expiration;
- The extension will not go into effect until the premium is paid when due;
- The insurer can price the extension based on several factors, but it will not exceed 200% of the annual premium;
- It is excess insurance over any other valid insurance; and
- It will reset the General Aggregate and the Products and Completed Operations aggregate to the limits stated on the declarations page.

Claim Information – An additional condition on the claims-made form is the policy owner's rights to *claim and occurrence information*. The insurance company will provide information on any current claims-made policy and any claims-made coverage it has issued for the prior three years. The report will show each occurrence with the date and a brief description. It will also summarize, by policy year, all amounts paid and any amounts held in reserve as they apply to the policy's aggregate limits.

When the insurer cancels the policy or opts not to renew it, the insurer will provide the occurrence and claim information at least 30 days before the last day of coverage. The first named insured can request the report in writing at any time up to 60 days after the policy ends. The insurance company will provide the report within 45 days of the request.

The claims information is seen as quantitative because the amounts claimed are known. The occurrence information is viewed as nonquantitative since claims have yet to be filed, and insurers cannot know future claim amounts.

Premises and Operations

Premises and operations include the use, maintenance, or ownership of the insured's premises and all business operations, excluding the exposures included in the products and completed operations hazard. All liability losses resulting from the insured's operations or premises are covered, subject to the policy exclusions and limits.

Products and Completed Operations

The *products and completed operations* hazard covers damage or injuries after the insured has finished a job and left the site. It also offers protection after the insured surrenders control of a manufactured or sold product. Coverage to protect against this hazard is optional, although the coverage is automatically included for some types of business risks.

Insured Contract

The CGL Coverage Form excludes property damage or bodily injury that the policy owner has assumed under any agreement or contract. The exclusion does not apply to specific contracts, provided the damage or injury occurs after the contract's execution. These insured contracts are in the definitions section of the coverage form as the following:

- Sidetrack agreements;
- Contracts for the leasing of premises;
- License or easement agreements, except in connection with demolition or construction within 50 feet of a railroad;
- Obligations to indemnify a municipality, except concerning work performed for a municipality;
- Elevator maintenance agreements; and
- Liability the policy owner assumes under any contract that would have been imposed by law even if the contract did not exist. Any agreement or contract indemnifying a surveyor, architect, engineer, or railroad under specified circumstances is not included.

Contractual liability is *excluded* from coverage regarding bodily injuries and property damage. The insurance provider must pay damages based on their assumption of liability in a contract. However, the exclusion would not apply to liability for damages that the insured would have in the absence of the agreement. It also does not apply to liability assumed in a contract, provided bodily injury or property damage occurs after executing the contract.

Example 7.2 – Josh hires Patrick to remodel his building. The contract between them specifies that Patrick will hold Josh harmless for any injury to members of the general public while Patrick is doing the work. Patrick hires Lamar to perform part of the renovation. He requires that Lamar provide a hold harmless agreement indemnifying Patrick if he is liable for an injury to anyone in the general public. "Hold harmless" refers to an agreement to assume the financial consequences of another individual's liability.

Through no fault of either Patrick or Lamar, a member of the general public is injured on the premises and successfully sues Josh. Josh seeks recovery from Patrick under their hold harmless agreement, and Patrick's liability insurer pays the claim. Patrick's insurer then seeks recovery from Lamar by claiming that Lamar assumed Patrick's liability for injury to the public. In this scenario, Lamar's insurer will not cover this claim. The contractual liability coverage under the General Liability policy covers assumed liability "that would be imposed by law in the absence of any agreement or contract." Patrick's liability in this case only exists because of an agreement with Josh.

Owners and Contractors Protective Liability

Owners and Contractors Protective Liability (OCP) is a liability policy used primarily in the construction industry. The project owner can require contractors to obtain this policy on their behalf. The policy covers the owner for property damage and bodily injury arising from the contractor's actions during construction. This policy pays on a primary basis; the owner's general liability policy would be excess coverage over the OCP policy.

Commercial Property

Coverage Forms

Several commercial property coverage forms are available to meet the needs of commercial property owners. We will discuss each of these different commercial property coverage forms separately.

Building and Personal Property Form

The *Building and Personal Property Coverage Form* is the main commercial package form used to insure buildings, business personal property, and the property of others. This *direct damage form* grants the insured an option to choose a Cause of Loss form. These forms include the same names as the dwelling property and homeowners policies (basic, broad, and special).

The insured must select the limits needed for coverage. Unlike the HO and DP policies, no percentage of building coverages, such as personal property or other structures, are automatically included. Suppose the policyholder wants a particular building covered. In that case, it needs to be listed on the declarations page with an appropriate limit of insurance. The same applies to business personal property; if there are no limits in the Declarations, no coverage exists.

Property Covered and Not Covered – *Building Coverage* insures the following: the building described in the Declarations, furniture and outdoor fixtures, items used to maintain the property, permanently installed equipment and machinery, and additions under construction including the supplies, materials, and equipment.

Business Personal Property (BPP) Coverage insures business personal property located in or on the structure or building described on the declarations page or in the open, within 100 feet of the structure or building, or within 100 feet of the premises, whichever is greater. BPP insures the following:

- Fixtures and furniture (that are not considered building items);
- Equipment and machinery (not permanently installed);
- Stock;
- All other personal property owned by the policyholder and used in their business;
- Materials, labor, or services provided or arranged on the personal property of others;
- The interest of tenant betterments or improvements; and
- Leased personal property for which the policy owner is contractually responsible unless otherwise specified in the personal property of others section of the policy.

Personal Property of Others covers items in the insured's control, custody, or care. The property must be located in the building described in the Declarations, within 100 feet of the building, or within 100 feet of the premises, whichever is greater.

The following types of property and costs are *not covered* in the Building and Personal Property Coverage Form:

- Money, currency, bills, accounts, or securities;
- Animals (unless boarded and owned by others or owned by the policyholder as "stock" while inside a building);
- Autos held for sale;
- Sidewalks, bridges, and other paved surfaces;
- Contraband or illegal property;
- Excavation costs;
- Foundations of structures, buildings, boilers, or machinery if their foundations are below the lowest basement floor or the surface of the ground if no basement exists;
- Land;
- Personal property while waterborne or airborne;
- Wharves, piers, or docks;
- Property insured under another coverage form;

- Retaining walls that are not a part of the described building;
- Underground drains or pipes;
- The cost to research or replace valuable records or papers (a minimal amount of coverage is provided in the coverage extensions);
- Electronic data, except as insured under the Electronic Data additional coverage;
- Self-propelled machinery or vehicles registered for use on the public highway or used primarily away from the described premises; and
- Plants, trees, shrubs, crops, and fences.

Additional Coverages – The Building and Personal Property Coverage Form will provide the following additional coverages:

- **Debris removal** – Debris removal is limited to no more than 25% of the loss. Debris removal covers the expense of removing debris following a covered loss. These costs must be reported to the insurance carrier within 180 days of the loss for coverage to apply. A separate section of the policy provides an additional $10,000 in coverage if the 25% limit is insufficient.
- **Preservation of property** – The policy will also cover any damage to property that is moved to protect it from additional damage. Coverage will only be for 30 days after the property is moved.
- **Fire department service charge** – If the policy owner is required to pay for fire department service calls, the policy will reimburse the insured for up to $1,000 for this charge. The policy owner can purchase a higher amount, as shown on the declarations page. A deductible does not apply to this coverage.
- **Pollutant cleanup and removal** – The policy will cover up to $10,000 for expenses incurred to remove pollutants if the discharge resulted from a covered cause of loss and is reported in writing within 180 days of the occurrence. This amount is the maximum the insurance provider will pay in 12 months.
- **Increased cost of construction** – The policy will pay the lesser of $10,000 or 5% of the limit of insurance that applies to the building for the added cost of construction resulting from building law enforcement.
- **Electronic data** – The policy will cover up to $2,500 for the cost to restore or replace electronic data that has been corrupted or destroyed by a covered cause of loss.

Coverage Extensions – The form also includes several *coverage extensions*. The following types of property can be insured if the policy has a value reporting period or an 80% or more coinsurance percentage:

- **Newly acquired or constructed property** – Coverage lasts 30 days for newly acquired buildings and personal property similar to the insured property. This extension will cover up to $250,000 for newly acquired buildings and up to $100,000 for business personal property.
- **Personal effects and property of others** – Coverage is for up to $2,500 for personal effects of the policyholder or their employees (coverage does not apply to theft). This coverage can also apply to the personal property of others in the control, custody, and care of the insured.
- **Valuable papers and records** – $2,500 for the cost to research, restore, or replace lost information from valuable papers and records, except electronic data.
- **Property off-premises** – Up to $10,000 for property, excluding stock, temporarily at the premises the policyholder does not lease, own, or operate. This coverage is not applied to personal property in a vehicle or a salesperson's possession.
- **Outdoor property** – Up to $1,000 for television and radio antennas (including satellite dishes) and fences, or $250 for plants, shrubs, and trees destroyed or damaged by lightning, fire, explosion, civil commotion or riot, or aircraft.
- **Non-owned detached trailers** – $5,000 of coverage applies only if the loss occurs when the trailer is in the insured's custody and only if they are contractually obligated to cover the loss or damage. Higher

limits may be shown on the declarations page, and this coverage is considered excess coverage over other insurance.

The most the insurance provider is obligated to pay is the limit of insurance specified in the policy declarations, minus any applicable deductible. The deductible will apply only once per occurrence, irrespective of the number of different properties involved.

Loss Conditions — The Building and Personal Property Coverage Form includes several conditions in addition to the common policy conditions and the commercial property conditions. These additional conditions include the following:

- **Abandonment** — The policy owner cannot abandon property to the insurance provider.
- **Appraisal** — If the insured and insurer cannot agree on the property's value, both parties can make a written demand for an appraisal of the loss. The decision agreed upon during the appraisal process will bind both parties.
- **Duties in the event of loss or damage** — In the event of loss or damage, the following duties are required of the policy owner:
    - Inform the police if a law has been broken;
    - Provide the insurer with prompt notice of the loss and a description of when, how, and where it occurred;
    - Take every reasonable step to protect the property from additional damage;
    - Provide an inventory of both damaged and undamaged property at the insurer's request;
    - Allow the insurance provider to inspect the property as often as necessary;
    - Send the insurer a signed, sworn proof of loss within 60 days of its request; and
    - Cooperate with the insurance provider in the investigation;
- **Loss payment** — In the event of damage or loss, the insurer has the option to do the following:
    - Pay the value of the damaged or lost property;
    - Pay the cost of replacing or repairing the damaged or lost property;
    - Take all or any part of the property at an appraised value or agreed value;
    - Replace, rebuild, or repair the property with other property of like kind and quality; or
    - The insurer must provide notice of their intentions within 30 days after receiving the sworn proof of loss and then pay the covered loss within 30 days after they resolve to pay the claim;
- **Recovered property** — If the property is recovered after the insurer has already made the claim payment, the policy owner can keep the property and return the amount paid.
- **Vacancy** — When a building has been unoccupied for more than 60 consecutive days before the loss, the insurance provider will not cover the damage caused by glass breakage, sprinkler leakage, water damage, vandalism, theft, or attempted theft. If any other peril causes the loss, the insurance provider will decrease the amount it would have paid by 15%. When a vacancy permit endorsement is attached to a Building and Personal Property Coverage Form, under the basic policy, the vacancy condition is waived during this period.
- **Valuation** — The insurance carrier will settle the loss on an ACV basis *except* under the following conditions:
    - If the limit of insurance satisfies the coinsurance clause and the amount of the loss is less than $2,500, the insurance carrier will pay the cost of replacing or repairing the property.
    - Stock sold but not delivered will be valued based on the selling price. Stock means merchandise held in storage or for sale, raw materials, and in-process or finished goods, including supplies used for shipping and packing.
    - If required by law, the glass will be valued at the cost of replacement with safety glazing material.

- Tenant's betterments and improvements will be valued at ACV if repairs are made promptly or a percentage of the original cost if the repairs are not made promptly.
- Valuable records and papers will be valued on the cost of blank material and the labor necessary to transcribe the records.

The following *additional conditions* apply as well as the common policy conditions and the commercial property conditions:

- **Coinsurance** — The coinsurance clause determines how much will be paid if the limits of insurance do not meet the policy's coinsurance requirement.
- **Mortgage holders** — Insurance providers can deny coverage because the policy owner failed to comply with the policy provisions. A mortgage holder can still receive a payment if they pay any premium due under the policy, submit a signed proof of loss within 60 days, and notify the insurer of any changes in occupancy or ownership. When the insurer cancels coverage due to nonpayment of premium, it must provide the mortgage holder a written notice of cancellation (*10 days* if for nonpayment of premium, and *30 days* for all other reasons).

Optional Coverages – The Building and Personal Property Coverage Form contains the following optional coverages, which must be listed on the declarations page and applied separately to each item:

- **Agreed value** — The insured and insurer will determine a value for the property. The carrier will pay no more for loss or damage to that property than the percentage the insurance limit for this coverage bears to the agreed value shown. Coinsurance will not apply to property with an agreed value.
- **Inflation guard** — Limits of insurance to which this coverage applies are automatically raised by an annual percentage shown in the Declarations and prorated over the policy term.
- **Replacement cost** — The actual cash value (ACV) in the valuation condition is replaced with replacement cost valuation. This coverage is not applied to the personal property of others, antiques or rare articles, works of art, contents of a residence, or stock unless stock is shown in the Declarations.
- **Extension of the replacement cost to personal property of others** — If the replacement cost option is selected, the policy owner can also purchase this option. Suppose a written contract outlines the policy owner's liability for third-party property. In that case, the policy will pay no more than what is specified in that contract. It will not exceed the replacement cost of the policy limit or the item.

Condominium Associations

Because of the unique ownership situation with condominiums due to multiple occupancy and ownership, two different coverage forms have been developed to address that situation. The Condominium Association Coverage Form covers common building property and other property that must be insured due to the condominium association agreement. The Condominium Unit-Owners Coverage Form insures the owner's personal property.

The *Condominium Association Coverage Form* covers buildings and permanent fixtures for condominium associations.

Covered property under the Condominium Association Coverage Form includes the building, business personal property, and the property of others. The actual coverage is similar to what is provided under the Building and Personal Property Coverage Form. However, the building coverage specifically includes the following:

- Fixtures;
- Alterations and improvements that are a part of the building; and

- Security, refrigeration, ventilation, cooking, dishwashing, laundering, or housekeeping appliances contained in individual units if the condominium association agreement requires the association to provide insurance protection.

Business personal property includes property owned by the Association or jointly by the unit owners and leased business personal property that the Association has a contractual agreement to insure. Business personal property is insured if within 100 feet of the described premises.

The exact causes of loss forms used with the Building and Personal Property Coverage Form are used with this coverage form. Also, the same additional coverages and extensions are included in the Condominium Association Coverage Form.

The coverage form also includes several other conditions *in addition* to the common policy and commercial property conditions. These conditions are the same as those found in the building and personal property coverage form, except for *unit owner's insurance*. When the unit owner has insurance on the same property, condominium association insurance is designed to be *primary* coverage and not contribute to the owner's insurance.

You may find it helpful to review the additional coverages, extensions, and other conditions in the Building and Personal Property Coverage Form.

Three optional coverages are built into the coverage form activated by an entry in the Declarations. These optional coverages include the following:

1. Agreed value;
2. Inflation guard; and
3. Replacement cost.

Condominium (Commercial) Unit-Owners – The *Condominium (Commercial) Unit-Owners Coverage Form* covers business personal property for commercial condominium unit owners. This form insures commercial condominium unit owners, not residential condominium unit owners, who are covered under the homeowners and dwelling policies.

It has many of the same provisions as the Condominium Association Coverage Form, with three principal differences. These differences are as follows:

1. No building coverage is provided because the condominium building is jointly owned and insured under the association coverage form.
2. Improvements and betterments are included as business personal property if owned by the insured unless the condominium association agreement states that the association will provide coverage for these items.
3. The condominium association insurance condition states that if both the unit owner and association have insurance covering the same property, the *condominium commercial unit-owners coverage insurance is excess* coverage and will not contribute to the association insurance.

Builders Risk

The *Builders Risk Coverage Form* is utilized to insure buildings or structures while under construction. It provides coverage similar to the building and personal property coverage form. This coverage is mainly written on a completed value form. Still, it may also be written on a reporting form basis.

Property covered under a Builder's Risk Coverage Form includes the building and any temporary structures. Also covered are foundations, fixtures, equipment, machinery, supplies, and materials within 100 feet of the premises if they intend on becoming a permanent part of the building.

Property *not covered* includes:

- Land or water;
- Trees;
- Outdoor lawns;
- Plants or shrubs;
- Satellite dishes;
- Television and radio antennas; or
- Signs (unless attached to the building, the coverage limit is $2,500 per sign in any one event).

The covered causes of loss forms used with the Building and Personal Property Coverage Form also apply to the Builders Risk Coverage Form.

There are *four additional coverages* under the Builders Risk Coverage Form:

1. **Debris removal** — Applies if reported within 180 days of the damage or loss or the end of the policy period. The policy covers up to 25% of the direct physical loss and any applicable deductible. Suppose a covered property has not sustained direct physical damage or loss. In that scenario, the most the insurance company will pay is $5,000 at each location. However, when the direct loss and the debris removal expenses exceed the limit of insurance, the policy will cover an additional sum for debris removal over and above the amount of insurance.
2. **Preservation of property** — Property that is moved to a temporary location to protect it from damage or loss is covered as it is transferred or stored at another location. Damage or loss must occur within 30 days after the property is moved. This coverage is not viewed as an additional amount of insurance.
3. **Fire department service charge** — Up to $1,000 in coverage is included. The deductible does not apply to this additional coverage.
4. **Pollutant cleanup and removal** — The policy will cover up to $10,000 for expenses incurred to remove pollutants if the discharge results from a covered cause of loss and is reported to the insurer in writing within 180 days of occurrence. This amount is the maximum the insurer will pay in any 12 months.

The policy also contains two coverage extensions:

1. **Building materials and supplies of others** — The policy owner may extend coverage to include construction materials that will become a permanent part of the building for up to $5,000. This extension is an additional amount of insurance.
2. **Sod, plants, shrubs, and trees** — The insured can also extend coverage to a loss outside the building. The damage or loss must have resulted from lightning, fire, explosion, civil commotion or riot, or aircraft. The most the insurer will pay for this extension is $1,000, but not more than $250 per plant, shrub, or tree.

Business Income

Coverage for indirect losses is not automatic in the Commercial Package Policy. The insured must purchase the coverage and choose an appropriate limit of insurance. There are three forms from which the policy owner can select coverage:

1. Business Income with Extra Expense;
2. Business Income without Extra Expense; and
3. Extra Expense.

An explanation of a few important concepts is essential for understanding these forms:

An indirect loss is only payable after a covered direct damage loss occurs. Because the Commercial Package Policy includes three Cause of Loss forms, the perils that trigger indirect coverage will vary.

Business income is also known as *business interruption coverage* or *time element coverage*. Coverage is triggered by a covered loss that leads to a required suspension of operations during the restoration period at the premises listed in the Declarations.

Extra expenses – *Extra expenses* are expenses incurred by the policy owner, above their regular operating costs, during the restoration period and to minimize the suspension.

To better comprehend the concepts previously discussed, you need to know the following terms and definitions:

Suspension — The cessation or slowdown of the insured's business activities.

Operations — Refers to any business activity at the premises described in the Declarations.

Period of restoration — Begins 72 hours after the direct physical loss of *business income*. It begins immediately for *extra expense* coverage.

Resumption of operations — A condition exists that allows the insurance provider to reduce the amount of the loss if the policyholder does not resume operations as quickly as possible.

Civil Authority — Coverage will be extended if the policy owner suffers a business income or extra expense loss at a neighboring property less than one mile from the premises. Damage from a loss covered in the insured's policy must require them to suspend business operations, or a civil authority needs unimpeded access to the damaged property. Coverage is limited to four weeks, and a *72-hour waiting period* will apply.

Extended business income — If a business income loss is paid, the policy provides time for the insured to resume their normal income levels. This additional coverage has a beginning and ending period as follows:

- Begins on the date the property is repaired (except finished stock) and operations are resumed; and
- Ends on the date the policyholder could restore operations with reasonable diligence and speed or 60 consecutive days following the date on which operations are resumed, whichever is earlier.

A policy owner can activate an option to extend this time frame by entering a new date in the policy's Declarations.

Coinsurance applies to business income coverage (it does not apply to extra expense coverage). The policy owner has three optional coverages to choose from that will waive the coinsurance; these coverages must be active in the Declarations to apply:

- **Maximum period of indemnity** — If the policy owner chooses this optional coverage, the coinsurance clause is replaced. The most the insurance provider will pay for loss of business income is the lesser of either of the following:
    - The amount of loss incurred during the 120 days immediately after the loss; or
    - The limit of insurance.
- **Monthly limit of indemnity** — When a policy owner chooses this optional coverage, the coinsurance clause is replaced. The most the insurance provider will pay every 30 days after a direct physical loss is the limit of insurance multiplied by a specified percentage listed on the declarations page.

- **Business income agreed value** — To activate this coverage, the policy owner must complete a business income report showing the business financial data for the previous 12 months. The policy owner must also provide an estimate for the next 12 months. This report becomes a part of the policy. The selected limit on the worksheet should be at least the percentage of coinsurance shown in the Declarations multiplied by the extra expenses and net income for the following 12 months. Coinsurance is suspended on the date the policy owner selected this optional coverage or when the policy expires, whichever is earlier.

Business Interruption

Business Income coverage does not apply when the destruction of electronic data causes a suspension of operations (business interruption). Coverage also does not apply to any loss or damage to electronic data, except as allowed under the Interruption of Computer Operations additional coverage. Under this additional coverage, the insurance provider will pay up to $2,500 for all losses sustained and expenses incurred in one policy year, irrespective of the number of interruptions or the number of premises. The additional coverage does not apply to losses occurring after the end of the period of restoration, even if the maximum amount of insurance ($2,500) has not been exhausted.

Extra Expense (Only) Form

The *Extra Expense Coverage Form* covers consequential losses. It can be used by a business that will likely not have a business income loss. For instance, insurance agents earning most of their income from outside sales away from their office may not be concerned about a loss to the office. The agent may be more concerned with extra expenses needed to open a temporary office while the original office is undergoing renovation.

The key points to note in this form are as follows:

- Damage must be to property described in the Declarations. If damage is to property that is out in the open or a vehicle, it must be within 100 feet of the premises;
- Direct loss needs to be from a covered cause of loss (this will vary depending on the cause of loss form);
- Extra expenses include any necessary costs incurred during the restoration period. The policy owner would not have incurred these costs if no direct damage to the covered property occurred. Extra expenses also include those associated with minimizing the suspension of operations;
- The period of restoration does not have a waiting period so that insurers can pay extra expenses immediately;
- Civil authority coverage begins immediately and is applied upon an authority prohibiting access to the premises and lasting for four consecutive weeks;
- Expenses to replace or repair property are not included;
- $2,500 can be extended for losses associated with the interruption of computer operations; and
- The insured must resume operations as quickly as possible, or the insurance carrier will have the option to limit the loss payment.

Coinsurance does not apply in the extra expense form. A limit of insurance is chosen by the policy owner to be used per loss. The method of paying the policy owner for extra expense losses is governed by the limit selected and percentages noted on the declarations page for the following periods:

- 1st percentage – 30 days or less;
- 2nd percentage – 31 days to 60 days; and
- 3rd percentage – More than 60 days.

Each period will have a percentage. For example, a policy owner chooses $200,000 as a limit of insurance, and the following percentages – 30%, 60%, and 100%. In this scenario, the limit of insurance would be as follows:

- 30 days or less = $60,000
- 31 days to 60 days = $120,000
- More than 60 days = $200,000

If a covered direct damage loss were to result in an extra expense loss for this policy owner and the loss lasted for 30 days, the most that could be collected is $60,000. If the policy owner incurred $75,000 in extra expenses, the insurer would only pay $60,000. If the policy owner incurs $50,000 in losses, the insurer would only pay this amount.

Legal Liability

The legal liability coverage form insures the tangible property of others in the insured's care, custody, or control. It covers the insured's legal liability for loss or damage to the property of others, including *loss of use*.

The Declarations must describe the covered property explicitly, and the limit of insurance is the most the insurance company will pay for any single loss. The policy will also pay for the insured's defense costs associated with a covered loss. No duty to defend the insured exists if the insurance does not apply.

This form also requires a cause of loss form. The exact Causes of Loss forms that apply to the Building and Personal Property Coverage Form apply to this coverage. Coverage will vary depending on the selected form (basic, broad, or special).

Additional Coverage – Six additional coverages apply in addition to the limit of insurance. They are the same as the supplemental payments found in the General Liability Coverage Form. Concerning any claim or suit, the insurance provider will also cover the following:

- All expenses they incur;
- The cost of bonds to release attachments;
- All warranted expenses incurred by the insured at the insurance provider's expense, including up to $250 per day for loss of earnings;
- All expenses taxed against the insured in a suit;
- All prejudgment interest awarded; and
- Interest that accrues on any judgment awarded before the insurance provider pays it.

Extensions of Coverage – The Legal Liability Coverage Form includes three extensions of coverage that cover the following:

- **Additional Insureds** — If the named insured is a partnership or corporation. Coverage also applies to the insured's partners, executive officers, directors, trustees, and stockholders; and
- **Newly Acquired Organization** — Other than partnerships or joint ventures, newly acquired organizations are also covered, but only for 90 days or until the end of the policy period, whichever is sooner.
- **Newly Acquired Property** — Coverage is available for buildings or personal property that comes under the insured's control, care or custody after the beginning of the current policy period. Coverage ends when the policy expires, 30 days after the property came under the insured's control, or when values are reported to the insurance provider, whichever happens first.

Conditions – The Legal Liability Coverage Form contains several conditions that apply in addition to the Commercial Property Conditions:

- **Duties in the event of an accident, claim, or suit** — In the event of a loss, the insured duties include the following:
    - Notify the insurance provider promptly of any accident that may result in a loss;
    - Send the insurer prompt written notice of any claim or suit brought against the insured;
    - Immediately send the insurer copies of any demands or notices in conjunction with a claim or suit;
    - Authorize the insurer to obtain records or other information;
    - Cooperate with the insurer in the investigation;
    - Assist the insurer in enforcing any right against another person; and
    - Not make any settlements or assume any obligations voluntarily.
- **Legal action against the insurer** — No one has a right to bring legal action against the insurance provider until they comply with all policy provisions.
- **Other insurance** — If other insurance applies, the insurance provider will settle on a pro-rata basis if the other insurance is written on the same basis.
- **Transfer of rights of recovery against the insurer (Subrogation)** — The insured must transfer any rights they possess to collect from another to the insurer after payment has been made.

The following additional conditions apply in addition to the common policy provisions:

- **Amendment of commercial property conditions** — None of the commercial property conditions apply to this coverage form *except*:
    - "Concealment, misrepresentation or fraud,"
    - "Insurance under Two or More Coverages," and
    - "Liberalization."
- **Bankruptcy** — The insured's bankruptcy does not relieve the insurance provider of their obligation under this coverage form.
- **Policy period, coverage territory** — The insurance provider will pay for damage or loss caused by an accident that happens during the policy period listed on the declarations page and within the coverage territory (the United States, Puerto Rico, and Canada).
- **Separation of insureds** — Insurance applies separately to the named insured and each additional insured, except for the limits of insurance.

Definitions

The following terms are defined for use in the Commercial Property coverage forms:

- **Operations** — Business activities occurring at the described premises.
- **Period of Restoration** — The period that starts with the date of direct physical damage or loss caused by any Covered Cause of Loss at the described premises and ends with the earlier of the following:
    - When the property at the described premises should be rebuilt, repaired, or replaced with similar quality and reasonable speed; or
    - When business resumes at a new permanent location.
- **Pollutants** — Any liquid, solid, gaseous, or thermal contaminant or irritant, including vapor, smoke, soot, fumes, acids, alkalis, chemicals, and waste.
- **Suspension** — The slowdown or the cessation of the insured's business activities.
- **Stock** — Merchandise held for sale or in storage, raw materials, and in-process or finished goods, including supplies used in packaging or shipping.

- **Rental Value** — Calculated according to the following:
    - Total anticipated rental income from tenant occupancy of the described premises and furnished and equipped by the insured; and
    - Amount of all charges that are the legal obligation of the tenants and which would otherwise be the insured's obligation; and
    - The fair rental value of any portion of the described premises occupied by the insured.

Causes of Loss Forms

Insurance providers can write commercial property coverage with one of three causes of loss forms that tell which perils are being protected against – *basic*, *broad*, or *special*. These are the same as the coverage forms discussed for the homeowners and dwelling policies; each form protects against a wider range of perils than the previous form.

Basic Form

The *basic* form is a named peril form that insures against 11 causes of loss. These causes of loss are similar to those previously discussed in the Dwelling and Homeowners sections:

1. **Lightning**;
2. **Fire**;
3. **Explosion** — Does not include an explosion of pressure relief vessels or if caused by the swelling of contents or accumulations from water;
4. **Windstorm or hail** — Loss to the interior of the building is not covered unless there is initial damage to the exterior of the building; signs, outdoor crops, television and radio antennas, shrubs, and plants are excluded;
5. **Smoke**, but not from industrial operations or agricultural smudging;
6. **Aircraft or vehicles** — Damage or loss caused by a vehicle operated or owned by the policy owner during business operations is not covered;
7. **Riot or civil commotion** — This cause of loss includes acts of employees striking while on the described premises and looting;
8. **Vandalism** — Damage caused by theft (except the damage resulting from breaking in or exiting the premises) is not covered;
9. **Sprinkler leakage** — Covers leakage or discharge from an automatic fire protective sprinkler system, including the collapse of a tank;
10. **Sinkhole collapse** — Covers direct loss resulting from the sudden sinking or collapse of land created by the action of water on dolomite or limestone. There is no coverage if the collapse is into an artificial hole. Also, coverage does not include filling the sinkhole; and
11. **Volcanic action** — Covers direct loss from volcanic eruptions if caused by dust, ash, lava, or airborne shockwaves. The cost to remove dust or ash that does not cause a direct loss is not covered. All volcanic eruptions occurring within 168 hours are considered one event.

The basic form contains the following *exclusions*:

- Ordinance or law;
- Governmental actions;
- War and military action;
- Nuclear hazard;
- Earth movement;
- Water;
- Wet rot, dry rot, fungus, and bacteria;

- Artificially generated electrical current;
- Bursting or rupture of water pipes, unless it resulted from another covered cause of loss;
- Discharge or leakage of water or steam;
- Explosion of steam pipes, steam boilers, or steam engines operated or owned by the insured;
- Mechanical breakdown;
- Neglect; and
- Utility services.

Special additional exclusions exist for certain forms attached to the package's property section. Exclusions exist for the legal liability, extra expense, and business income forms.

One additional coverage is added for limited coverage for wet rot, dry rot, fungus, and bacteria. Loss caused by these items has to be the result of a covered cause of loss other than fire. Coverage does not apply to plants, shrubs, trees, or lawns which are part of a vegetated roof. Coverage may also apply if the flood coverage endorsement is attached. There is a $15,000 sublimit for these losses to include testing, removal and tearing out, and replacing parts of the property to gain access. This coverage is not considered additional insurance.

Broad Form

The *broad* form includes the same 11 causes of loss as the basic form. In addition, the broad form contains three additional perils:

1. **Falling objects** — The insurer will not cover loss or damage to personal property in the open or the interior of a structure or building unless a falling object first damages an outside wall or the roof.
2. **Weight of snow, ice, or sleet** — Except for the loss or damage to personal property located outside of structures or buildings or for loss or damage to plants, shrubs, trees, or lawns that are part of a vegetated roof.
3. **Water damage** — Includes accidental leakage or discharge of water or steam as the direct result of the breaking apart of a heating, air conditioning, plumbing, or other system or appliance. Water damage *does not apply* to any of the following:
    - Leakage or discharge from a sump or related equipment, including overflow because of sump pump failure; an automatic sprinkler system; gutters, roof drains, downspouts, or similar fixtures;
    - The cost to repair defects that caused the water damage;
    - Loss or damage as a result of repeated or continuous leakage or seepage that occurs for at least 14 days; or
    - Loss or damage caused by freezing unless the policy owners do their best to maintain the heat or turn off the water supply and drain the system.

The *exclusions* in the broad form are the same as those in the basic form. There are also special exclusions regarding the extra expense, business income, leasehold interest, and legal liability coverage forms.

The broad causes of loss form will include the following additional coverages:

- **Collapse** — The policy will insure the collapse of the building if the loss is the result of a covered cause of loss. Such causes include insects or vermin, hidden decay, rain that collects on the roof, the weight of people, or the use of defective construction methods or materials if the collapse occurs during construction. Collapse does not include expansion, bulging, shrinkage, cracking, or settling.
- **Limited coverage for wet rot, dry rot, fungus, and bacteria** — Loss caused by these conditions must result from a covered cause of loss other than fire. Coverage does not apply to plants, shrubs, trees, or lawns which are part of a vegetated roof. If the flood coverage endorsement is attached, coverage may

also apply. There is a $15,000 sublimit for these losses, including testing, removal, and tearing out and replacing any parts of the property to gain access. This coverage is not additional insurance.

Special Form

The *special* form does not list the covered causes of loss and is referred to as *open perils*. Instead, all causes of loss are insured against except for the exclusions.

The following *exclusions* apply if the damage is directly or indirectly a result of the following:

- Ordinance or law;
- War and military action;
- Governmental action;
- Nuclear hazard;
- Earth movement;
- Utility services;
- Water damage, including sewer backup; or
- Wet rot, dry rot, fungus, and bacteria.

The policy will not pay for damage or loss resulting from any of the following:

- Loss of market, loss of use, or delay;
- Artificially generated electrical current;
- Expansion, shrinking, cracking, smog, decay, settling, corrosion, or wear and tear;
- Gas, vapor, or smoke from industrial operations or agricultural smudging;
- Changes, extremes of temperature, dryness or dampness to personal property;
- Infestation or nesting or discharge of waste products from birds, insects, rodents, or other animals;
- Scratching or marring;
- Explosion of steam pipes, steam boilers, or steam engines;
- Mechanical breakdown;
- Water or other liquids that leak from plumbing equipment caused by freezing (unless the policy owner maintains the heat or turns off the water supply and drains the system);
- Repeated or continuous leakage or seepage of water for 14 days or more;
- Voluntary parting with any property;
- Criminal or dishonest acts of the insured or their employees;
- Rain, sleet, ice, or snow that damages personal property in the open;
- Collapse unless specified in an additional coverage;
- Dispersal, discharge, or release of pollutants unless a loss from a specified cause of loss results; or
- Neglect of a policy owner to preserve or save property from additional damage at the time of the loss.

The following perils are not insured against unless they result in a covered cause of loss:

- Weather conditions, but only if they contribute to further damage from an excluded cause of loss;
- Decisions or acts, including the failure to decide or act; and
- Defective, inadequate, or faulty planning, zoning, design, development, specifications, quality of work, and materials used for repair, maintenance, or construction.

Special exclusions are also in the extra expense, business income, leasehold interest, and legal liability forms. Product loss or damage is another exclusion that applies only to the specific property. Losses caused by an error or omission in testing, planning, packaging, and processing are not covered.

In addition to the exclusions, the special form also contains several limitations. Certain types of property will only be covered for a specific amount or are only covered for certain causes of loss. The insurer will not pay for damage or loss to the following types of property unless the damage or loss is caused by one of the following specified causes of loss:

- Animals, but only if they are killed, or their destruction is necessary;
- Fragile articles, if broken; or
- Builder's tools, machinery, and equipment while away from the described premises.

Specified causes of loss include the following:

- Lightning;
- Fire;
- Explosion;
- Windstorm or hail;
- Aircraft or vehicles;
- Vandalism;
- Riot or civil commotion;
- Leakage from fire-extinguishing equipment;
- Falling objects (unless the outside is damaged and there is no coverage to items in the open)
- Sinkhole collapse;
- Volcanic action;
- Weight of snow, ice, or sleet; and
- Water damage (accidental leakage or discharge of steam or water from an appliance).

For any damage or loss caused by theft, the following types of property are insured only for the following limits that are not in addition to the limits of insurance:

- $2,500 for furs and fur garments;
- $2,500 for jewelry (unless worth less than $100), watches, precious and semiprecious stones, gold, silver, other precious metals, and bullion;
- $2,500 for dies and patterns; and
- $250 for tickets, including lottery tickets held for sale, stamps, and letters of credit.

Additional Coverages and Extensions – The additional coverage of collapse and limited coverage for wet rot, dry rot, fungus, and bacteria are applied and subject to the limitations previously discussed.

Coverage extensions include:

- Property in transit for specific perils up to a limit of $5,000;
- Cost to tear out and replace part of the structure or building resulting from a loss due to water damage or other liquid discharge from an appliance or system; and
- Expenses incurred to install temporary glass plates or board-up openings while glass is waiting to be replaced.

Commercial Property Conditions

Commercial property coverage contains numerous conditions that are in addition to the conditions found in the common policy conditions form. Some of these conditions are included directly in the individual coverage forms, and others can be attached by a separate endorsement, known as the commercial property conditions.

The following common conditions are in Commercial Property Conditions Forms:

- **Concealment, misrepresentation, or fraud coverage** — Insurers will cancel coverage if the policy owner commits fraud as it relates to the policy at any time.
- **Control of property** — This condition states that any negligence or act by individuals not under the direction of the policy owner will not void coverage.
- **Insurance under two or more coverages** — If the same loss triggers more than one coverage under the policy, the insurer will pay no more than the actual loss.
- **Legal action against the insurer** — No one may bring legal action against the insurer until they fully comply with all the policy terms. Policy owners must bring legal action within two years of the loss (this time can vary from state to state).
- **Liberalization** — If the insurance carrier adopts any provisions that would broaden coverage during the policy period or 45 days before the effective date, the broadened coverage will automatically apply without an endorsement.
- **No benefit to bailee** — No individual other than the policy owner who has custody of covered property can benefit from the insurance.
- **Other insurance** — If the policy owner has other insurance with identical terms, conditions, and provisions, the policy will respond by limits. Suppose the other insurance is different than that described above. In that case, the policy will contribute on an excess basis, paying only for the amount of any loss exceeding the other insurance.
- **Policy period, coverage territory** — The coverage territory includes the U.S., its possessions and territories, and Canada.
- **Subrogation (transfer of rights of recovery against others)** — To recover damages, the policy owner must transfer any rights to the insurance carrier after they make payment for the loss.

Selected Endorsements

Spoilage – The *spoilage* endorsement classifies any *perishable stock* as covered property when owned by the insured or when the property of others is in the insured's care, custody, and control. The endorsement extends coverage for the following causes of loss:

- Breakdown of refrigeration, cooling, or humidity control equipment when located at the described premises;
- Contamination by a refrigerant; and
- Power outage, on or off the premises, when beyond the insured's control.

This endorsement can add an extra condition for maintaining a refrigeration agreement at the insured location to provide coverage.

Earthquake – The *Earthquake and Volcanic Eruption Endorsement* has to be used with one of the Causes of Loss forms (Basic, Broad, or Special). It adds two perils for coverage:

- Earthquake; and
- Volcanic eruption (explosion, eruption, or pouring forth of a volcano).

This coverage provided by the other causes of loss forms is limited to above-ground volcanic eruptions, excluding ground shock waves. All volcanic eruptions or earthquake shocks occurring within 168 hours (7 days) are considered one earthquake or explosion. The deductible is a percentage of the loss listed in the property Declarations.

The Exclusions and Limitations sections of the Causes of Loss Form apply to coverage provided under this endorsement.

Flood Coverage – The *Flood Coverage* endorsement adds flood to the covered perils in a standard property policy. Flood refers to a general and temporary condition of complete or partial inundation of normally dry land areas due to the overflow of inland or tidal waters, the rapid or unusual runoff or accumulation of surface waters from any source, or mudslides or mudflows caused by flood, involving a river of liquid and flowing mud on the surface of typically dry land areas. All flooding in a continuous or protracted event is considered a single flood.

The flood endorsement is subject to a limit of insurance and a yearly aggregate amount. The exclusions and limitations of the policy cause of loss form apply to coverage provided under this endorsement with certain exceptions.

The flood coverage endorsement is considered excess coverage over any coverage available through the National Flood Insurance Program (NFIP). The coverage would be primary if, when the endorsement was written, the property was not eligible for an NFIP policy or if the insurer agreed to issue the endorsement without an underlying NFIP policy. When other insurance covers a flood loss through the NFIP, the insurance provider will pay its share of the loss up to the limit of insurance.

Ordinance or Law Coverage – *Ordinance or law* is a coverage endorsement that can be added to the property policy. It covers a building if the enforcement of any zoning, building, or land use law results in damage or loss, increased cost of reconstruction or repairs, or demolition and removal costs.

The endorsement is divided into three coverages, which the policy owner activates by purchasing each coverage. They can buy all or some of the coverages included. Policy owners can add the ordinance or law endorsement only to a property policy written on a replacement cost basis, and coinsurance does not apply.

The building listed in the endorsement must sustain covered direct damage to at least part of the structure. Only the part of the structure covered by a peril in the policy and subject to the ordinance or law will take advantage of this endorsement.

Coverage is for completing minimum requirements as specified by the ordinance or law. Insurers will provide no coverage for ordinances or laws the policy owner was required to comply with before the loss.

This endorsement can offer the following coverages when selected:

- **Coverage A** — Loss to the undamaged portion of the building-loss in value to the building's or structure's undamaged portion;
- **Coverage B** — Demolition cost of the undamaged portion of the covered building or structure; and
- **Coverage C** — Increased construction cost for the damaged and undamaged portions of the building or structure.

Protective Safeguards – Policy owners can add the protective safeguards endorsement to the Commercial Property form. When the insurer requires protective safeguards, coverage will be suspended if the insured fails to maintain the following protective devices or services:

- Automatic sprinkler system;
- Automatic fire alarm;
- Security service; and
- Service contract.

Commercial Inland Marine

Nationwide Marine Definition

Inland Marine coverage is either filed or unfiled with state regulatory authorities. Filed coverages have standardized coverage forms. Unfiled Inland Marine classes provide a unique exposure to loss, in which standardized forms have yet to be created.

The *Nationwide Marine Definition* defines the coverage types written on Ocean Marine and Inland Marine insurance forms. In 1953 the National Association of Insurance Commissioners (NAIC) implemented a Nationwide Marine Insurance Definition and revised it in 1976. This definition is used mainly for classification purposes rather than as a definition of underwriting powers.

Inland Marine coverage can be written on almost any type of property that is considered to be *portable*. In addition, instruments of communication and transportation, such as docks, piers, and bridges, are also covered on Inland Marine coverage forms. Personal inland marine policies are often referred to as *floaters* because the coverage *floats* with the insured property anywhere in the world. Inland Marine must be differentiated from Ocean Marine, which insures property being transported over water. Inland Marine exposures pertain to property that is located on land.

Inland marine policies will pay actual cash value (ACV), but the insurance provider reserves the right to repair or replace instead. The Nationwide Marine Definition defines four general classes of risks that can be the subject of Inland Marine coverage. These risks are as follows:

1. Domestic shipments and transportation risks;
2. Tunnels, bridges, and other instrumentalities of communication and transportation;
3. Personal property floater risks; and
4. Commercial property floater risks.

Bailee Insurance

Bailee's Customer coverage forms protect against customer property losses in the insured's custody, care, or control. Each of these coverage forms is unfiled.

- **Bailee's Customer Policy** — This coverage form insures customer property loss without regard to the insured's legal liability for the loss. It insures the interest of both the bailee and the bailor.
- **Furriers Block** — This coverage is written for insureds engaged in the fur business. It insures merchandise held for sale and customers' property that the insured has temporary custody of for storage, repair, or cleaning.
- **Cleaners, Dryers, and Laundries** — This coverage form covers insureds in the dry cleaning or laundry business from damage or loss to customers' property while in their possession.
- **Warehouseman's** — This coverage form protects customers' property while stored at a warehouse. It is typically written as excess coverage over the property owner's other valid and collectible insurance.

Conditions Form

The commercial inland marine conditions are *added* to the common policy conditions and any conditions that apply to a specific coverage form. They are similar to other common conditions previously discussed and include the following:

- **Obligations of the insured following a loss;**
- **Insurance under two or more policies;**
- **Other insurance covering the same loss;**
- **Appraisal;**
- **Abandonment;**
- **Loss payment;**
- **Pair, set, or parts;**
- **Salvage (recovered property);**
- **Subrogation (transfer of rights of recovery);**
- **Privilege to adjust with the owner** — Since inland marine coverages can insure the property of others in the insured's custody, care, or control, this condition states that the insurer will settle with the actual property owners in the event of loss;
- **Reinstatement of limit** — This condition says that payment of any claim will not reduce the limit of insurance, except in the case of a total loss on a scheduled item. In this case, the insurance provider will cancel the specific coverage and refund any unearned premium for the insurance on that item;
- **Misrepresentation, concealment, or fraud;**
- **Legal action against the insurance provider;**
- **No benefit to the bailee;**
- **The policy period; and**
- **Valuation** — This condition states that the insurance provider will determine the value of an item following a loss based on the *lesser* of
    - The reasonable costs to restore the property;
    - The actual cash value of the item; or
    - The cost of replacing the property with like kind and quality.

Coverage Forms

A *commercial floater* refers to any inland marine policy designed to insure movable commercial property, wherever it may be located worldwide.

Insurers can write commercial inland marine coverage as either a part of a commercial package policy (CPP) or a standalone policy. Forms are referred to as *filed* or *unfiled*. A *filed form* is a form that may require an insurance provider to file for rate and form approval. An *unfiled form* may not require an approved filing to the state insurance department. Regulations may vary from state to state.

A different inland marine declaration is used with each type of coverage written. Therefore, depending on written coverages, more than one inland marine declaration may be attached to a policy. Besides the endorsements, policy period, and general information concerning the insured's name, the commercial inland marine Declarations specifically describe the covered property.

Most filed forms include a $250 deductible for a single loss. In addition, the filed coverage forms are typically written on an open peril basis. The causes of loss forms for commercial property do not apply to these coverages. The following *exclusions* are commonly found in these forms:

- Governmental action;
- Military action and war;
- Nuclear hazard;
- Delay, loss of market (customer base or customer demand), or loss of use;
- Voluntarily parting with property by scheme, device, or fraudulent trick;

- Dishonest acts by the insured or the insured's representatives or employees;
- Unauthorized instruction to transfer property;
- An insured's failure to use all reasonable means to preserve and protect property from further loss or damage;
- Damage or loss caused by any of the following, but if loss by a covered cause of loss takes place, insurers will cover the additional loss in the following situations:
    - Acts or decisions, or the failure to act or decide;
    - Weather conditions;
    - Inadequate or defective planning, zoning, construction, or quality of work;
    - Collapse, other than that provided as an additional coverage; or
    - Wear and tear, gradual deterioration, or inherent device.

The table below includes a list of filed and unfiled forms used to write commercial inland marine coverage.

FILED FORMS		UNFILED FORMS
Accounts Receivable	Air Transit	Bailee's Customer
Equipment Dealers	Trip Transit	Warehouseman's
Camera and Musical Instruments Dealers	Annual Transit	Pattern and Die
Film	Parcel Post	Salespersons Samples
Floor Plans	Air Cargo	Processing Risk
Fine Arts	Motor Truck Cargo	Exhibition Floater
Jewelers Block	Bridges and Tunnels	Garment Contractors
Physicians and Surgeons Equipment	Radio and TV Towers	Installations
Mail Coverage	Furriers Block	Builder's Risk — Installation
Signs	Laundries and Dry Cleaners	Electronic Data Processing
Theatrical Property	Cold Storage Locker	Stamp and Coin Dealers
Commercial Articles	Processors Legal Liability	Fine Arts Dealers
Valuable Papers and Records	Contractors Equipment	

We will now describe only some of the forms listed above.

Accounts Receivable – *Accounts Receivable* coverage is one of the most popular and important inland marine coverage forms. Unlike most inland marine coverages, the coverage protects property located at a fixed location rather than mobile property. The Accounts Receivable Coverage Form is a filed form. It provides coverage for losses of due accounts from customers that become uncollectible because of a loss to the insured's accounts receivable records.

Coverage is written on an all-risk basis. Additional exclusions not including those already discussed include the following:

- Concealment, alteration, falsification, or destruction of records to hide a wrongful act;
- Accounting, bookkeeping, or billing records; or
- Electrical or magnetic disturbance, injury, or erasure.

The following totals will be deducted from the total:

- The total of accounts that the insured can re-establish and collect;
- The total of accounts in which there is no loss;
- A total for likely "bad debt" that the insured is ordinarily unable to collect; and
- All unearned service charges and interest on necessary loans.

In addition, the insured must store their accounts receivable records in a receptacle described in the Declarations when they are not in use.

Commercial Articles – The *Commercial Articles* form is a filed form that protects the owners' interest, as opposed to the dealers of musical instruments, commercial cameras, and similar property. This form also includes the same property of others in the insured's custody, care, or control. Property not covered includes property in illegal transportation or trade and contraband. Like every inland marine coverage form, coverage is provided on an all-risk basis. The form consists of each of the common exclusions previously discussed.

The coinsurance clause in this coverage form differs somewhat from other coinsurance clauses. It states that all items insured but not explicitly listed or described must be covered for their total value when the loss occurs to avoid a coinsurance penalty. Another condition exclusive to this coverage form relates to additional acquired property, which is automatically insured for up to 30 days if it is of the same type of property already covered. The insurer will pay 25% of the limit of insurance for the same property, up to a maximum of $10,000.

Contractors Equipment Floater – The *Contractors Equipment Floater* is an unfiled commercial inland marine coverage form that generates the most premium within the insurance industry. It insures mobile equipment and contractor's equipment rented, owned, or borrowed by other contractors, as opposed to dealers. It covers the equipment while it is located on the job site and temporarily stored between jobs or during transportation to and from the job site. Insurers can write coverage on either an open peril basis or a named peril basis.

Additionally (newly) acquired property – This form provides an added coverage that allows for a newly acquired property during the policy period to be covered for 60 days (but not beyond the policy period). This coverage extension is typically limited to 25% of the limit of insurance, or $50,000, whichever is less.

Equipment shipped by air within the United States, its territories and possessions, Puerto Rico, and Canada is considered to be in the form's coverage territory.

Coinsurance might apply and will be listed on the declarations page.

Electronic Data Processing – *Electronic Data Processing* coverage has grown in importance recently. Businesses that lease, own, or rent data processing equipment are eligible for coverage. These unfiled forms generally cover the following four coverages:

1. Data processing media, including paper tapes or magnetic tapes, discs, and punch cards;
2. Computer hardware that is purposely scheduled;
3. Extra expense incurred by the insured to continue business operations following a loss; and
4. Business interruption can also cover the loss of income when the business is interrupted due to damage to equipment media.

Equipment Dealers – The stock of construction equipment and mobile equipment dealers, including the similar property of others in the insured's custody, care, or control, may be covered under the filed *Equipment Dealers* coverage form. Property that is not protected includes the following:

- Automobiles, motorcycles, and motor trucks;
- Watercraft and aircraft;
- Currency, money, notes, bills, accounts, and deeds;
- Property during manufacturing;
- Property rented, leased, or sold;

- Fixtures, furniture, and office supplies;
- Improvements and betterments;
- Tools, machinery, fittings, molds, patterns, etc.; and
- Property in illegal transportation or trade, or contraband.

Insurers write this coverage on an all-risk basis, and the following additional *exclusions* apply:

- Flood, water, surface water;
- Unexplained disappearance;
- Damage related to processing or work performed on the property; and
- Artificially produced electrical current.

This coverage form provides the following *extensions of coverage*:

- Removal of debris;
- Pollution removal and cleanup; and
- Theft damage to a building.

There are several additional conditions listed in this coverage form:

- **Valuation** — This condition replaces the standard inland marine valuation clause. It states that the insurer will determine the value of the unsold property based on either the cost to reasonably restore the property, the actual cash value, or the cost of replacing the damaged property with the same property, whichever is less.
    - The value of sold yet undelivered property will be valued at the net selling price minus any discounts and allowances.
    - The value of the property of others will be the lesser of the following: the actual cash value of the property, including the cost of materials and labor the insured has added, or the amount for which the insured is liable, including the cost of materials and labor the insured has added.
- **Coinsurance** — Property must be covered up to *80%* of its replacement cost.
- **Records and Inventory** — The insured must maintain accurate records and inventory for three years after the end of the policy period. These records include a detailed list of all purchases and sales, stock in trade, and property of others. Also, a physical stock inventory must be sent to the insurance provider at least once each year.
- **Protective Safeguards** — If the insurer requires protective safeguards (e.g., automatic sprinkler, fire alarm), coverage will be suspended if the insured does not keep them in operation or in good working condition while the business is closed.

Installations Floater — The *Installations Floater* coverage form is unfiled and often purchased by contractors to insure items such as the heating and air-conditioning equipment in a building. The property is insured while in transit, during the unloading and equipment installation, and until the building owner takes control. Insurers can write coverage on either a named peril or open peril basis. Coverage ends when the work is finished and is accepted by the ultimate owner or user of the property.

Jewelers Block — The *Jewelers Block* coverage form is a filed dealer's form that insures merchandise held for sale by the insured and the property of others in the insured's custody, care, or control.

Usually, once the property leaves the premises, there is no additional coverage. Certain types of property *not covered* include the following:

- Property purchased under a deferred sales arrangement after it leaves the insured's premises;
- Property displayed in showcases away from the insured's premises;
- Property while it is at trade exhibitions;
- Property while being worn by any insured, representative, employee, or member of their family, friends, or relatives (an exception is made for watches being worn for the sole purpose of adjustments);
- Property in transit by:
    - Mail (excluding registered mail);
    - Express carriers;
    - Air carriers, railroad, or waterborne; or
    - Motor carrier;
- Other property in illegal transportation or trade, or contraband.

This coverage form provides several optional types of transit coverage, which will insure property in transit if one of the following is listed on the declarations page:

- Carriers operating solely as a merchant's parcel delivery;
- Armored car services;
- The baggage service or passenger parcel of railroads, passenger bus lines, airborne or waterborne carriers; or
- Registered mail.

One other condition not found in the other coverage forms is the Changes in the Premises condition. It states the policy does not insure the property if the risk has been substantially increased by changes in the premises unless agreed to in writing by the insurance company.

Signs – For attached outdoor signs, limited coverage for signs is provided in the commercial property coverage form, usually limiting coverage to $2,500. Protection under the filed *Signs* coverage form includes the insured's signs, including fluorescent, neon, automatic, or mechanical signs, and similar property of others in the insured's custody, care, or control. The form includes a 100% coinsurance requirement.

Valuable Papers and Records – One of the most popular and most important of the commercial inland marine coverages is the filed *Valuable Papers and Records Form*. This form provides coverage for the reconstruction of valuable papers and records, which include the following: printed, written, or inscribed documents, manuscripts or historical records, books, abstracts, deeds, films, drawings, blueprints, maps, or mortgages.

Valuable papers and records *do not include* any of the following:

- Money or securities;
- Converted data;
- Prepackaged software and instructions or programs used in data processing; or
- Material on which such data is recorded.

Insured property under this form *does not include* the following:

- Any property not explicitly listed in the Declarations if the insurer cannot easily replace the property with other property;
- Property held as samples or for delivery after a sale;
- Property in storage away from the listed premises; or

- Other property in illegal transportation or trade and contraband.

Insurers will cover the property on an all-risk basis, subject to the following additional exclusions:

- Errors or omissions by the insured, the insured's representatives or employees (except for-hire carriers); and
- Electrical or magnetic disturbance, injury, or erasure.

The valuable papers and records coverage form does not have a coinsurance provision. However, a special condition requires the insured to keep all valuable records and papers, when not in use, in a receptacle described in the Declarations.

Motor Truck Cargo Forms – The *Motor Truck Cargo Policy - Carriers Form* is unfiled and used by common carriers that transport the goods of others for a fee. This legal liability coverage insures the carrier against liability for damage to the goods. The property of others is insured on an open peril basis.

The property is insured until delivery to the final destination; coverage will last for 72 hours at a facility not listed in the Declarations. Carriers can purchase insurance to provide coverage at unspecified terminals.

Owners, or private carriers who ship their goods using their vehicles, are insured on the Motor Truck Cargo Policy Owners Coverage Form. Coverage is provided for direct damage to the owner's property. Similar to the Motor Truck Cargo Carriers Form, liability is not a factor in these forms. Insurers write coverage on an open peril basis. The form only covers goods in transit from where the shipment begins to the final destination.

Equipment Breakdown Protection Coverage Form

The *Equipment Breakdown Coverage Form*, formerly known as the Boiler and Machinery Coverage Form, is used to insure many types of business risks and all industrial risks. Coverage will pay for direct loss to covered property from the breakdown of covered equipment.

An equipment breakdown form is a one-peril form. That peril is the breakdown of covered equipment. Insurers will pay property damage as long as that property *sustains direct damage* to covered property at the premises listed in the Declarations.

Additional coverages provided by this form include:

- Expediting expenses up to $25,000 for expediting permanent repairs or temporary repairs or replacement of property. This coverage is not an additional amount of insurance;
- Spoilage damage to raw materials, finished products, or property in transit;
- Utility interruption if a breakdown directly causes the interruption. The covered equipment supplies electric power, air conditioning, heating, communication services, water, sewer, or gas to the premises. The interruption must last at least the consecutive period presented in the Declarations.
- Automatic coverage for newly acquired locations if the coverage is equal to the coverage at the currently insured location.
- Ordinance or law coverage is applied despite the law or exclusion ordinance. The enforcement of any law or ordinance in force when the breakdown occurs will require the increases in loss.
- Errors and omissions

- Brands and labels if branded or labeled merchandise that is covered property is damaged due to a breakdown. The insurance provider may accept an agreed or appraised value for all or any part of the property.
- Contingent business income and extra expense, or extra expense only coverage subject to the same terms and conditions. This coverage will pay for a loss to covered equipment caused by a breakdown.

This form includes a loss condition that affects the appraisal of covered property. Property is insured on a *replacement cost basis*. However, suppose damaged property is not replaced or repaired within *two years* after the accident. In that case, the insurance provider will pay the cost to replace or repair the property or the actual cash value, whichever is less.

The equipment breakdown form does not insure bodily injury liability or consequential losses, such as an interruption in business and extra expense. However, the insured may obtain optional coverage for business interruptions.

The form defines an *accident* as the accidental and sudden breakdown of an object, resulting in physical damage to the object. Accident does not include:

- Deterioration, depletion, corrosion, or erosion;
- Wear and tear;
- Leakage at joints, fittings, or valves;
- Breakdown of brushes, gas tubes, or vacuum tubes;
- Breakdown of a foundation supporting the object
- Breakdown of electronic data processing equipment or computers; or
- The performance of protective or safety devices.

Unless a higher limit appears in the Declarations, equipment breakdown coverage will pay for direct damage directly resulting from a breakdown to covered equipment up to *$25,000* for each of the following:

- Consequential loss;
- Data and media (the cost to replace, research, or restore the damaged data);
- Expediting expenses;
- Hazardous substance cleanup, or the replacement or repair of contaminated property;
- Ammonia contamination; and
- Water damage.

Following a covered breakdown, coverage for fungus, wet rot, or dry rot is usually limited to *one year* and *$15,000* for testing, removal, and restoration, regardless of the number of claims.

The insured generally can buy optional higher limits for each of these coverages. In addition, the losses are subject to a deductible presented in the Declarations. The highest deductible will be applied if more than one object is involved in an accident.

Equipment breakdown coverage *excludes* losses resulting from any of the following:

- Earth movement;
- Ordinance or law except for the operation and use of electrical supply and emergency generating equipment located on the premises of a hospital;
- Nuclear hazard;

- Water (surface water, flood, tidal waves and tsunami, overflow or spray of any body of water, mudflow and mudslides, drain or sewer backups, or water damage caused by the leakage or discharge of a sprinkler system);
- Military action or war;
- Fire or combustion explosion, including those resulting in or ensuing from a breakdown;
- Explosion of covered electric steam generators, steam boilers, steam piping, steam engines, steam turbines, or gas turbines, if not otherwise excluded. Rotating or moving machinery is covered if the explosion results from mechanical breakdown or centrifugal force;
- Explosion within the furnace of a chemical boiler or the path from the furnace to the atmosphere;
- Bacterium, virus, or other microorganisms (except if caused by a breakdown);
- Wet rot, dry rot, and fungus (unless a breakdown causes these conditions);
- Damage to covered machinery undergoing electrical or pressure tests;
- Deterioration, depletion, erosion, corrosion, or wear and tear. If a breakdown results from these causes, the insurer will pay for the resulting loss or damage;
- Water or other methods used to extinguish a fire, even when the attempt is unsuccessful;
- A mechanical breakdown caused by vehicles or aircraft, freezing caused by cold weather, sinkhole collapse, lightning, smoke, civil commotion or vandalism, riot, or weight of snow, sleet, or ice;
- An interruption of or a delay in any business, processing, or manufacturing activity except for coverage provided by the business income and extra expense, extra expense only, and utility interruption coverages;
- A breakdown resulting from hail or windstorm;
- Lack of or excess power, light, refrigeration, heat, or steam except for any coverage provided by the business income and extra expense, extra expense only, utility interruption, and spoilage damage coverages;
- Any indirect result of a breakdown to covered machinery except for any coverage provided by the business income and extra expense, extra expense only, utility interruption, and spoilage damage coverages; or
- The insured's negligence to use all reasonable means to preserve and save covered property from further damage during and after the loss.

No coverage is provided for the following circumstances under the business income and extra expense, extra expense only, and utility interruption coverages:

- Business that could not have been conducted if the breakdown had not taken place;
- The insured's failure to use due diligence and all reasonable means to operate the business at the premises presented in the Declarations;
- The lapse, suspension, or cancellation of a contract after a breakdown extending beyond the time business could have continued if the contract had not lapsed, been suspended, or canceled.

Utility interruption coverage *does not cover* the following:

- Lightning;
- Smoke;
- Collapse;
- Sinkhole collapse;
- Acts of sabotage;
- Intentional acts of load shedding by the supplying utility;
- Freezing caused by cold weather;
- The impact of objects falling from an aircraft or missile;
- The impact of a vehicle, aircraft, or missile;

- Civil commotion, vandalism, or riot; and
- The weight of snow, sleet, or ice.

Commercial property forms can cover many of these perils.

Since most of the premium pays for examinations and inspections, equipment breakdown insurance places a lot of emphasis on inspections and loss control. The policy contains a unique condition that allows the insurance company to immediately suspend coverage whenever an object is exposed to or found in a dangerous condition. The suspension will take effect when the insured is notified in writing, and no advance notice is required. The suspension only applies to losses resulting from a particular object, not to the entire policy (if more than one object is insured).

In the equipment breakdown form, covered objects are defined as covered equipment. They include electrical equipment, mechanical equipment, refrigeration equipment, high-pressure equipment, turbines, and production machinery.

If an accident causes other accidents, all related events will be considered a single accident. All accidents simultaneously at the same location and by the same cause will be treated as a *single accident*.

Commercial Crime

Insurers can add crime insurance to a commercial package policy or write it on a monoline basis. The crime program fills in some of the gaps in the building and business personal property form as they pertain to crime losses. Crime insurance is written on an all-risk or open peril basis. Both the basic and broad causes of loss forms do not cover the peril of theft. The special cause of loss form contains exclusions for dishonest acts of workers and sublimits for theft of patents, dies, molds, stamps, jewelry, and furs.

The crime program presents policies in two major sections: commercial and government entities. The insured can choose a discovery or loss sustained form for each section. Each form has different coverage triggers, and these trigger differences (occurrence and claims-made) are similar to the general liability form.

The crime policy consists of separate coverages that can be selected by the insured, regardless of the form chosen. Each coverage has its own insuring agreement, conditions, and exclusions. The declarations page of a crime policy activates the applicable coverages within the policy. As an example, a crime declarations page will illustrate the following coverage choices:

CRIME DECLARATIONS PAGE	
Employee Theft (Employee Dishonesty)	$_____
Alteration and Forgery	$_____
Inside-Theft of Money and Securities	$_____
Inside-Robbery or Safe Burglary of Other Property	$_____
Outside the Premises	$_____
Computer Fraud	$_____
Fund Transfer Fraud	$_____
Counterfeit Paper Currency and Money Order	$_____

Discovery and Loss Sustained Forms

Discovery — A covered occurrence happening at any time and identified during the policy period or extended reporting period. The extended reporting period to identify a loss in the discovery form is as follows:

- The loss has to be reported within 60 days of policy cancellation;
- The loss has to be reported within one year of policy cancellation regarding any employee benefit plan; and
- The extended reporting period ends upon replacement of coverage.

Loss Sustained — The policy will cover a loss discovered during the policy period and an extended reporting period. Coverage also applies if the loss took place under a prior policy, in whole or in part, based on the coverage and limits selected and the insurance company providing the coverage.

For a loss to be paid from a prior policy period, it must be insured in both policies. The insurance policy in place at the time of the loss has to be effective and with no lapse in coverage when the current policy is canceled. The most the insurance provider will pay is the limit available on this policy as of its effective date or the lesser of the limit of insurance in the prior policy.

The extended reporting period to identify a loss in a loss-sustained coverage form has the following features:

- The loss has to be reported within one year of cancellation; and
- The extended reporting period ends upon replacement of coverage in whole or in part.

Definitions

Employee — *Employee* can mean any of the following:

- A natural person in the insured's service for 30 days after termination;
- A temporary worker hired from an employment contractor;
- Managers, directors, or trustees performing acts within the usual duties of an employee; or
- Former managers, employees, partners, directors, or trustees performing consulting services for the insured.

Discover or discovered — The time when an insured first becomes aware of the facts that would lead a sensible person to assume that a loss occurred.

Banking premises — The inside of a premises occupied by a banking institution or similar establishment.

Occurrence — A single act or a series of acts that may or may not involve individuals.

Premises — The inside of a premises in which the insured conducts business

Money — *Money* denotes currency, coins, banknotes with a face value, register checks, travelers' checks, and money orders sold to the public.

Funds — *Funds* include money and securities.

Other property — *Other property* means property aside from money or securities.

Tangible property — *Tangible property* denotes any other property that has built-in value.

Securities — *Securities* are negotiable and non-negotiable contracts or instruments representing either money or other property such as revenue, tickets, tokens, other stamps, and evidence of debt issued in relation to credit cards or charge cards that are not issued by the insured.

Burglary — *Burglary* is the crime of forced entry into or out of another person's premises by an individual or individuals with criminal intent. Insurance policies covering the peril of burglary require that, after a loss, there are observable signs of forced entry or exit from the premises.

Theft — *Theft* refers to any act of stealing, including burglary and robbery.

Robbery — *Robbery* is the taking of property from the custody and care of an individual by someone who caused or threatened to cause that person bodily harm.

Safe burglary – *Safe burglary* is the unlawful taking of covered property from within a locked vault or safe inside the premises or the actual taking of the vault or safe from the premises.

Coverages

Common policy provisions that apply to crime coverage forms (both discovery and loss sustained) include the following *general exclusions*:

- **Acts carried out by the insured, the insured's partners or members** — Loss resulting from acts carried out by the insured or partners, or members of the insured, as well as the actions of employees, representatives, managers, or directors identified by the insured before the policy period;
- **Acts of managers, trustees, employees, or representatives**;
- **Acts of employees identified by the insured before the policy period**;
- **Confidential information** — Loss resulting from illicit disclosure of the insured's or other person's confidential information (e.g., customer lists, trade secrets, or patents);
- **Government action** — Loss from seizure or destruction of property due to a governmental authority;
- **Indirect losses** — Expenses incurred while determining the amount of loss;
- **Legal fees, expenses, and costs** — Legal expenses associated with legal action;
- **Nuclear hazards**;
- **Pollution** — Loss or damage resulting from or caused by pollution, including seepage, dispersal, discharge, release, or escape of any solid, liquid, gaseous or thermal pollutant (such as waste, chemicals, acids, fumes, vapor, or smoke); and
- **Military action and war** — Losses or damage caused by military action, war, revolution, rebellion, and similar actions.

Employees, independent contractors, and officers are not covered under commercial crime policies.

Employee Theft – *Employee Theft* covers losses caused by the theft of covered property by employees. Covered property under this form includes money, securities, and property aside from money or securities.

The policy contains an extension of coverage that applies for up to 90 days to employees who are temporarily outside the coverage area. One additional condition articulates that coverage on any employee is immediately canceled when the insured finds out the employee is involved in a dishonest act, whether or not the action occurred before employment.

The following exclusions apply:

- Loss caused by a worker whose coverage was previously canceled under similar coverage and never reinstated;

- Losses that can only be proven through an accounting of profit and loss or a shortage in inventory;
- Losses caused by trading; and
- Losses resulting from fraudulently issuing, signing, and canceling a warehouse receipt, or failing to cancel a warehouse receipt.

Forgery or Alteration – *Forgery or alteration* provides worldwide coverage for loss of money resulting from forgery and alteration of outgoing drafts, checks, or promissory notes. Defense coverage is also provided for the insured should the insured be sued in an action arising from failure to honor a financial instrument suspected of forgery.

This insuring agreement also has its own conditions:

- **Proof of loss** — the insured must provide the insurer with the altered or forged check;
- **Territory** — anywhere in the world; and
- **Electronic signatures** — treated as handwritten.

Inside - Theft of Money and Securities – *Inside the Premises (Theft of Money and Securities)* covers the loss of money and securities from inside the premises or banking premises caused directly by theft, disappearance, or destruction. Coverage also applies to damage to the premises or its exterior and damage or loss to a locked cash box, cash drawer, cash register, vault, or safe inside the premises caused by actual or attempted theft.

In addition to those in the general provisions, several additional *exclusions* also apply to this coverage. This insuring agreement does not cover losses caused by:

- Fire;
- Errors in accounting or arithmetic or omissions;
- Surrendering of property in any purchase or exchange;
- Loss of money from a money-operated device, unless the machine is equipped with a continuous deposit recording mechanism;
- Loss or damage to motor vehicles, semi-trailers, or trailers, or accessories and equipment attached to them;
- Voluntarily parting with any property or inducement;
- Loss of property resulting from unauthorized instructions or the threat of bodily injury after it is transferred to another individual or place outside the premises or banking facility (this exclusion does not apply to covered property in a messenger's care or custody);
- Malicious mischief or vandalism; or
- Voluntarily parting with a title to possess property.

Inside - Robbery or Safe Burglary of Other Property – *Inside the premises (Robbery or Safe Burglary of Other Property)* covers loss or damage to other property inside the premises caused by an actual or attempted robbery of a custodian or from a vault or safe inside the premises.

This insuring agreement includes the same exclusions in the inside theft of money and securities and the general crime exclusions.

In addition, certain property is defined explicitly as not covered, including motor vehicles, trailers, equipment, and accessories. A special limit of $5,000 per occurrence applies to loss or damage to precious metals, precious and semiprecious stones, pearls, furs, manuscripts, drawings, or records.

Outside - Theft of Money and Securities – *Outside the Premises (Theft of Money and Securities)* insuring agreements cover loss caused directly by theft, disappearance, or destruction of money, securities, and other property outside the premises in the custody and care of an armored motor vehicle company a or messenger. Exclusions are comparable to the inside the premises insuring agreements. The special limitation of $5,000 per occurrence to the same kinds of property is applied.

Computer Fraud – The *computer and funds transfer fraud* form will provide worldwide coverage for loss or damage to money, securities, and other property directly resulting from fraudulently using any computer to transfer that property from inside those premises. Coverage will not be provided if a loss results from a fraudulent entry or change by a person or organization with authorized access to that computer system.

Funds Transfer Fraud – The *funds transfer fraud* insuring agreement provides coverage for the loss of funds resulting from fraudulent instructions received by a financial institution to pay money from an insured's transfer account to another individual. Computer fraud is excluded from this coverage.

Money Orders and Counterfeit Paper Currency – *Money orders and counterfeit paper currency* covers loss resulting directly from the insured having accepted, in good faith, money orders issued by any express company, post office, or bank that are not paid upon presentation or counterfeit paper currency that is acquired during the course of business in exchange for money, merchandise, or services.

Identity Theft – *Identity Theft* insurance is currently one of the most frequently advertised types of insurance on the market. In today's global society, the ability to control personal identity is at risk every time an individual purchases on the Internet, uses a credit card, or shows a driver's license in the checkout line at a local retail store.

Identity theft can manifest itself in many forms. Consumers must always be aware that their personal information is at risk. The following are the most common areas where fraudulent transactions can occur, and that would indicate that someone's identity has been stolen:

- Bank account withdrawals;
- Bankruptcy claims;
- Incorrect information on credit reports;
- Fraudulent transactions on credit cards;
- Untrue criminal violations;
- Calls from debt collectors;
- Fraudulent use of driver's license;
- Suspicious activity on investment accounts;
- Stolen mail (bill payment not received);
- New phone service;
- Social Security issues;
- New student loans; or
- IRS issues for nonpayment.

Farm Coverage

Farm coverage is unique because it insures the property and liability exposures of the business operation of a farm. It also may include the personal residential property and liability exposures of a family living on the farm premises. As in any commercial package policy, farm coverage may be written together in a package or separately as a monoline policy.

In addition to the common policy conditions and common policy declarations, farm coverage must include a Farm Conditions and a Farm Declarations form and one or more farm coverage forms. There are four farm coverage forms:

1. Farm property;
2. Farm liability;
3. Mobile agricultural machinery and equipment; and
4. Livestock.

Farm Property Coverage Form

Farm property coverage forms are subject to the causes of loss described on the declarations page. Like the commercial package policy, the cause of loss form will dictate coverage and exclusions for each property form. Farm property can be insured in a basic, broad, or special form.

Coverage A - Dwellings – *Coverage A - Dwellings* is similar to Coverage A of the Homeowners policy. Towers, antennas, and satellite dishes are considered structures under Coverage A.

The limits in Coverage A will cover the following:

- A dwelling located on or away from an insured location;
- Structures attached to the dwelling; and
- Materials and supplies located on the described insured location used to construct, alter or repair the dwelling or attached structures; and
- If not covered by other insurance, building and outdoor equipment used to service the dwelling, its grounds, or other structures.

A special limit of insurance ($1,000) applies to outdoor radio antennas, TV antennas, and satellite dishes attached to a covered dwelling unless a higher limit is listed in the Declarations. This limit is not in addition to the Coverage A limits.

Coverage B - Other Private Structures – *Coverage B - Other Private Structures* is similar to homeowners coverage. However, Coverage B does not include coverage for any detached structure used primarily for farming purposes. Coverage B provides a special limitation of $1,000 for loss to satellite dishes or antennas. The policy provides an automatic limit of 10% of Coverage A as an additional limit of insurance for other private structures.

Coverage C - Household Personal Property – *Coverage C - Household Personal Property* applies to personal property owned by an insured when the property is located on the covered premises. The following special limits of insurance for Coverage C include:

- $200 for money, gold, silver, and platinum;
- $1,500 for securities, letters of credit, manuscripts, and passports;
- $1,500 for watercraft and their equipment, outboard engines, furnishings, and trailers;
- $1,500 for trailers not used for farming operations or watercraft;
- $2,500 for business property located on the insured premises;
- $500 for business property located away from the insured premises;
- In the event of loss by theft:
    - $2,500 for jewelry, furs, precious and semiprecious stones, and watches

- o $2,500 for silverware, goldware, platinum ware, and pewterware
- o $3,000 for firearms and related equipment;
- $1,500 for electronic equipment and accessories in or on a motor vehicle only if equipped to be operated from the vehicle's electrical system and other power sources;
- $1,500 for electronic equipment and accessories used mainly for business operations or farming while off the insured premises and not in or on a motor vehicle.

Coverage D - Loss of Use – *Coverage D - Loss of Use* provides coverage for extra living expenses if the principal living quarters of the insured become uninhabitable. This coverage also includes the fair rental value if the dwelling the owner rents to others at the described premises becomes uninhabitable because of a loss from an insured peril.

Coverage E - Scheduled Farm Personal Property – *Coverage E - Scheduled Farm Personal Property* pays for direct physical damage to or loss of insured property. The insured property includes farm personal property covered on a scheduled basis and may consist of the following property:

- Grain and grain in stacks;
- Straw, hay, and fodder;
- Supplies, materials, and farm products;
- Livestock (excluding livestock at a stockyard or in transit);
- Fish, worms, bees, or other animals (except for the Basic or Broad Covered Causes of Loss);
- Poultry in any building designated for poultry under the Declarations or while in the open (excluding turkeys, unless specified);
- Computers used for farm management;
- Miscellaneous equipment; and
- Portable structures and buildings.

Coverage E does not provide coverage for trees, growing crops, or household personal property, and has *special limits of liability* that apply to the following:

- Straw, hay, or fodder in the open — $10,000 per stack;
- Miscellaneous farm machinery or equipment with a maximum limit of $3,000 per item;
- Poultry with a market value; and
- Livestock not specifically covered is limited to the least of ACV — 120% of the amount obtained by dividing the limit of insurance on the type and class of animal by the number of heads of that kind of animal owned at the time of loss, or $2,000. Each head of cattle, mule, or horse one year of age will be counted as 1/2 head when the loss occurs.

Coverage F - Unscheduled Farm Personal Property – Under *Coverage F - Unscheduled Farm Personal Property*, a single limit of liability applies to all farm personal property on the insured premises unless specifically excluded. Off-premises coverage is provided for ground feed, grain, and other items while being processed, stored, or in the custody of a common carrier. Farm machinery, equipment, and livestock can also be covered off-premises. Excluded properties from this definition include automobiles, crops, racehorses, and household property.

Coverage F is subject to an 80% coinsurance clause to discourage underinsurance. This clause has a provision to provide for an insufficient amount of insurance carried due to the replacement or purchase of additional equipment. In the event of damage or loss to the replacement or additional equipment within 30 days of purchase, up to $75,000 of the replacement equipment value and $100,000 of the new equipment value will not be used to determine the required limit of insurance.

Coverage G - Other Farm Structures – *Coverage G - Barns, Outbuildings, and Other Farm Structures* will protect farming structures such as:

- Silos, farm structures, portable structures, or buildings;
- Fences (other than the field and pasture fences), pens, corrals, chutes, and feed racks;
- Outdoor television and radio equipment, towers, antennas, and masts; and
- Building supplies, materials, betterments, and improvements.

Coverage is subject to an 80% coinsurance clause.

Farm Liability Coverage Form

The *farm liability* coverage form is identical to the commercial general liability form. Coverages H, I, and J protect against bodily injury and property damage, personal and advertising injury, and medical payments.

Coverage H - Bodily Injury and Property Damage Liability – *Coverage H - Bodily Injury and Property Damage Liability* covers bodily injury and property damage claims from liability arising out of personal acts of the insured and the farming business. Although it protects the farming business, it excludes coverage for businesses other than farming. It contains the business pursuits and professional services exclusions similar to personal liability coverage.

Coverage I - Personal and Advertising Injury Liability – *Coverage I - Personal and Advertising Injury Liability* is similar to the coverage provided in the general liability coverage form. However, advertising injury is covered only if the offense is committed when advertising the insured's farm-related products, goods, or services.

Exclusions under this coverage include breach of contract, intentional acts, contractual liability, failure of goods to perform, and any offense committed by an insured in the business of broadcasting. The personal injury coverage is similar to the coverage provided in the general liability coverage form.

Coverage J - Medical Payments – *Coverage J - Medical Payments* agrees to pay reasonable medical expenses resulting from an accident, regardless of fault, if the expenses are incurred and reported to the insurance provider within three years of the accident date. Coverage applies only to an individual who is not an insured. This means that farm workers are excluded from this coverage. However, resident workers are included.

Chapter Review

This chapter explained the commercial package policy and its multiple coverage parts, exclusions, and limitations. Let's review them:

COMMERCIAL PACKAGE POLICY (CPP)	
Policy Types	• Packaged (single contract) or monoline (separate single coverages)
Coverage Parts	• General Liability • Commercial Property • Inland Marine • Commercial Auto • Equipment Breakdown (also known as boiler and machinery) • Crime • Farm

	COMMERCIAL PACKAGE POLICY (CPP) *(Continued)*
Modular Parts	- Policy coverage
- Common policy declarations and conditions
- Interline endorsements (endorsements that apply to more than one coverage part to eliminate redundancy)
- Line(s) of insurance declarations page(s) and coverage form(s) and conditions
- Causes of loss forms
- Endorsements
Common Policy Conditions	- *Cancellation* - the first named insured can cancel a policy with written notice
- *Changes* - term changes have to be made by endorsement
- *Examination of books and records* - insurers can audit an insured's records and books for a period of three years after the end of policy
- *Inspection and surveys* - insurance provider may make surveys, inspections, reports, and recommendations
- *Premiums* - the first named insured is responsible for making premium payments
- *Transfer of rights and duties* - a policy owner's rights and duties may be transferred to another with written consent
Common Policy Declarations	- Lists who, what, where, when, and how much coverage exists
- Policies take effect at 12:01 a.m. at the mailing address of the insured
	COMMERCIAL PROPERTY
Coverage Forms	- *Building and Personal Property* - covers buildings, business personal property, and the property of others
- Direct damage form
- Basic, broad, and special causes of loss forms
- *Condominiums* - association and commercial unit-owners forms
- *Builders Risk* - covers buildings under construction
- *Business Income and Extra Expense* - combined or separate coverage for losses
Common Conditions	- *Concealment, misrepresentation, or fraud coverage* - coverage will be voided in the event the policyholder committed fraud at any time as it relates to the policy
- *Control of property* - this condition states that any act or negligence by individuals not under the direction of the policyholder will not void coverage
- *Insurance under two or more coverages* - if more than one coverage under the policy can respond to the same loss, the insurance provider will pay no more than the actual loss
- *Legal action against the insurer* - no individual can bring legal action against the insurance provider until all policy terms have been complied with, and then only if the legal action is brought within 24 months of the loss
- *Liberalization* - if the insurer adopts any provisions that expand coverage during the policy period or within 45 days before the effective date, the expanded coverage is applicable without having to be endorsed on the policy
- *No benefit to bailee* - no individual who has custody of covered property, other than the policy owner, can benefit from the insurance

Common Conditions *(Continued)*	• *Other insurance* - if the insured has other insurance with identical terms, conditions, and provisions, the policy will contribute by limits; if the other insurance is different, the policy will respond on an excess basis, paying only for the amount of a loss in excess of the other insurance • *Policy period, coverage territory* - the policy territory includes the United States, its possessions/territories, and Canada • *Subrogation (transfer of rights of recovery against others)* - the policy owner must transfer any rights they have to recover damages from another person to the insurance provider after the insurer makes payment for the loss
COMMERCIAL INLAND MARINE	
Features	• Filed (standardized) or unfiled (unique exposure) with state regulatory authorities • Coverage is available on any property that is portable • Policies are called floaters because the coverage floats with the insured property anywhere in the world

Nationwide Marine Definition	• The coverage written on Inland Marine and Ocean Marine forms
	• Defines four classes of risk:
	   ○ Domestic shipments and transportation risks
	   ○ Tunnels, bridges, and other instrumentalities of transportation and communication
	   ○ Commercial property floater risks
	   ○ Personal property floater risks

COMMERCIAL GENERAL LIABILITY	

CGL Coverages	• *Coverage A – Bodily Injury and Property Damage* - Covers the bodily injury and property damage of a third party
	• *Coverage B – Personal and Advertising Injury Protection* - Covers non-physical injury (libel and slander)
	• *Coverage C – Medical Payments* - covers medical, surgical, ambulance, hospital, professional nursing, and funeral expenses of the third party
	• *Supplementary payments* - additional amounts up to the stated policy limits
	• Limits of liability:
	   ○ *Per occurrence* - maximum amount payable per occurrence or accident
	   ○ *Aggregate limit* - the most insurers will pay for losses in a policy period

Occurrence vs. Claims-Made (Coverage Triggers)	• *Occurrence* - pays for bodily injury and property damage during the policy period, even if it has ended; trigger: the date on which injury or damage occurs • *Claims-made* - pays for bodily injury and property damage reported during the policy period; BI and PD not reported are not covered; trigger: date the claim is made
Commercial General Liability Exposures	• *Premises and operations* - includes the use, maintenance, or ownership of an insured's premises; includes business operations; subject to limits and exclusions • *Contractual liability* - the insurer pays for bodily injury or property damage the insured has agreed to assume under written contractual agreement • *Product and completed operations* - includes injuries or damage occurring after the insured completed their job and left the site or relinquishes control of the product

	COMMERCIAL CRIME
Coverage Triggers	• *Discovery form* - losses occurring at any time and discovered during the policy period or extended reporting period • *Loss sustained form* - losses discovered during the policy period and an extended reporting period and must be reported within one year of cancellation
Coverages	• *Employee theft* - covers theft committed by insureds' employees; includes money, securities, and other property • *Forgery or alteration* - covers loss of money as a result of forgery on alteration of outgoing checks, drafts, or promissory notes • *Inside – theft of money and securities* - covers theft of money and securities inside premises or banking premises • *Inside – robbery or safe burglary of other property* - covers loss or damage to other property inside the premises as a result of actual or attempted robbery • *Outside* – covers loss occurring outside the premises in the care of a messenger or armored motor vehicle • *Computer fraud* - covers loss from the use of any computer to fraudulently transfer money, securities, and other property • *Funds transfer fraud* - covers loss of funds resulting from fraudulent instructions to transfer money • *Money orders and counterfeit paper currency* - covers loss resulting from acceptance of non-paid money orders or counterfeit paper currency • *Extortion – Commercial Entities* - provides payment in response to bodily threats against an insured
	FARM COVERAGE FORM
Features	• Insures property and liability exposures, and personal residential exposures of property and liability of a family living on farm premises • Written as a single package or as separate coverages (monoline)
Coverage Forms	• *Coverage A – Dwellings* is similar to Coverage A of the Homeowners program • *Coverage B – Other Private Structures* is similar to the homeowners coverage • *Coverage C – Household Personal Property* applies to personal property owned by an insured while the property is on the insured location • *Coverage D – Loss of Use* provides coverage for additional living expenses if the insured's principal living quarters become uninhabitable • *Coverage E – Scheduled Farm Personal Property* pays for direct physical loss of or damage to covered property • *Coverage F – Unscheduled Farm Personal Property*, a single limit of liability applies to all farm personal property on the insured premises unless excluded • *Coverage G – Barns, Outbuildings, Other Structures* covers farming structures • *Coverage H – Bodily Injury and Property Damage* (*Liability*) - covers bodily injury and property damage arising out of farming • *Coverage I – Personal and Advertising Injury* (*Liability*) - similar to the general liability coverage form, but advertising injury is covered only if the offense is committed while advertising the insured's farm-related products and services • *Coverage J – Medical Payments* (*Liability*) - covers medical expenses reported within three years of the accident date

CHAPTER 8: Businessowners Policy

Businesses need insurance just as much as individuals but usually require higher coverage limits. In this chapter, you will learn the businessowners policy's purpose, characteristics, and requirements for underwriting. You will also examine businessowners property and liability coverage forms in great detail, including conditions and limits for each.

- Purpose and Eligibility
- Section I – Property
- Section II – Liability
- Section III – Common Policy Conditions
- Selected Endorsements

Purpose and Eligibility

The *businessowners policy (BOP)* is a combination policy that provides several different coverages for businesses that meet the eligibility requirements. The program was established in 1976 and has been revised extensively.

The BOP is a stand-alone policy with its own forms. Like the homeowners policy, the businessowners policy delivers property and liability coverage in a single contract. Also, like the homeowners policy, there is a single premium with no itemization or division of premium charged for property or liability. The businessowners policy rules require that all buildings and personal property under one owner be covered in the same policy.

The businessowners policy is a package policy designed to meet the needs of small to medium-sized businesses. Instead of choosing the individual's coverages to be insured, the insurer offers a package of coverage, which includes property and liability coverage. The policy owner usually cannot exclude coverage automatically provided in the package.

The following are several advantages of self-contained prepackaged policies:

- Insurance providers realize expense savings and can avoid adverse risk selection;
- Underwriting and rating are simplified, which lowers the insurance provider's costs and aids agents and brokers in quoting;
- Property and liability coverage will come in one predesigned package (what this means for insureds is that there are fewer policies to manage, which reduces the risk of overlapping coverages or coverage gaps);
- The options most frequently needed by small business owners are included or available for an additional premium;
- The rates for the entire package are very favorable because the eligible types of risks typically have a lower potential for loss; and
- Broader coverage and lower premiums will result in a competition that benefits business owners.

The *premium* amount for the businessowners policy is indivisible, meaning there is no separate premium for property and liability coverage. A special package rate applies to all mandatory coverages. The final premium will depend on the limits selected, deductibles, and any optional coverages. While the BOP coverage is written with *no coinsurance* requirement, insureds are encouraged to insure to value if they want to collect the total replacement cost. *Replacement cost* is a standard valuation for BOP policies, provided the limit of insurance equals at least 80% of the covered property replacement cost. If it is less than 80%, a loss is valued at *actual cash value* (optional valuation). Some insurance providers might agree to waive insurance-to-value by endorsement.

Insurance companies cannot insure every business under a BOP even though these insureds are generally lower-risk businesses. These businesses predominantly conduct business on their premises and typically do not have extensive product or completed operations exposure. Under the businessowners policy, specific businesses that are eligible include the following:

- Office buildings;
- Residential or commercial condominiums and apartments;
- Service, processing, and mercantile establishments;
- Contractors (such as plumbers, painters, electricians, or carpenters);
- Fast-food or limited cooking restaurants; or
- Convenience stores.

All insurers issuing businessowners policies have eligibility rules. Besides general eligibility rules regarding the type of business, there are typically additional underwriting criteria imposed by insurance companies, such as income or size limitations:

- *Office buildings* up to 100,000 square feet and no more than six stories high;
- *Retail or service businesses* up to 25,000 square feet in floor space and up to $3,000,000 in annual gross sales;
- *Convenience stores with gas pumps*, no auto service or auto washing services, and no more than 50% of gross sales may come from gasoline sales; and
- *Fast-food restaurants* up to 7,500 square feet (beer and wine sales are allowed up to 25% of gross sales).

Businesses that are usually *ineligible* include the following:

- Automobile sales and servicing operations;
- Manufacturing operations;
- Bars and grills;
- Places of amusement;
- Financial institutions; and
- Self-storage facilities and certain types of contractors.

Proprietary businessowners policy programs can have different eligibility rules.

Section I – Property

Covered Property

Businessowners property coverage must be activated in the Declarations and is available for buildings, business personal property, or both. Building and personal property definitions are similar to those in the Building and Personal Property Coverage Form. A separate limit of insurance for the property of others is not used in the businessowners form as it is included in the business personal property (BPP) limit. The exact radius of 100 feet in the commercial package section applies to the BPP of the policy owner in the businessowners form.

PROPERTY COVERED

1. Business personal property, buildings, or both

PROPERTY NOT COVERED

1. Money and securities;
2. Bills, accounts, and other evidence of debt;
3. Watercraft while afloat;
4. Aircraft and vehicles;
5. Computers permanently installed in any vehicle, watercraft, or aircraft (unless being held as stock);
6. Property or contraband in the course of transportation or illegal trade;
7. Lawns, crops, water, or land;
8. Plants and shrubs, trees, detached signs, satellite dishes, radio and television antennas, outdoor fences;
9. Electronic data, except as covered under the Electronic Data additional coverage and except for the policy owner's stock of prepackaged software; or
10. Animals (unless owned by others and boarded with the policy owner).

Causes of Loss, Limitations and Exclusions

The Businessowners Property Coverage Form insures risks of direct physical loss to covered property, contingent upon certain limitations and exclusions.

This form contains several limitations in coverage, so the policy will not pay for loss or damage to the following:

- Hot water boilers and other water heating equipment for occurrences inside the equipment, not including an explosion;
- Hot water boilers, steam pipes, steam boilers, or other water heating equipment caused by any condition inside the equipment; however, loss to the equipment caused by an explosion of fuel or gases in the device is covered;
- Missing property with no physical evidence to demonstrate what happened to the property or if only an inventory shortage is detected (mysterious disappearance);
- Property transferred to a place or person outside the premises listed in the Declarations based on unauthorized instructions;
- Loss to the interior of any structure or building caused by dust, sand, ice, sleet, snow, or rain unless the outside of the structure or building is damaged first. Coverage also applies if the loss results from the melting of sleet, ice, or snow on the structure or building;
- Restrictions on coverage for porcelain, marble, glassware, and animals unless loss or damage is caused by a list of named perils known as specified causes of loss. These perils are described in the Definitions section of the property portion of the policy and include water damage, sleet, ice, the weight of snow, falling objects, volcanic action, sinkhole collapse, sprinkler leakage, vandalism, riot or civil commotion, aircraft or vehicles, smoke, windstorm or hail, explosion, lightning, fire; or
- Special limits of liability exist for losses resulting from theft. The $2,500 sublimit applies to dies, molds, patterns, precious stones, gold, silver, platinum, watches, furs, and jewelry. Watches and jewelry worth $100 or less are not subject to the limitation.

The *exclusions* in the businessowners property coverage are similar to those previously discussed:

- Earth movement;
- Ordinance or law;
- Governmental action;
- Utility service (power failure);
- Nuclear hazard;
- War and military action;
- Water (waterborne material, mudflow, waves, and flood);
- Certain computer-related losses (malfunction, failure, or inadequacy of software, hardware, networks, etc.);
- Virus or bacteria;
- Wet rot, dry rot, and fungi except as covered in the additional coverage for wet or dry rot and fungi;
- Electrical apparatus (artificially generated electrical current);
- Consequential losses (delay, loss of market, or loss of use);
- Smoke, gas, vapor (smoke from industrial operations or agricultural smudging);
- Explosion of a steam apparatus;
- Frozen plumbing;
- Dishonesty;
- False pretense (voluntarily parting with the property if induced by device, scheme, or trick);

- Collapse (except as specified in the additional coverage);
- Exposed property damaged by sleet, ice, snow, or rain;
- Neglect;
- Pollution;
- Expected losses (gradual deterioration, wear and tear, mechanical breakdown, etc.);
- Errors or omissions;
- Electrical disturbance;
- Installation, testing, repair;
- Constant or continual seepage or leakage of water;
- Weather conditions that only contribute to an otherwise excluded cause of loss;
- Negligent work;
- Decisions or acts, including failure to decide or act;
- Loss or damage to products caused by an error or omission;
- Business income and additional expense resulting from delays or cancellation of a lease; and
- Accounts receivable – Loss or damage resulting from bookkeeping, accounting, or billing errors or omission; and falsification, alteration, destruction, or concealment of records of accounts receivable done to conceal the wrongful taking, giving, or withholding of money, securities, or other property.

Additional Coverages

The businessowners property coverage includes several *additional coverages* explained below. Be sure to pay close attention to the numbers associated with each coverage:

Debris removal: 25% / 180 days / $10,000 — Up to 25% of the direct loss is covered, plus the deductible if reported within the end of the policy period or 180 days of the loss, whichever is earlier. If the direct loss and debris removal amounts exceed the limit of insurance, or if the debris removal cost exceeds the 25% limitation, the policy will pay an additional $10,000 under the coverage for debris removal.

Preservation of property: 30 days — Commonly called removal coverage, this coverage provides 30 days of coverage for property that is removed temporarily to protect it from damage.

Fire department service charge: $2,500 — The limit of $2,500 is included as an additional amount of coverage unless a different limit is shown in the Declarations.

Collapse — The collapse of a building is covered if it is caused by one of the specified causes of loss. These include the weight of people or property, insects or vermin, hidden decay, or the use of defective materials if the collapse happens during construction. This additional coverage is provided only in the special form.

Water damage, other liquids, powder, or molten material damage — If damage or loss results from any of these causes of loss, the insurer will pay to tear out and replace any part of the structure or building. It will also repair the appliance or system from which the water or other substance leaked. This additional coverage is provided only in the special form.

Business income: Actual loss sustained / 12 months / Ordinary payroll / 60 days / 72-hour waiting period — Loss of business income is covered during the restoration period following a direct loss to covered property. Coverage is limited to one year following the loss of business income and 60 days following the immediate loss of ordinary payroll. The limit of insurance does not apply to this additional coverage.

Extended business income: 30 days — The policy will pay for the necessary postponement of business operations from the time property is rebuilt, repaired or replaced, and operations are resumed to the date operations are re-established to the level that would have existed without the loss, or 30 days after the property is rebuilt, repaired, or replaced, and operations are resumed, whichever is earlier.

Extra expense: Actual loss sustained / 12 months / No waiting period — Extra expense coverage in the businessowners policy is provided for up to 12 months after a direct loss to covered property. The limit of insurance does not apply to this additional coverage.

Pollutant cleanup and removal: $10,000 / 12 months / 180 days — The policy will cover up to $10,000 for expenses incurred in 12 months. These expenses are to remove pollutants from water or land at the described premises if the pollution is caused by a covered cause of loss and is reported to the insurance provider within 180 days. This coverage is an additional amount of insurance. This coverage does not apply to the cost of testing for the existence or effects of pollutants.

Civil authority: 72 hours / 4 weeks — Loss of business income or extra expense caused by an act of civil authority is also covered. This act must prevent access to the premises due to a direct loss elsewhere. Coverage for business income will start 72 hours after the action and continues for up to four consecutive weeks.

Money orders and counterfeit paper currency: $1,000 — The policy also will cover up to $1,000 for losses that result from the good faith acceptance of unpaid money orders or counterfeit currency. The limitation for money and securities does not apply to this coverage.

Forgery and alteration — Up to $2,500 for losses resulting from forged or altered checks or drafts is also covered, including defense coverage.

Increased cost of construction: $10,000 — Structures or buildings insured on a replacement cost basis are covered for increased costs incurred to comply with a law or ordinance. The enforcement of such regulations must occur while repairing, rebuilding, or replacing damaged parts of the property if the damage resulted from a covered cause of loss. This coverage is not subject to the law or ordinance exclusion and is subject to a $10,000 sublimit.

Glass expenses — The policy will pay for expenses incurred to install temporary plates or board-up openings in the damaged glass. It will also cover the cost of replacing or removing obstructions when repairing or replacing glass that is not part of a building.

Business income from dependent properties: $5,000 — Loss of business income due to physical damage or loss at the premises of a dependent property resulting from a covered cause of loss is covered up to a limit of $5,000. This coverage does not apply to loss or damage to electronic data.

Fire extinguisher systems recharge expense: $5,000 — The policy will cover up to $5,000 for replacing or recharging fire extinguishers if discharged on or within 100 feet of the premises. Loss from an accidental discharge of chemicals from extinguishers is also covered.

Electronic data: $10,000 — The policy will pay up to $10,000 (or more if a higher limit is listed in the Declarations) for the cost to restore or replace electronic data damaged by a covered cause of loss. Losses are valued at the replacement cost of the media on which the data is stored. Viruses are a covered cause of loss for this particular coverage.

Interruption of computer operations: $10,000 — The coverage provided under business income and extra expense may be broadened to apply to the suspension of business resulting from an interruption in computer operations due to damage of electronic data caused by a covered cause of loss, including a computer virus. The policy will pay up to $10,000 for this coverage unless a higher limit is indicated in the Declarations.

Limited coverage for wet rot, dry rot, and fungi: $15,000 — The policy will cover up to $15,000 for loss or damage by wet rot, dry rot, or fungi. The loss must result from a specified cause of loss other than lightning or fire.

Coverage Extensions

Coverage can be broadened from the business personal property or building coverage section when the applicable limit of insurance is specified on the declarations page. The policy contains several coverage extensions that are in addition to the limit of insurance:

Newly acquired or constructed property: $250,000 for buildings / $100,000 for BPP — The policy owner may extend coverage up to $250,000 to buildings being built on the premises and buildings acquired at a new location. Up to $100,000 is available for newly obtained business personal property. Coverage will only apply for 30 days after the policy owner acquires the property or the end of the policy period, whichever comes first.

Personal property off premises: $10,000 — Coverage up to $10,000 is available for business personal property. This coverage does not include securities and money during transportation or temporarily at the premises the policy owner does not operate, lease, use, or own.

Outdoor property: $2,500 total / $1,000 per tree, shrub, or plant — The policyholder may extend the coverage to apply to detached signs and trees, outdoor radio and television antennas, shrubs, and plants if the loss results from an explosion, lightning, fire, riot or civil commotion, or aircraft. The insurance provider will pay up to $2,500 for this coverage extension but not more than $1,000 for any shrub, plant, or tree.

Personal effects: $2,500 — Business personal property coverage may be broadened to apply to personal belongings owned by the policy owner, officers, partners, and employees. The insurance provider will pay up to $2,500 at each described premises.

Valuable papers and records: $10,000 on-premises / $5,000 off-premises — Coverage up to $10,000 is available for the cost to research, restore, or replace lost information for which copies are not available on the premises. It will also cover $5,000 for valuable papers and records not at the described premises. Insurers will value losses at the cost of replacement or restoration.

Accounts receivable: $10,000 on-premises / $5,000 off-premises — The policyholder may extend business personal property coverage to apply to *accounts receivable*. The policy will pay the following:

- All amounts due from the policy owner's customers that the policy owner is unable to collect;
- Interest charges on any loan required to offset uncollectible amounts pending the insurance provider's payment of these amounts;
- Collections expenses exceeding standard collection costs that are made necessary by damage or loss; and
- Other reasonable expenses that the policy owner incurs to restore records of account receivables. Such expenses result from direct physical damage or loss by a covered cause of loss to the policy owner's accounts receivable records.

The most the policy will cover under this extension for damage or loss in any one occurrence is $10,000 unless a higher limit of insurance for accounts receivable is described in the Declarations. For accounts receivable that are not at the indicated premises, the most the extension will pay is $5,000.

Limits of Insurance

The policy will cover up to the *limits of insurance* shown in the Declarations. The following specific limits apply:

- In any one occurrence, outdoor signs attached to the building are covered for $1,000 per sign;
- The following additional coverage extensions are paid in addition to the limits of insurance:
    - Pollutant cleanup and removal;
    - Fire department service charge;
    - Business income from dependent properties;
    - Increased cost of construction;
    - Interruption of computer operations; and
    - Electronic data.

The Business Property Coverage Form includes two provisions that pertain to automatic coverage increases:

1. **Building Limit (Automatic Increase)** — The building's limit of insurance will automatically increase annually by *8%* or the percentage amount listed in the Declarations; and
2. **Business Personal Property Limit (Seasonal Increase)** — The business personal property limit will automatically increase by *25%* for seasonal fluctuations unless stated in the Declarations. This increase is only applicable if the policyholder carries insurance equal to 100% of the average monthly values for the past 12 months.

Deductibles

The most the insurance provider will pay for any loss is the limit of insurance after the policy owner pays the deductible. The deductible *does not apply* to any of the following:

- Fire extinguisher systems recharge expense;
- Fire department service charge;
- Extra expense;
- Business income;
- Optional coverage selections; or
- Civil authority coverages.

Property Loss and General Conditions

The following *conditions* found in the Business Property Coverage Form apply in addition to the common policy conditions:

- **Appraisal**;
- **Abandonment**;
- **Duties in the event of loss or damage** — The following are the policy owner's duties in the event of loss or damage:
    - Inform the police if a law has been broken;
    - Give the insurance provider prompt notice of loss and a description of when, how, and where it took place, including a description of damaged property;
    - Take all reasonable steps to protect covered property from additional damage and keep a record of every expense;
    - Provide an inventory of the damaged and undamaged property at the insurer's request;
    - Allow the insurer to examine the property and inspect the insured's records and books;

- o Send the insurance provider a signed, sworn proof of loss within 60 days of the request;
- o Cooperate with the insurance provider in the investigation and settlement;
- o Resume business operations as soon as possible; and
- o The insurance provider has a right to examine any policyholder under oath;
- **Legal action against the insurer** — The policy owner must be in full compliance with all policy provisions before bringing legal action against the insurer, and the action must be brought within 24 months of the date of loss;
- **Loss payment** — In the event of damage or loss, the insurance company has the option to do the following:
    - o Pay the value of the damaged or lost property;
    - o Pay the cost to replace or repair the damaged or lost property;
    - o Take all or any part of the damaged or lost property at an appraised or agreed upon price;
    - o Replace, rebuild, or repair the damaged or lost property with like kind and quality;
    - o The insurer will provide notice of intentions within 30 days of receiving the sworn proof of loss;
    - o At the time of the loss, the policy will pay on a replacement cost basis if the property is insured for 80% or more of the full replacement value;
    - o The policy will pay the greater of ACV or the coinsurance formula if the property is not insured to 80% of the full replacement value; and
    - o Replacement cost payment will not occur until all repairs are made in a timely fashion. The policy owner can choose to settle the loss on an ACV basis. If the cost to replace or repair is less than $2,500, then the insurance company will not require replacement or repair of the property;
- **Recovered property** — If the property is recovered after loss settlement, the policy owner may either keep the property and return any loss settlement payment or surrender the property to the insurance provider;
- **Resumption of operations** — The insurer will decrease the amount of business income and extra expense losses to the extent the policyholder can resume operations by using damaged and undamaged property;
- **Vacancy** — If a building is vacant for more than 60 consecutive days, insurers will not cover losses caused by the following: theft or attempted theft, vandalism, building glass breakage, sprinkler leakage (unless the insured takes protective measures), and water damage. Insurers will cover losses in a building unoccupied for more than 60 days caused by any other covered perils for an amount that is 15% less than normal coverage under the policy. It is worth noting that buildings under renovation or construction are not considered unoccupied. When a policy is issued to a tenant, a vacancy occurs when the building does not contain sufficient business personal property to conduct normal operations. When the policy is issued to the general lessee or owner of a building, a vacancy occurs when at least 65% of the square footage is not rented or is unused.

General Conditions

The *four general conditions* in *Section I – Property* of the businessowners policy include:

1. **Control of property** — Any act of neglect of any person other than the policy owner beyond the policy owner's control or direction will not affect this coverage. The breach of any condition of this insurance form at any location will not affect coverage where the breach of condition does not exist at the time of loss or damage.
2. **Mortgage holders** — Protection for a mortgage holder exists in the policy as long as the mortgage holder meets certain conditions. We covered these conditions earlier, so be sure to review them.
3. **No benefit to bailee** — No organization or person (other than the policy owner) having custody of covered property will benefit from this coverage.

4. **Policy period, coverage territory** — The insurance provider will cover damages or losses during the policy period and within the coverage territory. Insurers will also cover property in transit between ports in the coverage territory. The U.S. (including its territories and possessions), Puerto Rico, and Canada are included in the coverage territory.

Optional Coverages

The businessowners property coverage form has several optional coverages built into it. For coverage to apply, a policy must indicate a limit and premium on the declarations page. The optional coverages include the following:

- **Outdoor signs** — All outdoor signs owned or in the policy owner's control, custody, or care can be insured. The signs are usually insured on an open peril basis for an amount of coverage specified in the Declarations. Common exclusions include mechanical breakdown, corrosion, rust, hidden or latent defects, and wear and tear. Without additional coverage, the businessowners policy will pay $1,000 per sign in any one occurrence for loss or damage to outdoor signs *affixed to the building*. However, this additional coverage allows the policy owner to purchase more insurance for outdoor signs.
- **Money and securities** — Loss of money and securities resulting from destruction, disappearance, or theft can be covered. The policy owner must maintain records of the money and securities so that the insurance provider can verify the amount of loss or damage. For coverage to apply, the money or securities must have been located at a financial institution, the insured premises, the policy owner's or employee's home, or in transit from one of these locations. Separate limits are specified for losses inside and outside the premises.
- **Employee dishonesty** — Loss to money and securities or business personal property caused by dishonest acts of employees is covered. Under this additional coverage, employees refer to anyone currently employed or terminated within the past *30 days*. Acts committed by the policyholder or partners are excluded. The policy Declarations will indicate the applicable limit of insurance. In addition, coverage on any employee automatically ends once the policyholder learns of previous acts of dishonesty.
- **Equipment breakdown protection** — This additional coverage protects against a direct loss or damage to covered property, including mechanical or electrical equipment and machinery, resulting from a mechanical breakdown or electrical failure to pressure.

Definitions

Definitions found in the BOP coverage form include, but are not limited to, the following:

- *Money* means currency, bank notes, coins, and traveler's checks or money orders held for sale;
- *Period of restoration* for business income coverage will start immediately for extra expense coverage or 72 hours after the direct loss. The period of restoration ends on the date business has resumed or the property has been repaired;
- *Pollutants* include any thermal, gaseous, liquid, or solid contaminant or irritant;
- *Specified causes of loss* refers to water damage, snow or sleet, the weight of ice, falling objects, volcanic action, sinkhole collapse, leakage from fire-extinguishing equipment, vandalism, riot or civil commotion, aircraft or vehicles, smoke, windstorm or hail, explosion, lightning, and fire; and
- *Valuable papers and records* inscribed, manuscripts, written or printed documents, and records (including mortgages, deeds, maps, films, drawings, books, or abstracts). Money or securities are included in the term valuable papers and records.

Section II – Liability

Coverages

Business liability – The liability coverage contained in the BOP is written on a businessowners liability coverage form. This section is included in every policy and cannot be written on a monoline basis. It applies to all operations and premises owned or operated by the insured. The BOP liability form has the following features:

- Usually issued with an occurrence coverage trigger;
- Supplemental payment features are covered in addition to the limit of insurance in the Declarations;
- Includes coverage for property damage, bodily injury, and personal and advertising injury for an occurrence within the coverage territory and coverage period;
- The limit of liability is the most the insurance company will pay contingent upon an aggregate amount for the policy term; and
- The insurer's responsibility to defend terminates when the limits of insurance are depleted.

Medical expenses – Medical payments coverage will pay for hospital, medical, dental, and funeral services sustained within *one year* from the date of an accident. It covers an individual who suffers bodily injury from an accident on or near the policy owner's premises or because of the policy owner's operations.

Exclusions

The business liability and medical payments coverages contain the following *exclusions*:

- **Expected or intended injury** — This exclusion does not apply to bodily injury that is caused by the use of reasonable force to protect the property or an individual;
- **Contractual liability** — This exclusion does not apply to the insured contracts;
- **Liquor liability** — There is no coverage for liability arising out of the following: causing or contributing to a person's intoxication, providing alcohol to a minor or a person who is already intoxicated, or any ordinance or regulation relating to the distribution, sale, or gift of alcoholic beverages. This exclusion applies only to policy owners involved in any business that manufactures, distributes, sells, serves, or furnishes alcohol (host liquor);
- **Workers compensation and similar laws** — There is no coverage for any duty the policy owner has under workers compensation or similar laws;
- **Employer's liability** — Bodily injury to an employee during employment, including the employee's spouse, children, or siblings, is not covered. Any liability assumed under an insured contract does not apply to this exclusion;
- **Pollution** — Property damage or bodily injury resulting from alleged or actual pollution is excluded. The exclusion does not apply to fumes, smoke, or heat from a hostile fire;
- **Aircraft, auto, or watercraft** — Property damage or bodily injury resulting from the use, maintenance, ownership, or entrustment to others of any auto, aircraft, or watercraft is not covered. This exclusion does not apply to the following perils and property that insurers will cover:
    - Watercraft while on shore at the premises owned by the policy owner;
    - Non-owned watercraft *less than 51 feet long* and not being used to transport property or individuals for a fee;
    - Parking an auto on or next to the premises rented or owned by the policy owner. The auto cannot be rented, owned, or loaned to the policyholder;
    - Liability assumed under an insured contract;

- o If not subject to a compulsory or financial responsibility law, property damage or bodily injury arising out of the operation of equipment or machinery attached to or part of a vehicle that meets the definition of mobile equipment; and
- o Property damage or bodily injury that results from the operation of a cherry picker or similar equipment mounted on trucks, pumps, air compressors, and generators.
- **Mobile equipment** — The transportation of mobile equipment by an auto or the use of mobile equipment in any speed, demolition, or racing contest is not covered;
- **War** — War, including undeclared civil war, insurrections, warlike actions, revolutions, rebellions, or actions taken by government authority are not covered;
- **Professional services** — There is no coverage for property damage, bodily injury, or personal or advertising injury due to the rendering or failure to render professional services described in the exclusion;
- **Property damage to property the policy owner owns or is in their control, custody, or care**;
- **Damage to the policy owner's product or work**;
- **Damage to tangible property or property not physically injured**;
- **Recall of work, products, or tangible property**;
- **Personal and advertising injury exclusions** — These are the same as the exclusions discussed in the CGL coverage form;
- **Electronic data** — Damages arising out of damage to electronic data or its loss of use are not covered;
- **Criminal acts of the policy owner**;
- **Recording and distribution of information which violates the law** — Property damage, bodily injury, or personal and advertising injury caused by a violation of laws such as the CAN-SPAM Act, the Telephone Consumer Protection Act, the FCRA, and any federal, state, or local regulation, ordinance, or statute is not covered;
- **Medical expense exclusions** — These are the same exclusions previously discussed for medical payments in the CGL coverage form; and
- **Nuclear energy liability exclusion** — This applies to all liability coverages.

Who is an Insured

When the named insured is listed on the declarations page as *an individual or sole proprietor*, that individual and their spouse are insureds, but only regarding the business.

When the named insured is specified as a *partnership or joint venture*, the named insured, their spouse, and partners also are insureds, but only concerning the business.

When the named insured is listed as a *limited liability company (LLC)*, the named insured and members are also insureds, but only regarding the conduct of the business. Managers are also insureds, but only regarding their duties as managers.

The named insured and trustees are covered when the insured is designated as *a trust*.

When the named insured is listed as an organization other than a joint venture, partnership (corporations), or LLC, the named insured is covered. Directors and executive officers are insureds, but only concerning their duties as directors and officers. Stockholders are also insureds, but only regarding their liability as stockholders.

Each of the following can also be considered an insured:

- A volunteer while executing the duties related to the insured business or its employees;
- An employee during employment;

- Any individual (other than a volunteer or employee) of any organization acting as the policy owner's real estate manager;
- Any organization or individual having temporary custody of the property if the named insured dies; and
- The legal representative if the named insured dies, but only regarding their obligations as such.

No organization or person is considered an insured regarding the conduct of any past or current partnership, joint venture, or LLC that is not listed as a named insured on the declarations page.

Limits of Insurance

The amount of insurance listed in the Declarations is the most the policy will cover regardless of the number of insureds, organizations, individuals bringing suit, or claims filed or lawsuits brought.

Medical expenses are paid per person and are also contingent upon the limit in the Declarations.

Similar *aggregate limits* exist in the businessowners policy as in the CGL policy. The policy includes an aggregate for completed operations exposures and products, which is double the occurrence limit. Another aggregate similar to the general aggregate in the CGL policy applies to all property damage, bodily injury, personal and advertising injury, and medical expense claims not associated with completed operations or products. This aggregate is also double the occurrence limit shown in the Declarations.

In addition, the policy includes a *separate limit* of insurance for fire damage liability which can be incorporated in aggregate based on the nature of the claim.

The limits of insurance under the liability section apply separately to every successive yearly period and any remaining period of less than one year, beginning with the start of the policy period listed on the declarations page.

General Conditions

In addition to the common policy conditions, the following conditions apply to the liability coverage:

- **Bankruptcy** — Insolvency or bankruptcy of the policyholder does not relieve the insurer of any obligation.
- **Duties in the event of an occurrence, claim, or suit** — In the event of a loss, the policyholder's responsibilities include the following:
    o Promptly informing the insurance provider of the occurrence (when, how, where, names, and addresses of any injured individuals);
    o Prompt written notice of a claim;
    o Promptly informing the insurance provider of any legal papers received related to the loss; and
    o Assisting and cooperating in the investigation of a claim.
- **Legal action against the insurance provider** — No party can join or bring the insurer into legal action against the policy owner. Also, no party can sue the insurer unless full compliance with policy terms exists. A party can sue the insurer to recover an agreed-upon settlement; however, the payment cannot surpass the policy limits nor include items not insured by the policy.
- **Separation of insured** — The limit of insurance is only paid once per occurrence, irrespective of the number of insureds or the number of claimants covered by the policy.

Definitions

The Definitions section of the business liability coverage form contains definitions of personal and advertising injury, bodily injury, coverage territory, mobile equipment, products/completed operations hazard, and other terms related to liability and medical expenses forms. The definitions are similar to other policies you have previously studied. However, some definitions are unique to businessowners liability coverage and essential to know for your exam.

Insured product – *Insured product* refers to any good or product (besides real property) manufactured, handled, sold, distributed, or disposed of by the insured, others trading under the insured's name, or an individual or organization whose business or assets the insured has acquired. It also includes containers, parts, materials, or equipment furnished in connection with the insured's goods or products.

Insured contract – An *insured contract* means any of the following:

- A contract for a lease of premises (except for the portion of the contract that indemnifies any individual for damage by fire to premises while rented to or temporarily occupied by the insured);
- A sidetrack agreement;
- An easement or license agreement (except in relation to demolition or construction on or within 50 feet of a railroad);
- An obligation, as required by ordinance, to indemnify a municipality, except in
- connection with work for a municipality;
- An elevator maintenance agreement; or
- Part of a contract on the insured business under which the insured assumes the tort liability of another party to cover bodily injury or property damage to a third person. Tort liability is a liability imposed by law in the absence of any agreement or contract.

Section III – Common Policy Conditions

The businessowners policy contains the *common policy conditions* applicable to *Section I – Property* and *Section II – Liability*, in addition to the conditions included in those separate coverage sections. These conditions are similar to the previously discussed commercial property conditions, commercial liability conditions, and common policy conditions. The businessowners common policy conditions are listed below:

Cancellation — The policy owner can cancel the policy at any time by mailing a written notice to the insurer. Only the first named insured may request the cancellation in a policy listing two or more insureds in the Declarations. The insurance provider can cancel the policy by mailing the first named insured a written notice of cancellation.

The insurer requires advance written notice of policy cancellation so the policy owner can obtain other insurance. Additional requirements for *notice by mail* include the following:

- Delivered or mailed to the policy owner *five days* before the date of cancellation, provided that any of the following conditions exist at the insured building:
    o The building is vacant for 60 or more consecutive days (buildings with 65% or more of the floor area or rental units vacant are considered unoccupied);
    o Permanent repairs for damage caused by a covered loss have not been arranged for within 30 days of the initial payment of loss;
    o The building has a demolition order, outstanding order to vacate, or has been declared unsafe by a government authority;
    o Salvageable and fixed items have been removed from the building and are not being replaced;

- The policy owner fails to furnish necessary utilities (water, heat, sewer) for 30 or more consecutive days (except during seasonal vacancy); or
- The policy owner fails to pay property taxes owed or outstanding for more than one year;
- Must be delivered or mailed to the policy owner *ten days before* the date of cancellation if nonpayment of premium is the reason for cancellation;
- Must be delivered or mailed to the policy owner *30 days before* the date of cancellation for any other reason (may vary by state);
- The insurer only has to verify that the notice was mailed to the first named insured at the mailing address on file with the insurance provider, not that the notice was actually delivered; and
- When cancellation results in a return of premium, the refund is forwarded to the first named insured.

Changes — This condition states that the policy makes up the entire contract between the policy owner and the insurer. The policy can be revised only by a written request from the first named insured and with approval from the insurer.

Concealment, misrepresentation, or fraud — The policy will be voided if any policy owner commits fraud relating to the policy or intentionally misrepresents or conceals a material fact regarding the policy, covered property, the policy owner's interest in the covered property, or a claim under the policy.

Examination of books and records — The insurer can audit and examine the policy owner's records and books at any reasonable time during the policy period. Such audits can occur up to *three years* after a policy is no longer in force.

Inspections and surveys — The insurer has the right to inspect the policyholder's premises and operations at any time during the policy period. These inspections aim to determine the insurability of the property and operations, set proper insurance premiums, and make loss control recommendations. Such inspections do not guarantee that the property or operations are safe and in compliance with state laws.

Insurance under multiple coverages — If two or more coverages in the policy apply to the same loss, the insurance provider will not pay more than the actual amount of the loss.

Liberalization — If the insurer adopts any change that extends coverage without an additional premium within 45 days before or during the policy period, that coverage will immediately apply to the policy.

Other insurance — When a loss is covered by other insurance, the insurer will pay only the amount exceeding the other coverage, regardless of whether or not the policy owner can collect from the other insurance.

Premiums — The first named insured must pay the premium under the policy. In addition, if the insurance company ever gives any refund, it will be sent to the first named insured.

Premium audit — The policy is subject to an audit if a premium is designated as an advanced premium in the Declarations. The final premium due will be calculated when actual exposures are determined. The first named insured must maintain records of information necessary for premium calculation and send copies to the insurer at the insurer's request.

Subrogation (transfer of rights of recovery against others to the insurance provider) — The insurer has the right to recoup its claim payment from a negligent third party.

Transfer of rights and duties under the policy — The policy owner may not transfer any rights or duties under the policy to any other entity or individual without the insurer's written consent. Also, the policy owner's rights and duties are automatically transferred to the policy owner's legal representative upon death.

In New York, cancellation requirements for the businessowners policy are as follows:

- When the policy has been effective for 60 days or less, the insured must be given 30 days' notice before the cancellation unless it is due to nonpayment of premium. In this case, a 15-day notice is required.
- When a policy has been effective for more than 60 days, a 15-day notice must be given by the insurance provider to the first named insured.

Nonrenewal – Notice of nonrenewal must be given to the insured within 60 days of the expiration but not more than 120 days. Conditions are also set for conditional renewals with coverage amendments and premium increases exceeding certain thresholds.

Selected Endorsements

Hired Auto and Non-owned Auto Liability

The *hired and non-owned auto liability* endorsement provides coverage for liability arising from the use or maintenance of a hired or non-owned auto. These coverages are purchased separately and are scheduled on the endorsement. This endorsement can be added to the businessowners policy only if the insured does not have commercial auto insurance. This insurance is excess coverage over any primary insurance coverage on the hired or non-owned auto.

This endorsement adjusts who is considered an insured. An insured is any of the following under this endorsement:

- The named insured;
- Any other individual using a hired auto with the insured's permission;
- For a non-owned auto:
    - Any executive officer or partner of the insured; or
    - Any employee of the insured but only while the non-owned auto is being used in the insured business.

The following are expressly *excluded* from the definition of an insured:

- Any individual while employed in or otherwise engaged in duties related to an auto business (other than the insured's auto business);
- The owner or lessee of a hired auto or the owner of a non-owned auto, or any agent or employee of such owner or lessee; and
- Any individual or organization for the conduct of current or past partnerships or joint ventures that are not shown as a named insured on the declarations page.

Named Perils

The *named perils* endorsement revises coverage under the Businessowners Coverage Form. It removes the property coverage's cause of loss and limitation sections; insurers replaced them with a list of named perils. The optional coverage for money and securities is replaced with burglary and robbery coverage for business personal property and money and securities. Insurers also removed the additional coverages for water damage and collapse, other liquids, and powder or molten material damage from the form.

The *exclusions* are also revised to the following:

- Burst piping;
- Electrical apparatus;
- Water discharge;
- Mechanical breakdown;
- Steam apparatus;
- Errors from installation, testing, and repair;
- Errors or omissions;
- Electrical disturbance; and
- Continuous or repeated leakage or seepage of water.

Chapter Review

This chapter discussed the characteristics, purpose, and underwriting requirements of a businessowners policy. Let's review some of the key points:

BUSINESSOWNERS – CHARACTERISTICS AND PURPOSE	
Purpose	• For small to medium-sized businesses • A prepackaged policy that contains both property and liability coverages • Coverage is included in a package policy that cannot be excluded by the insured
Eligible Businesses	• Apartments • Office buildings • Mercantile/processing/service establishments • Contractors (certain types) • Convenience stores • Fast-food restaurants
Ineligible Businesses	• Auto sales and servicing operations • Household personal property • Manufacturing operations • Places of amusement • Bars/grills • Banks • Contractors (certain types) and self-storage facilities
SECTION I – PROPERTY	
Coverage Features	• Property covered: buildings and business personal property • Direct physical loss to covered property • Coverage limitations and exclusions - the policy will not pay for certain losses or damages (similar to the CPP) • Additional coverages (e.g., debris removal, fire department service charge, etc.) • Coverage extensions - extends policy limits

	SECTION I – PROPERTY *(Continued)*
Policy General Conditions	- *Control of property* - Any act of neglect of any individual other than the insured beyond the insured's direction or control will not affect this insurance
- *Mortgage holders* - Protection for a mortgage holder provided certain conditions are met
- *No benefit to bailee* - No person or organization (besides the insured) having custody of covered property may benefit from insurance coverage issued
- *Policy period, coverage territory* - The insurance provider will cover losses or damages commencing during the policy period listed in the declarations and within the coverage territory or, regarding property in transit, while it is between ports in the coverage territory
Optional Coverages	- *Outdoor signs* - can be insured on an open peril basis for an insurance amount specified in the Declarations
- *Money and securities* - coverage for loss of money and securities resulting from theft, disappearance, or destruction
- *Employee dishonesty* - coverage for loss to business personal property or money and securities resulting from employees' dishonest acts
- *Equipment breakdown protection* - protection for a direct loss or damage to covered property caused by an electrical failure or mechanical breakdown to pressure, mechanical or electrical machinery, and equipment
	SECTION II – LIABILITY
Features	- Similar to CGL policies
- Cannot be written on a monoline basis
- Covers bodily injury, property damage, personal injury, advertising injury, and medical expenses
- Pays for medical, dental, hospital, and funeral services on or near insured premises within one year of an accident
Exclusions	- Expected/intended injury
- Contractual liability
- Liquor liability
- Pollution
- Mobile equipment
- Professional services
- Electronic data
- War
Who is Insured	- *Individual (sole proprietor)* - named insured and spouse
- *Partnership/joint venture* - named insured, spouse, members, partners
- *Limited liability company (LLC)* - named insured, members
- *Trust* - named insured, trustees
- *Corporations* - named insured, executive officers, directors
Limits of Insurance	- An aggregate limit for product and completed operations exposures (two times occurrence limit)
- An aggregate limit for bodily injury, property damage, personal/advertising injury, and medical expenses (two times occurrence limit)
- A separate limit for fire damage legal liability

General Conditions	- *Bankruptcy* - does not relieve obligations - *Duties in the event of occurrence, claim, or suit* - insured must provide the insurer with notification of occurrence, written notice, related legal papers, cooperation with an investigation - *Legal action against the insurer* - insurers cannot bring legal action brought against an insured, nor can the insurance provider be sued without complying with policy terms - *Separation of insured* - limit paid once per occurrence
**SECTION III – COMMON POLICY CONDITIONS**
Conditions (Sections I and II)	- *Cancellation* - an insured can cancel with a written notice - *Changes* - the policy can be changed with a written request - *Concealment/misrepresentation/fraud* - policy voided if insured conceals, misrepresents, or commits fraudulent acts - *Examination of books and records* - the insurer's right to examine/audit insured's records up to three years after the policy term - *Inspections and surveys* - the insurer can inspect an insured's premises and operations to determine insurability - *Insurance under two or more coverages* - the insurer will pay the actual amount of loss if two or more policies cover the same loss - *Liberalization* - any revision broadening coverage must be applied to policy - *Other insurance* - in response to multiple coverages, the insurer pays for loss in excess of the other coverage - *Premiums* - first named insured responsible for payments - *Premium audit* - calculation of final premium due - *Subrogation* - an insurer's right to seek damages from a third party after reimbursing the insured - *Transfer of rights and duties* - an insured can transfer their rights and duties to another with a written consent

CHAPTER 9:
Workers Compensation

This chapter describes workers compensation insurance and the state and federal laws related to it. You will learn about the parts of a policy, the calculation of premiums, and selected endorsements. You will also learn about alternative sources of workers compensation insurance available in the state.

- Workers Compensation Laws
- Workers Compensation and Employers Liability Insurance
- Volunteer Firefighters and Ambulance Workers Endorsements
- Premium Computation
- Other Sources of Coverage
- New York State Disability Benefits Law
- Paid Family Leave

Workers Compensation Laws

Types of Laws

Monopolistic vs. Competitive – In some states, employers must purchase workers compensation insurance from an entity operated by the state. These are called *monopolistic state funds*. Private insurers may not write workers compensation insurance in competition with these state funds.

In other states, employers purchase workers compensation from those insurance companies authorized to write casualty insurance. State regulations mandate the benefits and coverage, known as a *competitive market*.

Compulsory vs. Elective – From state to state, the workers compensation laws vary. Most states have *compulsory laws* requiring every employer to provide workers compensation coverage for anyone meeting the definition of an employee. These laws do not apply to employers that are excluded due to employment type or staff size.

The remaining few states have *elective laws*, which means the employer does not have to be subject to the state's workers compensation laws. When an employer elects not to be subject to the state's laws, it loses its common law defenses against liability suits.

New York Workers Compensation Law

Exclusive Remedy – Workers Compensation is designed to be the exclusive or sole remedy for injuries that occur during covered employment without regard to fault or negligence. Employees cannot sue their employer, but they can collect medical and work loss benefits as outlined in the workers compensation law. These codes were amended in 1996 to limit the rights of third parties to prosecute an injured plaintiff's employer for compensation or damages unless grave injuries have occurred. For example, if a piece of equipment injures an employee, the employee cannot sue the employer. Suppose the employee sues the equipment manufacturer. In that case, the manufacturer brings suit against the employer for contributing to the injury. Section 11 of the workers compensation law defines a *grave injury* as any of the following:

- Death;
- Loss of multiple fingers or toes or loss of an index finger;
- Permanent and total loss of use or amputation of a leg, arm, foot, or hand;
- Paraplegia or quadriplegia;
- Total and permanent blindness or deafness;
- Loss of nose or ear;
- Permanent and severe facial disfigurement; and
- An acquired injury to the brain caused by an external physical force causing permanent total disability.

Employment Covered – Nearly all employers are required to provide workers compensation benefits, with some exceptions. Employers *must cover* the following employees:

- Employees engaged in a business, trade, or occupation carried on by the employer for profit, including lease employees, borrowed employees, family members, and volunteer workers;
- Employees of counties and municipalities engaged in work defined as hazardous;
- Public school teachers, excluding those employed by New York City and public-school aides;
- New York state employees;

- Domestic workers employed 40 or more hours a week by the same employer;
- Farm workers whose employer paid $1,200 or more for farm labor in the previous calendar year;
- Most workers of a nonprofit organization;
- Corporate officers depending on the number of officers, stockholders and if the entity has employees or not (provisions exist for the officers to exclude themselves in a one or two-person corporation); and
- Any other worker determined by the NY Workers Compensation Board to be an employee not explicitly excluded.

Independent and Subcontractors – Although the definition of an employee is extensive, independent contractors or subcontractors are not protected under workers compensation law if they are not employees. The employee relationship is determined based on the following factors:

- Right to control;
- The character of work of the employee is consistent with the employer's business;
- Method of payment and what an employee is required to do to obtain wages;
- Furnishing equipment and materials; and
- Right to hire and fire.

Independent contractors can be evaluated on such parameters as:

- Who controls the time and manner of work?
- Is there a separate business establishment?
- Does the contractor have a federal employer identification number?
- Is the work performed differently than the hiring business (non-construction businesses)?
- Is there a work contract?
- Does the contractor carry their own liability insurance?

The difference between *employees* and *independent contractors* is essential. Employers who classify employees as independent contractors to save workers compensation costs, may face fines and penalties.

Covered Injuries – *Injury* is only an accidental injury arising out of and during employment. The term *injury* does not apply to a solely mental injury. It is based on work-related stress if the mental injury results from a lawful personnel decision involving a work evaluation, disciplinary action, job transfer, demotion, or termination accepted in good faith by the employer.

Typically *excluded* from coverage are injuries that:

- Occur while the insured is traveling to and from work;
- Result from the employee's intoxication;
- Are intentionally caused by the employee;
- Result from a deliberate failure to follow safety precautions; and
- Occur from activities not part of the job.

Occupational Disease – An *occupational disease* is a term used to describe a disease resulting from the nature of employment and contracted while performing such work for the employer. Some occupational diseases naturally result from a specific occupation. To collect workers compensation, the employee would have to demonstrate that these diseases would not develop from ordinary life experiences. For example, someone could prove that many employees working in a particular field all developed a particular disease. Workers do not have to verify with 100% certainty that an injury was related to the job, only that it is more probable than not.

Benefits Provided – Workers compensation benefits for a *loss of wages* are paid based on the following formula:

Weekly Benefit = 2/3 x Average weekly wage x Percent of disability

No compensation will be allowed for the first *seven days of disability*, except the benefits provided by workers compensation laws. If the injury results in a disability of more than 14 days, insurers will provide compensation from the date of the disability. The weekly benefit is subject to a maximum, which is determined annually.

Medical benefits and *rehabilitation benefits* are paid for the treatment and care of injured employees. In all states, medical payments are unlimited. There are no dollar limits or time limits set out to pay for necessary medical and surgical expenses, except possibly for certain types of care. Examples of services that will be paid for include the following:

- Medical, surgical, optometric, or other treatment;
- Nurse and hospital service;
- Medicine;
- Optometric services; and
- Eyeglasses, false teeth, artificial eyes, crutches, orthotics, functional assistive and adaptive devices, and apparatus.

Death benefits for a compensable injury are payable to a surviving spouse, minor children, or other dependents as defined by law. Benefits are equal to two-thirds (2/3) of the average weekly wage for the year before the accident. Weekly benefits are subject to the weekly maximum. A lump-sum payment may be available to surviving parents or the deceased's estate if no dependents exist. *Funeral benefits* and can also be paid.

Claims Reporting Requirements – Suppose a covered employer has a workers compensation claim. In that case, the employer must maintain records of all employee injuries or illnesses incurred on the job and keep those records for *at least 18 years*.

All workplace accidents must be reported to the Workers Compensation Board and New York State Insurance Fund if:

- There is loss of time from regular duties exceeding one day beyond the workday or shift in which the accident occurred;
- Medical treatment beyond regular first aid is required; or
- More than two first aid treatments are required.

Any accident meeting the above criteria must be reported immediately. Failure to do so within ten days after the employer learns of the injury is a misdemeanor punishable by a fine.

The time element is important because it impacts the speed with which benefits are paid or determined in each case. The workers compensation law requires that the first payment of compensation is due no more than 18 days after disability starts.

The presiding officer of the Board must appoint one or more physicians to examine any claimant. When an employee's disease or death is determined as a result of silicosis or other compressed air illnesses, the employer is liable for total compensation. Additionally, any blood-borne disease contracted within 24 hours of performing the duties of a safety and security officer or treatment assistant employed by the office of mental health, court officer, reporter, clerk, or interpreter would be eligible for total compensation.

When a disease other than those previously mentioned originated from previous employment, the past employer can appeal to the Board for apportionment of compensation among several affected employees. Compensation is proportional to the time spent as an employee. If requested by the last employer or the Board, an employee or their dependents must provide a listing of all prior employers over the previous 12 months.

Within *30 days* of the final disposition or settlement of a workers compensation claim under the alternative dispute resolution system, the employer must file a completed ADR-2 form with the Workers Compensation Board.

At least once annually and as required by the chair, each employer must submit a report to the presiding officer containing the following information:

- The number of employees in the alternative dispute resolution program;
- The number of claims filed;
- The total lost wage benefits paid within the program;
- The total medical expenditures paid within the program; and
- The number of decisions made, settlements paid, and appeals taken.

In addition to the reporting requirements summarized above, all parties must promptly comply with the data collection requests of the New York State School of Industrial and Labor Relations. Workers compensation statutes require employers to meet capital reserves requirements sufficient to cover any claims that could arise. Employers can meet such requirements through competitive state funds, assigned risk, and self-insurance plans.

Federal Workers Compensation Laws

Federal Employers Liability Act (FELA) – The *Federal Employers Liability Act (FELA)* is an employers liability law rather than a workers compensation law. It preceded workers compensation and made an interstate railroad liable for bodily injury sustained by employees. Unless directly excluded, liability coverage under FELA is covered under Section II of the workers compensation and employers liability policy.

Although most state workers compensation laws limit recovery only to economic losses, the FELA usually permits railroad employees to recover the following damages:

- Lost earnings (past and future);
- Medical expenses if the injured employee paid out of pocket;
- Compensation for the reduced ability of an employee to earn a wage because of the injuries suffered; and
- Payment for pain and suffering.

All actions of the FELA must begin within *three years* from the day the cause of action commenced.

U.S. Longshore and Harbor Workers Compensation Act – Individuals (other than seamen) engaged in maritime employment are covered under a federal workers compensation statute, the *U.S. Longshore and Harbor Workers Compensation Act (LHWCA)*. A worker is protected under the LHWCA only if they meet a situs and a status test. The injury must occur on navigable waters or on an adjoining pier, wharf, dock, or similar facility used in loading, unloading, building, or repairing vessels. In addition, the individual must have been engaged in maritime employment when an injury occurred. When coverage is required for LHWCA, it can be added by endorsement to a workers compensation policy.

The LHWCA, and its extensions, provide compensation for lost wages, medical benefits, and rehabilitation services to employees injured during employment or who contracted a work-related disease due to work. Survivor benefits also are provided if the occupational injury causes the death of an employee.

The Jones Act – The *Jones Act* is a federal act that covers ships' crews with the same remedy available to railroad workers. Usually, anyone spending more than 30% of their time on a vessel that is in navigation will qualify as a seaman under the Jones Act. Seamen may sue their employer for injuries sustained through the negligence or fault of the employer. The act applies to navigable waters used for interstate or international trade.

Any employee who does not qualify as a Jones Act seaman will typically be covered under longshore or maritime law and not under the Jones Act. An example would be an individual working as a contract employee who moves back and forth between multiple ships not under common ownership.

Workers Compensation and Employers Liability Insurance

General Section

Every workers compensation and employers liability (WC&EL) policy is based on the National Council on Compensation Insurance's (NCCI) standard policy. However, they might contain slight variations by different insurance companies.

The general section of a workers compensation policy is split into five subsections as follows:

1. **The Policy** — This subsection summarizes every component of the policy. The information page, which is a substitute for the declarations page in other liability insurance policies, all endorsements, and any schedules constitute the policy. Policy terms cannot be altered unless there is an endorsement. The contract is between the employer stated on the information page and the insurance provider.
2. **Who is Insured** — The insured is the employer named on the information page. In the case of a partnership, a partner is only insured as an employer of the partnership's employees.
3. **Workers Compensation Law** — This is an essential policy subsection because the language refers to the workers compensation laws for states listed on the information page (3A). Employers in "3A states" have employees. Workers compensation policies are very different from other policies discussed in this book. No coverage amounts for statutory benefits are listed in the policy or on the information page. The policy will pay the amount in the applicable state where a covered injury occurs. Employers must list every state in which they have employees in section 3A.
4. **State** — This subsection defines a state which is any state in the United States, including the District of Columbia (Washington, D.C.).
5. **Locations** — Coverage applies to every location listed on the information page and in section 3A unless states listed in section 3A have self-insurance or other insurance.

Part One – Workers Compensation Insurance

Workers compensation coverage applies to work-related disease, accidental bodily injury, or death. It covers the lawful benefits required under the state's workers compensation regulations. The policy also states that the workers compensation insurance provider will not pay benefits for intentional self-injury, willful misconduct, or a violation of safety.

Supplemental payments are also included and comparable to those found in other insurance policies. They consist of the following:

- Defense expenses;
- Costs incurred at the insurance provider's request;
- Premiums for specific bonds;

- Litigation expenses;
- Interest on judgments required by law until a settlement is offered by the insurance provider; and
- All expenses incurred by the insurance provider.

The *other insurance* clause is also contained in the workers compensation section. It states that the insurance company will pay equal shares when other insurance, including self-insurance, can also respond to the loss.

Part Two – Employers Liability Insurance

Employers liability insurance coverage defends the insured from circumstances not covered under a state's workers compensation law. Unlike the workers compensation coverage section, which does not explicitly show the statutory limits provided, the employer's liability limits are shown on the information page. The basic limits provided are:

- $100,000 per worker for disease;
- $100,000 for bodily injury per accident; and
- $500,000 policy limit for each disease claim within the policy term.

Most insurance companies allow the insured to buy higher employers liability limits for an added premium. In some states, these limits do not apply. In addition to the basic coverage, this section also provides supplemental coverage, similar to other policies.

Coverage is provided for the employers liability associated with bodily injury by work-related disease or accident. It includes resulting death and is initiated if:

- Injury results from employment by the insured;
- Takes place in a state or territory noted in section 3A of the information page;
- Takes place during the policy period; and
- If a lawsuit is brought in the United States, its territories, possessions, or Canada.

Several *exclusions* apply to employers liability coverage:

- Assumed liability under a contract;
- Exemplary or punitive damages;
- Workers intentionally employed in violation of the law;
- Injury knowingly caused by the insured;
- Injuries that take place outside the United States, its possessions, or Canada;
- Damages caused by the policies or employment practices of the insured, including harassment, defamation, humiliation, discrimination, or termination of any worker;
- Although coverage is typically available by endorsement, workers who are subject to federal workers compensation or employer's liability laws;
- Penalties or fines levied because of a violation of state or federal laws; and
- Damages payable under laws that protect migrant and seasonal agricultural workers.

The *other insurance* clause explains that insurers will pay losses based on a contribution by equal shares. The limit of liability provision states that the limits for bodily injury by accident on the information page apply per accident, and bodily injury by disease applies per person subject to the bodily injury by disease policy limit for any losses during the policy term. The final two provisions refer to actions against the insurer and the insurer's subrogation rights.

Part Three – Other States Insurance

Other states' insurance coverage extends a policy owner's coverage for incidental or new operations in other states (excluding the monopolistic states) on a temporary and automatic basis, subject to certain conditions and time limits.

The state where a temporary or new operation exists must be listed in the 3C section of the information page. It is common for this section to list or describe all states other than monopolistic states. This section also provides the insured with the greatest protection for incidental or new exposures. If the state is not listed, no coverage will apply.

A critical component of this coverage is when the work was started. Suppose it is after the policy's effective date and the insured has made no other arrangements for coverage (self-insurance). In that case, coverage will apply as if the state were listed in 3A – mandatory coverage. However, coverage will only apply when work gets underway on the effective date if the insurance provider is notified within 30 days.

Example 9.1 – An insured has a calendar year policy and starts work in June in a new state. The state in which work is conducted is not listed in 3A of the information page. Provided this state is listed in 3C, coverage will apply as if it were listed in 3A. The insured's work continues in policy period two of the following year. An injury takes place in March of the second policy term. To have coverage, the insured had to notify the insurance provider by the end of January of policy period two. If this is the case, the state would be listed in 3A, and coverage would apply. If the insured did not notify the insurance provider, there would be no coverage even if the state continued to be listed in 3C.

Injuries that take place in states in which the employer and employee do not reside can get complicated. It is easier to think of work performed when completed by employees who live and work in a particular state, even if the headquarters of the employer is not in that state.

Part Four – Your Duties if Injury Occurs

The *Your Duties if Injury Occurs* section explains the insured's responsibilities in case of an injury to an employee. These duties include the following:

- Notifying the insurer at once;
- Providing immediate medical care mandated by the law;
- Providing the names and addresses of the injured employee and any witnesses to the injury;
- Promptly sending any legal papers or other notices;
- Cooperating with the insurance provider; and
- Not making any voluntary payments or assuming any responsibilities.

Part Five – Premium

The premium section describes how premiums are determined, what the requirements are for the insured's record retention, and what rights the insurance company has in auditing the books and records of the insured.

Premiums are determined *by classification*. In most cases, classifications are not specific to any industry. Instead, they are for job types, such as clerical, executive, inside sales, outside sales, and many others. Each classification will have a corresponding premium associated with it. The higher the hazard, the higher the premium. These rates are determined by the insurer and often require approval by state insurance departments.

Remuneration is another component in determining rates and includes payroll and other compensation methods. The insured must keep records on all remuneration to workers so the final premium can be determined. The rate per job classification is charged per *each $100 of the annual payroll* of every job-related classification.

Because the insured does not know the final payroll until the end of the policy period, the initial premium is considered a deposit. It is subject to being adjusted at the end of the term. This adjustment occurs during the premium audit, which can be conducted during regular business hours during the policy period and up to three years following the policy's expiration.

Part Six – Conditions

The conditions found in workers compensation and employers liability policies include

- **Inspection** — At any time, the insurer has the right to inspect the workplace.
- **Long-term policy** — All policy provisions will apply as though a new policy was issued on each anniversary date if the policy period is longer than one year and 16 days.
- **Assignment (transfer of your rights and duties)** — The rights and duties of the insured may not be transferred to anyone without the insurer's written consent.
- **Cancellation** — The insurer must provide the insured with at least ten days' advanced written notice for any cancellation. The insured may cancel the policy with a written notice to the insurer.
- **Sole representative** — The first named insured will act on behalf of every insured under the policy.

Selected Endorsements

Voluntary Compensation – The *voluntary compensation* endorsement added to workers compensation policies will cover workers who do not fall under a state's workers compensation law. Such workers include some types of domestic employees and farmworkers working fewer than 40 hours per week for one employer. This endorsement stipulates that the insurance provider will pay statutory benefits to the insured person in exchange for the injured employee releasing the insurance provider and the employer from further liability. Any additional compensation under the endorsement ends if the worker does not sign the release.

Foreign Coverage Endorsement – The *foreign coverage* endorsement extends coverage to lawsuits filed in foreign jurisdictions. This endorsement frequently provides for the insured's expenses to return to the U.S.

Waiver of Subrogation

The *waiver of subrogation* endorsement waives the insurance provider's right to recover from others, for an additional premium, against a particular organization or person named in the endorsement. It also waives the insurer's right of subrogation on a blanket basis for all individuals or organizations for whom the named insured has agreed by written contract to provide such a waiver

Volunteer Firefighters and Ambulance Workers Endorsements

The Volunteer Firefighters and Volunteer Ambulance Workers endorsements include volunteer firefighters and volunteer ambulance workers under workers compensation policies. To qualify, a volunteer firefighter must be an active volunteer with a fire company in a county, city, town, village, or fire district. A volunteer ambulance worker must be an active volunteer with an ambulance company.

Coverage can be written under a group policy or purchased as a single policy to insure a town's firefighting and ambulance districts. It can also be issued as a group policy to cover all areas within in county. Volunteers are not required to contribute to the policy premium.

Coverage allows a volunteer firefighter or ambulance worker to receive benefits in case of injury while in the line of duty. Line of duty can include training activities, attendance at a convention, travel to a fire or accident, equipment testing, meetings with the company, inspections, or fundraising activities.

Activities not considered in the line of duty include

- Participation in recreational or social functions;
- Work performed for a private employer;
- Work while on leave or suspension from duty; and
- Competitive events, such as baseball, basketball, and other volunteer sporting events.

As with all workers compensation claims, compensation is not based on fault by the volunteer, and liability is not increased because of fault by the company. However, injuries arising from intoxication from alcohol or drugs will render the volunteer ineligible for benefits.

Benefits are set according to state statutes and are based on the volunteer's ability to perform on a 5-day or 6-day work week in the volunteer's regular occupation.

Premium Computation

Job Classification – Payroll and Rates

A workers compensation rating is established by applying a rating bureau job classification to every $100 of an employer's payroll. Estimated payroll amounts are used when a policy is issued, and an audit decides the final premium. Payroll refers to remuneration. It includes wages, salaries, bonuses, commissions, vacation and sick leave pay, and noncash compensation.

Experience Modification Factor

A rating bureau determines the *experience modification factor*. These calculations relate to an employer's losses, payroll, and premiums. They are separated according to the classification of operations and reported to the bureau by the employer's insurer.

Premium Discounts

A *premium discount* is applied when an insured owes more than $5,000 in total standard premium.

Participation (Dividend) Plans

In some states, insurers or state workers compensation funds are permitted to write participating policies, also known as safety groups. The insured is eligible for a *partial premium refund* (dividends) if the experience during the policy term falls within parameters established by the insurance provider at the beginning of the policy term. Dividends are not guaranteed. To be eligible to participate, the insured is required to meet the associated underwriting participation requirements.

In the case of a group policy, the group has to qualify for the dividend. In the event the loss experience of the group is low, participating members may receive a dividend. No penalties are imposed for a high loss experience.

Other Sources of Coverage

New York State Insurance Fund

The State Insurance Fund insures employers against liability for work-related injuries, occupational diseases, or the death of their employees.

The New York Workers Compensation Fund is part of the New York State Insurance Fund (NYSIF). The NYSIF's and the NY Workers Compensation Fund's mission is to do the following:

- Provide appropriate and timely indemnity and medical payments to injured workers;
- Drive down the cost of workers compensation insurance for businesses operating in this state;
- Ensure that all New York businesses have a market for workers compensation insurance available to them at a fair price; and
- Maintain a solvent state insurance fund always available for New York businesses.

The NYSIF is a nonprofit agency in the State of New York. NYSIF was established in 1914 to offer a guaranteed source of workers compensation coverage at the lowest possible cost to employers within the state. It is a self-supporting insurance carrier that competes with private insurance providers in the workers compensation and disability benefits markets. The NYSIF is the largest workers compensation insurance provider in New York State.

Self-Insured Employers and Employer Groups

Almost every state permits employers to retain the risk of workers compensation losses. Employers who are authorized may self-insure their workers compensation obligation. The amount of a group self-insurer's security must be re-evaluated yearly after the receipt and review of the annual financial and other reports.

An employer that provides a self-insured workers compensation plan may wish to limit liability by purchasing excess insurance coverage to cover catastrophic losses. Excess workers compensation coverage usually is one of two types:

1. *Aggregate excess* coverage, a form of stop loss coverage, requires the employer to pay the initial portion of all monetary claims up to a retained limit. Once a claim exceeds the plan's limit, the excess coverage pays all additional monetary claims to the stated limit of the aggregate excess policy.
2. *Specific excess* coverage also requires a retention limit. However, the limit is for a single loss or all losses resulting from one occurrence. If covered losses exceed the retention limit, the insurance provider will pay additional losses up to the policy limits.

New York State Disability Benefits Law

Purpose

Employers with one or more employees are subject to the New York State Disability Benefits Law, which is part of the workers compensation law. The law provides for payment of cash benefits to employees who become disabled because of sickness or injuries and disabilities from pregnancies.

The New York State Disability Benefits Law is a nonoccupational disability law that provides disability income benefits for nonoccupational injuries or diseases preventing employees from earning a living. The law provides income benefits only and does not provide medical or other benefits. The Workers Compensation Board of New York administers this law.

In *workers compensation* cases, the insurance company carries the cost of medical treatment. In *disability benefits* cases, the law *does not provide* for medical care payments.

Definitions

State Fund – The State Insurance Fund created under the Workers Compensation Act.

Employer — An *employer* is a person, partnership, corporation, association, or legal representative of a deceased employer. It also refers to the receiver or trustee of a person, partnership, corporation, or association who has individuals in employment. This definition does not include the state, a municipal corporation, a local governmental agency, other political subdivisions, or public authority.

Employee — An *employee* is a person engaged in the services of an employer in any employment as defined by workers compensation law. An employee can be any professional musician or individual engaged in the arts who performs services for a radio station, television network, film production, hotel, restaurant, theatre, nightclub, or similar establishment. However, suppose such a musician or individual is stipulated by a written contract to be an employee of another employer covered by workers compensation in New York. In that case, they will not fit the definition of employee.

Disability — *Disability* includes disability caused by or in connection with a pregnancy.

Benefits — *Benefits* are the money allowances during a disability payable to an employee who qualifies to receive such benefits, as provided by law.

Carrier — A *carrier* includes stock corporations, mutual corporations, the state fund, and reciprocal insurance providers. Carriers insure the payment of benefits provided, and employers and associations of employers or employees and trustees authorized or permitted to pay benefits.

Wages — Wages refer to the money rate at which employment with a covered employer is paid under the hiring contract with the covered employer. Wages include the reasonable value of board, rent, lodging, housing, or similar advantage received under the hiring agreement.

Average weekly wage – *Average weekly wage* is the amount determined by dividing either:

- The total wages of such employee in the employment of their previous covered employer for the eight weeks or portion that the employee was employed immediately preceding and including their last day worked before the commencement of such disability; or
- The total wages of the previous eight weeks or portion immediately preceding and excluding the week the disability began, whichever is higher, by the number of weeks or portion of such employment.

Employment Covered

Under the New York State Disability Benefits law, the following are *covered employers and employees*:

- An employer who has in employment one or more individuals on each of at least 30 days in any calendar year or four weeks after the 30th day of employment, whichever is the later;
- An employee or recent employee of a covered employer who has worked at least four consecutive weeks;
- Employees of an employer that selects voluntary coverage, which requires a particular filing that extends coverage to certain types of employees;

- Employees who change jobs from one covered employer to another are eligible on day one of the new jobs. Former employees on unemployment for the first 26 weeks provided they are eligible and claiming unemployment benefits;
- Domestic employees who work 40 or more hours for the same employer;
- Spouses of an employer unless excluded by a special filing; and
- Out-of-state employers who are considered covered employers under the law.

Benefits

Benefits refer to the money allowances during disability payable to an eligible employee, as the Workers Compensation Act provides. Disability benefits must be payable to an eligible employee for disabilities *starting with the 8th consecutive day* of disability (after a 7-day waiting period), and after that, during the continuation of disability, subject to the limitations regarding maximum and minimum amounts and duration and other conditions. The maximum benefit period is 26 weeks out of 52 consecutive weeks. Subsequent periods of disability caused by the identical or corresponding injury or sickness will be considered a single period of disability only if separated by less than three months.

The weekly benefit the disabled employee is qualified to receive for disability must be 50% of the employee's weekly wage, not exceeding $170, unless the employee's average weekly wage is less than $20. In that circumstance, the benefit must be the average weekly wage. Provisions are also made for employees with multiple employers.

Paid Family Leave

Starting January 1, 2018, private employees in the state of New York are eligible for Paid Family Leave (PFL). PFL extends compensation for disability to include time off work because of caring for a seriously ill family member or bonding time with a newly adopted child or newborn.

Through PFL, eligible employees are guaranteed:

- 12 weeks of paid time off;
- Job protection when the employee returns to the job; and
- Continuation of health insurance while the employee is on leave.

Private employers conducting business in New York must *provide PFL insurance*. This insurance is usually added as a rider on existing disability policies. For employees to use PFL, they must request it by giving at least *30 days advance notice*. If PFL is unforeseeable and requires immediate time off, the employee must inform the employer as soon as possible.

For employees to qualify, they must be employed by the employer for at least 26 straight weeks if they work more than 20 hours per week or 175 days if they work fewer than 20 hours a week. Self-employed individuals can obtain PFL insurance on their own. However, PFL will only take effect 26 months after being self-employed.

Chapter Review

This chapter explained workers compensation insurance and the state and federal regulations associated with it. Let's review some of the key points:

TYPES OF LAWS	
Monopolistic vs. Competitive	• *Monopolistic* - employer purchases from a state-operated entity • *Competitive* - employer purchased from authorized insurers
Compulsory vs. Elective	• *Compulsory laws* - require employers to provide workers compensation • *Elective laws* - an employer is not required to follow state workers compensation laws
FEDERAL WORKERS COMPENSATION LAWS	
Federal Employers Liability Act (FELA)	• Liability law • Insured interstate railroad workers may sue an employer for negligence • Covered under Section II of workers compensation
U.S. Longshore and Harbor Workers Compensation Act	• Offers workers compensation benefits to workers engaged in maritime employment • Provides medical benefits, lost wage compensation, and rehabilitation services
Jones Act	• Covers ships' crew who are injured working on a vessel • Applies to navigable waters for international/interstate commerce
WORKERS COMPENSATION AND EMPLOYERS LIABILITY	
General Section	• *Policy* - summarizes all components of the policy • *Who is insured* - employer/insured named • *Workers compensation law* - provides statutory benefits • *State* - defines the state • *Locations* - coverage applies to all locations listed on the information page

Part One - Workers Compensation Insurance	• Benefits are referenced in the individual states' law
	• Supplemental payments:
	  o Defense costs
	  o Expenses incurred
	  o Bond premiums
	  o Litigation costs
	  o Interest in judgments
	  o An expense incurred by the insurer

Part Two - Employers Liability Insurance	• Basic limits:
	  o Bodily injury per accident - $100,000
	  o Per employee for disease - $100,000
	  o Policy limits for disease - $500,000
	• Insurers can allow the purchase of higher limits
	• *Other insurance clause* - losses paid on a contribution are on an equal share basis
	• *Limit of liability provision* - accident applies per accident, bodily injury by disease applies per individual

Part Three - Other States Insurance	• Allows coverage for employees in different states than the employer • States other than those in which the policy is written must be included for coverage to apply • Automatic/temporary basis

Part Four - Your Duties if Injury Occurs	• Insured must: 　○ Notify the insurer 　○ Provide immediate medical care 　○ Provide names and addresses of injured workers and witnesses 　○ Send notices/legal papers 　○ Cooperate with insurer 　○ Prevent voluntary payments or obligation assumptions
Part Five - Premium	• Explains premium determination, record retention requirements, and insurer auditing rights • Determined by classification • The initial premium is considered a deposit, subject to adjustment at the end of the policy period • *Remuneration* - includes payroll and other compensation
Part Six - Conditions	• *Inspection* - an insurer's right to inspect the workplace • *Long-term policy* - all provisions apply to a policy period longer than one year and 16 days • *Assignment* - rights and duties cannot be transferred without a written request • *Cancellation* - an insurer must provide a 10-day advanced written notice before cancellation • *Sole representative* - first named insured acts on behalf of all insureds under the policy
PREMIUM COMPUTATION	
Job Classification - Payroll and Rates	• Rating developed by applying bureau job classification rate to each $100 of payroll • An audit determines the final premium
Experience Modification Factor	• Developed by the rating bureau • Coverage based on employer losses, payroll, and premiums
Premium Discounts	• Occurs when the insured owes a total standard premium greater than $5,000

CHAPTER 10:
Other Coverages and Options

This chapter explains other coverages and options, such as umbrella and excess liability policies and surplus lines. As you read about each policy type and its features, ask yourself who it would benefit the most. This chapter includes several new terms and numbers for time limits and dollar amounts, so review them carefully.

- Umbrella and Excess Liability Policies
- Specialty Liability Insurance
- Excess Lines
- Surety Bonds
- National Flood Insurance Program
- Other Policies – Watercraft
- New York Property Insurance Underwriting Association

Umbrella and Excess Liability Policies

Some personal and commercial insurance policies are not designed to insure first-party property exposures. A policy owner uses *umbrella policies or excess policies* when required or when they choose to purchase limits higher than what is offered through the primary policy. Here are a few essential terms related to these types of policies:

Underlying policy (primary liability policy) – The underlying policy is a policy that is covered by the excess or umbrella policy. For example, suppose a policy owner has a homeowners policy, automobile policy, and watercraft policy. In that case, these policies are underlying insurance for a personal umbrella policy. The limits of insurance for liability coverage (not property) of the underlying policies are used first, and then the limits available in the excess or umbrella coverage.

Umbrella (stand-alone) – Umbrella policies differ from excess policies because the coverage can be greater or less than the underlying policies.

Excess (follow form) – Excess policies do not restrict or expand coverage concerning the underlying insurance. The coverage parallels the underlying policy but increases the limit of liability based on the amounts chosen by the policy owner.

Personal

An excess or umbrella policy, also known as catastrophe insurance, provides coverage over the underlying policy. These policies are commonly issued to give a minimum of $1,000,000 worth of additional coverage. There is generally a minimum limit of liability the insured must carry and maintain on the basic policies.

When an underlying policy provides primary coverage, in a covered loss, no deductible has to be satisfied to access the excess or umbrella policy limits. However, in the case of true umbrella policies, the potential exists for coverage on a primary basis within the umbrella. In other words, the underlying or primary policy does not cover the loss, but the umbrella does.

In these cases, the insured must pay the *self-insured retention (SIR)* deductible.

The personal umbrella policy will cover damages exceeding the underlying or primary insurance for property damage or bodily injury due to a covered occurrence. It also covers personal injury for which a policy owner becomes legally liable because of one or more offenses listed under the definition of personal injury.

The personal umbrella policy defines an *insured* as any of the following:

- The named insured;
- A family member;
- Any individual using an auto or recreational motor vehicle (golf cart, dune buggy, all-terrain vehicle, snowmobile, or any other motorized land vehicle designed for recreational use off public roads) owned by the policy owner and covered under the policy;
- Any individual using a temporary substitute for such an auto or recreational vehicle is also an insured;
- Any other individual or organization, but only regarding the legal responsibility for acts or omissions of the policy owner or any family member while using an auto or recreational vehicle. However, the owner or lessor of an auto or recreational vehicle loaned or hired for use by a policy owner is not considered an insured); or

- Any individual or organization legally responsible for animals owned by the policy owner or any family member. However, an individual or organization using or having custody of such animals during any business or without the owner's consent is not considered an insured.

The umbrella policy mirrors the underlying policies' coverage for recreational vehicles and watercraft. However, optional endorsements to exclude coverage for designated recreational vehicles are available to the insurance company.

When a claim made or lawsuit brought against a policy owner is caused by an offense to which coverage applies, the umbrella insurer can participate in the investigation and settlement of a claim. However, the umbrella insurer will not contribute to any expenses incurred by the underlying insurer.

If underlying coverage is not effective, the umbrella insurer will provide defense at the insurer's expense by the counsel of the insurer's choice. The insurer can settle any claim without the consent of the policy owner.

Coverage provided by the umbrella policy *will not apply* to the following:

- Intentional damage or injury;
- Personal injury stemming from the published material, if done by or at a policy owner's direction with knowledge of its falsity;
- Property damage or bodily injury from the ownership, use, maintenance, loading, or unloading of any recreational vehicle owned by any policy owner;
- Loss from the use of any motor vehicle without the belief that the individual is entitled to do so;
- Loss from the use of any motor vehicle or watercraft while in operation or preparing for a prearranged speed contest or race; or
- Property damage or bodily injury from an act or omission of a policy owner as an officer or board member of a corporation.

The umbrella policy also excludes uninsured motorist/underinsured motorist coverage. Still, it can be reinstated through an endorsement in states that require such coverage.

A policy owner must maintain the underlying insurance at the full limits stated on the declarations page with no change to more restrictive conditions during the policy term. When any underlying insurance is canceled or not renewed or replaced, the policy owner must notify the insurance provider immediately.

When the insured does not maintain underlying insurance, the insurer will not be liable for more than it would have been if the underlying insurance was effective.

The policy's general provisions and other conditions are in line with the ISO personal lines format.

Commercial

The primary function of a commercial umbrella policy is to provide excess protection through higher limits of liability over general liability policies, business automobile liability policies, and many other types of liability programs. There is typically a minimum limit of liability the policy owner must carry and maintain on the basic policies, such as $1,000,000 for commercial risks. Also, there are retained limits known as a self-insured retention (SIR) that the policy owner must satisfy before the umbrella policy responds to certain losses. The SIR applies only for losses not covered by any underlying insurance.

The difference between a commercial umbrella policy and an excess policy is determined the same way as with personal umbrella policies. Once a liability claim is filed for recovery of damage or injury, the primary policy pays up to the policy limits, after which the umbrella policy will apply. If there is no primary underlying insurance, the excess policy will apply after the insured paid the self-insured retention.

Specialty Liability Insurance

Errors and Omissions

Errors and omissions coverage protects insurance brokers and agents from financial losses if a policy owner sues to recover their losses. Policy owners can take legal action against a broker or agent because they did not place requested coverage, gave incorrect advice, or hid potential issues. Insurers typically write coverage on a claims-made basis. States will vary in how they interpret mistakes made by brokers and agents. The coverage provided is very similar to professional liability.

Professional Liability

Individuals providing professional services to others for a fee require *professional liability* coverage. It protects the professional against legal liability caused by errors and omissions, negligence, and the rendering or failing to render professional services. Insurers typically write a professional liability policy on a claims-made basis. We will describe the primary types of available professional liability coverages below.

The *Physicians, Surgeons, and Dentists Malpractice Form* offers coverage for liability from malpractice, error, or mistakes made in rendering or failing to render professional services.

Attorneys perform multiple services today, such as providing financial advice or drawing contracts. In addition to giving legal advice and other legal services, they are open to a wide range of liability exposures to potential errors and omissions claims. Lawyers Professional Liability coverage protects lawyers from these claims.

Under the *consent to settle a loss provision*, when a claim is filed under a professional liability policy or errors and omissions policy, the insurer cannot settle the claim by offering to pay the claimant without the policy owner's consent. Even though, at times, it would be cheaper to pay an award instead of defending the lawsuit, there is more at risk than money. For example, settling a claim could harm the professional's reputation. When the policy owner feels that they are not negligent, the policy owner can require the insurer to defend the action in court.

Directors and Officers Liability

Directors and officers liability coverage will protect the directors and officers of an organization from any claims for losses resulting from a wrongful act made while acting in an official capacity.

Wrongful acts will trigger coverage instead of being triggered on an occurrence or accident basis. Wrongful acts include neglect, breach of duty, and misstatements by directors and officers.

Directors and Officers liability policies will only pay damages that the corporation would, under the law, be required to reimburse the individual director or officer. The policy usually will not cover penalties, fines, or punitive damages.

Fiduciary Liability

Fiduciary liability covers individuals who administer employee benefit plans or pensions and have a fiduciary responsibility to manage the funds in the best interests of the plan's participants. Professional liability can cover losses associated with negligence, errors or omissions, or poor management of these plans.

By law, if *the fund pays the premiums* for fiduciary liability insurance, the policy has to allow for subrogation against the individual trustees involved in the loss.

Liquor Liability

Liquor liability (also called *dram shop liability*) is the exposure that restaurants, bars, and other similar establishments experience due to the selling, distributing, manufacturing, or serving of alcoholic beverages. Liquor liability protects the insured in the event of legal action against the insured for selling alcohol to a customer who is subsequently involved in an accident and sustains bodily injury or property damage.

Businesses that manufacture, distribute, sell, serve, or furnish alcoholic beverages can have liability exposure to legal actions under state or local statutes. These statutes establish the duties for those injuries arising from distributing or using alcoholic beverages and causing injuries to the user or caused to others by the user.

Employment Practices Liability

Employment practices liability refers to the exposures employers face in their role. Commercial general liability or the employers liability portion of workers compensation will not cover these claims. This coverage offers protection for liability resulting from the following:

- Refusal to employ, demotion or failure to promote, termination of the individual's employment, negative evaluation, discipline, reassignment, humiliation, or defamation of the individual based on discrimination;
- Work-related sexual harassment; or
- Other work-related physical, verbal, emotional, or mental abuse directed at the individual relating to color, race, gender, national origin, age, marital status, sexual orientation, mental or physical condition, or any other protected characteristic or class established by any local, state, or federal law.

Environmental Liability

Pollution liability coverage is written on a claims-made basis. Limited coverage existed in both the commercial package and the businessowners policies for these types of losses. Insurers can write the coverage a separate policy or as an endorsement attached to a General Liability Policy. It provides two types of coverage:

1. Bodily injury or property damage liability resulting from a pollution accident; and
2. Clean-up costs mandated by a government entity. (Coverage can be purchased for voluntary clean-up costs, which are necessary to prevent or curtail a pollution accident and in which the insurer provides written consent for an additional premium).

The common *exclusions* in the coverage form include:

- Emissions from an abandoned or closed site;
- Acid rain; and
- Escape of fluids from oil, gas, mineral, water, or geothermal wells.

All claims must transpire after the retroactive date and be reported during the policy period. The policy offers an optional one-year extended reporting period if the insurance carrier:

- Cancels or nonrenews coverage;
- Replaces it with another type of policy; or
- Renews it with a new retroactive date.

The insured must request this extended reporting period within 30 days following the end of the policy period and pay any added premium due.

Limited Pollution Liability coverage is similar to the Pollution Liability coverage form. It covers bodily injury or property damage caused by a pollution accident but does not provide clean-up costs.

The *pollution liability endorsement* can be used to provide *limited* pollution coverage. It covers a separate aggregate limit of liability for pollution coverage, but discharges from underground storage tanks are excluded. This endorsement only covers third-party injury or damage caused by pollution. No coverage exists for clean-up costs.

Cyber Liability and Data Breach

The ISO has recently established a new line of insurance that covers cyber risks, called the Internet Liability and Network Protection Policy. The policy contains five separate agreements listed below:

1. **Website publishing liability** — Provides coverage against perils related to Internet publishing, including libel, and trademark, service mark, or copyright infringement;
2. **Network security liability** — Protects the insured against claims for failing to maintain the security of a computer system;
3. **Replacement or restoration of electronic data** — Pays for the cost of replacing or restoring data lost because of a virus, denial-of-service attack, or malicious instruction;
4. **Cyber extortion** — Covers expenses, including ransom payments, incurred from extortion threats; and
5. **Business income and extra expense** — Covers expenses incurred due to an e-commerce incident or extortion threat.

Each agreement provides its own aggregate limit of coverage, subject to an overall policy limit. Defense expenses are included within the policy limits. All coverage is written on a claims-made basis and allows the addition of endorsements for worldwide protection.

Excess Lines

Definition of Excess Lines

Excess lines insurance is purchased from insurance providers who do not have a certificate of authority to operate as an admitted insurer. Retail brokers and agents who do not have a surplus lines license must access these insurers through an excess/surplus lines broker.

Licensing Requirements

The Superintendent can issue an excess lines broker's license to any person, firm, corporation, or association that is domiciled or maintains an office in this state and is a licensed insurance agent. *Nonresidents* with an excess lines broker's license in their home state can be issued licenses in New York, provided the applicant's home state grants nonresident licenses to residents of this state on the same basis. However, that reciprocity is not required regarding the placement of liability insurance on behalf of a purchasing group or its members. The Superintendent may suspend or revoke a license when they judge it to be in the best interests of the people of this state.

Before the Superintendent issues an excess lines broker's license, the person, firm, corporation, or association applying for the license must file a completed application with the Superintendent's office containing the information prescribed by the Superintendent.

Licenses will expire with the expiration of the qualifying broker's license. Licensees can renew the license for *24 months* by filing an application and paying the prescribed fee.

Total Cost Form

A copy of the *Total Cost Form* must be given to all insureds for each excess line policy. The surplus lines broker will provide it *before binding* coverage for a particular risk. The form will account for all policy commissions, fees, and taxes.

Affidavit

For each new policy or renewal acquired from an unauthorized insurer, excess lines brokers must file an *affidavit* that meets the Insurance Law with the Excess Line Association of New York (ELANY) requirements. The excess lines broker must obtain a properly completed and executed affidavit from the producing broker. It must document *three declinations* from authorized insurers or if the producing broker provided the insured with the required written notice.

Export List

Before the excess lines broker can place the risk with an eligible excess lines insurer, New York Insurance Law requires that an excess lines broker (or producing broker) demonstrates that three licensed insurers have declined to write the particular risk. The *Export List* is a list of insurance coverages for which the Superintendent has determined declinations are not required.

Disclosure (No Guaranty Fund)

Excess line brokers can only deliver an insurance policy or contract issued by the insurance provider. The excess lines broker or producing broker can deliver written confirmation of coverage with an unauthorized insurer if the confirmation identifies the insurer by name and address. It must also accurately describe the coverage, terms, and premium. All excess line insurers must print the "no guaranty fund" disclosure on all documents used for solicitation and binding coverage for excess line policies. The disclosure must confirm that the New York State Securities Funds do not protect the insurer in the event of insolvency.

Surety Bonds

A *surety* refers to someone who guarantees someone else's performance. The surety issues a bond on one party who must perform as required and financially compensates the other party when contractual obligations are not met. In the traditional sense, *surety bonds* are not insurance and differ in several ways. At the outset, insurance is a two-party agreement between the insured and the insurer. A surety is involved in a three-party contract between a principal, obligee, and surety.

When it comes to compensation for losses, insurance covers insureds without recourse for recovery against the insured. Unlike insurance, surety bonds do not pay for losses. Instead, they guarantee the individual(s) will fulfill specific responsibilities or obligations. If the duty is not performed as promised, the surety pays the bond amount to the individual to whom the promise had been made and broken. A bond is written for a fixed limit, and the surety will be liable only for this amount. This limit is known as the *bond penalty*.

The three parties to a bond include the principal, obligee, and surety.

Principal – The *principal* or *obligor* is the individual who purchases the bond and who promises to fulfill the obligation. This person or entity goes through the underwriting process. The underwriting for surety bonds considers the credibility and financial stability of the principal or obligor. The underwriting process can be as simple as an application or as complex as a thorough financial review.

Obligee – The *obligee or insured* is the person to whom the bond is payable and to whom the promise has been made as a result of the principal defaulting on its obligation. This party requires a bond for entering into a contract with the principal. For example, an entity that enters into an agreement with a construction firm to build an office building may require the contractor to be bonded to the amount of the project to ensure its completion. The building owner would be the obligee or insured.

Surety – The *guarantor or surety* (the bonding company) provides the financial backing for the guarantee, known as a bond penalty. If the principal or obligor defaults on its obligation, the surety will pay damages to the obligee or insured in the amount specified in the bond.

Example 10.1 – A business owner (obligee) may require a contractor (principal) to complete a specified job by a particular date. The contractor would purchase a bond from a surety company (guarantor) for a specified amount, which would be payable to the business owner if the contractor cannot meet the deadline. The bond guarantees that if the principal defaults on the agreement, the surety bond will pay the obligee. The surety bond acts like an insurance policy between the insurer and the insured; the surety guarantees that a particular outcome will occur as agreed. If it does not, the bond will pay the financial consequences to the obligee or claimant. However, unlike insurance, the obligor or principal is accountable for reimbursing the guarantor or surety the amount paid under the bond.

Types of Bonds

License and permit bonds – State and local governments typically require a *license and permit bonds*. They guarantee that the laws and regulations of a particular profession are followed. These bonds guarantee that the recipient of a permit will comply with the laws, ordinances, and regulations related to the use of the permit.

Bid bonds — The obligee usually requires a *bid bond* when construction projects are granted based on the lowest bid. The bid bond promises that if the contractor is awarded the contract, the contractor will accept the contract, and a performance bond will be issued.

Performance bonds — These bonds guarantee that the principal will complete the contract as agreed.

Labor and materials bonds — These bonds guarantee that work and materials will be delivered free and clear of any liens or other financial burdens. They are sometimes called payment bonds.

National Flood Insurance Program

Floods cause more property damage in the U.S. than any other type of natural disaster. The federal government established the *National Flood Insurance Program (NFIP)* to mitigate the coverage gap left by the private insurance industry. The NFIP was implemented by the Federal Insurance and Mitigation Administration (FIMA) through the Federal Emergency Management Agency (FEMA).

Congress created the NFIP in 1968 to respond to the increasing cost of disaster relief for flood victims and the rising damage resulting from floods. The program consists of three primary components:

1. Insurance;
2. Floodplain management; and
3. Floodplain mapping.

Nearly 20,000 communities across the U.S. and its territories participate in the NFIP by adopting and enforcing floodplain management laws to reduce potential flood damage. In exchange for participation, the NFIP makes flood insurance backed by the federal government available to renters, homeowners, and business owners in these communities.

Since the adoption of flood insurance was slow to take effect, in 1973, the federal government passed the Flood Disaster Protection Act, which required flood insurance in the following situations:

1. Flood insurance is a requirement in certain flood-prone regions as a condition for receiving loans through, or backed by, the federal government; and
2. Property owners who do not purchase flood insurance within 12 months after it becomes available will not qualify for full disaster relief funding. The amount of disaster relief will be decreased by the insurance amount that property owners could have purchased.

These participating communities are in the regular or standard flood program. They are eligible for coverage under the three policy forms that will be discussed later, to the full limits of insurance available through the program. The NFIP offers limits of insurance up to maximum amounts that may or may not be sufficient to cover an insured's loss. Insurance markets exist to provide flood coverage above the amounts of the NFIP.

For communities in the process of fulfilling floodplain management requirements, the full benefits of an NFIP policy are not available until their community is in full compliance with these requirements. In this interim stage, an emergency program offers reduced benefits until the requirements are met.

"Write Your Own" vs. Direct

National Flood Insurance is written and serviced *directly through the NFIP* or a *write your own (WYO)* insurance program. The private insurance carriers participating in a WYO program sell and service policies on a no-risk-bearing basis through a special arrangement with the Federal Insurance Administration (FIA). They retain a portion of the flood insurance premium to pay administrative costs and commissions. The remaining premiums, plus any investment, are used to pay for losses. The NFIP reimburses the insurance carriers for the excess costs if the premium is insufficient to cover losses. The coverage purchased through the NFIP and the WYO insurance plan is the same. All licensed property and casualty producers can write business with the NFIP.

NFIP flood insurance has a *policy term of one year*. Every policy expires at 12:01 a.m. on the last day of the effective term. The insureds remain covered for 30 days after the expiration.

Eligibility

To be eligible for the flood program, a policy owner must reside in a community that has met the minimum floodplain management requirements. An eligible structure must have a roof and two solid walls, be mainly above ground, and not entirely over water.

FIMA can deny coverage through a provision in the 1968 Act for any property that violates state or local laws, ordinances, or regulations.

Certain restrictions also apply to any property located within areas determined by the federal government as part of the Coastal Barrier Resource System or as an Otherwise Protected Area.

Upon purchasing a flood policy, a *30-day waiting period* begins from the time of application and premium payment. This waiting period can sometimes be waived surrounding new or revised loans or map revisions. It can also be waived if a loan exists on a property that should have acquired flood insurance but did not.

Flood Definition

As defined by the NFIP, the key to triggering a flood policy is the damage caused by a flood. Water damage not meeting this definition will not be considered a flood.

According to the NFIP, a flood is a temporary and general condition of complete or partial inundation of two or more acres of normally dry land or two or more properties (at least one owned by the insured).

Floods can be caused by:

- Tidal waters or overflow inland;
- Rapid and unusual runoff or accumulation of surface waters from any source;
- Mudflow (a river of liquid and flowing mud on surfaces of normally dry land) and collapse; or
- Subsidence or collapse of land along a lake shore or similar body of water due to undermining or erosion caused by currents or waves of water exceeding projected cyclical levels that result in a flood.

The following losses are excluded from coverage or do not meet the definition of a flood: backup of sewers unrelated to a flood, landslides, windblown rain, snow, or sleet. Flooding that is within the policyholder's control is not covered.

Forms

Dwelling – The *Dwelling Policy Form* is used to insure residential structures and their contents. The coverage is up to $250,000 in building coverage and $100,000 for personal property. Qualified structures include the following:

- Single-family structures;
- 1-4 family structures;
- Condominium units;
- Manufactured mobile/trailer home;
- Townhouse/Rowhouse structures; and
- Timeshares.

General – The *General Property Policy Form* covers other residential (more than four units) and nonresidential structures and their contents:

- Up to $250,000 for the building and $100,000 for personal property for other residential structures; and
- Up to $500,000 for the building and $500,000 for business property for nonresidential structures.

Residential Condominium Building Association Policy – The *Residential Condominium Building Association Policy (RCBAP)* is used for residential condominium building associations. It covers the entire building under one policy, including all units, improvements, and personal property owned in common. The RCBAP does not protect from loss or damage to personal property owned exclusively by the condo unit owner.

The limits of coverage are as follows:

- Up to $250,000 times the number of units in the building for building coverage; and
- Up to $100,000 in personal property per building.

Other Policies – Watercraft

General Policy Structure

Like many other policy forms, the Watercraft policy starts with an insuring agreement and definitions. It is further split into the following sections:

- Part A – Liability Coverage;
- Part B – Medical Payments Coverage;
- Part C (not currently used);
- Part D – Coverage for Damage to Your Watercraft;
- Part E – Your Duties after Accident or Loss; and
- Part F – General Provisions.

Definitions

Some of the terms and definitions unique to the watercraft policy include:

Personal watercraft — A recreational watercraft powered by an inboard motor capable of carrying one or more individuals in a standing, sitting, or kneeling position.

Non-owned watercraft — Any watercraft, including its motor and watercraft trailer, which is not owned or available for regular use by the insured.

Outboard motor — Any motor intended to be attached to a watercraft, including fuel tanks and electric starting equipment or controls required for the operation of the motor.

Watercraft trailer — A vehicle that is intended to be pulled by a private passenger auto, pickup, or van and transport a watercraft on land.

Boating equipment — Accessories and other equipment (other than outboard motors) owned by the insured, integral to the operation and maintenance of the watercraft, and are in or on the covered watercraft.

Covered watercraft — Any watercraft, outboard motor, and watercraft trailer listed on the declarations page and newly acquired property.

A watercraft, outboard motor, or watercraft trailer will be considered owned by an individual if leased under a written agreement to that individual and for a continuous period of at least six months.

Part A – Liability Coverage

Part A – Liability Coverage will pay for damages for property damage or bodily injury for which any insured becomes legally liable due to a watercraft accident. The insurance carrier will settle or defend any claim or lawsuit asking for these damages as considered appropriate. In addition to the limit of liability listed on the declarations page, the insurance provider will pay all defense costs it incurs.

Liability coverage supplementary payments will not reduce the limit of liability and are as follows:

- Up to 10% of the limit of liability for Part A;
- Up to $250 for the cost of bail bonds required due to an accident;

- Premiums on appeal bonds;
- Interest accruing after a judgment is entered in the lawsuit;
- Up to $200 per day for loss of earnings (other income is excluded) due to attendance at hearings or trials at the insurer's request; and
- Other reasonable expenses.

Exclusions – Some of the major *exclusions* to liability coverage include:

- Intentional property damage or bodily injury;
- Property damage to property used by, rented to, or in the insured's care;
- Bodily injury to an individual who is entitled to workers compensation benefits, benefits under the Jones Act, or Federal Longshore and Harbor Workers Compensation benefits;
- An insured's liability for watercraft while it is rented to others, hired for charter or conveyance, or used as a public livery;
- Losses incurred while the insured is engaged or employed in the business of selling, servicing, repairing, storing, or docking watercraft;
- Using a watercraft without a reasonable belief that the insured is entitled to do so;
- Bodily injury or property damage for an insured under a nuclear energy liability policy; and
- Watercraft being operated in any stunt activity, prearranged or organized race, or other speed competition.

Part B – Medical Payments Coverage

Part B – Medical Payments Coverage covers expenses incurred for essential medical and funeral services sustained by an insured. The policy will only cover services rendered within three years from the accident date.

Part B exclusions are similar to those listed in Part A. The main distinction is that bodily injury sustained *while occupying* a personal watercraft will not be covered.

Part D – Coverage for Damage to Your Watercraft

Part D – Coverage for Damage to Your Watercraft covers direct and accidental loss of the covered watercraft and boating equipment minus any applicable deductible listed on the declarations page. If a loss to more than one item of covered property arises from the same loss, only one deductible will apply.

The *limit of liability* for Part D will be the *lesser* of:

- The amount listed in the Declarations;
- The actual cash value (ACV) of the stolen or damaged property; or
- The amount necessary to replace or repair the property.

The insurance provider will adjust for depreciation and physical condition in determining actual cash value in the event of a total loss.

Additional Coverages – This policy section also provides the following *additional coverages*:

- **Salvage expense coverage** – Covers up to 25% of the Part D limit of liability. This coverage is additional insurance without a deductible.
- **Towing and assistance expense coverage** – If the watercraft becomes disabled, the insurance provider will pay reasonable expenses for

- Towing it to the nearest repair place;
- Delivery of oil, gas, or repair parts at the site of disablement;
- Watercraft trailer roadside repair; and
- The coverage limit is $500 for any single disablement, subject to a maximum of $1,000 for any policy period.
- **Personal effects coverage** — The insurance provider pays for direct and accidental loss to personal effects owned by the insured or the insured's guests (at the insured's request). Personal effects include cell phones, cameras, clothing, fishing equipment, water skiing, and other sporting equipment. However, it does not include coverage for animals, money, jewelry, watches, or permanently attached equipment. This coverage is limited to $500; it is additional insurance with no deductible.

Part E – Duties after an Accident or Loss

Duties of the insured after an accident or loss under the watercraft policy form are similar to any other policy form and can be summarized as follows:

- Promptly notify the insurance provider of how, when, and where the accident or loss occurred;
- Cooperate with the insurance provider and provide any documentation as requested;
- Take reasonable steps after a loss to protect the damaged property from additional loss;
- Promptly notify the police, Coast Guard, or other authorities if the covered property is stolen; and
- Allow the insurance carrier to inspect and appraise the damaged property before its repair or disposal.

Part F – General Provisions

The following *general provisions* apply to watercraft policies. Most of these provisions have previously been discussed in other types of property and liability coverages:

- **Abandonment;**
- **Bankruptcy;**
- **Changes;**
- **Financial responsibility** — when the policy is certified as future proof of financial responsibility, it must comply with the law to the extent required;
- **Fraud;**
- **Lay-up period** — the insurance provider will not provide coverage while a watercraft is operated during the lay-up period or not stored in the lay-up location;
- **Legal action against insurer;**
- **Loss payable clause;**
- **Insurer's right to recover payment;**
- **Out-of-state coverage;**
- **Policy period;**
- **Policy territory** — coverage only applies to accidents and losses that occur within the Custom Policy Territory shown in the Declarations, or if not specified, coverage applies on land, in inland waters, in coastal waters within 12 miles of the shoreline, or the Great Lakes within the U.S., its territories or possessions, Puerto Rico, or Canada;
- **Termination** (including cancellation, nonrenewal, automatic termination, and other termination provisions);
- **Transfer of insured's interest in this policy**; and
- **Two or more watercraft policies.**

New York Property Insurance Underwriting Association

Purpose

New York Property Insurance Underwriting Association (NYPIUA) is a joint underwriting association. It was created under New York's laws to meet the public's basic insurance needs. The Association was designated as a FAIR Plan (Fair Access to Insurance Requirements) to write certain types of property insurance. Since its inception, the Association has evolved into a precise residual market mechanism responsive to the varied needs of the insuring public.

Any individual with an insurable interest in the property who has made a diligent effort in the standard insurance market to procure homeowners insurance, fire insurance extended coverage, and coverage for additional perils and broad form coverage is entitled to apply to the Association for such coverage if determined necessary by the Superintendent.

Every authorized insurer who sells these policies must remain a member of the Association as a condition of its authority to continue transacting fire, extended coverage, and homeowners insurance in this state.

At least once every 30 days, the Association must report to the Superintendent, the Speaker of the Assembly, and the temporary president of the senate on the number, location, and type of policies written through a coastal market assistance program.

Coverage

Initially, the Association only offered Basic Fire and Extended Coverage. It was later recognized early that these basic coverages alone were not meeting the property owners' needs, and insurance carriers added additional coverages. The Association currently offers fire, extended coverage, sprinkler leakage, vandalism and malicious mischief, and time element coverages.

Coastal Market Assistance Program (C-MAP)

The Coastal Market Assistance Program (C-MAP) was created in 1997 by the State of New York Department of Financial Services. It is administered by the New York Property Insurance Underwriting Association (NYPIUA).

C-MAP's purpose is to help homeowners living in New York's coastal areas in obtaining home insurance. To increase availability, insurers voluntarily participate in C-MAP by insuring property they might otherwise reject because of proximity to the coast.

The following are eligible properties for coverage under C-MAP:

- 1-4 family owner-occupied dwelling, apartment unit, or condominium unit;
- Property on Long Island's south shore, Queens, Brooklyn, Staten Island, and Long Island's forks within one mile of the shore; or
- Property on Long Island's north shore, in the Bronx and Westchester, within 2,500 feet of the shore.

The following property owners qualify for coverage under C-MAP:

- Homeowners with homes in these areas who have received a cancellation notice, nonrenewal notice, or conditional renewal notice from their insurance carrier for a reason other than nonpayment;
- The NYPIUA policyholders whose property satisfies the geographic criteria defined above; and
- New purchasers of property residing in these areas.

There are two ways C-MAP coverage can be obtained:

1. **Direct Method** — A company issues coverage through an agent with whom it has a contract. As a C-MAP participant, a company can accept an application for property that would not usually qualify under the company's proximity to shore underwriting guidelines. A particular C-MAP application is not required. The application process follows routine company procedures.
2. **Rotation** — Here, C-MAP applications are submitted to the NYPIUA by brokers, agents, or homeowners. Applications are checked for completeness and eligibility by the NYPIUA and then transmitted to participating C-MAP companies for consideration. The NYPIUA will then communicate the insurance carrier's binding decision to the applicant and the broker of record, instructions for binding coverage. Depending on internal policy, a company can submit policies, endorsements, commissions, and cancellation notices to the NYPIUA for transferring or conducting business directly with the originating producer.

The NYPIUA's policy offers a choice of two policy forms to insure homes in the C-MAP program.

The first offers coverage protecting property against loss or damage caused by fire, lightning, hail, windstorm, riot, riot attending a strike, civil commotion, vehicles, aircraft, smoke, vandalism, and malicious mischief.

The second includes the following protection in addition to the previously mentioned perils: property damage by burglars (not theft of property), the weight of ice, snow, or sleet, falling objects, accidental discharge of steam, sudden cracking of hot water or steam systems, freezing, and sudden damage from artificial electric currents.

Neither NYPIUA policy form is a homeowners policy. It will cover only those perils named in the policy.

The NYPIUA policies are written on an Actual Cash Value (ACV) basis, except for policies written in conjunction with a voluntary market policy that includes an approved "wrap-around" endorsement. Upon the producer's request, building coverage will be written on a repair or replacement cost basis.

Chapter Review

This chapter explained several coverages that can apply to personal and commercial insurance. Let's review some of the major points:

	UMBRELLA AND EXCESS LIABILITY
Types of Policies	• *Underlying policy* – the primary liability policy • *Umbrella (stand-alone)* – coverage can be > or < the underlying policy • *Excess (follow form)* – mirrors the underlying policy and increases the limits of liability
Personal Umbrella	• Also referred to as catastrophe insurance • Protects the insured from large claims and lawsuits • Offers a minimum of $1,000,000 in additional coverage • *Self-insured retention (SIR)* – retained limits that the policy owner must pay before the umbrella policy responds to certain losses • The policy owner must maintain underlying insurance • The insurance provider is not liable beyond what it would pay if underlying insurance were in effect

	UMBRELLA AND EXCESS LIABILITY *(Continued)*
Commercial	- Provides higher limits of liability over other liability coverage - Minimum limit of liability - The insured pays self-insured (SIR) before the umbrella pays for certain losses
	SPECIALTY LIABILITY INSURANCE
Professional Liability	- Used by individuals who provide professional services for a fee - Protects against legal liability - Written on a claims-made basis - Primary types: - Physicians, surgeons, and dentists malpractice form - Lawyers professional liability
Errors and Omissions	- Protects insurance brokers and agents from financial loss due to a lawsuit with an insured - Financial loss resulting from incorrect advice, not placing correct coverage, not informing the insured of essential issues - Written on a claims-made basis
Directors and Officers Liability	- Protects directors and officers from losses arising from wrongful acts while in an official capacity - Triggered by a wrongful act - Does not pay for fines, penalties, or punitive damages

Employment Practices Liability	- Protects the employer against liability resulting from:
	  - Refusal to employ, termination, demotion, failure to promote, negative evaluation, reassignment, discipline, defamation, humiliation based on discrimination
	  - Sexual harassment
	  - Verbal, physical, mental, and emotional abuse relating to race, color, national origin, gender, marital status, age, sexual orientation, physical or psychological condition

Fiduciary Liability	- Covers those who administer and manage pension or employee benefit plans - Errors and omission, negligence, and poor management covered under the plan - Subrogation provision must be included if paid by the fund
Liquor Liability	- Protects bars and restaurants from legal action brought against them for selling, distributing, manufacturing, or serving alcoholic beverages - Lawsuits due to a customer being served alcohol and later causing/suffering property damage or bodily injury as a result
	NATIONAL FLOOD INSURANCE PROGRAM (NFIP)
Components	- Insurance - Floodplain management - Floodplain mapping
Eligibility	- Community must meet the minimum floodplain management guidelines - Eligible structures: A roof, two solid walls, and mostly above ground - 30-day waiting period - Damage must be a result of a flood as defined by the NFIP

Types of Coverage	• Direct through the NFIP • *Write your own insurance program (WYO)* – through private insurance providers • Identical coverage through both
Flood Definitions	• Overflow of inland or tidal waters • Rapid and unusual accumulation or runoff of surface waters from any source • Mudflow (a river of flowing mud and liquid on surfaces of typically dry land) and collapse • Collapse of land along a lake's shore or similar body of water exceeding anticipated cyclical levels that result in flood
BONDS	
Definitions	• *Surety* – someone who guarantees the performance of another • *Surety bond* – the 3-party contract between a principal, obligee, and surety • *Penalty* – a set limit for which the surety is liable
Principal, Obligee, and Surety	• *Principal (or obligor)* – the person who promises to fulfill an obligation and purchases the bond; goes through the underwriting process • *Obligee (or insured)* – the person to whom the promise is made and to whom the bond is paid when the principal defaults on the obligation • *Guarantor (or surety)* – the surety or bonding company providing financial backing; only pays if the principal defaults on the obligation

CHAPTER 11:
Accident and Health Insurance

This chapter will discuss a variety of accident and health policy provisions, disability income insurance, and medical plans. State-specific benefits and offers required in New York will be explained, as well as long-term care, Medicare supplements, and group health insurance.

- Individual Health Insurance Policy General Provisions
- Disability Income and Related Insurance
- Individual Disability Income Insurance
- Medical Plans
- Group Health and Blanket Insurance
- New York Mandated Benefits and Offers (Individual and/or Group)
- HIPAA Requirements
- Medicare Supplements
- Federal Patient Protection and Affordable Care Act (PPACA)

Individual Health Insurance Policy General Provisions

Required Provisions

The National Association of Insurance Commissioners (NAIC) developed the *Uniform Individual Accident and Sickness Policy Provisions Law*, which was adopted in every state. This law introduced standard provisions included in every individual health insurance policy. Although the wording may differ from one insurance carrier to another, the basic provisions are the same. The law provides for 12 mandatory policy provisions and 11 optional policy provisions.

These provisions define the duties and rights of the policy owner and the insurance provider. The insurance provider may reword any provision so long as the modification does not make the provision less favorable to the policy owner or beneficiary.

Entire Contract; Changes – The *entire contract* provision stipulates that the health insurance policy, a copy of the signed application, and any attached riders and amendments make up the entire contract. Neither party can change the policy without the express written consent of both parties, and any changes must also be a part of the contract. Only an insurance company's executive officer, not an agent, has the authority to make any changes to the policy.

Time Limit on Certain Defenses – The *time limit on certain defenses* provision is analogous to the incontestability provision contained in a life insurance policy. Insurance providers cannot use any statement or misstatement made in the application (except fraudulent ones) to deny a claim when the policy has been in force for *two years*. Unlike in life insurance, fraudulent misstatements on a health insurance application can be contested at any time *unless the policy is guaranteed renewable*. If the policy is guaranteed renewable, the fraudulent misstatements cannot be contested after the 2-year contestable period.

Grace Period – The *grace period* is the time beyond the premium due date. Policyholders can still pay premiums before the policy lapses for nonpayment of the premium. Grace periods may differ according to individual state laws. In most cases, the grace period cannot be less than *seven days for policies with a weekly premium payment mode, ten days for policies with a monthly premium payment mode, and 31 days for every other mode*. During the grace period, coverage continues in force.

Reinstatement – When the policy owner does not pay the premium by the end of the grace period, the policy will lapse (terminate). This provision states under what conditions the insured may *reinstate coverage*. If the insurance company or an authorized representative accepts the policy premium and does not require a reinstatement application, reinstatement is automatic. However, when a reinstatement application is needed, and an insurer issues a conditional receipt for the premium payment, the insurance company may approve or disapprove the reinstatement application. Insurers automatically reinstate coverage if they do not refuse the reinstatement application within 45 days from the date the conditional receipt was issued. Accidents will be covered immediately following the reinstatement; however, *insurance providers will cover sickness after ten days*. This stipulation helps to protect the insurance provider from *adverse selection*.

Claims Procedures – The *notice of claim* provision specifies the insured's responsibility to provide the insurance company with reasonable notice in the event of a loss. Notice is required as soon as possible or within *20 days* of the loss. Notice to the agent is the same as notice to the insurance company.

Upon receipt of a notice of claim, the insurance company must supply claims forms to the insured within 15 days. If forms are not furnished, the claimant must submit written proof of the occurrence, nature of the loss, and extent of loss to the insurance provider.

After a loss occurs, the claimant has to submit proof of loss as soon as reasonably possible or within 90 days of the loss, but not to exceed one year. However, the 1-year limit is not applicable if the claimant is not legally competent to comply with this provision.

The time of payment of claims provision states that claims are to be paid immediately upon written proof of loss. If the claim involves disability income benefits, they must be paid no less frequently than monthly. The time of payment for claims is typically stated in different policies as 60 days, 45 days, or 30 days.

The payment of claims provision specifies who receives the claims payments when they are to be made. All benefits are payable to the insured during their lifetime. If the insured is deceased, pending claims are paid to the beneficiary. If there is no beneficiary, benefits will be paid to the deceased's estate, unless the insured has allocated the benefits to be paid directly to a doctor or hospital who has rendered services. Some states allow a provision that gives the insurance carrier the right to expedite payments of urgently needed claim funds and pay up to $3,000 in benefits to a relative or individual who is considered equitably entitled to payment. This provision is called the facility of payment clause.

Legal Actions – This provision limits the time a claimant can seek recovery from an insurance provider under a policy. The insured has to wait *60 days*, but not later than *three years* (in most states), after proof of loss before legal action can be brought against the insurance company.

Change of Beneficiary – The change of beneficiary provision states that the policyholder can change the beneficiary at any time. They must provide a written request to the insurance carrier unless the beneficiary is *designated as irrevocable*. The beneficiary's consent is not required. If the beneficiary designation is irrevocable, the policy owner must first obtain the beneficiary's permission before the insurer can make any change.

Other Provisions

In addition to the mandatory provisions discussed above, the insurer can include any of the following optional provisions.

An insurer can change the wording of the optional policy provisions as long as the rewording is not less favorable to the policy owner.

Change of Occupation – The insured's occupation is a crucial underwriting consideration, particularly for disability income insurance. Health insurance policies typically include a provision that allows the insurance company to adjust benefits if the insured changes occupations. Suppose the insured changes to a more hazardous occupation. Upon a claim, the insurer will reduce benefits to that which premiums paid would have purchased assuming the more hazardous occupation. When the change is to a less dangerous occupation, the insured must apply for a rate reduction with the insurer.

Misstatement of Age – Suppose the applicant has misstated their age on the application. In that circumstance, the insurance provider can adjust the benefits to an amount that the premium at the correct age would have obtained. This provision is similar to the one found in a life insurance policy.

Other Insurance in this Insurer – This provision will be applied when an insured obtains several policies with the same insurer and over-insures. This provision allows a pro-rata benefit reduction and return of premium in the event of multiple policies with the same insurance company when the benefits exceed a specified maximum.

Expense-incurred basis – Suppose the insured has two or more policies from different insurers that provide benefits on an expense-incurred basis, and the policies cover the same expenses. In that circumstance, if the insured did not notify the insurers that the other coverage existed, each insurer would pay a proportionate share of any claim, meaning benefits will be pro-rated.

Other Benefits – The same principle applies when the policy pays specific benefits instead of paying on an expense-incurred basis.

Relation of Earnings to Insurance – The danger of being over-insured is always a potential risk with health insurance coverage, but this is especially true concerning disability income. Insurers must protect the concept of indemnity.

Every disability income insurer uses the *Relation of Earnings to Insurance* rule, which allows the insurance provider to check the insured's income for a specified period prior to the submission of an income claim. There will be a percentage cap that the insurer will enforce.

A disability income insurer does not want a situation where an insured has no incentive to seek rehabilitation. This situation could occur because the insured receives a higher income while disabled than they received while working.

Suppose an insured is covered by multiple policies. In that case, insurance providers are liable for only a proportionate amount of the disability benefits the insured will receive. This is calculated by comparing the amount a single insurer will pay with the amount that all insurers would pay. However, the total monthly benefits must stay within $200 or the sum of the monthly benefits stated in the coverage, whichever is less.

Unpaid Premium – Upon payment of a claim, the insurer will deduct any past-due premiums from the claim, and it will pay the policy owner the net amount.

Cancellation – Within the first 90 days after the issue date, the insurance provider can cancel a policy by written notice delivered to the insured or sent by first class mail to their last address as shown by the insurer's records. The notice must state when the cancellation will be effective, but not less than ten days after that. In the event of cancellation, the insurance provider will return the unearned portion of any paid premium. Cancellation must be without prejudice to any claim originating before the date of cancellation.

Conformity with State Statutes - This provision specifies that any policy provision, on its effective date, conflicting with the state statutes where the insured resides on that date is automatically amended to ensure conformity with the minimum requirement of the statutes. Although this is an optional provision, most states require it to be included in every health insurance policy.

Illegal Occupation – This provision states that liability will be denied if the insured is engaged in an illegal occupation or is injured while committing an unlawful act.

Intoxicants and Narcotics – The insurance provider is not liable for any claims that result when the insured is intoxicated or under the influence of drugs (unless administered by a doctor). Treatment for substance abuse is typically a covered benefit under health insurance policies. This provision excludes any injury or sickness resulting from the insured's intoxication.

Other General Provisions

All individual health insurance policies must include specific standard provisions. These are called Uniform Mandatory Provisions. In addition to these mandatory provisions, some provisions, such as the free look provision, are required in individual policies. In contrast, other provisions are necessary for both individual and group policies. Insurance providers can use additional provisions that do not conflict with the uniform provisions as long as they receive approval from the state where the policy is delivered. Although it is impossible to list all the provisions used by insurance companies, the following are the most commonly used:

Right to Examine (Free Look) – The right to examine (free look) provision gives the insured a period to review a policy upon delivery. It provides the right to return the policy for any reason. The insured is then entitled to a full refund of all premiums paid. New York law mandates that health policies issued in this state must have a free-look period of at least 10, but not more than 20 days.

Insuring Clause – The *insuring clause* or agreement is typically on the first page of the policy. It is a general statement that identifies the basic contract between the insured and the insurer. It identifies the insured and the insurer and specifies what kind of losses (perils) are covered.

Examples of insuring clause statements include the following:

- "The company will cover total disability losses due to injuries or sickness subject to the policy provisions."
- "We will pay the benefits provided in this policy for loss resulting from injury or sickness."

Consideration Clause – The *consideration clause*, which is usually on the first page of the policy, makes it clear that both parties to the contract are required to give some valuable consideration. The consideration given by the applicant is the payment of the premium and the statements in the application. The insurance provider's consideration is the promise to pay claims under the contract terms.

Renewability Clause – The health insurance policy will also define the insurance carrier and the insured's right to cancel or renew coverage. Insureds should carefully examine every policy to determine which renewal provision it includes, as these are essential provisions.

Noncancelable – The insurer cannot cancel a *noncancelable* policy, nor can the premium be raised beyond what is in the policy. The policy may call for an increase in a particular year, like "age 65," which the insurer must write in the original contract. The insured has the right to renew the policy for the contract's life. The insurance company cannot increase the premium above the amount for which the insurer initially issued the policy. However, the guarantee to renew coverage typically only applies until the insured reaches age 65. At this time, the insured is usually eligible for Medicare. For disability income insurance, the policy will be renewed beyond age 65 only if the insured can prove that they have continued to work a full-time job.

Guaranteed Renewable – The *guaranteed renewable* provision is similar to the noncancelable provision, except that the insurance company can raise the policy premium on the anniversary date. However, the policy owner has the unilateral right to renew the policy for the contract's life. The insurance provider can only raise premiums *on a class basis* and not on an individual policy. As with noncancelable policies, coverage usually is not renewable beyond the insured's age of 65. Insurers must write long-term care and disability insurance policies and Medicare Supplements as guaranteed renewable contracts. The insurance company cannot cancel them when the insured reaches age 65.

Disability Income and Related Insurance

Qualifying for Disability Benefits

A significant risk that individuals will face in their lifetime is becoming disabled and unable to perform work-related duties. Recent statistics show a 30% chance of a 25-year-old being disabled for more than 90 days before age 65. It is far less likely that the same 25-year-old will suffer a premature death before age 65.

For most people who cannot work, employment income would end after a brief period. Consequently, most individuals would have to use their savings to pay everyday expenses such as rent, food, and utilities. Each person should ask themselves how long they could survive without an income.

Therefore, disability income insurance is a critical component of a comprehensive insurance program designed to replace lost income in the event of this contingency. Disability income insurance provides a reasonable and predetermined income to a disabled party for a set period subject to a "time deductible" termed an *elimination period*. Disability income coverage provides, after a specified waiting period, a monthly benefit for a stated amount and a period for total and partial disability due to injury (accidents) or illness (sickness). Disability income insurance can be purchased individually or on a group basis through an employer.

Disability income benefits are limited to a percentage of an insured's earned income. The insurance provider wants a claimant to have a financial incentive to return to work. An individual becomes eligible for regular disability benefits when they satisfy the insurer's definition of disability because of either sickness or injury. This definition of disability varies from insurer to insurer. The applicant and the agent need to be fully aware of the eligible causes of loss that activate this critical benefit trigger in the disability income policy's insuring clause.

Inability to Perform Duties

A disability income policy requires the insured not to be able to perform the duties of their occupation to pay benefits. The benefits will also depend on the policy's chosen definition of disability.

Own Occupation – An own occupation policy will provide benefits when the insured cannot perform any duties of their own occupation due to a sickness or an accident.

This definition is typically limited to the first 24 months following a loss. It allows insureds (claimants) to receive benefits if they cannot perform the duties of their normal occupation because of disablement. Claimants will receive benefits even though they might be able to earn income from a different occupation. After 24 months, if the insured still cannot perform the duties of their own occupation, the definition of disability narrows to mean the inability to perform *any occupation* for which the insured is reasonably suited by experience, training, or education. This narrow definition dramatically reduces the insurance provider's liability because claimants can likely find something they can do for financial gain. The "own occupation" definition is commonly used for highly trained, skilled occupations like trial attorneys, surgeons, etc.

Any Occupation – A policy containing an "any occupation" provision will provide benefits when the insured cannot perform any of the occupation's duties for which they are suited because of experience, training, or education. "Own occupation" is considered the more liberal definition and provides the insured with a better benefit.

Some insurance companies still use the two-tier approach by combining both definitions in a single disability income policy. It is much easier for an insurer to justify the "any occupation" definition when issuing a policy from an underwriting perspective.

Individual Disability Income Insurance

Individual disability income policies are applied for and paid for by the person rather than through the employer, like group disability income. Individual Disability Income premiums are paid with after-tax dollars, and benefits are not taxable.

Basic Total Disability Plan

A *total disability* plan protects an individual or the family against the economic loss that comes with the total disability of the wage earner.

Income Benefits (Monthly Indemnity) – Most often, benefits are paid monthly but could be paid weekly in some policies. The benefit amount is specified in the policy. It is typically limited to a percentage of one's income at the time of application to prevent over-insurance.

Elimination and Benefit Periods – The *elimination period* is a waiting period imposed on the insured from the start of disability until benefit payments begin. It is a deductible that measures days instead of dollars. The elimination period eliminates coverage for short-term disabilities; insureds will be able to return to work in a relatively short amount of time. The elimination periods contained in most policies range from 30 days to 180 days. Just as a higher deductible amount translates into lower premiums for medical expense insurance, a longer elimination period results in a lower premium for disability income insurance. An essential consideration in selecting the elimination period is stipulating payment in arrears. In other words, if the insured chooses a 90-day elimination period, the insured will be eligible for benefits on the 91st day; however, payments will not begin until the 121st day. In selecting the duration of the elimination period, the insured needs to determine how long they can go without benefit payments following disability.

The *benefit period* refers to the time the monthly disability benefit payments will last for each disability after the elimination period has been satisfied. Most policies include benefit periods lasting one year, two years, five years, and until age 65. Some plans offer a lifetime benefit period; however, a longer benefit period will result in higher premiums.

Injury can be defined using either the accidental means definition or the accidental bodily injury definition. The accidental means definition indicates that the cause of the accident must be unintended and unexpected. Accidental bodily injury suggests the damage to the body is unintended and unexpected. A policy that uses the accidental bodily injury definition provides broader coverage than a policy that uses the accidental means definition.

Illness or sickness is defined as a disease or *sickness* contracted after the policy has been effective for 30 days. It can also refer to a condition or disorder that manifests after the policy becomes effective (in force).

Often, the insurer will allow the insured to have different benefit periods for sickness and injury. For example, the insured could apply for benefit periods of five years for illness but to age 65 for an accident.

Recurrent disability is in a policy provision that specifies the period (typically within six months) during which the recurrence of an illness or injury will be considered a continuation of a previous disability period. The importance of this feature is that the recurrence of a disabling condition will not be treated as a new period of disability so that the insured is not subject to another elimination period.

Waiver of Premium Feature – Waiver of premium is typically included in a basic disability income policy. This benefit allows the insured, when disabled, to forego paying the premiums once they qualify for benefits. Premiums paid by the insured during the elimination period are typically refunded once the insured qualifies to receive benefits.

Coordination with Social Insurance and Workers Compensation Benefits

To avoid over-insurance, the insurance providers have several options to coordinate with Social Security and workers compensation benefits.

Additional Monthly Benefit (AMB) – Some insurers offer the *Additional Monthly Benefit rider* in the approximate amount that Social Security would pay. The benefit is only provided for one year. It is then anticipated that Social Security benefits would begin at the end of one year.

Social Insurance Supplement (SIS) – The insurance provider can offer a *Social Insurance Supplement* rider, which will pay a benefit in the approximate amount that Social Security would pay. Suppose Social Security does pay. In that case, the Social Insurance Supplement benefit is reduced dollar for dollar by the amount of the Social Security benefit payment.

Social Insurance Supplements (SIS) or *Social Security Riders* supplement or replace benefits that might be payable under Social Security Disability. These allow for the payment of income benefits, usually in three different circumstances:

1. When the insured qualifies for Social Security benefits but before the benefits commence (typically, there is a 5-month waiting period for Social Security benefits);
2. If the insured has been denied coverage under Social Security (roughly 75% of individuals who apply for Social Security benefits are denied coverage because of their rigid definition of total disability); or
3. When the amount payable under Social Security is less than the amount payable under the rider (in this situation, the insurer will pay only the difference).

These riders can also supplement or replace benefits payable under a social insurance program like workers compensation.

Occupational vs. Nonoccupational Coverage – Health insurance, including disability insurance, is written on an *occupational* or *nonoccupational* basis. Occupational coverage provides benefits for injury, illness, or disability resulting from accidents or sicknesses occurring *on or off* the job. Nonoccupational coverage, on the other hand, only covers claims resulting from accidents or illnesses occurring *off* the job. Insurers will assume that workers compensation coverage will cover accidents or injuries on the job.

Medical Plans

Medical Plan Concepts

Basic medical expense insurance includes various essential medical, hospital, and surgical benefits. The broad category of medical expense coverage can offer a wide range of benefits, or policies can be narrowly written and provide only one or two types of coverage.

Fee-for-Service Basis vs. Prepaid Basis – Medical expense plans could be *fee-for-service* where providers receive a payment for their billed charges for each service provided. Prepaid plans offer hospital and medical benefits in services rather than dollars. In *prepaid plans*, the providers are regularly compensated whether or not they deliver services. However, there is no additional compensation when a provider renders services.

Specified Coverages vs. Comprehensive Care – *Specified coverage* policies limit coverage to one illness or one limiting group of coverages (e.g., cancer policies, dental plans, prescription drug coverage, and other limited coverage plans). These policies are commonly written as stand-alone individual policies to complement a traditional fee-for-service Major Medical Expense Policy.

Comprehensive care policies cover most types of medical expenses. It is a comprehensive health care service package that typically includes preventive care, immunizations, routine physicals, outpatient services, and hospitalization, such as HMOs.

Benefit Schedule vs. Usual, Customary, and Reasonable Charges – Some medical expense insurance plans contain a *benefit schedule*, specifically specifying what is covered in the plan and for how much. Other plans can incorporate the term *usual, customary, and reasonable*. Usual, customary, and reasonable means the insurer will pay an amount for a particular procedure based on the average charge in that geographic region.

Any Provider vs. Limited Choice of Providers – More traditional reimbursement-type comprehensive medical expense plans allow the insured to be treated by almost any qualified doctor. The newer managed care type of plans limit their benefits to doctors and care centers on their specific list of providers.

Insureds vs. Subscribers and Participants – The participants in a plan are either considered insureds or subscribers. *Insureds* are individuals receiving benefits, and subscribers are individuals responsible for the premium payments.

Commercial insurance providers issuing fee-for-service contracts refer to the individuals eligible for benefits under the policy as "insureds." Those organizations, like Blue Cross, HMOs, and PPOs that offer prepaid plans, use the term "subscribers" rather than "insureds." The words "insured" and "subscriber" refer to the people eligible for coverage under the plan.

Most commercial health insurance providers refer to their policyholders as insureds. When Blue Cross organizations formed, they developed pre-paid plans with hospitals for their members. These organizations chose to call their members subscribers rather than insureds mainly due to the pre-paid mechanism. To this day, Blue Cross/Blue Shield groups refer to their members as subscribers.

Types of Plans

Today, healthcare insurance providers are:

- Stock and mutual insurers.
- Blue Cross/Blue Shield.
- Health maintenance organizations (HMOs).
- Preferred provider organizations (PPOs).

Care is administered not only in a doctor's office or the hospital but also in skilled nursing facilities, urgent care centers, and surgicenters.

Basic Hospital, Basic Medical, Basic Surgical

Characteristics – Insurers commonly group basic hospital, surgical, and medical policies and major medical policies under the banner of *Medical Expense Insurance*. These policies deliver benefits for covering the cost of medical care resulting from sickness or accidents. The three basic coverages (hospital, surgical, and medical) can be purchased separately or as a package. These coverages are known as *first-dollar coverage* because they do not require the insured to pay a deductible. This coverage differs from Major Medical Expense insurance; however, the basic medical coverages generally have more limited coverage than the Major Medical Policies.

A basic hospital insurance policy in New York provides coverage subject to no deductible exceeding $500 for at least 60 continuous days of a hospital stay.

Coverage includes the following services:

- Daily room and board, consisting of bed and board, including special diets and general nursing care, in an amount of at least the lesser of:
    - 80% of the costs for semiprivate accommodations;
    - 100% of the costs for semiprivate accommodations for the first 20 days of confinement and at least 50% of such expenses for the next 40 days; or
    - $240 per day (can be reduced to $165 for policies delivered outside the metropolitan area).
- Miscellaneous hospital services for at least 80% of the costs incurred, up to at least $5,000, or 20 times the daily room and board rate if specified in dollar amounts.
- Outpatient services including:
    - Hospital services on the day surgery is performed;
    - Hospital services rendered within 24 hours after accidental injury; and
    - X-ray and laboratory tests performed in the outpatient department of a hospital.

In New York, a basic medical insurance policy must include coverage for the following:

- Surgical services, including operating and endoscopic procedures, for
    - At least 80% of the reasonable costs; or
    - If specified in dollar amounts, a fee schedule providing amounts for any procedure at least equal to those provided for in a fee schedule with a maximum of $2,600 based on values found in the State of New York Certified Surgical Fee Schedule or an equivalent fee schedule approved by the superintendent.
- Anesthetic services for at least 80% of the reasonable costs or 15% of the benefit provided in an approved fee schedule.
- In-hospital medical services for at least 80% of the reasonable expenses or $25 per day for at least 60 days.

Common Limitations

Basic hospital expense coverage – Hospital expense policies cover hospital room and board charges and miscellaneous hospital expenses. These expenses can include medicines, lab and x-ray charges, and the use of the operating room and supplies when a hospital admits the insured. The insurer sets the limits on room and board at a specific dollar amount per day up to a maximum number of days, and there is no deductible. These limits may not cover the total hospital room and board costs incurred by the insured. For instance, if the hospital expense benefit was $500 per day, and the hospital charged $600 per day, the insured would be responsible for the additional $100 per day.

Miscellaneous Hospital Expenses – *Miscellaneous hospital expenses* generally have a separate limit. This amount pays for the various costs associated with a hospital stay. This separate limit appears as a multiple of the room and board charges, such as ten times the room and board charges or a flat amount. A policy might specify the maximum limit for certain expenses, such as $100 for drugs or $150 for using the operating room. As with the room and board charges, the miscellaneous hospital expense limits may not cover the total amount needed by the insured during a lengthy hospital stay.

Basic Medical Expense Coverage – *Basic medical expense coverage* is also known as Basic Physicians' Nonsurgical Expense Coverage. It offers coverage for nonsurgical services a physician provides. However, the benefits are typically limited to visits to patients confined in the hospital. Some policies will also cover office visits. There is no deductible, but coverage is usually limited to a certain number of visits per day, a specified limit per visit, or a specific limit per hospital stay.

In addition to nonsurgical physician's expenses, insureds can purchase basic medical expense coverage to cover maternity benefits, emergency accident benefits, mental and nervous disorders, home health care, hospice care, outpatient care, and nurses' expenses. Regardless of the type of plan or coverage purchased, these policies usually offer only limited benefits contingent upon time limitations. The insured must often pay a considerable sum of money and the benefits paid by the medical expense policies.

Basic surgical expense coverage – This coverage is usually written together with Hospital Expense policies. These policies cover the costs of surgeons' services, whether they perform the surgery in or out of the hospital. Coverage includes the surgeons' fees, an anesthesiologist, and the operating room when it is not a miscellaneous medical item. Similar to the other basic medical expense coverage types, there is no deductible, but coverage is limited. All contracts have a *surgical schedule* that lists the types of operations covered and their assigned dollar amounts. If the procedure is not on the schedule, the contract may pay for a similar operation. Special schedules may list a specified amount, express the amount payable as a percentage of the maximum benefit, or assign a relative value multiplied by its conversion factor.

Exclusions from Coverage – The following are *excluded* from coverage in a basic medical plan:

- Self-inflicted injuries;
- War, acts of war, or injuries and illness while on active military service;
- Injuries while committing a felony;
- Injuries or death while under the influence of drugs or alcohol;
- Cosmetic surgery (except when required as the result of an accident);
- Vision correction;
- Experimental procedures;
- Sexually transmitted diseases;
- Infertility services; and
- Organ transplants.

Provisions Affecting Cost to Insureds – When insurers use the *relative value* approach, they will assign each surgical procedure a point value relative to the points assigned to the maximum benefit. The maximum points are usually assigned to major surgical procedures, such as open-heart surgery. The points for this maximum benefit are generally high, like 1,000 points. Other surgical procedures, like an appendectomy, can only have an assigned point value of 200. The assigned points (relative value) of 200 are multiplied by a *conversion factor* to determine the amount payable for the appendectomy. This conversion factor represents the total amount payable *per point*. For example, if the conversion factor were 10, the policy would pay $2,000 for the appendectomy (200 x 10) and $10,000, the maximum benefit, for the open-heart surgery (1,000 x 10).

Major Medical Insurance (Indemnity Plans)

Major medical expense policies were a natural outgrowth of basic medical expense policies. Since basic medical expense policies had low dollar protection limits, the need for a more comprehensive form of protection was realized and provided in the form of major medical policies. Usually, a major medical policy provides a substantial dollar amount of protection, typically $1,000,000. That amount could be more or less; it will depend on the insurer writing the policy. New York sets the following minimal limitations for a major medical insurer:

1. No less than a $100,000 benefit;
2. Coinsurance cannot exceed 25%; and
3. Deductibles cannot exceed 5% of basic coverage benefits if greater.

Characteristics – Major medical expense contracts feature blanket coverage, high maximum limits, coinsurance, and a deductible. Dollar deductibles are paid upfront, and the coinsurance, or sharing of the cost, is paid after the deductible is satisfied and the claim is submitted.

Common Limitations – Usually most major medical plans cover most medical expenses in and out of the hospital, and they have high maximum benefit limits. These plans are also known as covered or eligible expense plans.

Exclusions from Coverage – The following are among the *exclusions* included in major medical insurance policies:

- Intentionally self-inflicted injuries;
- Injuries caused by war;
- Custodial care;
- Regular dental/vision/hearing care;
- Injuries covered by workers compensation insurance; and
- Cosmetic surgery (unless necessitated by an accident or a congenital disability).

Provisions Affecting Cost to Insureds – Major medical policy premiums vary depending on the deductible amount, the coinsurance percentage, the stop-loss amount, and the maximum benefit amount.

Most insurers incorporate an annual *deductible* into their major medical policy. A typical deductible may range from $100 to $2,500. The deductible amount is the portion of medical expenses paid by the insured each year before the insurance benefits commence. The higher the deductible, the lower the annual premium will be for coverage. In other words, if an insured accepts more risk through a higher deductible, the insurer lowers their premium.

Once the deductible has been satisfied, the insured and the insurer share the following expenses. This sharing of costs is known as *coinsurance*. Usually, the insurer pays the larger share of 90/10, 80/20, 70/30, or 50/50. The smaller the percentage the insurer pays, the less the premium will be. Coinsurance helps to keep costs down by requiring the insured's participation in the ongoing expense.

Many insurers include a *stop-loss feature* in their major medical policies. The stop-loss amount is the amount the insured pays out of pocket during the year. When the insured's out-of-pocket expenses reach the stop-loss, the insurer provides coverage at 100% of eligible expenses for the remainder of the year. The out-of-pocket expenses that qualify for the stop-loss are the insured's portion of the coinsurance, which may or may not include the deductible. The higher the stop-loss, the lower the premium will be for the insured.

Health Maintenance Organizations (HMOs)

Through the Health Maintenance Act of 1973, Congress vigorously supported the growth of *Health Maintenance Organizations (HMOs)* in this country. The act required employers with more than 25 employees to offer the HMO as an alternative to their regular health insurance plans.

Preventive Care Services – The primary goal of the HMO Act was to lower the cost of health care by utilizing *preventive care*. While most insurance plans did not provide any benefits for preventive care before 1973, HMOs offer free annual check-ups for the entire family. Through these visits, the HMOs hope to identify diseases in the earliest stages, when treatment is most likely to succeed. The HMOs also offer members free or low-cost immunizations to prevent certain illnesses.

General Characteristics – The HMO offers benefits in the form of services rather than reimbursement for a physician's or hospital's services. Usually, the insurance carriers provide the financing, while the doctors and hospitals provide the care. The HMO concept is distinctive in that it offers both patient care and financing for its members.

Limited Service Area – The HMO provides health care services to individuals living within specific geographic boundaries, like city limits or county lines. If a person lives within the boundaries, they are eligible to enroll in the HMO. They are ineligible if they do not live within the service area.

Limited Choice of Providers – The HMO limits costs by only offering care from physicians that meet their standards and are willing to provide care at a pre-negotiated price.

Copayments – A *copayment* or copay is a flat dollar amount or a specific part of the cost of care that the member must pay. For example, the member might pay $5, $10, or $25 for each doctor's office visit.

Prepaid Basis – HMOs operate on a *capitated* basis. The HMO receives a flat monthly amount attributed to each member, whether they see a physician. Essentially, it is a prepaid medical plan. As a plan member, you will receive all the necessary services from the member physicians and hospitals.

Primary Care Physician vs. Referral (Specialty) Physician – Care is provided to the HMO's members by a limited number of physicians approved to practice in the HMO.

Primary Care Physician (PCP) – When a person becomes a member of the HMO, they will select their *primary care physician (PCP)* or *gatekeeper*. Once selected, the insurer will pay the primary care physician or HMO regularly for being responsible for the care of that member, whether or not care is provided. It should be in the best interest of the primary care physician to keep this member healthy to prevent future treatment of disease.

Referral (Specialty) Physician – For the member to see a specialist, the primary care physician (gatekeeper) must refer the member. The referral system prevents the member from seeing higher-priced specialists unless it is essential. Many HMOs impose a financial cost to the primary care physician for referring a patient to a more expensive specialist. Therefore, the primary care physician is incentivized to use an alternative treatment before providing a referral. HMOs must have mechanisms to handle complaints that sometimes result in the delay of a referral or complaints about coverage concerns or other patient care.

Hospital Services and Emergency Care – The HMO offers the member inpatient hospital care, in or out of the service area. The services may be limited when treating mental, emotional, or nervous disorders, including drug or alcohol treatment or rehabilitation.

Emergency care must be provided for the member whether they are in or out of the HMO service area. Suppose a member receives emergency care outside the service area. In that situation, the HMO will be eager to get the member back into the service area so salaried member physicians can provide care.

Preferred Provider Organizations (PPOs) and Point of Service (POS) Plans

Preferred Provider Organizations (PPOs) are the traditional medical systems' answer to HMOs. Under the PPO system, the physicians are paid fees for their services instead of a salary. Nevertheless, the member is encouraged to visit approved member physicians who previously agreed upon the fees to charge. This incentive comes in the form of benefits. Members can utilize any physician they choose. However, the PPO will cover 90% of the cost of a physician on their approved list while only covering 70% of the cost if the member uses a physician not included on the PPO's approved list.

The *Point-Of-Service (POS)* plan is simply a combination of HMO and PPO plans.

General Characteristics – A PPO is a group of physicians and hospitals that contract with insurance companies, employers, or third-party organizations to provide medical services at a reduced fee. PPOs differ from HMOs in two ways. First, providers do not offer medical care on a prepaid basis; physicians are paid a discounted fee for services. Secondly, subscribers do not have to use physicians or facilities that contract with the PPO. The PPO traditionally offers a more extensive selection of providers compared to HMOs.

With the Point-Of-Service plan, employees do not have to be locked into one plan or choose between the two. Employees can make a different selection whenever a need arises for medical services.

Primary Care Physician Referral – The insured does not have to choose a primary care physician in a PPO. The insured can select medical providers not found on the preferred list and retain coverage. The insured can receive medical care from any provider. Yet, if the insured chooses a PPO provider, the insured will incur lower out-of-pocket costs. Conversely, if an insured utilizes a non-network provider, the insured's out-of-pocket costs will be higher. In a PPO, all network providers are "preferred." The insured can visit any of them, even specialists, without seeing a primary care physician first. Certain services might require plan pre-certification, which evaluates the medical necessity of inpatient admissions and the number of days needed to treat the condition.

The Point-Of-Service (POS) plan combines the ability to self-refer at increased out-of-pocket costs with gatekeeping arrangements. A patient can acquire higher benefits at a lower cost when care is arranged through or provided by the primary care physician (PCP). Benefits for covered services when self-referring without having a PCP arrange for the service are usually more expensive.

Indemnity Plan Features – If a non-member physician is used under the POS plan, the attending physician will receive a fee for service. Member patients will have to pay a higher coinsurance amount or percentage for using a non-member physician.

Group Health and Blanket Insurance

Characteristics of Group Insurance

In a group policy, the contract is between the insurer and the group sponsor (the employer, union, trust, or other sponsoring organization), as opposed to the individual policy, where the contract is between the insurer and the insured.

Group Contract – In group insurance, the policy is also referred to as the *master policy*. It is issued to the policy owner, which could be an association, employer, union, or trust.

Certificate of Coverage – The individuals covered under a group insurance plan are issued evidence of coverage in the form of *certificates of insurance* or certificates of coverage. The certificate of insurance cannot include provisions or statements that are misleading, unfair, or deceptive. The certificate consists of the policy coverage, how to file a claim, how long the coverage will last, and how to convert the policy to an individual policy.

Experience Rating vs. Community Rating – Group health insurance is typically subject to *experience rating*, where the experience of this particular group as a whole determines the premiums. Individual policies are subject to *community rating* or pool rating, where the premium is based upon the overall claims experience of the insurer. Experience rating helps employers with low claims experience because they receive lower premiums.

Under New York state law (Chapter 501, Regulations 145 and 146), all medical expense health insurance sold to individuals or small groups (2 - 50 employees) must be community rated. All insureds, regardless of sex, age, or occupation, pay the same premium into a predetermined geographic pool. The claims from that geographic area are paid from the pool's collection. Different rates are allowed for different regions. For example, New York City would likely have higher rates per insured than those utilized in Syracuse. Before the enactment of this law, experience rating was used by all commercial carriers. This rating penalized individuals and employers with exorbitant renewal increases based on their poor individual claims experience.

New York Mandated Benefits and Offers (Individual/Group)

Dependent Child Age Limit

As defined by the Insurance Laws of New York, dependent children include any children under a specified age.

The Affordable Care Act mandates every insurance company offering health insurance policies to provide coverage for the insured's dependent children. They must provide coverage for children *up to the age of 26*.

Group health policies that provide coverage for the insured's dependents must cover any married and unmarried dependent children *until age 26*. This stipulation exists regardless of financial residency, dependence, employment, or student status. Policy owners can extend coverage to age 29 for unmarried children upon request.

Policy Extensions for Disabled Children

There are policy extensions for unmarried dependent children, irrespective of age, who cannot self-sustain employment due to developmental disability, mental illness, mental retardation, or physical handicap. Coverage will not end as long as the policy stays in force and the dependent child remains in this condition.

The dependent child must have become disabled before attaining the limiting age. Policy owners must submit proof of the dependent's incapacity *within 31 days* of the day the notice of termination of coverage is sent to the policy owner.

Newborn Child Coverage

Any coverage for families must provide coverage for newborns from birth. This coverage includes newborns adopted by the insured if the insured takes physical custody of the infant upon the infant's release from the hospital.

Newborns are insured for sickness or injury, including the necessary care and treatment of medically diagnosed congenital disabilities and birth abnormalities, including premature birth (except cases involving adoption). Coverage of the initial hospital stay is not required if a natural parent has insurance coverage for the infant's care.

Suppose notification or payment of an additional premium or contribution is required to make coverage effective for a newborn infant. In that case, the insured can provide payment within at least 30 days of the newborn's birthday to make coverage effective from birth. This provision must include 48 hours of hospitalization coverage for natural childbirth and 96 hours for caesarian delivery.

HIPAA Requirements

Legislation in July of 1997 ensures the "portability" of group insurance coverage. It includes various required benefits that affect small employers, the self-employed, the mentally ill, and pregnant women. HIPAA (Health Insurance Portability and Accountability Act) regulates protection for group health plans for employers with *two or more* employees and individual insurance policies sold by insurers.

HIPAA includes the following protection for coverage:

Group Health Plans

- Prohibiting discrimination against employees and their dependents based on health conditions;
- Allowing individuals in special circumstances the opportunity to enroll in a new.

Individual Policies

- Guaranteeing access to individual policies for qualifying individuals;
- Guaranteeing renewability of individual policies.

Eligibility

HIPAA has regulations concerning eligibility for employer-sponsored group health plans. These plans cannot set up eligibility rules for enrollment under the plan that discriminate based on any health factor relating to an eligible individual or their dependents. *Health factors* include any of the following:

- Health status;
- Medical conditions (both physical and mental);
- Receipt of health care;
- Claims experience;
- Genetic information;
- Medical history;
- Disability; or
- Evidence of insurability, including conditions arising from acts of domestic violence and participation in activities such as skiing, snowmobiling, motorcycling, etc.

Employer-sponsored group health plans can apply waiting periods before enrollment as long as they are applied uniformly to all participants.

To be eligible under HIPAA regulations to convert health insurance coverage from a *group plan* to an *individual policy*, a person must meet the following criteria:

- Have been covered under a group plan in the most recent insurance;
- Have 18 continuous months of creditable health coverage;
- Have exhausted any COBRA or state continuation coverage;
- Not be eligible for Medicaid or Medicare;
- Not have any other health insurance;
- Apply for an individual health insurance policy within 63 days of losing prior coverage.

Such HIPAA-eligible individuals have a guaranteed right to obtain individual coverage.

Guaranteed Issue

If the new employee satisfies the requirements, the employer has to offer coverage on a guaranteed issue basis.

Renewability

At the direction of a plan sponsor, the issuer of group health coverage must renew or continue the current coverage. However, the group health coverage can be discontinued or nonrenewed due to the following: fraud, nonpayment of premium, violation of participation or contribution rules, discontinuation of that particular coverage, association membership cessation, or movement outside the service area.

Privacy Protection

The HIPAA Privacy Rule defines protected information as "individually identifiable health information" held or disseminated by a covered entity or its business associate, whether paper, electronic or oral. It is also known as *protected health information (PHI)*.

Individually identifiable health information includes demographic data relating to payment information or physical or mental health conditions that could quickly identify the individual.

A covered entity has to obtain the individual's written authorization to disclose information that is not for health care operations, treatment, or payment.

The *Security Rules* of HIPAA apply to electronically protected health information that is individually identifiable in electronic form. This information includes a patient's past, present, or future medical condition and payment for health care. The Security Rules were established to protect the integrity, confidentiality, and availability of electronically protected health information.

Covered entities must comply with the security provisions of HIPAA by maintaining reasonable administrative, technical, and physical safeguards against any reasonably anticipated risks.

Medicare Supplements

Purpose

Medicare supplement plans, also called *Medigap*, are policies issued by private insurers to fill in some of the gaps in Medicare. These plans intend to fill the gap in coverage attributable to Medicare's co-payment requirements, deductibles, and benefit periods. The federal Social Security program does not administer these plans. Instead, they are sold and serviced by private insurance companies and HMOs. These policies must meet specific requirements and receive approval from the state insurance department. Medicare supplement policies pay some or all of Medicare's co-payments and deductibles.

Under the *Omnibus Budget Reconciliation Act (OBRA)* of 1990, Congress passed a law that authorized the NAIC to create a standardized model for Medicare supplement policies. This model requires Medigap plans to meet specific requirements regarding participant eligibility and the benefits provided. This law aimed to eliminate questionable marketing practices and provide consumers with a degree of protection by standardizing the coverage.

Open Enrollment

Anyone who qualifies for Medicare can also obtain a Medicare supplement and pay the required premium for those additional benefits. Under OBRA, Medicare supplement insurance cannot discriminate in pricing or be denied based on an applicant's claims experience, health status, medical condition, or receipt of health care. An open enrollment period is a 6-month period that guarantees applicants the right to purchase Medigap once they first enroll in Medicare Part B. To buy a Medigap policy, the applicant must usually have both Medicare Part A and Part B.

In New York, applicants must be accepted throughout the year for any Medicare Supplement insurance benefit plan available from an issuer.

Standardized Medicare Supplement Plans

The NAIC established "standard" Medicare supplement benefit plans identified with the letters A through N. They did this to standardize the coverage offered under Medicare supplement plans. *The core benefits found in Plan A must be in every plan*, in addition to the variety of benefits these other plans offer. Any insurer selling Medigap plans must at least provide Plan A, while the other plans are optional.

Once an individual becomes eligible for a Medicare supplement policy, and during the open enrollment period, insurers offer coverage on a guaranteed issue basis. Under these circumstances, an insurance provider must do the following:

- Sell the patient a supplement policy;
- Identify all pre-existing conditions incurred more than six months from the effective date of coverage; and
- Not charge more for a Medicare supplement policy due to past or present health conditions.

Core Benefits – Medicare Supplement Plan A includes only the *core benefits*. The core benefits, also called basic benefits, cover the following:

- Part A coinsurance/copayment (not the Part A deductible);
- Part A hospital costs up to an additional 365 days after Medicare benefits are exhausted;
- Part A hospice care coinsurance/copayment;
- Part B coinsurance/copayment;
- The "blood deductible" for Parts A and B (first 3 pints of blood).

Additional Benefits – In addition to Plan A, which includes only the core benefits, most insurance companies offer some or all of the additional plans. Insurance providers are not permitted to change the benefits provided in these supplemental plans, nor can they change the designation letter of any of the following plans:

Plan B – Core benefits plus the Medicare Part A deductible.

Plan D – Core benefits, Medicare Part A deductible, skilled nursing facility coinsurance, and the foreign travel benefit.

Plan G – Core benefits, Medicare Part A deductible, skilled nursing facility coinsurance, 100% of Medicare Part B excess charges, and the foreign travel benefit. This plan has to pay for services of activities of daily living (ADL) that Medicare does not cover.

Plans C, E, F, H, I, and J are no longer available. These plans will remain effective for those insureds who purchased them when they were still available.

Medicare Supplement Plans K and L have lower premiums with higher out-of-pocket costs. The core benefits of these two plans are different as well:

- Approved hospital costs for the copayments for days 61 through 90 during any Medicare benefit period.
- Approved hospital costs for the copayments for lifetime reserve days 91 through 150.
- Approved hospital costs for an additional 365 days after all Medicare benefits are utilized.
- 50% of charges for the first 3 pints of blood in Plan K, 75% of charges for the first 3 pints of blood in Plan L.
- 50% of the Part B coinsurance amount in Plan K, 75% of the Part B coinsurance amount in Plan L.
- 50% of respite care and hospice cost-sharing expenses for Part A in Plan K, 75% of respite care and hospice cost-sharing expenses for Part A in Plan L.

Plan K provides 50% of the Medicare Part A deductible and 50% of skilled nursing facility coinsurance.

Plan L provides 75% of the Medicare Part A deductible and 75% of skilled nursing facility coinsurance.

Plans M and N include benefits similar to Plan D, but the co-pays and deductibles may differ.

Medigap Plan	Core Benefit	Skilled Nursing Coinsurance	Part A Deductible	Part B Excess (100%)	Foreign Travel Emergency
A	•				
B	•		•		
D	•	•	•		•
G	•	•	•	•	•
K	•	50%	50%		
L	•	75%	75%		
M	•	•	50%		•
N	•	•	•		•

New York Regulations and Required Provisions

Standards for Marketing – The following are standards for marketing Medicare Supplement policies:

- Every insurer must establish marketing procedures to ensure that any comparison of policies by their agents will be fair and accurate;
- Insurers must establish marketing guidelines to ensure that excessive amounts of insurance are not sold or issued;
- There must be an established formula to determine whether a replacement policy contains benefits clearly and substantially greater than those under the policy being replaced;
- The first page of the policy must include a Notice to Buyer informing them that this policy may not cover all of their medical expenses.

Insurers must reasonably ascertain whether a prospective applicant or enrollee for Medicare Supplement insurance already has accident and sickness insurance and the type and amounts they currently own. The insurer must establish procedures to verify that they comply with these rules.

Producers cannot utilize twisting, misleading advertising, and high-pressure tactics. They also cannot use the terms *Medigap, Medicare Supplement, Medicare Wrap-Around*, or similar words unless the policy fully complies with the law.

Permitted Compensation Arrangements – An insurer can pay compensation to an agent for the sale of a Medicare Supplement policy. The term *compensation* includes any monetary and nonmonetary compensation or payment relating to the sale or renewal of the policy, including but not limited to bonuses, prizes, gifts, awards, and finder's fees.

The first-year commission cannot be more than 200% of the renewal commission for servicing the policy in the second year. The commission in renewal years must be the same as the second year. Insurers must provide it for at least five renewal years.

Insurers cannot pay greater compensation to agents. Producers or agents cannot receive compensation greater than the *renewal compensation payable by the replacing insurer* if a policy is being replaced. Exceptions are made if the benefits of the new policy are clearly and significantly larger than the benefits provided by the policy being replaced.

Appropriateness of Recommended Purchase or Replacement – Any producer selling a Medicare supplement must make reasonable efforts to determine the appropriateness of a recommended replacement or purchase. The application for Medicare supplement insurance must include a statement signed by the producer that confirms they have reviewed the applicant's current health insurance coverage. The statement must also ensure that additional coverage of the type and amount applied for meets the applicant's needs.

Any sale of a Medicare supplement policy that would give the insured more than one such policy is prohibited.

Replacement – Every insurer's application for Medicare supplement insurance must include a question designed to determine if the applicant has another Medicare supplement policy. The question must also determine if this policy will replace any other accident and health policy. The application must also ask if the applicant is eligible for Medicaid and advise that counseling services may be available. It is the responsibility of the issuers, agents, and brokers to ensure that Medicare supplement policies are not being replaced unnecessarily.

If replacement is involved, the insurer or its producer must furnish the applicant with the "Notice Regarding Replacement" before issuing or delivering the policy. The insurer must retain one copy signed by the applicant and the producer. The "Notice Regarding Replacement" must inform the applicant of the *30-day free-look* provision of the policy.

When a Medicare supplement policy replaces another, the replacing insurer must waive any periods regarding the following in the new Medicare supplement policy: pre-existing conditions, elimination periods, waiting periods, and probationary periods. Suppose a Medicare supplement policy replaces another that has been effective for six months or more. In that situation, the replacing policy cannot have any time requirements on pre-existing conditions, elimination periods, waiting periods, or probationary periods similar to the original policy.

Disclosure Statement – Medicare Supplement policies must include a renewal or continuation provision that is appropriately captioned and on the first page of the policy. It needs to include any reservation by the insurer of the right to change premiums and any automatic renewal premium increases based on the policy owner's age (attained age policies). Issue age policies do not permit an increase in premiums based on age; they allow an increase in premiums only because of increased benefits.

Insurance providers must also furnish an outline of coverage with each Medicare supplement policy that informs the insured or applicant of the basic nature and provisions of the policy.

Medicare Supplement policies must not allow for payment of benefits based on the standards described as *reasonable and customary, usual and customary, or similar words.*

Insurance providers that issue Medicare Supplement insurance policies in New York must provide the disclosure statement to the applicant along with the application. The disclosure statement must be issued in straightforward language and format, in at least *12-point type*, and has to consist of four parts, all of which must be prominently displayed:

1. A cover page;
2. Premium information – on the cover page or immediately following it;
3. Disclosure pages; and
4. Charts displaying the features of each benefit plan offered by the insurance provider, displayed on the cover page.

Renewability – The *guaranteed issue* provision stipulates that during the six months after a person eligible for Medicare coverage due to age signs up for Part B, an insurer issuing this type of plan cannot:

- Deny or implement conditions on the issuance or effectiveness of any Medicare supplement policy available for sale in this state;
- Discriminate in the pricing of that policy because of the health status, receipt of health care, claims experience, or medical condition of an applicant;
- Impose an exclusion of benefits because of a pre-existing condition under the policy.

This provision does not prevent the exclusion of benefits during the first six months based upon a pre-existing condition. The policy owner must have received treatment or a diagnosis six months before the policy became effective.

Each Medicare Supplement policy has to be *guaranteed renewable*, meaning that the insured has the right to continue the Medicare Supplement insurance coverage by paying the premiums. The issuer has no right to make any changes to policy provisions except for the following:

- Change benefits intended to cover cost-sharing amounts under Medicare to coincide with any changes in the applicable copayments and deductibles;
- Amend the policy to meet the minimum standards for Medicare Supplement insurance; or
- Revise premium rates on a class basis.

Federal Patient Protection and Affordable Care Act (PPACA)

The *Patient Protection and Affordable Care Act (PPACA or ACA, or the Act)* was signed into law on March 23, 2010, as part of the Health Care and Education Reconciliation Act of 2010 (Public Law 111 through 148). The ACA is a comprehensive bill implemented in phases until fully effective in 2018. Since the bill is a federal law, the Act supersedes state regulations and must conform accordingly.

The Act mandates increased educational, preventive, and community-based health care services. To help lower health insurance costs, the ACA intends to do the following:

- Establish a new competitive private health insurance market;
- Hold insurance companies accountable by keeping premiums low, preventing denials of care, and allowing applicants with pre-existing conditions to obtain coverage (the ACA eliminated pre-existing conditions exclusions as of January 2014);
- Stabilize the economy and the budget by reducing the deficit through cutting government spending; and
- Extend coverage for dependent children until age 26 in individual and group health plans.

Also, it gives small businesses and nonprofits a tax credit for an employer's contribution to health insurance for employees. It prohibits insurers from rescinding health coverage when an insured becomes ill and eliminates lifetime benefit limits.

Specific health coverage plans, such as stand-alone dental, retiree-only, Medigap, and long-term care insurance, are usually *exempt* from the ACA changes.

These provisions are controversial, and health care laws are constantly being challenged in the courts. Agents should review current laws to ensure they give up-to-date information and advice.

Eligibility – The Health Insurance Marketplace makes health coverage available to uninsured individuals. To be eligible for health coverage through the Marketplace, the person:

- Has to be a U.S. citizen or national or be legally present in the United States;
- Has to live in the United States; and
- Cannot be currently incarcerated.

If a person has Medicare coverage, that person is *not eligible* to use the Marketplace to buy a health or dental plan.

Health status (no discrimination) – A group health plan or insurer offering group or individual health coverage cannot establish eligibility rules based on any of the following health status-related factors linked to insureds or their dependents:

- Claims experience;
- Health status;
- Medical condition (including both physical and mental illnesses);
- Medical history;
- Receipt of health care;
- Genetic information;
- Evidence of insurability (including conditions resulting from acts of domestic violence);
- Disability; or
- Any other health status-related factor.

When health insurance providers set their premium rates, they are only allowed to base those rates on four standards:

1. Location of residence within the state (geographic rating area);
2. Single or family enrollment (family composition);
3. Age; and
4. Tobacco use.

For individual plans, the location refers to the insured's home address; for small group plans, the location relates to the employer's principal place of business.

Essential benefits – Essential benefits include hospitalization, emergency services, wellness and preventive services, chronic disease management, and maternity care.

It is essential to note that all Health Insurance Marketplace plans are required to cover pregnancy and childbirth, even if pregnancy begins before the coverage becomes effective

Guaranteed issue – Insurers must accept any eligible applicant for individual or group insurance coverage. Enrollment for coverage can be restricted to open or special enrollment periods.

Guaranteed renewability – An insurer that offers either group or individual health coverage must renew or continue the policy at the option of the individual or the plan sponsor.

Pre-existing conditions – Under the ACA, the Pre-Existing Condition Insurance Plan offers coverage to those who private insurers have denied health insurance due to a pre-existing condition.

Appeal rights – When insurers rescind individual or group coverage for fraud or an intentional misrepresentation of material facts, they must provide at least 30 days' advance notice to give the insured time to appeal. All insureds or enrollees have the right to review their files, present evidence and testimony as part of the appeal process, and keep their coverage in force pending the outcome of the appeals process.

Coverage for children of the insured – The Act extends coverage for the insured's children to age 26 irrespective of their residency, marital status, financial dependence on their parents, or eligibility to enroll in their employer's health plan. Coverage for dependent children can continue beyond the limiting age (the child's 26th birthday) if the child continues to be:

- Unable to self-sustain employment due to a physical or intellectual disability; and
- Predominantly dependent upon the policy owner or subscriber for support and maintenance.

Lifetime and annual limits – Health plans are restricted from applying a dollar limit on essential benefits. They cannot establish a dollar limit on the benefits paid during an insured's lifetime.

Emergency care – Emergency services must be covered, even at an out-of-network provider, for amounts that would have been paid to an in-network provider for delivering the same services.

Preventive benefits – The ACA stipulates that 100% of preventative care will be covered without cost sharing. Preventive care includes counseling, screenings, and routine checkups to prevent health problems.

Cost-sharing under Group Health Plans – A group health plan has to ensure that any imposed annual cost-sharing does not exceed provided limitations.

The Act established *insurance exchanges* that administer health insurance subsidies and facilitate enrollment in private health insurance, Medicaid, and the Children's Health Insurance Program (CHIP). An exchange can assist the applicant in doing the following:

- Compare private health plans;
- Obtain information concerning health coverage options to make educated decisions;
- Obtain information concerning eligibility or tax credits for the most affordable coverage;
- Enroll in a health insurance plan that meets the applicant's needs.

Essential Health Benefits

The Affordable Care Act requires every health care plan to include the following *ten essential benefits*:

1. Emergency services;
2. Ambulatory patient services;
3. Hospitalization;
4. Maternity, pregnancy, and newborn care;
5. Services for mental health and substance abuse disorder, including behavioral health treatment;

6. Prescription drugs;
7. Rehabilitative and habilitative services and devices;
8. Laboratory services;
9. Chronic disease management and preventive and wellness services; and
10. Pediatric services, including oral and vision care.

Metal Levels

Under the Affordable Care Act, plans in the Marketplace are classified into five coverage categories, including four "metal level" plans and catastrophic plans.

The metal level plans cover different amounts of an average individual's care costs. The actual percentage the insured will pay per service or in total will depend on the services used during the year. Generally, the metal level plans will pay as follows:

1. Bronze: 60%
2. Silver: 70%
3. Gold: 80%
4. Platinum: 90%

For example, under the bronze plan, the health plan is expected to cover 60% of the cost for an average population, and the participants would cover the remaining 40%. Participants with severe diseases can pay significantly more.

Every insurer that offers adult and family coverage under the metal levels must also offer child-only coverage.

Young adults under age 30 and individuals who have a hardship exemption (cannot buy affordable coverage) may be able to obtain individual catastrophic plans that cover essential benefits. These plans have lower monthly premiums and high deductibles (several thousand dollars). The insured is typically required to pay up to a certain amount of medical costs. After the insured satisfies the deductible, the catastrophic plan will cover essential health benefits costs.

Exchanges

Every state is required to establish *Affordable Insurance Exchanges, known as Marketplaces*. These exchanges will either serve both individual and small business clients separately or have a combined exchange to serve individuals and small businesses under one organization. In states that have chosen not to build their own Marketplace, a *Federally-Facilitated Marketplace* (healthcare.gov) is available that assists with eligibility and enrollment, plan management, and consumer support. Coverage can be purchased through the Marketplace's website, call center, or by postal mail.

Under these regulations, states that choose to set up an Exchange for Small Business Health Options Program (SHOP) must implement the federal standards for the program. States can also enact a law or regulation adopting federal standards to set up insurance options for small employer participation. A SHOP provides small employers with the same purchasing power as large employers. It also allows them to make a single monthly payment and offers a choice of plans.

The ACA defines *small employers* as those with at least one but not more than 100 employees. In 2017, states allowed large employers to obtain coverage through SHOP exchanges.

Insurance exchanges may or may not have open enrollment periods for small employers but have to admit small employers whenever they apply for coverage.

The *NY State of Health (NYSOH)* is an organized marketplace that helps individuals shop for and enroll in health insurance coverage. Individuals, families, and small businesses use the Marketplace to compare insurance options, calculate costs, and choose coverage. The Marketplace helps individuals check their eligibility for health care programs like Medicaid and sign up for them if they are eligible. The Marketplace also specifies what type of financial assistance is available to applicants to help them afford health insurance obtained through the Marketplace.

Enrollment

State insurance exchanges must allow an *initial open enrollment* period, *annual open enrollment* periods after the initial period (currently scheduled from November 1 through January 31), and *special enrollment* periods. Enrollees or individuals have 60 days from the date of a triggering event to choose a qualified health plan unless expressly stated otherwise. Triggering or qualifying events include the birth or adoption of a child, marriage, divorce, change in employment, or termination of health coverage.

Enrollees and qualified individuals can enroll in or change from one qualified health plan to another due to the following triggering events:

- A qualified individual or dependent loses their minimum coverage;
- A qualified individual adds a dependent or becomes a dependent through birth, marriage, adoption, or placement for adoption;
- A person who was not previously a citizen or lawfully present individual who gains such status;
- A qualified individual's enrollment or non-enrollment in a qualified health plan is erroneous or unintentional and is the result of the misrepresentation, error, or inaction of an employee, officer, or agent of the exchange;
- An enrollee adequately establishes that the qualified health plan in which they are enrolled substantially violated a material provision of its contract;
- A person is deemed newly eligible or newly ineligible for advance payments of the premium tax credit or has a change in eligibility status for cost-sharing reductions, irrespective of whether the individual is enrolled in a qualified health plan;
- An enrollee or qualified individual gains access to new qualified health plans due to a permanent move;
- A Native American, as defined by the Indian Health Care Improvement Act, can enroll in a qualified plan or change from one qualified health plan to another qualified plan once per month; and
- A qualified individual or enrollee establishes that they meet other exceptional circumstances as the exchange may allow.

Individual Mandate

Initially, the Affordable Care Act required every U.S. citizen and legal resident to have qualifying health care coverage. This requirement was the *individual mandate* and part of the Act's *Shared Responsibility Provision*. A federal tax penalty would be assessed if the person did not have qualifying health care. The penalty would be based on the individual's taxable income, dependents, and joint filing status.

As of 2019, the individual mandate and shared responsibility penalty *no longer apply*. However, many states have an individual health insurance mandate. In these states, an individual must have qualifying health coverage or pay a *state tax penalty*.

Employer Penalties – The following are penalties for employers with more than 50 full-time employees if at least one employee receives a premium tax credit for health care coverage:

Coverage	Penalty Tax
Employer *does not* offer coverage	$2,000 per full-time employee (first 30 employees are excluded)
Employer *offers* coverage	The lesser of $3,000 per employee who receives a premium tax credit or $2,000 per each full-time employee (first 30 employees are excluded)

Employers with fewer than 50 full-time employees are exempt from these penalties.

Benchmark Plans

A *benchmark plan* is the second-lowest-priced silver plan available within a state's health insurance exchange in a particular geographical region. Benchmark plans establish the specifics of the Essential Health Benefits required of every ACA plan sold in New York. Tax credit amounts are calculated on the cost of this benchmark plan. They are then adjusted according to an enrollee's annual income. Consumers eligible for premium tax credits do not have to purchase the benchmark plan in their region. They will not lose out on these credits by selecting a different plan.

Chapter Review

This chapter explained a variety of accident and health policy provisions, disability income insurance, and medical plans. Let's review some of the key concepts:

	INDIVIDUAL HEALTH INSURANCE POLICY PROVISIONS

Uniform Required Provisions	• *Entire contract* - policy (with riders and amendments) and a copy of the app
	• *Grace period* - time period after the premium is due during which the policy will not lapse
	• *Reinstatement* - a policy can be restored within a specified period with proof of insurability
	• *Change of beneficiary:*
	   ○ *Revocable* - can be changed at any time
	   ○ *Irrevocable* - can only be changed with the beneficiary's consent
	• *Notice of claim* - the insured must provide the insurer with reasonable notice after a loss; notice is required within 20 days of loss, or as soon as possible
	• *Claim form* - the insurer must supply the insured with claims forms within a specific period
	• *Proof of loss* - claimant must submit proof of loss within 90 days of a loss
	• *Time of payment of claims* - claims must be paid upon written proof of loss
	• *Payment of claims* - specifies to whom claims payments will be made
	• *Physical examination and autopsy* - provides the insurer the right to examine the insured as often as necessary while a claim is pending
	• *Time limit on certain defenses* - misstatements on an application cannot be used to deny a claim after the policy has been in force for two years
	• *Legal action* - an insured must wait 60 days after written proof of loss before bringing legal action against the insurer

Uniform Optional Provisions *(Continued)*	• *Misstatement of age* - benefits are adjusted according to what the paid premium would have purchased at the correct age • *Change of occupation* - allows the insurer to adjust benefits if the insured changes occupations • *Illegal occupation* - liability will be denied if the insured is engaged in an illegal occupation or is injured while committing an illegal act • *Other insurance in this insurer* - pro rata benefit reduction in response to over-insurance • *Insurance with other insurers* - separate insurers pay proportionate benefits for any one claim • *Unpaid premium* - past due accounts are deducted from the claim amount • *Cancellation* - the insurer can cancel the policy with a written notice • *Conformity with state statutes* - conflicting policies are automatically amended • *Intoxicants and narcotics* - the insurer is not liable for claims resulting from intoxicants or drug use
Other Provisions and Clauses	• *Insuring clause* - a basic agreement between the policy owner and the insurer • *Free look* - the policy can be returned for a refund within a specified period • *Consideration* - the parties to a contract exchange something of value • *Probationary period* - states that a period must lapse before coverage for specified conditions goes into effect • *Elimination period* - a period of days that must pass after the occurrence of an accident or onset of an illness before disability income benefits will be payable • *Coinsurance* - allows the sharing of expenses between the insured and the insurer; expressed as a percentage after the insured pays the policy deductible • *Exclusions* - specifies causes of loss for which the insurer will not pay, including losses from military duty, war, self-inflicted injuries, cosmetic medical expenses, dental expense, eye refractions, or care in government facilities
MEDICAL PLANS CONCEPTS	
Major Medical Insurance (Indemnity Plans)	• High maximum limits • Blanket coverage is provided • Deductibles are paid up front • Costs are shared after meeting the deductible
Health Care Services Organization (HMOs)	• Preventive care; prepaid basis; limited to the service area • *Basic benefit services* - physician, hospital inpatient, outpatient medical, preventive, urgent care, emergency, diagnostic lab, out-of-area coverage • *Optional benefits* - long-term care, nursing services, home health, prescription drugs, dental/vision care, mental health care, substance abuse services
Preferred Provider Organizations (PPOs)	• Physicians are paid on a fee for service basis • No primary care physician referrals • Members can use any physician they choose, but are encouraged to use approved physicians who have previously agreed upon fees
Point-of-Service Plans (POS)	• Combines HMO and PPO plans • Employees are not locked into one plan; they are allowed to choose depending on the need for medical services • Non-member physicians are paid service fee; patient pays higher coinsurance

MEDICARE SUPPLEMENT POLICIES	
Basics	- Also referred to as Medigap
- Policies issued by private insurers to fill in gaps in Medicare coverage
- Open enrollment period of six months
Coverage	- *Plan A* - core benefits, such as coinsurance/copayment; additional Part A hospital costs; hospice care coinsurance/copayment; Part B coinsurance/copayment; Three pints of blood under Parts A and B
- *Plans B – N* - core benefits plus various additional benefits
FEDERAL PATIENT PROTECTION AND AFFORDABLE CARE ACT (PPACA)	
Features and Coverages	- Mandates preventive, educational, and community-based health care
- Premium rates can be based on geographic rating area, family composition, age, and tobacco use
- Children are covered until age 26
- Coverage for pre-existing conditions
- *Enrollment period* - November 1 to January 31
- Metal levels/plan covers:
- Bonze 60%
- Silver 70%
- Gold 80%
- Platinum 90%
- *Grandfathered plan* - existing provisions that are not required to change in response to new laws, restrictions, or requirements
Eligibility	- Must be a U.S. citizen or U.S. national or be lawfully present in the U.S.
- Must live in the United States
- Cannot be currently incarcerated
Ten Essential Health Benefits	- Ambulatory patient services
- Emergency services
- Hospitalization
- Pregnancy, maternity and newborn care
- Mental health and substance use
- Prescription drugs
- Rehabilitative and habilitative services and devices
- Laboratory services
- Preventive and wellness services and chronic disease management
- Pediatric services, including oral and vision care
Insurance Exchanges (Marketplace)	- Federally-facilitated marketplace
- State exchanges
- SHOP
- Helps applicants to:
- Compare private health plans
- Obtain information about health coverage and eligibility or tax credits
- Enroll in an appropriate health plan

KEY FACTS

Knowing the key facts can be the difference between passing and failing your exam. Read through each chapter for a quick review of essential terms and concepts presented in this book.

Insurance Regulation

Licensing

Definitions

- Agents are also known as producers.
- Any individual or business entity acting as an insurance producer must be licensed by the state.
- Insurance providers must appoint an agent that they represent.
- A home state is defined as the District of Columbia or any state or territory of the U.S. where the applicant maintains a principal place of business or residence and is licensed to act as an insurance producer.
- A resident licensee has declared New York as their home state.
- A domestic insurer is domiciled in this state.
- An alien insurer is domiciled in a foreign country.
- A foreign insurer is domiciled in another state.
- An agent is an individual who solicits, negotiates, or sells insurance on behalf of an insurance provider.
- Selling refers to the exchange of an insurance contract for money.
- Soliciting refers to the attempt to sell insurance.

Process

- To qualify for a New York resident license, an applicant must be at least 18, complete any necessary pre-licensing education, pass the appropriate exam (if required), submit an application for a license to the Department within two years of passing the exam, and pay the required licensing fee.
- Candidates for a life and health agent or broker license must complete 40 hours of required pre-licensing education unless they hold the CLU (Chartered Life Underwriter) designation.
- For applicants who are currently licensed or who have been licensed in another state and are relocating to New York, the exam and education requirements can be waived if they submit a Letter of Clearance stating that they have been licensed in good standing in their initial state within the last 90 days.
- In addition to their state life insurance license, producers require a federal FINRA securities license to sell variable products like variable life or variable annuities.

Types of Licenses

Agent

- An insurance provider authorizes an agent to solicit or negotiate insurance.
- Agents represent the insurance providers rather than the insured.

Brokers

- An insurance broker is any individual that solicits, negotiates, or sells insurance on behalf of an insured.
- Applicants for a Life Settlement Broker license can be exempt from an examination if they are licensed for at least one year as a life insurance agent or broker.
- A Life Settlement Broker is a person who, for compensation, solicits, negotiates, or offers to negotiate a life settlement contract on behalf of a policy owner.

Consultants

- A Life Insurance Consultant provides clients with professional and expert advice on insurance.
- A Life Insurance Consultant provides professional and expert advice on insurance to clients.

- Consultants cannot solicit, negotiate, or sell insurance unless licensed as agents.
- A consultant's compensation needs to be based upon a written agreement signed by their client.

Adjusters

- An adjuster must be licensed as an independent or a public adjuster.
- Independent adjusters adjust claims on behalf of an insurance provider.
- Public adjusters adjust claims on behalf of an insured.

Nonresident

- A nonresident licensee has declared a state other than New York as their home state and has a license in good standing in that state.
- Nonresident licenses are based upon reciprocal agreements between states. They can be issued without an exam if the applicant is appropriately licensed in their home state.

Business Entities

- Business entities like partnerships, legal liability companies, and corporations can be licensed as producers. The sub-licensee named in the licensing application will be held responsible for the entities' compliance with the New York Insurance Code.

Temporary

- The Superintendent can issue a temporary license for up to 90 days, without an exam, to the surviving next of kin of a deceased producer or a producer who becomes totally disabled.
- The Superintendent can issue a temporary license for up to six months, without an exam, to the designee of a licensed producer entering the armed forces.
- Licensees must report to the Superintendent any administrative action taken against them in another jurisdiction or by another government agency in New York within 30 days of the matter's final disposition.

Maintenance and Duration

- Producer licenses expire biennially on the licensee's birthday.
- All licensed brokers, agents, consultants, and public adjusters must complete 15 hours of continuing education courses every two years.
- Although they are required to obtain a license, agents who sell only accident or baggage insurance are exempt from an examination and continuing education requirements.
- The Insurance Superintendent requires the filing of an assumed name to be used by a producer before use.
- A producer cannot use an assumed name unless it has first been filed with the Superintendent.
- A licensee must inform the Superintendent of a change of address, including an email address, within 30 days of the change.
- Every insurance provider, upon receipt of any inquiry from the Department respecting a claim, must furnish the Department with the available information requested within ten business days.

Disciplinary Actions

- If, after a hearing, the Superintendent concludes that a method of competition or practice is deceptive or unfair, they can issue an order requiring an individual to cease and desist from participating in such a practice.
- If the Superintendent determines that a licensee is guilty of fraud, they can revoke, suspend, or refuse to renew the license. Still, they cannot place a licensee on probation.

- The Superintendent can revoke or suspend a producer's license for writing controlled business. Controlled business is when a producer receives more than 10% of commissions in 12 months from insurance sold to a business associate, immediate family member, or spouse.
- The Superintendent can impose a civil penalty not exceeding $5,000 plus payment of the claim against anyone who commits a fraudulent insurance act.
- All insurance applications must include a notice to the applicant regarding the penalties for committing a fraudulent insurance act.
- Anyone who violates a cease and desist order can be liable for a penalty of up to $5,000 per violation.

State Regulation

Superintendent's General Duties and Powers

- The New York State Governor appoints the Superintendent of Financial Services (Superintendent) to preside over the Department of Financial Services and administer and enforce the New York State Insurance Code.
- The Superintendent supervises the business of and the individuals providing financial products and services, including anyone subject to the provisions of the banking law and the insurance law.
- The Superintendent has the authority to conduct investigations of matters affecting the interests of consumers of financial products and services.
- The Superintendent protects users of financial products and services by doing the following: reviewing complaints, referring matters to the Attorney General, making recommendations to the Governor, initiating consumer financial education programs, and continuing and expanding the prevention, detection, and investigation of insurance fraud.

Company Regulation

- Insurance providers must obtain a Certificate of Authority from the Superintendent admitting or authorizing them to transact insurance in New York.
- To prove solvency, authorized insurance providers must file audited annual financial statements with the Superintendent, proving that they have adequate legal reserves to pay claims.
- Offering to settle a claim for less than a reasonable person would expect is an unfair claims settlement practice.
- It is an unfair claims settlement practice to not attempt in good faith to bring about a fair, prompt, and equitable claims settlement where liability has become apparent.
- Insurance providers cannot engage in unfair claims settlement practices with such frequency as to indicate a general business practice.
- Insurance providers must submit a certificate of appointment for every producer with the Superintendent.
- Notice of appointment has to be given to the Superintendent within 15 days from the date the agency contract is executed.
- When terminating an agent's appointment for cause, insurance providers must submit a statement stating the facts to the Superintendent within 30 days.

Unfair and Prohibited Practices

- When there is reason to believe that an individual has committed an unfair trade practice, the Superintendent can conduct a hearing by giving ten days advance written notice.
- Every insurance provider must establish an internal department to investigate and resolve complaints filed with the Department of Financial Services.
- It is considered a misrepresentation when an agent makes misleading statements regarding past or future dividends.

- It is considered misrepresentation for an agent to make an incomplete comparison of insurance policies to induce someone to lapse, forfeit, or surrender a policy.
- A misrepresentation by an insured will not void the policy unless it was material in that the insurance provider would not have issued the policy if it knew the facts.
- If an insured makes a material misrepresentation on their application, the policy can be rescinded or voided.
- Dividends cannot be guaranteed.
- Advertisements cannot include deceptive, untrue, or misleading statements.
- Defamation is defined as making a false oral or written statement derogatory to the financial condition or affecting the solvency or financial standing of an insurance provider.
- Insurance providers cannot discriminate based on color, race, sex, marital status, national origin, creed, or disability.
- Offering a customer an inducement to encourage them to obtain a policy (like a return of commission) is a prohibited and unfair practice called rebating.
- Articles of merchandise with a stamped or printed advertisement of the broker, agent, or insurer are not considered rebates if they are valued at $25 or less.

License Regulation

- Writing coverage on one's own life, business associates, or family members is prohibited and considered controlled business.
- Fiduciary duties include handling premiums.
- Upon notification of a claim, every insurance provider must acknowledge the receipt of such notice within 15 working days.
- The license of each supervising or responsible individual must be prominently displayed at each broker's or agent's office.
- Producers have 30 days to file written comments with the Superintendent relating to the content of a notice of termination
- The Superintendent must audit the records and books of every authorized domestic insurance provider at least once every five years.
- Insurers must maintain a record for each contract for six years after the policy termination date.
- The Insurance Fraud Prevention Act was passed to address the potential for illegal activities and abuse in issuing policies and the payment of claims.
- All individuals and corporations are prohibited from soliciting or negotiating an insurance or annuity contract without a license.
- Under the Consumer Privacy Regulation, no later than the delivery time of a new policy and at least once every year after that, insurance providers must give insureds a notice explaining their privacy policies.
- Under the Consumer Privacy Regulation, customers have the right to opt out of having their information shared with an unaffiliated third party.
- All financial services companies must implement and maintain a cybersecurity program to prevent cyberattacks and implement recovery procedures if one occurs.
- Insurance providers must also maintain a cybersecurity program to prevent cyberattacks and implement recovery procedures if one occurs.

Commissions and Compensation

- An insurance provider cannot pay a commission to an individual not licensed in New York.
- If an individual was licensed at the time of the sale of an insurance policy, they could receive renewal or deferred commissions even if they are no longer licensed.

- The Producer Compensation Transparency regulation sets forth minimum disclosure requirements regarding the role of insurance producers and their compensation.
- Suppose a buyer wants more information about the producer's compensation, the amount, nature, and the source of the payment to be received. Under the Producer Compensation Transparency regulation, the producer must disclose it in writing to the buyer, and a copy has to be retained by the producer for at least three years.
- A producer compensation disclosure must include a description of the producer's role in the transaction and the buyer's right to request information regarding the producer's compensation.

Federal Regulation

Fair Credit Reporting Act

- The federal Fair Credit Reporting Act (FCRA) stipulates that consumer reports must be ordered according to federal law.
- The FCRA gives customers the right to question reports made about them by consumer reporting agencies.

Fraud and False Statements Act

- A person convicted of violating the federal Fraud and False Statements Act in New York can be fined and imprisoned for up to 15 years and prohibited from working in the insurance industry without the Superintendent's prior consent.

General Insurance

Key Concepts

- Insurance is the transfer of pure risk to the insurer in consideration for a premium.
- The chance of loss without any chance of gain is known as pure risk.
- Speculative risk has the opportunity for gain or loss and is not insurable.
- Risk is the chance of loss.
- A condition that could end up in a loss is called exposure.
- A hazard increases the possibility of loss.
- The presence of a physical hazard increases the probability of a loss occurring.
- A peril is a cause of loss, like a fire.
- To be insurable, losses have to be calculable.
- The law of large numbers allows insurance providers to predict claims more accurately.
- The law of large numbers applies to groups of people, not to individuals. The larger the group, the more accurate the predictions will be.
- Most insurance providers buy reinsurance to protect themselves from a catastrophic loss.
- Insurance laws do not have to be uniform from one state to another.

Insurers

- A stock insurer can pay dividends to its shareholders (stockholders), but they cannot be guaranteed.
- An attorney-in-fact manages a reciprocal insurer.
- The government offers insurance primarily based on social needs, like workers compensation and flood insurance, but does not offer insurance to prevent fraud.

- An unincorporated association of individuals who insure each other is called a reciprocal insurer.
- A foreign insurer has a home office in another state.
- An insurer incorporated outside of the U.S. who sells in the U.S. is an alien insurer.

Producers and General Rules of Agency

- A producer can be personally liable when violating the producer's contract.
- Producers represent the insurer, not the insured.
- Independent producers own their accounts and are not insurance company employees.
- Producers have express, implied, and apparent authority.
- The authority a producer has written in their contract is called express authority.
- A producer's binding authority (if any) is expressed (written down) in the producer's contract with the insurance provider the producer represents.
- The authority not expressly (written) granted, but is the actual authority the producer has to transact regular business activities, is called implied authority.

Contracts

- The elements of a legal contract can be remembered by the acronym C-O-A-L (consideration, offer, acceptance, legal purpose, and legal capacity).
- A requirement for a valid contract is a mutual agreement or offer and acceptance.
- Advertising the availability of insurance is not an offer.
- A specific proposal to enter into a contract is known as an offer.
- The consideration of a policy does not need to be equal.
- A policy cannot be voided because of unequal consideration.
- Under the consideration clause, something of value needs to be exchanged.
- Since insurance contracts are contracts of adhesion, policy ambiguities always favor the insured.
- Insurance policies are considered unilateral contracts in that only one party makes an enforceable promise to the insurance provider.
- The principle of indemnity specifies that the purpose of insurance is to restore the insured to the same position as before the loss took place.
- The principle of utmost good faith stipulates that all parties to an insurance transaction are honest.
- A representation is considered the truth to the best of one's knowledge.
- A warranty is a sworn statement of truth, guaranteed to be true.
- A breach of warranty can void a contract.
- Concealment is defined as the failure to disclose a material fact.
- When an insurance provider voluntarily gives up the right to obtain information that they are entitled to, they have made a waiver.

Property and Casualty Basics

Terms and Concepts

- A direct cause of loss is also referred to as a proximate cause of loss.
- A deductible represents a form of risk retention.
- The higher the deductible, the lower the premium, and vice versa.
- Rates are a factor when calculating the premium.

- All-risk property policies are also known as open peril policies.
- To see what is covered on an all-risk or open-peril policy, an applicant must read the exclusions.
- Strict or absolute liability is liability without negligence.
- Strict liability is not a defense against a negligence lawsuit.
- Under the principle of comparative negligence, benefits payable to an injured party are reduced according to their own negligence, preventing an injured party from collecting damages related to their own negligence.
- Under contributory negligence, the injured party cannot recover if they are partly at fault.
- The purpose of subrogation is to prevent the insured from collecting twice.
- A binder of coverage can be either oral or in writing.

Policy Structure

- The four parts of a policy can be remembered by the acronym D-I-C-E (declarations, insuring agreement, conditions, and exclusions).
- The declarations list the named insured, policy limits, and the premium and policy periods.
- The limits of liability are found on the policy's declarations page.
- The insuring agreement lists the covered perils and describes the coverages provided.
- The conditions list the obligations of both parties, the insured and the insurance provider.
- The exclusions list the perils that are not covered.
- Exclusions exist in an insurance policy to clarify coverage.
- Supplementary payments included in the liability section of a policy are paid in addition to the liability limits.
- An endorsement modifies the terms of the policy, not policy conditions.

Provisions and Clauses

- The policy period is defined as the time the policy is effective.
- When an insured transfers their right of ownership to another party, it is called an assignment.
- Appraisal is used on property policies to determine the amount payable.
- Arbitration is used on liability policies to determine if coverage applies.
- If the insurance provider and the insured disagree that the liability policy does or does not provide coverage, the claim will go to arbitration.
- In arbitration, there are three arbitrators.
- The cancellation provisions are found in the conditions section of the policy.
- The insured must promptly notify the insurance provider about a claim.
- The maximum amount an insurance provider will pay is specified in the limits of liability.
- The purpose of coinsurance is to ensure the client carries adequate limits.
- The other insurance (or pro-rata liability) clause on a property policy allows two or more policies insuring the same property to pay claims proportionately.
- Pro-rata means proportionate; it does not mean equal.
- On property policies, abandonment of the property to the insurance provider is prohibited.
- The liberalization clause allows the insurance provider to increase coverage immediately at no charge.
- Insurance providers can sell the salvage to offset the claims expenses.
- Vacancy means a person has moved out of their home and taken their furniture.
- Unoccupied means a person is on an extended vacation. However, their furniture is still in their home, and they will return.

Key Facts

Dwelling Policy

- The primary difference among the various dwelling policy (DP) forms is the insured against property perils.
- DP policies do not cover personal liability; however, it can be added as a Personal Liability Supplement for an additional premium.
- DP policies include general exclusions for damage due to nuclear hazards, war, and floods but not wind.
- On a dwelling policy, Other Structures coverage applies to a structure rented as a private garage.
- DP policies will not cover the breakage of glass after 60 days of a vacancy.
- DP policies will not cover frozen plumbing unless the heat is on when the plumbing freezes.
- Insurers cannot cover the land on which the policy owner's dwelling sits.
- Inflation guard, also called the automatic increase endorsement, has to be added by endorsement to a DP policy.
- Insurers would only cover a loss from dust or rain if an opening in the dwelling's walls or the roof was first created by wind or another covered cause of loss.
- When a dwelling is insured by more than one policy, losses are shared pro rata under the other insurance clause. This clause may also be called the pro rata liability clause.
- The Basic dwelling form DP-1 is a specified or named peril policy.
- The DP-1 Basic Form does not cover additional living expenses under Coverage D; only fair rental value is covered.
- On the DP-1 form, the Extended Coverage Endorsement is added to the Standard Fire Policy.
- A DP-2 Broad Form is a named peril policy on the dwelling and its contents.
- On the dwelling broad form DP-2 (Coverages A and B), building structures are issued with an 80% coinsurance requirement.
- On a DP-2 Broad Form, Coverage B (Other Structures) exceeds other coverage limits.
- The DP-3 policy provides identical coverage as the DP-2 (Contents Broad) policy for personal property coverage.
- Although the DP-1 Basic Form does not provide coverage for lawns, plants, shrubs, and trees, the DP-2 and DP-3 forms offer this coverage.
- When a dwelling policy is referred to as DP-2 ('02), it relates to the Dwelling Property Broad Form. The ('02) designates that it is the ISO policy form introduced in 2002.

Homeowners Policy

- Every HO policy is a package policy combining property and liability coverages.
- The limit of liability is the most a policy will pay under the liability section.
- An insured includes residents of a household who are relatives or any other individual under age 21 who is in the care of the insured.
- All HO policies exclude coverage for mudslides, landslides, or floods.
- The homeowners policy does not cover the theft of fish, birds, or animals.
- Personal injury liability for defamation, slander, libel, false arrest, and invasion of privacy is not automatically covered by a HO policy. It can be added by endorsement for an added premium.
- Insurers cannot cover the land on which a house is located on HO policies.

- Section II (Liability) will pay for damage to the property of others up to $1,000 per occurrence.
- The HO policy will not cover the property of a renter or boarder; it will protect the property of a residence employee or guest.
- The HO policy will cover contents worldwide, including theft.
- The HO policy written on a dwelling during construction will not cover theft.
- Medical coverage will pay for charges related to medical, hospital, nursing, ambulance, x-ray, surgical, dental, prosthetic devices, and funeral services.
- Medical payments do not apply to regular household members.
- The bankruptcy of a policyholder does not relieve the insurance provider of their duties under the policy.
- Most property policies do not cover claims resulting from the enforcement of a law or ordinance. However, limited coverage can be provided as additional coverage.
- The insurance provider's responsibility to defend a lawsuit is stated in the insuring agreement.
- Additional coverages (such as for plants, shrubs, and trees) are over and above the policy limit.
- HO liability pays for bodily injury to a third party.
- If an insurance provider cancels the HO policy, they must send advance written notice to the named insured and the mortgage company.
- The HO policy will not cover the cost of defense on an excluded claim.
- The HO policy covers contents in total while in transit for up to 30 days.
- Coverage C will not pay for the property of a tenant, roomer, or boarder unless they are related to the policy owner.
- Most property policies do not cover claims resulting from the enforcement of a law or ordinance. However, limited coverage can be provided as additional coverage.
- Damage resulting from rain is not covered on a property policy unless the wall or roof was first damaged by hail or wind, allowing the rain to enter.
- Property policies will not pay for damage to motorized vehicles other than those used to maintain the premises (e.g., riding lawn mowers).
- Personal liability and medical coverage will pay for the policyholder's activities on and off the premises.
- Loss of use pays for only additional living expenses.
- The insurance provider's responsibility to defend a lawsuit ends when the amount paid out for damages equals the limit of liability.
- A person hired to maintain the premises is called a residence employee.
- At the policy owner's option, recovered property will be returned to the policy owner or retained by the insurance provider. If the property is returned, the insurer must adjust the loss payment.
- After a loss, if the cost of reconstruction for a home exceeds its market value, the insurance provider will consider it a constructive total loss.
- The HO-2 protects against losses caused by named perils on the dwelling and its contents.
- The HO-3 protects the dwelling and other structures on an open peril basis, and personal property is covered only for broad perils.
- The HO-3 special form policy covers the theft of a resident employee's personal property.
- The HO-4 are property policies issued to tenants to insure against losses caused by a covered peril to alterations, improvements, and additions made to the described location at the tenant's expense.
- Under the HO-6 policy, contents coverage protects against losses caused by named perils.
- The HO-6 (condominium unit owners) form does not insure common area buildings.
- The HO-8 form was created specifically for older homes.

Auto Insurance

Liability

- Liability covers PD and BI to others for which a policy owner is negligent.
- The Auto Assigned Risk Plan provides a method for individuals rejected in the normal market to obtain insurance coverage.
- All authorized insurance companies selling auto insurance must participate in the Auto Assigned Risk Plan.
- Supplementary payments under a personal automobile policy (PAP) do not cover the policy owner's loss of earnings except when they attend a trial or hearing at the insurer's request. The policy owner's injuries are not covered.
- The Personal Auto Coverage Form insures tape decks and radios if they are permanently installed in the dash.
- The medical payment section of the PAP will pay necessary medical and funeral expenses resulting from an accident sustained by a policy owner.
- The medical payments coverage listed in the PAP will not pay for lost wages.
- Auto medical in a PAP covers the policy owner and any passengers in the car. It is no-fault, optional coverage, and is not a supplementary payment.
- On a PAP, medical coverage pays for an at-fault driver's injuries.

Physical Damage

- Part D on a PAP is called Coverage for Damage to Your Auto and is optional. It is divided into two coverages: Collision and Other Than Collision.
- Part D has a deductible and is written on an ACV basis. Other Than Collision coverage is also called comprehensive coverage.
- Hitting a pole with an insured automobile is an example of a collision.
- In the PAP, hitting a deer is an example of other than collision.
- If a bird were to hit the policyholder's windshield, the windshield is covered under other than collision coverage.
- Collision coverage on the PAP covers colliding with other objects, rollover, and upset. All others would be covered by Other Than Collision coverage.
- Towing and labor coverage is optional on the PAP and will cost extra.
- The optional coverage limit for towing and labor pays per occurrence or event.
- Under a PAP, flood damage is covered but not included in property policies.
- In an accident, the injured policy owner's PAP is always the primary policy. The driver's PAP, if different, is always the excess policy.

Uninsured Motorists

- Policy owners purchase uninsured motorist coverage because of their concern of being in an auto accident with a person who has no insurance and is at fault.
- An uninsured motorist refers to hit-and-run drivers, drivers whose insurer has gone bankrupt, and drivers who do not carry the minimum state-required limits.
- If a person is concerned about being in an auto accident with someone with inadequate liability insurance limits and who is at fault, they may purchase underinsured motorist coverage.

Exclusions

- A PAP does not offer coverage in Mexico.
- A PAP does not cover a policy owner's property in transit.
- Auto medical covers the policy owner and passengers but does not cover injured pedestrians.
- A personal automobile policy will cover small pick-up trucks, even if they are used for ranching or farming. It will not cover dump trucks, farm implements, or motorcycles driven on the highway.
- On the PAP, exclusions for the Other than Collision coverage include freezing, wear and tear, and mechanical breakdown.
- The PAP does not cover autos used as livery or taxis, but carpools are covered.

Business Auto

- In a business auto policy, insurers would cover damage to an insured vehicle resulting from a falling object under comprehensive coverage.
- The business auto coverage form does not cover an injured employee driving a company car.
- In a business auto policy, if the employer's partner uses their car during company business, the partner must add owned auto coverage.
- In a business auto policy, if the employer wants to cover their employees while driving their own cars on company business, the employer needs to add hired and non-owned auto coverage.
- In garage insurance, car dealers with fluctuating inventories are encouraged to use reporting forms.
- Garage liability covers a product's liability but does not cover the cost of a product recall.
- The garage coverage form was established for repair shops, auto dealers, parking garages, service stations, and similar risks.
- In a garage form, the garagekeepers coverage insures property in the policy owner's control, custody, and care.

Commercial Lines

Commercial Package Policy (CPP)

- The common conditions section of a CPP allows either the policy owner or the insurance provider to cancel the policy.
- CPPs are subject to a premium audit for three years after a policy's expiration.
- Business income insurance is considered a type of time-element coverage.

Commercial Property

- On a commercial property, ordinance or law coverage and replacement cost coverage value reporting forms are all optional endorsements. Valuation is a loss condition in the insurance policy.
- Commercial property insurance covers the building's unattached signs as business personal property.
- The leasehold interest coverage form protects a policy owner for the value of their lease if it is canceled due to loss or damage from a covered cause of loss.
- The causes of loss forms in commercial property are the basic, broad, and special forms.
- The coverage territory on a commercial property policy includes the U.S., Puerto Rico, and Canada.
- The legal actions clause on a commercial property policy states that the policy owner has a maximum of two years to file a lawsuit against the insurance company.
- Commercial fire policies only cover plants, shrubs, and trees up to $500 each.

Inland Marine
- A list of risks eligible for inland marine coverage published by the National Association of Insurance Commissioners (NAIC) is called the Nationwide Definition.
- On equipment breakdown coverage, the insurance provider may inspect the policy owner's equipment. However, they are not required to do so.
- The scheduled personal property endorsement covers personal property with high values, such as jewelry, antiques, and furs.
- An individual would buy a data processing floater to insure computer equipment properly.
- A fine arts floater will automatically cover newly acquired fine art for 90 days.
- A scheduled personal property floater provides coverage on an ACV basis.
- If a loss to a pair or set occurs, the insurance provider can repair or replace the set to its value before the loss. It can also pay the difference in value before and after the loss. To calculate the difference, the insurance company would subtract the remaining value from the value of the full set.

CGL Coverage
- In a commercial general liability (CGL) policy, the occurrence limits are applied separately for each claim. The aggregate limit applies to each claim submitted during the policy period.
- The CGL policy includes three coverage sections: Part A – Liability, Part B – Personal Injury and Advertising Injury, and Part C – Medical Payments to others. These coverages do not have a deductible.
- A CGL policy will provide liability protection anywhere in the world, provided the product was made within the policy territory, and the lawsuit is filed there.
- The CGL policy territory includes the United States, Puerto Rico, and Canada.
- In a CGL policy, the Medical to Others coverage is applied per person.
- In a CGL policy, Fire coverage is applied per occurrence.

Exposures
- Products liability is applied only after the product is out of the policy owner's control.
- Products liability does not cover the cost of a product recall or the resulting lost income.

Occurrence vs. Claims-Made
- An occurrence basis liability policy covers claims that occur in the policy period, even if a claim is submitted after the expiration date.
- The retroactive date on a claims-made CGL policy only applies to Coverage A (BI and PD).
- All claims-made CGL policies include a basic extended reporting period (ERP) that allows an insured with a pending claim an additional 60 days after expiration to notify their insurer.
- If the claimant notifies the insurance provider within 60 days of the pending claim, they have up to five years to complete the claim. The basic ERP is free.
- The CGL policy does not include coverage for pollution liability. This coverage can be added by optional endorsement for an additional premium.
- A claims-made liability policy requires that the claim occurs after the retroactive date and is submitted during the policy period or within the extended reporting period.

Businessowners Policy

- A businessowners policy (BOP) covers property damage (PD), bodily injury (BI), and personal injury liability, but it does not cover employer liability.
- In a BOP, if the building has been unoccupied for longer than 60 consecutive days, there is no coverage for glass breakage, sprinkler leakage, vandalism, water damage, or theft.
- Auto liability is not covered by an unendorsed BOP, including liability for the operation of a non-owned auto.
- In a BOP, loss of business income is insured without a dollar limit for a maximum of one year.
- Under a businessowners policy, the optional endorsement designed to cover an employee's personal property does not cover theft.
- According to the common conditions section of a BOP, an insurance provider can cancel a policy if the building has been unoccupied or vacant for 60 or more consecutive days.
- Manufacturing companies are not insurable under a BOP.
- A BOP cannot insure a bank or credit union.
- If a policyholder purchases a special policy to cover their printing presses in addition to a BOP, a claim will be pro-rated.
- In a BOP, the protective safeguards warranty allows the insurance provider to deny a claim if systems are not adequately maintained.
- Unendorsed businessowners policies will pay claims on an all-risk basis.
- A BOP written for a tenant will automatically cover betterments and improvements.
- In the BOP, the inflation guard endorsement automatically raises policy limits by 8% on each anniversary date.
- The BOP protects on an all-risk basis for the building and its contents and contains an 80% coinsurance clause. It is issued on a replacement cost basis, and the policy covers theft.
- The BOP automatically covers business liability for PD, BI, personal injury and advertising injury, medical, and fire legal liability.
- When attached to a BOP, the protective safeguard endorsement requires the policy owner to maintain the alarm system or the sprinkler system in good working order.
- The aggregate limit of liability contained in the CGL policy and the BOP is the most the insurance provider will pay for all occurrences during the policy period.

Workers Compensation

- When workers compensation must be purchased from a state fund, it is known as monopolistic.
- When workers compensation can be purchased from either the state fund or any other authorized insurer, it is known as competitive.
- The state establishes workers compensation statutory coverages.
- Workers compensation covers both disease and occupational injury.
- Workers compensation coverage cannot be added to a package policy. It is always a stand-alone policy.
- Under workers compensation, permanent partial disability means the inability to perform job-related functions due to disease or injury.

- If the employee cannot fulfill their job duties but will be able to do so after recovering from a disease or injury, the employee is considered to have a temporary disability.
- Workers compensation covers medical expenses on an unlimited basis.
- An employee who cannot return to work due to a disability is classified as totally disabled.
- If an insurance company issues a workers compensation policy that does not comply with a state's requirements, they must pay the required coverages in case of a claim.
- Upon work-related death, workers compensation will pay income benefits to surviving spouses and children.
- Payroll determines workers compensation premiums and will not be known until after the policy period concludes.
- Under workers compensation insurance, Other States coverage only applies to those states listed in the policy's Declarations.

Other Coverages

- The minimum deductible listed in an earthquake policy is $250. The deductible on earthquake insurance is a percentage of the policy limit.
- When a boatowners policy owner has both a liability and a personal umbrella policy, the liability limits on the boatowners policy would be the primary coverage.
- Farm policies do not insure growing crops or autos driven on the highway.
- In a farm policy, the definition of a dwelling excludes a building used for agricultural purposes.
- Farm risks are not covered under DP or HO forms.

National Flood Insurance Program (NFIP)
- The Federal Insurance Administration (FIA) establishes flood insurance rates. A community is required to cooperate with the FIA to qualify for NFIP.
- Flood refers to the temporary inundation of normally dry land.
- Flood insurance will not cover docks, piers, or wharves.
- NFIP flood insurance does not insure seepage or sewer backup through walls.
- Flood insurance is sold by the government and participating private insurance companies, but the federal government pays claims.
- The maximum insurance allowed under the regular NFIP program is $250,000 for a single-family home.
- To qualify for federal flood insurance, the community must participate in the NFIP.

Umbrella and Excess Liability
- Personal umbrella liability policies will pay on an excess basis only after the primary policy has already been paid.
- An excess limits policy, such as an umbrella policy, is written in addition to the primary liability policy's limits of insurance.
- Umbrella policies include a retention requirement that is like a deductible and must be paid by the policy owner in case of a claim.
- An umbrella policy is not written on a standardized industry form.
- In a personal umbrella policy, the retained limit refers to the policy limits of the primary policies.

Professional Liability

- Lawyers errors and omissions (E&O) does not cover PD and BI, only claims for financial damages.
- Malpractice liability provides medical professionals with bodily injury liability.
- A directors and officers (D&O) policy will cover a lawsuit brought by a shareholder against a director who unintentionally falsified the company's financial reports.
- Directors and officers liability covers the management mistakes of board members and corporate officers.
- An Employment Practices Liability policy covers harassment, discrimination, and unlawful termination. This coverage is not included in a workers compensation policy.

Accident and Health Insurance Policy General Provisions

Uniform Required Provisions

- Mandatory provisions, like the grace period, protect the insured. Optional provisions, like probationary periods, protect the insurer.
- Except for fraud, health insurance policies are incontestable after they have been effective for two years.
- The probationary period is different from the time limit on certain defenses provision (incontestability); the maximum probationary period is 12 months, and the incontestability provision is typically two years.
- The incontestability clause protects the insurer. Under this clause, the insurer can contest a claim for the first two years but not after that unless it can prove fraud. Insurers are reluctant to charge fraud because it requires proof of intent to deceive and is difficult to prove.
- The time limit on certain defenses clause is another name for the incontestability clause (usually up to two years, except for fraud).
- If a reinstatement application is required, a policyowner is reinstated when the insurer specifies or after 45 days, whichever comes first. When a policy owner is reinstated, a 10-day probationary period starts for sickness only.
- If no reinstatement application is required, a policy owner is reinstated effective upon payment of the late premium to either the insurer or the producer.
- Under the legal actions provision, if a claim is not paid immediately, the claimant has to wait at least 60 days before filing a lawsuit for failure to pay. Such lawsuits must be filed within three years of the original loss.
- Health insurance providers should pay individual claims as soon as possible, as specified in a provision called timely payment of claims.
- The time payment of claims provision gives the claims department time to investigate (maximum of 60 days).
- Claims can be denied if they occur after policy expiration.
- Insurance providers do not have to pay unsubstantiated claims.
- After receipt of notice of a claim, the insurance provider must send out claim forms.
- If the insurer does not provide claim forms within the required time frame, the insured can submit proof of loss in writing.

Uniform Optional Provisions

- The change of occupation provision allows the insurance provider to change the benefit amount or premium if the insured changes occupations during the coverage period.
- Under the misstatement of age clause, benefits are adjusted, not the premiums.

- To reinforce the principle of indemnity by preventing a policy owner from collecting more than they lost, most disability income policies include an insurance with other insurers clause, which requires insurers to share a claim proportionately.
- If an insured pays the overdue premium on a lapsed health insurance policy and does not hear from the insurance provider, the insured is automatically reinstated in 45 days.
- Under the unpaid premium provision, if a policy owner has a claim in the grace period, the insurance provider can subtract the overdue premium from the amount of the claim paid.
- A cancellable health insurance policy can be canceled by the insured or the insurance provider.
- Insurers must refund unearned premiums to a policy owner whose policy was canceled midterm. A pro rata refund is sent when the insurer cancels. A short-rate refund is sent when the policy owner cancels.
- Cancellation will not affect a pending claim.
- The illegal occupations provision would allow an insurance provider to deny coverage if the insured became injured or died while committing a felony.

Other General Provisions

- If a health insurance policy can be nonrenewed by the insurance provider at the end of any policy period, the policy is considered to be optionally renewable.
- On a noncancelable policy, the insurer cannot change the coverage or the rates. However, it does not have to offer renewal.
- If a policy is guaranteed renewable and noncancelable, the insurer cannot change anything, and it has to offer renewal.
- On a guaranteed renewable policy, the insurer cannot change the coverage. It can change the rates by class (not individually).
- A guaranteed renewable policy is renewable at the option of the insured (by paying the premium) up to a certain specified age (typically age 65). The insurance provider can change rates by class.
- A conditionally renewable policy has to be renewed if the insured meets the specified conditions.

Medical Plans

Medical Plan Concepts

- Major medical insurance is regarded as a comprehensive insurance plan.
- The purpose of preadmission certification is to eliminate unnecessary treatment, ultimately lowering premiums (cost saving).
- Medical expense policies must cover the insured's newborn child from birth.
- On medical expense insurance, the scheduled benefit limit shown is the most that the insurance provider will pay.

Types of Providers and Plans

- The term health care service organization (HCSO) can be used interchangeably with the term health maintenance organization (HMO).
- An HMO primary care physician provides general care, authorizes treatment, makes referrals, and acts as the gatekeeper between HMO members and their health care providers.
- Health care service organizations (HCSOs) emphasize preventive care.
- HCSOs pay reimbursements to their providers directly rather than to their insureds.

- When a physician works on behalf of an HCSO in an independent group clinic, it is a group practice model.
- HMO primary care physicians can include those in family practice, obstetrics, pediatrics, and gynecology, but not internists.
- HMOs typically do not cover adult hearing exams as a preventive care service.
- Except for emergencies, HMO services need to be provided in-network.
- HMOs cover out-of-network emergency treatment without pre-authorization, although providers must inform the HMO after treatment has been rendered.
- The term managed care includes medical services provided by HMOs, PPOs, and POS (point-of-service) plans but excludes indemnity plans.
- Medical expense claims are frequently paid on a fee-for-service basis.
- Major medical expense policies frequently have a comprehensive calendar year deductible.
- In utilization management, pre-certification differs from a concurrent review because pre-certification is performed before treatment.
- Basic medical expense plans cover in-hospital only, with first dollar coverage. There is no coinsurance or deductible, but coverage is subject to inside (maximum) limits.
- Major medical and comprehensive major medical plans have coinsurance requirements and deductibles.
- The stop loss feature on a major medical policy applies after the insured pays the deductible. It limits the amount of coinsurance the insured must pay on a large claim.
- Medical expense policies are typically written as cancelable, which means the insurer can cancel at any time as long as it provides advance notice.
- Medical expense policies typically include a probationary period for pre-existing conditions. Insurers will not cover these conditions if they take place during this period.
- A family deductible limits the total amount the family has to pay during the year, no matter how many family members become sick or injured.
- The assignment of benefits provision on medical expense insurance facilitates claims handling by allowing the insurance carrier to pay benefits directly to the provider.
- When calculating how much the insurer will pay on a claim, subtract the deductible first, then apply the coinsurance percentage.
- PPO subscribers who go out of network for services will receive reduced benefits.
- To encourage an insured covered by a point-of-service (POS) plan to seek coverage in-network. Out-of-network coverage is frequently subject to higher deductibles.

Patient Protection and Affordable Care Act

Affordable Care Act
- The Patient Protection and Affordable Care Act (PPACA) is also known as the Affordable Care Act (ACA).
- This legislation requires children to remain a dependent on their parent's health insurance policy up until age 26, regardless of dependency, college status, or marital status.
- The Marketplaces are websites that permit individuals and small businesses to procure health insurance.
- Premiums can vary based on the following factors:
    - Age (older people can be charged more than young people)
    - Geographic location
    - Tobacco use
    - Individual vs. family enrollment
    - Plan category (bronze, silver, gold, platinum, catastrophic)

- The Marketplaces will qualify individuals for Medicaid or the Children's Health Insurance Plan (CHIP).
- The Marketplaces are also designed to ascertain if an individual qualifies for cost reduction measures.
- Two cost reduction measures are available when an individual qualifies based on need and purchases coverage on a Marketplace: A Premium Tax Credit and a cost-sharing subsidy.
- These two cost reduction measures are only available if coverage is obtained through a Marketplace.
- Policies sold on the Marketplace include five levels of coverage: four metal levels – Bronze, Silver, Gold, Platinum, and a catastrophic plan.
- The metal levels of coverage provide identical coverage; the differences are found in how much the insurance provider covers (actuarial value) and how much the policy costs (premium).
- The Premium Tax Credit applies to any level of coverage obtained (except catastrophic).
- Catastrophic coverage can only be obtained in certain situations.
- Grandfathered plans do not have to follow all requirements of the ACA.
- The ACA mandates health benefit plans to include coverage for the ten essential health benefits.
- The ACA does not require a small business with less than 50 full-time equivalent (FTE) employees to provide health coverage to its employees.
- The coverage offered to employees must include an offer of coverage for the employee's dependents.
- Spouses are not considered dependents.
- A full-time employee under the ACA is an individual who works 30 hours or more, on average, per week.
- An employer subject to the ACA that does not offer health coverage to full-time employees and dependents will be subject to an Employer Shared Responsibility Payment (penalty).
- An employer that offers health coverage to only employees but not dependents can also face a penalty.
- An employer that offers the required coverage to employees will also trigger the Employer Shared Responsibility Payment (penalty) if a full-time employee instead obtains coverage for themselves on the Marketplace with a Premium Tax Credit.
- A full-time employee can purchase coverage through the Marketplace for the following reasons: coverage was not offered to this employee, the coverage offered did not provide a minimum value, or the coverage offered was not affordable.
- Minimum value is met if the plan includes an actuarial value of 60% or more (comparable to a bronze level of coverage through the Marketplace).
- A full-time employee offered affordable healthcare coverage by their employer will not be able to qualify for the Premium Tax Credit or cost-sharing subsidy towards their coverage. This employee's spouse or dependents can purchase Marketplace coverage and qualify for one or both cost-saving measures.
- A part-time employee or an employee's spouse or dependents who purchase Marketplace coverage with a Premium Tax Credit will never trigger the Employer Shared Responsibility Payment.

Insurance for Seniors and Special Needs Individuals

Medicare Supplements

- Private insurers and their agents sell Medicare Supplements.
- There is a 6-month open enrollment period for purchasing a Medigap policy.
- Individuals age 65 or older cannot be denied Medigap coverage for health problems during the open enrollment period.
- Medicare Supplement plans do not have to be approved by Medicare.
- Medicare Supplements must cover Medicare's Part A and Part B coinsurance and the first 3 pints of a blood transfusion as basic or core benefits.

- Only standardized Medigap plans can be offered.
- Insurers can offer only standardized Medigap plans.
- The maximum probationary period on a Medicare Supplement policy is six months.
- When selling a Medicare Supplement, producers must give out an Outline of Coverage no later than the time of application and obtain a signed receipt from the applicant.
- Medicare Supplements include a 30-day free-look period.
- Selling a person more than one Medicare Supplement is prohibited. Replacing one Medicare supplement policy with another is allowed as long as it is not detrimental to the insured.
- Medicare supplement policies do not have to include guidelines for Medicare eligibility.

GLOSSARY

Abandonment – The relinquishment of insured property into the hands of another or into possession of no one in particular.
Absolute Liability – A liability that occurs due to hazardous operations, such as working at extreme heights or using explosives.
Accident – An unforeseen, unplanned event occurring suddenly and at a specific place.
Actual Cash Value (ACV) – The required amount for property loss or to pay damages is determined based on the property's current replacement value minus depreciation.
Additional Coverage – A provision in an insurance policy that allows for more coverage for specific loss expenses without a premium increase.
Additional Insureds – Individuals or businesses that are not named insureds on the declarations page but are protected by the policy, typically regarding a specific interest.
Adhesion – An insurance provider offers a contract on a "take-it-or-leave-it" basis. The policy owner's only option is to accept or reject the contract. Any contract ambiguities will be settled in favor of the policy owner.
Admitted Insurer – An insurance company licensed and authorized to transact business in a particular state.
Adverse Selection – The tendency of risks with a higher probability of loss to buy and maintain insurance coverage more often than those with a lower probability.
Agent – An individual licensed to negotiate, sell, or effect insurance contracts on behalf of an insurance provider.
Aggregate Limit – The maximum coverage limit available under a liability policy during a policy year irrespective of the number of accidents that may occur or the number of claims that may be made.
Agreed Value – A property policy with a provision agreed upon by the insurance provider and policy owner regarding the amount of insurance representing a fair valuation for the property when the coverage is written.
Aleatory – A contract where the participating parties agree to an exchange of unequal amounts. Insurance contracts are aleatory in that the amount the insurance provider will pay in the event of a loss is unequal to the amount the policy owner will pay in premiums.
Alien Insurer – An insurance company that is incorporated outside the United States.
Apparent Authority – The appearance or assumption of authority based on the principal's words, actions, or deeds or because of circumstances the principal created.
Appraisal – An assessment of the property to determine the correct amount of insurance to be written or the amount of loss to be paid.
Arbitration – Method of claim settlement used when the policy owner and insurance provider cannot agree upon the amount of the loss.
Assignment – The transfer of an interest in an insurance policy or a legal right. In property and casualty insurance, assignments of policies are generally valid only with the prior written consent of the insurance provider.
Authorized Insurer – An insurer that has qualified and received a Certificate of Authority from the Department of Insurance to transact insurance business in the state.

Auto – Any land motor vehicle, trailer, or semi-trailer intended for use on public roads, including attached equipment or machinery; auto does not include mobile equipment.

Avoidance – A method to deal with risk by deliberately avoiding it. For instance, if an individual wanted to avoid the risk of dying in a helicopter crash, they might choose never to fly in a helicopter.

Bailee – A person or entity that has possession of personal property entrusted to them by the owner. For example, a computer repair person possessing a customer's computer would be a bailee.

Beneficiary – The individual who receives the proceeds from an insurance policy.

Binder – A temporary contract that puts an insurance policy into force before the premium is paid.

Blanket Bond – A bond that covers losses caused by dishonest employees.

Blanket Insurance – A single property policy that offers insurance for multiple classes of property at a single location or provides insurance for one or more classes of property at multiple locations.

Bodily Injury Liability – Legal liability arising from physical trauma or death to an individual due to a purposeful or negligent act and omissions by an insured.

Boycott – An unfair trade practice where one person refuses to do business with another until they agree to certain conditions.

Builder's Risk Coverage Form – A commercial property form that insures buildings under construction.

Building and Personal Property Coverage Form – A particular commercial property form that insures buildings and their contents.

Burglary – The forced entry into another person's premises with felonious intent.

Cancellation – Terminating an in-force policy before the expiration date by the insurer or insured.

Casualty Insurance – A type of insurance that insures against losses caused by injury to individuals or damage to the property of others.

Cease and Desist Order – A demand to stop committing an act violating a provision.

Certificate of Authority – A document that authorizes a company to start transacting business and specifies the kind(s) of insurance a company can transact. It is illegal for an insurer to transact insurance business without this certificate.

Certificate of Insurance – A legal document stating that an insurance policy has been issued and indicating the types and amounts of insurance provided.

Claim – A demand made by the insured to cover a loss protected by the insurance policy.

Class Rating – The practice of calculating a price per unit of insurance that applies to all applicants possessing a given set of characteristics.

Coercion – An unfair trade practice where an insurance company uses mental or physical force to persuade an applicant to purchase insurance.

Coinsurance – An agreement between an insurance provider and policy owner in which both parties are expected to pay a portion of the potential loss and other expenses.

Combined Single – A single dollar limit of liability applies to the total damages for property damage and bodily injury combined, resulting from one accident or occurrence.

Commercial Lines – Insurance coverage for business, manufacturing, or mercantile establishments.

Commissioner (Superintendent, Director) – The administrative officer and chief executive of a state insurance department.

Common Law – An unwritten body of law based on past judicial decisions, customs, and usages.

Complaint – A written statement of a liability claim provided by the claimant; a reason for a lawsuit.

Components – Factors that determine rates, including loss adjusting expenses, loss reserves, operating expenses, and profits.

Comprehensive Coverage – Also known as Other Than Collision coverage, it insures against losses by fire, falling objects, vandalism, theft, etc.

Concealment – The intentional withholding of known facts that, if material, could void a contract.

Conditional Contract – An agreement in which both parties must perform specific duties and follow rules of conduct to make it enforceable.

Conditions – The section of an insurance policy stating the general rules or procedures that the insurance provider and insured agree to follow under the terms of the policy.

Consideration – The binding force in any contract that involves something of value to be exchanged for the transfer of risk. The consideration on the policy owner's part is the representations made in the application and the premium payment. The consideration on the insurer's part is the promise to pay in the event of a loss.

Consultant – An individual who, for a fee, offers any counsel, advice, opinion, or service regarding the advantages, disadvantages, or benefits promised under a policy of insurance.

Consumer Reports – Written or oral statements regarding a consumer's credit, reputation, character, or habits collected by a reporting agency from credit reports, employment records, and other public sources.

Contract – An agreement or arrangement between two or more parties that is enforceable by law.

Controlled Business – An entity that obtains and possesses a license to write business on the owner, relatives, immediate family, employees, and employer.

Concurrent Causation – Multiple events leading to a loss

Death Benefit – The amount payable upon the death of the individual whose life is insured.

Declarations – The section of an insurance policy that contains the basic underwriting information, such as the policy owner's name, address, amount of coverage and premiums, and a description of insured locations, as well as any supplemental representations by the policy owner.

Deductible – The portion of the loss to be paid by the policy owner before the insurance provider may pay any claim benefits.

Defamation – An unfair trade practice where an insurer or agent makes a defamatory statement about another intending to harm the reputation of a person or company.

Deposit Premium Audit – A condition allowing the insurer to audit the policy owner's records or books at the end of the policy term to ensure sufficient premium is collected for the exposure.

Depreciation – The reduction of the value of real and personal property because of wear and tear and age.

Direct Losses – Physical damage to buildings or personal property caused by a direct consequence of a particular peril.

Director (Superintendent, Commissioner) – The head of the state insurance department.

Disability – A mental or physical impairment, either congenital or resulting from a sickness or injury.

Disclosure – An act of identifying the name of the representative, firm or producer, limited representative, or temporary producer on any policy solicitation.

Domestic Insurer – An insurance company incorporated in the state.

Domicile of Insurer – An insurer's location of incorporation and the legal ability to transact business in a state.

Economic Loss – An accident's projected cost (insured and uninsured).

Endorsement – A printed addendum to the contract that changes the insurance policy's original coverages, terms, or conditions.

Estoppel – A legal obstruction to denying a fact or restoring a right that has been previously waived.

Excess Policy – A policy that pays for a loss only after the primary policy has paid its limit.

Exclusions – Causes of exposures, loss, conditions, etc., listed in the policy for which insurance benefits will not be paid.

Exclusive or Captive Agent – An agent who represents only one insurance company and is compensated by commissions.

Experience Rating – The method of determining the premium based on the policy owner's previous loss experience.

Exposure – A unit of measure used to calculate rates charged for insurance coverage.

Express Authority – The authority granted to an agent through the agent's written contract.

Extensions of Coverage – A provision in certain insurance policies that allows the extension of a major coverage to include specific types of loss or damage to property that is not specifically insured.

Fiduciary – An agent or broker handling an insurer's funds in a trust capacity.

First Named Insured – The individual whose name appears first on the policy's declarations page.

Flood – A temporary and general condition of complete or partial inundation of usually dry land areas from overflow of inland or tidal waters or the rapid and unusual accumulation or runoff of surface waters from any source.

Foreign Insurer – An insurance company incorporated in another state.

Fraternal Benefit Society – A life or health insurance company formed to provide insurance for members of an affiliated lodge, fraternal, or religious organization with a representative form of government.

Fraud – Intentional deceit or misrepresentation with the intent to induce a person to part with something of value.

Functional Replacement Cost – The cost of replacing damaged property with less expensive and more modern equipment or construction.

Gross Negligence – Irresponsible behavior that shows disregard for the lives or safety of others.

Hazard – A circumstance that increases the probability of a loss.

Hazard, Moral – The effect of a person's character, reputation, living habits, etc., on their insurability.

Hazard, Morale – The effect a person's indifference toward loss has on the risk to be insured.

Hazard, Physical – A type of hazard that arises from a person's physical characteristics, such as a physical disability because of either current circumstance or a condition present at birth.

Implied Authority – Authority that is not written into the contract or expressed. The agent is assumed to have implied authority to conduct the insurance business on the principal's behalf.

Indemnity – Compensation to the policy owner that restores them to the same financial position they held before the loss.

Independent Agents – Agents that sell the products of several insurance companies and work for themselves or other agents.

Indirect Losses – Losses caused by a peril but not directly resulting from it. Indirect losses may include extra expenses, business disruption, renters insurance, and other consequences that occur over time.

Inflation Guard – A coverage extension that annually automatically increases the amounts of insurance on buildings by an agreed-upon percentage.

Insurable Interest – Any interest an insured might have in the property that is the subject of insurance coverage so that damage or destruction of that property would cause the policy owner financial loss.

Insurance – The transfer of the possibility of a loss (risk) to an insurance carrier that spreads the costs of unexpected losses to many individuals.

Insurance Policy – A contract between an insured and an insurance provider which agrees to pay the policy owner for loss caused by specific events.

Insured – The individual or organization that is protected by insurance; the party to be indemnified (can also be the "policy owner" or "policyholder").

Insured Contract – A definition of liability forms that explains the types of contracts where liability is assumed by the insured and included for coverage in the policy. Several examples of insured contracts are elevator maintenance agreements, leases of premises, easement agreements, and other agreements about the insured's business.

Insurer – An entity that indemnifies against losses, provides benefits, or renders services (can also be the "company" or "insurance company" or "carrier" or "insurance carrier" or "provider" or "insurance provider").

Insuring Agreement – The section of an insurance policy containing the perils insured against, the description of coverage provided, and the insurance provider's promise to pay.

Intentional Tort – A deliberate act that results in harm to another person.

Interline Endorsement – A written amendment intended to minimize the number of endorsements in the policy and eliminate redundancy.

Judgment Rating – An approach used when no credible statistics are available, or exposure units are so varied that it is challenging to construct a class.

Law of Large Numbers – A principle stating that the larger the number of similar units of exposure, the more closely the reported losses will equal the probability of loss.

Legal Liability – A liability under the law occurs when an individual is responsible for damages or injuries to another because of negligence.
Liability – An individual's responsibility under the law.
Liberalization – A property insurance clause that expands broader regulated or legislated coverage to current policies, as long as it does not cause a premium to increase.
Lien – A security, charge, or encumbrance on a property.
Limit of Liability – The maximum amount for which an insurer is liable.
Lloyd's Associations – Organizations that support underwriters or groups that accept insurance risk.
Loss – The decrease, disappearance, or reduction of value of the property or person insured in a policy by a covered peril.
Loss Payable Clause – A property insurance provision used to protect a secured lender's interest in personal property.
Loss Ratio – A calculation insurance carriers use to relate income from loss expenses: loss ratio = (loss adjusting expense + incurred losses) / earned premium.
Loss Valuation – A factor in calculating the charged premium and the amount of required insurance.
Market Value – A rarely used method of valuing a loss based on the amount a buyer would pay to a seller for the property before the loss.
Misrepresentation – A lie or false statement that can void a contract.
Monoline Policy – A separate policy written as a single coverage.
Mutual Assessment Insurer – A mutual insurer with the right to charge additional premium amounts to meet operational needs.
Mutual Companies – Insurance companies with no capital stock that their policyholders own.
Mysterious Disappearance – The disappearance of any property where the time, location, or manner of the loss cannot be explained.
Named Insured – The individual(s) whose name appears on the policy's declarations page.
Named Peril – A cause of loss covered explicitly by the policy. No coverage is provided for perils not listed in the policy.
Negligence – Failing to use the care that a prudent, reasonable individual would use under the same or similar circumstances.
No Benefit to the Bailee – A provision excluding any assignment or granting of any policy provision to any organization or person moving, repairing, storing, or holding insured property for a fee.
Non-admitted Insurer – An insurance provider that has not applied or has applied and been denied a Certificate of Authority and cannot transact insurance.
Nonconcurrency – A situation where other insurance is written on the same risk but not on the same coverage basis.
Nonrenewal – A policy termination by an insurance provider on the renewal or anniversary date.
Notice of Claim – A provision that details an insured's responsibility to provide the insurer with reasonable notice in the event of a loss.
Occurrence – A broader definition of loss, which differs from an accident. It encompasses losses caused by repeated or continuous exposure to conditions resulting in damage to property or injury to individuals that is neither expected nor intended.
Open Peril – A term used in property insurance to describe the scope of coverage provided under an insurance policy form that covers "any risk of loss" that is not explicitly excluded.
Pair and Set Clause – In many inland marine and property policies, the insurance provider is not required to pay for the total value of a set of items if only one thing has been destroyed, damaged, or lost.
Partnership – A legal entity in which two or more individuals agree to share the profits and losses of the business.
Passive – A description of an anti-theft system or device for autos that automatically activates when the driver turns the ignition key to the off position and removes the key.

Peril – The cause behind a possible loss.

Personal Injury Liability – Legal responsibility for an injury to another individual's character caused by slander, libel, invasion of privacy, false arrest, and other acts.

Personal Lines Insurance – A type of insurance coverage available to families and individuals for non-business risks.

Policy Limits – The maximum amount a policy owner can collect or for which a policy owner is protected under the terms of the policy.

Policy Period – The period or "term" when a policy is effective.

Policyholder – The individual possessing an insurance policy. This person may or may not be the policy owner or the insured.

Policy Owner – The individual entitled to exercise the privileges and rights in the policy. This person may or may not be the insured.

Premium – A periodic payment to the insurance provider keeping the policy in force.

Primary Policy – A fundamental, basic policy that pays first concerning any other outstanding policies.

Pro Rata – Proportional distribution of loss shares for every insurance policy written on a piece of property.

Producer – An individual who acts on behalf of the insurance provider to negotiate, sell, or effect insurance contracts. This person is also called an agent.

Proof of Loss – A sworn statement typically provided by the insured to an insurance carrier before any loss under a policy is paid.

Property Damage Liability – Legal liability stemming from physical damage to the tangible property of others caused by the negligence of a policy owner.

Proximate Cause – An event or act that is the actual or immediate cause of a loss.

Pure Risk – Situations that can only result in no change or a loss; a gain is never possible. Pure risk is the only type of risk that insurance carriers are willing to accept.

Rebating – Any enticement or kickback offered in the sale of insurance products not specified in the policy.

Reciprocal – Insurance resulting from an interchange of reciprocal indemnity agreements among individuals known as subscribers.

Reduction – Lessening or reducing the probability or severity of a loss.

Reinsurance – A form of insurance where one insurer (the reinsurer), in consideration of a premium, agrees to indemnify another insurer (the ceding company) for part or all of its liabilities from any policies it has issued.

Replacement Cost – The cost to replace damaged property with a similar kind and quality at the current price, without any depreciation deduction.

Representations – A statement made by the applicant for insurance that is believed to be true but is not guaranteed to be true.

Retention – A way of dealing with risk by intentionally or unintentionally retaining a portion of it for the policy owner's account. It is the amount of responsibility assumed but not reinsured by the insurer.

Retrospective Rating – A self-rating plan under which the policy period's actual losses determine the final premium (contingent upon a minimum and maximum premium).

Right of Salvage – A policy provision in property insurance requiring that after payment of a total loss to insured property, the policy owner must transfer the property's title (or ownership) to the insurance provider.

Risk – Uncertainty regarding the outcome of an event when two or more possibilities exist.

Risk, Pure – The chance of a loss occurring in a situation that can only result in no change or a loss.

Risk, Speculative – The chance or uncertainty of a loss occurring in a situation involving the opportunity for a gain or a loss.

Robbery – The theft of property from another through the use of violence or the threat of violence.

Salvage – The amount of money realized from selling damaged property or merchandise. A salvage clause is included in ocean marine insurance and typically states that the rescuers of a ship are entitled to the salvage of the vessel and cargo.

Settlement – The process through which agreements are reached and claims are resolved in liability insurance.

Severability of Interests – A provision in which insurance is applied separately to each insured in a policy, treating each person as the only insured.

Sharing – A way to handle risk for a group of businesses or individuals with the same or similar exposure to loss who share the losses within that group.

Specific Insurance – A property insurance policy insures a specific unit or property for a particular amount of insurance.

Speculative Risk – The chance or uncertainty of a loss taking place in a situation that involves the opportunity for either a gain or loss.

Split – Separately stated limits of liability for different coverages, which can be stated on a per occurrence, per person, or per policy period basis, or divided between property damage and bodily injury.

Stated Amount – An amount of scheduled insurance in a property policy that is not contingent upon any coinsurance requirements if a covered loss occurs.

Statute Law – The written law as enacted by a legislative body (e.g., the laws of the state), which usually takes precedence in cases where both statute law and common law apply.

Stock Companies – Companies owned by their stockholders whose investments provide the necessary capital to establish and operate the insurance company.

Strict Liability – A liability that refers to damages resulting from defective products even though the manufacturer's negligence or fault cannot be proven.

Subrogation – The acquisition by an insurance provider of an insured's rights against any third party for indemnification of a loss or other payment to the extent that the insurance provider pays the loss.

Superintendent (Commissioner, Director) – The head of a state's insurance department.

Surety Bond – An assurance that debts and obligations will be fulfilled, and the benefits will be paid for losses resulting from nonperformance.

Surplus Lines – A type of insurance for which there is no readily available, admitted market.

Theft – Any act of removing or stealing property from its rightful owner. Theft embodies both burglary and robbery.

Third-Party Provisions – A set of insurance provisions that address the rights of another person besides the insured to have a secured financial interest in the covered property.

Tort – A wrongful act or violating another person's rights that leads to legal liability. Torts are identified as intentional or unintentional (also referred to as negligence).

Transfer – A basic concept of insurance under which the risk of financial loss is transferred to another party.

Twisting – A misrepresentation in which an agent or producer persuades an insured or policy owner to cancel, switch, or lapse policies, even when it is not to the advantage of the insured.

Umbrella Liability Policy – Coverage that includes extra protection against liability and an excess amount of insurance over and above the primary policy.

Unauthorized Insurer – An insurer that has not applied or has applied and been denied a Certificate of Authority to transact insurance business.

Underwriter – An individual who evaluates and classifies risks to accept or reject them on behalf of the insurance company.

Underwriting – The process of reviewing, accepting, or rejecting insurance applications.

Unilateral Contract – A contract that binds only one party to contractual obligations once the premium is paid.

Underinsured Motorist Coverage – Coverage in an auto policy under which the insurance provider will pay for costs up to specified limits for bodily injury if the liable driver's policy limits are depleted and they cannot pay the total amount for which they are liable.

Uninsured Motorist Coverage – Coverage that permits the named insured, passengers, and resident relative(s) in a covered auto to collect sums another driver would be legally liable to pay for bodily injury caused by an auto accident. The accident must be caused by an uninsured motorist, a hit-and-run driver, or a driver whose insurance provider is insolvent.

Unintentional Tort – The result of acting without care, usually referred to as negligence.

Unoccupied – A property with furnishings or contents but is not being lived in or used
Utmost Good Faith – The equal and fair bargaining by both parties in forming the contract, where the applicant must disclose risk to the insurer fully, and the insurer must be fair in underwriting the risk.
Vacant – A property that has no occupants, furnishings, or contents.
Valued Policy – A policy used when it is hard to determine the actual cash value of the insured property following a loss because of its uniqueness or rarity. This policy provides for payment of the entire policy amount if a total loss occurs without regard to depreciation or actual value.
Vicarious Liability – A liability in which one individual is responsible for the acts of another individual. For instance, parents can be held accountable for negligent acts of their children, and employers can be vicariously liable for the actions of their employees.
Waiting Period – The time between the start of a disability and the beginning of disability insurance benefits.
Waiver – The voluntary abandonment of a legal or known advantage or right.
Warranty – The material stipulation in a policy that, if breached, can void coverage.
Workers Compensation – Benefits required by state law to be paid by an employer to an employee in the case of disability, injury, or death due to an on-the-job hazard.

PRACTICE EXAM: 1

Test your readiness

You are about to take a New York Property and Casualty Insurance Agent/Broker Practice Examination. This exam consists of *150 Questions (plus five to ten non-scored experimental questions)* and is *2 hours and 30 minutes* long. If you do not have enough time to complete this exam right now, it is better to wait until you can fully devote your attention to completing it in the allotted time.

Any skipped questions will be graded as incorrect. The following chart breaks down the number of questions in each chapter and by topic.

Chapter	% of Exam
Insurance Regulation	9%
General Insurance	9%
Property and Casualty Insurance Basics	13%
Dwelling Policy	6%
Homeowners Policy	14%
Auto Insurance	11%
Commercial Package Policy (CPP)	11%
Businessowners Policy	8%
Workers Compensation Insurance	8%
Other Coverages and Options	7%
Accident and Health Insurance	4%
Total	**100%**

To calculate your score, subtract the number of incorrectly answered questions from 150. Take this number and divide it by 150. For example, if you incorrectly answered 45 questions, your score would be 70%, the minimum score needed to pass the exam.

#1. A customer was injured in a grocery store parking lot when a shopping cart collided with the customer. Coverage for this customer's claim would be provided under

a) Premises and operations.
b) Completed operations.
c) Contractual liability.
d) Product liability.

#2. In an insurance policy, the causes of loss insured against are called

a) Risks.
b) Hazards.
c) Perils.
d) Losses.

#3. The criminal act of forced entry into the premises of another by an individual or individuals with felonious intent is

a) Breaking and entering.
b) Theft.
c) Robbery.
d) Burglary.

#4. Under a commercial property policy, which of the following situations would NOT be covered by the basic causes of loss form?

a) The automatic fire protective sprinkler system inside New Wisdom Book Store leaks, causing damage to the store
b) Harley's Truck Depot is damaged by the sudden sinking of land caused by the action of water on limestone
c) The Sea Side Waterfront Cafe is damaged when flood waters rise and seep into the eatery
d) Shady Mike's Bistro has its door broken by vandals trying to get inside

#5. Professional liability coverage protects the insured against legal liability resulting from

a) Liability assumed under a contract.
b) Dishonest acts.
c) An employee's unprofessional conduct.
d) Errors and omissions.

#6. Which part of an insurance policy covers claims-related expenses, defense expenses, or reasonable expenses incurred by a policy owner to protect damaged property from additional loss?

a) Insuring agreement
b) Additional coverage
c) Exclusions
d) Declarations

#7. A policy owner's 8-year-old daughter threw a rock, accidentally breaking a plate glass window at a neighbor's house. The policy owner was held legally liable for the cost of replacing the window. This scenario is an example of

a) Intervening cause.
b) Juvenile delinquency.
c) Absolute liability.
d) Vicarious liability.

#8. In a personal auto policy (PAP), the medical payments coverage is similar to

a) Accident insurance because it pays medical expenses irrespective of fault.
b) Accident insurance because it has the same limits.
c) Bodily injury coverage because it pays the insured's doctor's bills.
d) Bodily injury coverage because it provides legal protection if the insured causes injuries to others.

#9. Which of the following best describes the reason for a stated amount contract?

a) To establish the value of property subject to loss by robbery or theft
b) To provide a maximum limit for which the insurer might become liable for casualty losses
c) To pre-establish the amount of coverage available for property items that are hard to value
d) To ensure that the indemnification principle is applied

#10. An agent who fails to segregate premium monies from their own personal funds is guilty of

a) Commingling.
b) Larceny.
c) Embezzlement.
d) Theft.

#11. Under a liability policy during a policy year, which of these is defined as the maximum limit of coverage available regardless of the number of claims made or the number of accidents that occur?

a) Per occurrence limit of liability
b) Split limit of liability
c) Aggregate limit of liability
d) Combined single limit of liability

#12. Under OBEL (Optional Basic Economic Loss) coverage, a policy owner in New York can purchase how much extra coverage?

a) $35,000
b) $15,000
c) $20,000
d) $25,000

#13. Which of the following is NOT considered a misrepresentation regarding unfair trade practices?

a) Comparing different insurance policies
b) Claiming that the insurance policy is a share of stock
c) Exaggerating the insurance policy's benefits
d) Stating that competitors will randomly increase their policy premiums every year

#14. When rating workers compensation insurance, all of these are factors EXCEPT

a) Payroll.
b) Loss experience.
c) Job classification.
d) Sales.

#15. More than one insured has become liable due to a single loss. How will the personal auto policy's limit of liability be affected?

a) A personal auto policy can have no more than one insured
b) The full limit applies to each insured individually
c) No more than the per occurrence limit applies, regardless of how many insureds are involved
d) Pro rata liability applies

#16. The general property policy form is used for other-residential and non-residential structures and their contents, like

a) Commercial structures.
b) Cooperative associations.
c) Apartment buildings.
d) Insurers would cover any of the above under this form.

#17. Workers compensation statutes require employers to meet capital reserves requirements sufficient to cover any claims that could arise. Employers can meet such requirements through all of the following EXCEPT

a) Assigned risk plans.
b) Competitive state funds.
c) Second injury funds programs.
d) Self-insurance plans.

#18. Regarding employee dishonesty, an optional coverage under the businessowners policy, all of the following statements are true EXCEPT

a) It covers losses caused by dishonest acts of the insured's employees.
b) Coverage includes all property, including money and securities held or owned by the insured.
c) It offers coverage for every employee, even those who were terminated in the previous 90 days.
d) It offers coverage for direct loss or damage to business personal property.

#19. A policyholder wants to obtain as much additional personal injury protection (APIP) coverage as possible. What is the maximum available APIP?

a) $25,000
b) $50,000
c) $100,000
d) $150,000

#20. Following a loss, an insured covered by business property coverage is NOT required to

a) Resume operating the business as soon as possible.
b) Send the insurance provider a sworn proof of loss within 60 days.
c) Take all reasonable steps to protect property from additional damage.
d) Reconstruct a timeline of activities leading up to the loss for the insurance provider to use in an investigation.

#21. Regarding contractual agreements with third parties, what is the term for the entity an agent represents?

a) Designee
b) Insured
c) Principal
d) Client

#22. Termination of an insurance policy that is in force before the expiration date listed in the policy is known as

a) Cessation.
b) Cancellation.
c) Rescission.
d) Nonrenewal.

#23. Damage to insured property resulting from earth movement or earthquake is covered under which homeowners forms?

a) None
b) HO-2
c) HO-3
d) HO-5

#24. Under the Fair Credit Reporting Act, when a consumer challenges the accuracy of the information in a consumer or investigative report, the reporting agency must

a) Send a certified copy of the entire report to the consumer.
b) Respond to the consumer's complaint.
c) Defend the report if the agency believes it is accurate.
d) Revise the report.

#25. A tow truck was stolen from the insured's premises. The insured has loss of use coverage on their commercial auto policy. How much will the insured collect from the coverage if they cannot use the tow truck in its operations for 40 days?

a) $200
b) $400
c) $600
d) $800

#26. The policy provision in property insurance policies that prevents the policy owner from collecting twice for the same loss is called

a) Consent to settle the loss.
b) Right of salvage.
c) Appraisal.
d) Subrogation.

#27. In property insurance policies, the abandonment provision states that

a) The legal rights of the insured property can be transferred.
b) The insured cannot relinquish ownership of the damaged property to claim a total loss. Still, it must protect damaged property from further loss.
c) The insurance is for the insured's benefit, not for someone else who has temporary custody of the insured property.
d) The insurance provider can take all or any part of damaged or lost property at an appraised or agreed value.

#28. Under New York Workers Compensation Laws, coverage must be provided for all residence employees who work less than

a) 10 hours per week.
b) 20 hours per week.
c) 32 hours per week.
d) 40 hours per week.

#29. Bonds are written for a set limit, and the surety will be liable only for this amount of the limit. This limit is called the

a) Limit of liability.
b) Penalty.
c) Face value.
d) Stated amount.

#30. In a personal umbrella policy, the amount paid by the policyholder for specific losses not covered under the primary coverage is known as

a) Self-insured retention.
b) Stop-loss.
c) Coinsurance.
d) Participation requirement.

#31. Which of the following other structures would be covered in a dwelling policy?

a) Structures used as part of a farming operation
b) Structures used by the insured in which to operate a retail business
c) Structures used by the insured to house a manufacturing operation
d) Structures rented to a neighbor for use as a private garage

#32. All of these are exclusions that apply to all three types of Dwelling Policies EXCEPT

a) Government action
b) Water damage
c) Earth movement
d) Fire or lightning

#33. Which of these would be the insured's duty if a loss occurs according to the duties in the event of an occurrence, claim, or suit condition?

a) Providing specific details about an occurrence
b) Delivering a claim to the insurance provider in person
c) Initiating the investigation of a claim
d) Promptly notifying the insurance provider of a claim by phone

#34. All of these are characteristics of the dwelling policy EXCEPT

a) Dwellings up to four family units are eligible.
b) The dwelling needs to be owner-occupied.
c) Coverage includes the dwelling only, contents only, or both.
d) Incidental occupancy of limited service-type exposure is allowed.

#35. Commercial auto coverage forms do not automatically include medical payment coverage because

a) The business that owns the vehicles has to be self-insured for medical payment coverage.
b) Commercial auto coverage is only for damage to vehicles.
c) Any individual occupying a commercial vehicle must have a personal auto policy to cover any medical payments resulting from an accident.
d) Often, any individual occupying a commercial vehicle would be insured under a workers compensation policy.

#36. In a farm policy, which coverage would reimburse the insured for a loss of rental income after damage to the insured dwelling by an insured peril?

a) Coverage A
b) Coverage C
c) Coverage D
d) Coverage E

#37. The personal injury liability endorsement to a homeowners policy applies to all the following EXCEPT

a) Invasion of privacy.
b) False arrest.
c) A third party breaks an arm when the insured knocks them down.
d) Slander.

#38. Vandals damaged a grave marker. It would cost $3,000 to have the damage repaired. Under these circumstances, how much would a homeowners policy cover?

a) $3,000
b) $0
c) $500
d) $1,000

#39. All of these are examples of risk retention EXCEPT

a) Premiums.
b) Deductibles.
c) Copayments.
d) Self-insurance.

#40. What endorsement can be added to a homeowners policy to protect against property damage resulting from a sump pump overflow?

a) Scheduled personal property
b) Water backup and sump discharge or overflow
c) Sump pump overflow
d) Special limit of liability

#41. What part of the National Flood Insurance Program insures residential structures, including individual condominium units, and their contents?

a) Basic coverage form
b) Residential Condominium Building Association Policy (RCBAP)
c) General property policy form
d) Dwelling policy form

#42. Which workers compensation condition states that the first named insured will act on behalf of all insureds under the policy?

a) Cancellation
b) Sole representative
c) Transfer of your rights and duties (assignment)
d) Inspection

#43. Under the builders risk form, which of the following is true concerning the fire department service charge?

a) It is not available in this form
b) It is a high-deductible endorsement
c) It is additional coverage
d) It is an automatic coverage for $500

#44. The Fair Credit Reporting Act (FCRA)

a) Prevents money laundering.
b) Regulates consumer reports.
c) Protects customer privacy.
d) Regulates telemarketing.

#45. A commercial auto coverage form that is intended for insureds employed in the business of transporting goods for others is called a

a) Truckers coverage form.
b) Commercial carrier coverage form.
c) Garagekeepers coverage form.
d) Cargo carriers coverage form.

#46. The Terrorism Risk Insurance Act of 2002

a) Provides a uniform exclusion of damage from terrorist attacks.
b) Shares the risk of loss from terrorist attacks with the federal government.
c) Protects the insured public against insurer insolvency.
d) Provides terrorism insurance for those unable to obtain it on the normal market.

#47. All of these statements regarding the New York Automobile Insurance Plan are correct EXCEPT

a) Each insurer participating in the Plan must maintain an office in New York.
b) The Plan is not allowed to reject any applicant for any reason.
c) All insurers writing motor vehicle insurance must participate in the Plan.
d) In addition to the minimum limits required to satisfy the financial responsibility laws, the Plan must offer specified excess limits.

#48. Which of the following describes the concept that the insured pays a small premium for a large amount of risk on the insurer's part?

a) Warranty
b) Aleatory
c) Adhesion
d) Subrogation

#49. A truck belonging to Kerry's Towing Service is stolen. The policyholder can acquire coverage for transportation expenses subject to which of the following limits?

a) $15 per day; $300 maximum
b) $15 per day; $450 maximum
c) $25 per day; $450 maximum
d) $20 per day; $600 maximum

#50. An insured obtained a disability income policy with a 10-year benefit period. The policy specified a 10-day elimination period for sickness plus a 30-day probationary period. The insured was hospitalized with an illness three weeks after the policy was in force. How much will the policy pay?

a) The insured will receive a return of the premium
b) It will pay up to ten years of benefits
c) It will pay until the insured is released from the hospital
d) Nothing, sickness is not covered during the first 30 days of the contract

#51. Under Coverage E – Scheduled Farm Personal Property, which of the following is NOT covered?

a) Turkeys while out in the open
b) Portable structures
c) Livestock
d) Farm machinery

#52. The policy conditions define

a) The amount of coverage.
b) How parties to the contract must act following a loss.
c) The basic underwriting information.
d) The excluded perils.

#53. If an insurer wants to order a consumer report on an applicant to assist in the underwriting process, and if a notice of insurance information practices has been provided, the report can contain all of the following information EXCEPT the applicant's

a) Prior insurance.
b) Ancestry.
c) Credit history.
d) Habits.

#54. Which of the following endorsements is used to insure Coverage C (Personal Property) for values beyond the limitations of the homeowners policy?

a) Personal property replacement cost endorsement
b) Blue skies endorsement
c) Personal property injury endorsement
d) Scheduled personal property endorsement

#55. Who does the agent represent?

a) Managing general agents (MGAs)
b) The insured
c) The insurer
d) The public

#56. A $100,000 house covered by a policy with an 80% coinsurance requirement has a fire that resulted in $40,000 worth of damage; the policy owner has $60,000 in coverage. How much can the policy owner collect for the loss?

a) $20,000
b) $30,000
c) $40,000
d) $60,000

#57. Under Inside the Premises - Robbery or Safe Burglary of Other Property coverage, which of the following would NOT be covered?

a) An employee is caught stealing from the cash register
b) Someone breaks in after business hours, pries open a wall vault, and steals several expensive paintings
c) A store clerk is locked in the storage room while the criminal steals valuable merchandise
d) Two intruders break a window during an attempted robbery

#58. In the equipment breakdown basic policy, all of the following are excluded EXCEPT

a) Explosion of steam boilers.
b) Ordinance or law coverage.
c) Business interruption.
d) Loss of power, lights, refrigeration, heat, or steam.

#59. Under the crime coverage Inside the Premises – Theft of Money and Securities Form, which of the following would be covered?

a) Loss or damage to a locked vault, safe, or cash register
b) Loss resulting from the surrendering of property in any purchase or exchange
c) Dishonest acts of representatives, trustees, directors, or employees
d) Accounting or arithmetic errors or omissions

#60. When would a misrepresentation by an applicant on the insurance policy application be considered fraud?

a) Never; statements made by the applicant are only representations
b) When the application is incomplete
c) Any misrepresentation is considered fraud
d) If it is material and intentional

#61. Which exposure is insured under Coverage I – Personal and Advertising Injury Liability?

a) Breach of a written contract
b) Unintentional acts arising from operating a farming business
c) Failure of goods to perform
d) Statements made by an insured during their farm radio show

#62. An insured has a Social Insurance Supplement (SIS) policy. After she becomes disabled in a sailing accident, she receives payments from her insurer. Shortly after that, she also begins receiving Social Security benefit payments. Which of the following will happen?

a) The SIS payment will be reduced dollar-for-dollar by the Social Security benefit payment
b) Social Security will discontinue benefits until the SIS plan ends
c) The SIS plan will discontinue paying benefits
d) Both plans will continue to pay fully

#63. Which of the following will be covered by the contractors equipment floater in an unfiled inland marine insurance form?

a) Mobile equipment only while it is on the job site
b) Mobile equipment owned by construction equipment dealers
c) Any type of mobile equipment
d) Mobile equipment during transportation to and from the job site

#64. Under the conditions of the dwelling policy, within how many days does an insurance provider have to pay for a loss once the proof of loss form has been received, and an agreement with the insured as to the amount payable has been reached?

a) 60 days
b) 30 days
c) 31 days
d) 45 days

#65. What does the term "standard" mean regarding the standard Medicare Supplement benefits plans?

a) All plans must include basic benefits A - N
b) Coverage options and conditions are developed for average individuals
c) All providers will have the same coverage options and conditions for each plan
d) Coverage options and conditions comply with the law but will differ from provider to provider

#66. Which of the following would participate in a Write Your Own (WYO) flood insurance program?

a) Businesses requiring National Flood Insurance policies
b) Private insurers that want to write and service National Flood Insurance policies on a no-risk-bearing basis
c) Lloyd's associations
d) Government insurance providers that write and service National Flood Insurance policies

#67. Which of the following is NOT a duty of the employer or insured if an injury occurs at work?

a) Furnish the name and address of the injured worker and any witnesses to the injury
b) Make voluntary payments for the treatment of the worker's injury
c) Provide immediate medical care required by the law
d) Notify the insurance carrier at once

#68. What will occur if a house insured by a standard mortgage clause results in a total loss?

a) The mortgagee controls no rights to any contracts involving the policy
b) The insured receives the full benefit and gives the mortgagee's share to the mortgagee
c) The mortgagee receives the full benefit and gives the insured's share to the insured
d) The insurance provider pays the mortgagee according to the mortgagee's interest in the property

#69. All of the following are true of Coverage B – Other Structures EXCEPT

a) This coverage does not apply to the HO-4 policy form.
b) The amount of coverage provided by Coverage B is an amount that is equal to 10% of Coverage A.
c) Land, where the other structures are located, is not covered.
d) It must be attached by endorsement to a homeowners policy.

#70. While Charlie was towing a utility trailer with his vehicle, the trailer came loose. Unfortunately for him, it crashed into the front of a grocery store. What part of Charlie's auto policy would pay for the damage to the grocery store?

a) Property damage liability
b) Collision coverage
c) Other-than-collision coverage
d) This loss would not be covered

#71. Directors and officers liability insurance will defend actions against a corporation or its directors and officers alleging wrongful acts. Regarding the coverage provided, wrongful acts include any of the following EXCEPT

a) Embezzlement.
b) Misstatements.
c) Neglect.
d) Breach of duty.

#72. What is the maximum number of roomers or boarders for insured properties covered under the dwelling policy?

a) Two
b) Three
c) Five
d) Six

#73. An agent fails to promptly remit the premiums collected from the insured to the insurer. The agent can be found guilty of

a) Controlled business.
b) Rebating.
c) Fraud.
d) Embezzlement.

#74. What type of information is NOT found in a certificate of insurance?

a) How to file a claim
b) How long the coverage will last
c) The company's cost for monthly premiums
d) What is covered in the policy

#75. Under the Business Personal Property Limit – Seasonal Increase provision, if no percentage is stated on the declarations page, seasonal fluctuations will automatically increase the business personal property limit by

a) 10%.
b) 15%.
c) 25%.
d) 50%.

#76. Which valuation type would be best suited for property whose value does not fluctuate very much?

a) Stated amount
b) Inflation guard
c) Agreed value
d) Market value

#77. Accidents that are not reportable do not impact an employer's premium rates provided

a) The New York State Insurance Fund is notified 21 days before the employer pays the claim.
b) The employer pays for any treatment directly or reimburses the New York State Insurance Fund for treatment expenses.
c) The employer documents the in-house claim and maintains such records for a minimum of ten years. The employee agrees to such a settlement by signing a notice of consent.
d) The employer and the employee file the appropriate documentation with the Labor Standards Board before the New York State Insurance Fund pays the claim.

#78. Which statement regarding the New York Disability Benefits Law is NOT correct?

a) Coverage is provided for unlimited medical expenses
b) Coverage is required for disability arising from nonoccupational injuries
c) Benefits are limited to 50% of an employee's average weekly wage, or $170 per week
d) An employer can qualify as a self-insurer, purchase coverage from a private insurer, or the State Insurance Fund

#79. What insurance concept is related to the names Weiss and Fitch?

a) Types of mutual companies
b) Index used by stock companies
c) Guides describing insurer financial integrity
d) Policy dividends

#80. According to the Nationwide Marine definitions, risks that can be the subject of inland marine insurance include all of the following EXCEPT

a) Large pleasure boats.
b) Property while stored at a warehouse.
c) Shipments made by a freight train.
d) Cargo transported by truck.

#81. When a producer uses stationery with an insurer's logo, applicants for insurance assume that the producer is authorized to transact on behalf of that insurance carrier. What type of agent authority does this describe?

a) Express
b) Implied
c) Assumed
d) Apparent

#82. On a DP-3 Dwelling Property Special Form policy, the coverage provided for personal property is

a) All-risk.
b) Open peril.
c) The same as coverage provided on the DP-1 Basic Form.
d) The same as coverage provided on the DP-2 Broad Form.

#83. Under an inland marine policy, which can be covered by the electronic data processing coverage form?

a) Computer hardware that is expressly scheduled
b) Extra expense the insured incurs to continue the business after a loss
c) Data processing media, including paper tapes, punch cards and discs, or magnetic tapes
d) All of these are covered

#84. When is a hired and non-owned auto liability endorsement available in a businessowners policy (BOP)?

a) Only if the policyholder has four or more employees
b) Never
c) Only if the policyholder does not have commercial auto coverage
d) Only in addition to commercial auto coverage

#85. Which of the following must an insurance carrier obtain to transact insurance business in this state legally?

a) Certificate of Authority
b) Power of Attorney
c) Business entity license
d) Certificate of Insurance

#86. Which of the following is a statement guaranteed to be true, and if untrue, could void an insurance policy?

a) Indemnity
b) Representation
c) Warranty
d) Concealment

#87. When USA Mower's marketing stated that its mower was the only safe mowing machine available for purchase in town, USA Mower was sued by Patriot Lawn and Garden. USA Mower's coverage would come from which part of its commercial general liability coverage?

a) Product liability
b) Personal and advertising injury liability
c) The insurer would not cover this claim
d) Premises and operations

#88. What is the maximum penalty for habitual, intentional noncompliance with the Fair Credit Reporting Act (FCRA)?

a) Revocation of license
b) $2,500
c) $1,000
d) $100 per violation

#89. Which of these homeowners endorsements covers liability exposures stemming from an incidental business conducted within a building on the residence premises?

a) Business income – report of values
b) Permitted incidental occupancies
c) Special limit of liability
d) Professional liability

#90. For the reported losses of an insured group to become more likely to equal the statistical probability of loss for that particular class, the insured group needs to become

a) More active.
b) Larger.
c) Smaller.
d) Older.

#91. Regarding homeowners policies, the term "business" refers to

a) An enterprise.
b) Full-time employment only.
c) Hobbies and avocations.
d) A trade, profession, or occupation.

#92. New York has compulsory insurance and financial responsibility laws that apply to motor vehicle owners and operators. Proof of financial responsibility can be fulfilled by any of the following EXCEPT

a) Posting sufficient cash or securities with the state treasurer.
b) Obtaining automobile liability insurance.
c) Maintaining a surety bond.
d) Submitting a hold-harmless agreement with the Motor Vehicle Department.

#93. Basic dwelling policies automatically protect against fire, lightning, and

a) Riot.
b) Windstorm.
c) Internal explosion.
d) Smoke.

#94. On the dwelling form, the broad theft coverage endorsement specifies all of the following limitations EXCEPT

a) $1,500 on jewelry.
b) $1,000 on silverware.
c) $200 on money.
d) $1,500 on securities.

#95. An insurer is domiciled in Wyoming and transacts insurance in Montana. Which term best describes the insurance provider's classification in Montana?

a) Unauthorized
b) Foreign
c) Alien
d) Domestic

#96. Which of the following personal auto coverages would apply to damage resulting from a bird hitting the windshield?

a) Property damage coverage
b) Uninsured motorist coverage
c) Collision coverage
d) Other-than-collision coverage

#97. Whether named or not, individuals covered under an insurance policy are known as the

a) Named insureds.
b) First named insureds.
c) Additional insureds.
d) Insureds.

#98. Which of these would NOT be considered personal property for insurance purposes?

a) Equipment
b) Furniture
c) A house
d) A vehicle

#99. Under the commercial auto policy, which endorsement provides the insured's employees additional protection while using a vehicle not hired, owned, or borrowed for the insured business?

a) Hired autos
b) Employees as insureds
c) Drive other car
d) Deductibles liability

#100. Under a personal auto policy, which of these statements is true regarding underinsured motorist coverage?

a) Coverage applies only to the extent that the underinsured motorist limits exceed the bodily injury limits the operator of the other vehicle carried
b) It will pay up to the limits of insurance for any loss that involves an underinsured driver
c) Limits must equal the bodily injury limits of the policy
d) Limits may differ from the limits for uninsured motorist coverage

#101. Which of the following is true of a Preferred Provider Organization (PPO)?

a) Members complete claim forms on every claim
b) No copayment fees are involved
c) Its goal is to direct patients to providers that offer discount services
d) The most common type of PPO is the staff model

102. According to the HO policy's appraisal condition, what procedure can be followed if the insured and insurance provider disagree on the size of a loss?

a) The policyholder can hire an appraiser, and the insurance provider will pay the amount determined
b) Either party can make a written request for an appraisal
c) The insured must accept what the insurance provider is willing to pay
d) The parties must pursue a lawsuit

#103. What will an employer lose in a state with elective workers compensation laws if it chooses not to be subject to those laws?

a) Its common law defenses against liability suits
b) Its ability to provide group health insurance
c) Its right to hire individuals with disabilities
d) Its eligibility for workers compensation insurance

#104. Which of these businesses would be eligible for a businessowners policy?

a) Johnny's Bar & Grill
b) Hometown Savings Bank
c) Norton & Hill Funeral Home
d) Summer Fun Amusement Park

#105. Which of the following common policy conditions prohibits the insured from changing the rights or duties as defined under the policy to any other individual or entity without the insurance company's written consent?

a) Subrogation
b) Reassignment and modification
c) Changes
d) Transfer of rights and duties under the policy

#106. Which of the following best defines the unfair trade practice of defamation?

a) Making derogatory oral statements about another insurance provider's financial condition
b) Assuming the name and identity of another individual
c) Issuing false advertising sales material
d) Refusing to deal with other insurers

#107. Which of the following limits in a policy's Declarations applies to medical expenses?

a) Per injury
b) Per incident
c) Per person
d) Per occurrence

#108. Under a homeowners policy, all of the following information must be included in the insured's signed, sworn proof of loss EXCEPT

a) The interest of all insureds in the property.
b) The insured's income and net worth at the time of loss.
c) The time and cause of the loss.
d) Other insurance on the property.

#109. When must a business purchase a liquor liability policy?

a) When employees consume alcoholic beverages
b) When it does not have a general liability policy
c) When it entertains employees or customers at events where liquor is served
d) When it is in the business of manufacturing, distributing, furnishing, or serving alcoholic beverages

#110. What premium computation method relates an employer's premiums, payroll, and losses to the rating bureau's classifications of operations?

a) Workers classification factor
b) Merit rating plan
c) Arbitration plan
d) Experience modification factor

#111. According to the New York State Disability Benefits Law definitions, the term for the money allowances during disability payable to an eligible employee is

a) Earned compensation.
b) Premiums.
c) Severance pay.
d) Benefits.

#112. All of the following statements about coinsurance are true EXCEPT

a) The policy owner agrees to maintain insurance equal to some specified percentage of the property's value.
b) If the insurance carried is less than required, the insurance might not cover the whole loss.
c) The coinsurance formula will also apply to total losses.
d) It is used to help adequacy and equity in rates.

#113. A businessowners policy (BOP) is

a) A special policy developed for large retail operations.
b) Part of a commercial package policy.
c) A monoline policy.
d) A self-contained prepackaged policy.

#114. The HO policy covers collapse resulting from all of the following EXCEPT

a) Weight of snow.
b) Hidden vermin or insect damage.
c) Weight of too many individuals attending a party hosted in the house.
d) Cracks in the foundation.

#115. The homeowners policy provides coverage for

a) The land under the residence.
b) Property of roomers, boarders, or tenants not related to any insured.
c) Business property while on the residence premises.
d) Losses caused by off-premises power failure.

#116. An insured with a homeowners policy has removed property from an insured location to protect it from a loss that a covered peril could cause. The removal coverage applies for

a) 5 days.
b) 30 days.
c) 60 days.
d) 90 days.

#117. In a businessowners policy, the cancellation provision specifies all of the following EXCEPT

a) The method of transferring the owner's rights.
b) The method of refunding unearned premiums.
c) The insured's cancellation requirements.
d) The insurer's cancellation requirements.

#118. Which of the following is NOT true regarding the reason for the Insurance Fraud Prevention Act?

a) It allows the Department to receive assistance from federal and state law enforcement agencies.
b) It allows the Superintendent and Department to investigate insurance fraud.
c) It helps to stop fraudulent acts more effectively.
d) It helps insurance carriers refrain from selling policies to applicants who are high risks.

#119. A trucking business exchanges trailers with other carriers. What coverage is necessary to cover loss to the other's trailer while in the borrower's possession?

a) Interstate carrier coverage
b) Mobile equipment
c) Owner-operator motor carrier coverage
d) Trailer interchange coverage

#120. A municipality can protect itself against the repair or construction of properties that do not conform to the building codes specified by ordinance by mandating the contractors to obtain

a) Bid bonds.
b) License and permit bonds.
c) Fidelity bonds.
d) Performance bonds.

#121. Employers liability insurance, Part Two of a standard workers compensation and employers liability (WC&EL) policy form, excludes

a) Liability to a third party for claims arising from an injury to an employee.
b) Bodily injury resulting from an accident when the injury occurs during the policy period.
c) Bodily injury resulting from or aggravated by disease during the policy period.
d) An intentional act caused by the insured.

#122. The uninsured motorist bodily injury coverage limits are set

a) At least 30 days after the vehicle is acquired.
b) When the auto policy is obtained.
c) When the vehicle is acquired.
d) At least 30 days before the vehicle is acquired.

#123. A producer has recently changed their email address. What must the producer do to comply with the change of address regulation?

a) Notify all their customers within 30 days
b) Nothing, email addresses are not subject to such regulations
c) Report the address change to the NAIC
d) Notify the Department within 30 days

#124. Which bond guarantees the principal will complete the contract as agreed?

a) Labor and materials bonds
b) Performance bonds
c) Fidelity bonds
d) Bid bonds

#125. Which HO coverage will respond if a lawsuit is brought or a claim is made against an insured for damages due to property damage or bodily injury from an occurrence to which the coverage applies?

a) Coverage D - Loss of Use
b) Coverage E - Personal Liability
c) Coverage F - Medical Payments to Others
d) Coverage C - Personal Property

#126. Which of the following types of property would be covered in any of the homeowners coverage forms?

a) Structures rented to others who are not tenants of the dwelling other than a garage
b) Birds, animals, or fish
c) Landlord furnishings in an on-premises apartment
d) Structures used for business purposes

#127. Under a homeowners policy, Coverage F (Medical Payments) would cover

a) A residence employee who is injured on the job.
b) A tenant who is injured while on the premises.
c) An injured family member while residing in the insured premises.
d) The insured for injuries suffered while working at home.

#128. In a liability insurance policy, supplementary payments are made

a) As part of the limit of liability.
b) At the option of the insured.
c) At the insurer's option.
d) In addition to the limit of liability.

#129. In a businessowners policy, the inspections and surveys condition

a) Obligates the insurance provider to make annual safety inspections.
b) Guarantees that all working conditions are healthful and safe.
c) Allows the insurance producer the right to inspect the insured's premises.
d) Validates that the insured is compliant with state and federal guidelines.

#130. Which federal act covers crews of ships?

a) Federal Employers Liability Act (FELA)
b) The Jones Act
c) U.S. Longshore and Harbor Workers Compensation Act
d) Federal Employees Compensation Act

#131. Which of the following personal property coverages would protect contents damaged by fire?

a) Coverage A
b) Coverage B
c) Coverage C
d) Coverage D

#132. A prospective licensee for a life and health agent license must complete how many hours of pre-licensing education?

a) 20
b) 40
c) 50
d) 90

#133. Regarding a Certificate of Authority, which of the following is NOT true?

a) It is the equivalent of an insurance license.
b) It is issued by a state's department of insurance.
c) It is issued to participants of group insurance.
d) It may be necessary for conducting business in a specific state.

#134. If an insurance provider makes a change to broaden coverage in a dwelling policy while it is in force, the changes will apply

a) Within 60 days.
b) Automatically.
c) When the new policy is written.
d) When the policy is up for renewal.

#135. In earthquake coverage provided by endorsement in the homeowners policy, one or more earthquake shocks would be regarded as a single earthquake if they occur within what maximum period?

a) 1 hour
b) 12 hours
c) 24 hours
d) 72 hours

#136. It would be unfairly discriminatory to ask an applicant for insurance about which of the following and then use that information as a rating factor to determine insurability?

a) Gender
b) Address
c) Sexual orientation
d) Age

#137. In personal auto policies, the term "you" refers to

a) The named insured.
b) Any individual injured in a covered accident.
c) Any individual reading the policy.
d) The insurance provider.

#138. Property insurance that provides $50,000 of coverage for personal property located at a single site and $100,000 of coverage for a building is called

a) Described coverage.
b) Specific coverage.
c) Schedule coverage.
d) Blanket coverage.

#139. Which of the following is a required part of an insurance policy that changes with each policy?

a) Conditions
b) Exclusions
c) Insuring Agreement
d) Declarations

#140. What is the forgery or alteration coverage limit in the businessowners policy?

a) $500
b) $1,000
c) $2,500
d) $5,000

#141. While an insured mows their yard with their brother's borrowed lawnmower, the fuel line ruptures, and the lawnmower is destroyed in the fire. How will the insured's homeowners liability react?

a) It will not cover the damage because the insured is not liable
b) It will pay the insured's brother's property insurance deductible
c) The insured's homeowners liability and their brother's property coverage will share on a prorated basis
d) It will cover the damage

#142. If a policy owner failed to maintain the underlying limits required by a personal umbrella policy, which of the following statements would be correct?

a) The policy owner would have to pay the self-insured retention limit
b) The policy owner would be responsible for the amount required as underlying limits in the event of a claim
c) It would have no effect on the umbrella policy
d) The policy will be canceled

#143. Concerning insurance, an offer is typically made when

a) The agent hands the policy to the policy owner.
b) An agent explains an insurance policy to a prospective applicant.
c) An insurance applicant turns in an application to the insurer.
d) The insurance company approves the application and receives the initial premium.

#144. The common policy condition is a modular part joined with other components to form the contract. The common policy condition section includes provisions applied to all lines of coverage that can be included in the policy. Which of the following provisions would be included in the common policy conditions section?

a) Before the insurance provider makes inspections, surveys, and reports relating to the insurance, approval from the insured has to be obtained
b) Requests for changes in the policy from the insured can be made by the second named insured
c) The insurance provider is given the right to audit the insured's books and records relating to the policy for up to five years following the end of the policy
d) The first named insured can cancel the policy at any time by giving written notice to the insurance provider

#145. In Medigap insurance, which of the following is NOT covered under Plan A?

a) The Medicare Part A deductible
b) Approved hospital costs for 365 additional days after Medicare benefits end
c) The 20% Part B coinsurance amounts for Medicare-approved services
d) The first three pints of blood every year

#146. Personal business property left out in the open is insured under a commercial property policy only while

a) Within 150 feet of the described premises.
b) Within 100 feet of the described premises.
c) Located on the described premises.
d) Specifically described on the declarations page.

#147. How long does a licensee have to inform the Superintendent of any change of address?

a) Immediately
b) 30 days
c) 60 days
d) 90 days

#148. The transfer of an insured's right to seek damages from a negligent party to the insurance provider is found in which of the following clauses?

a) Salvage
b) Appraisal
c) Subrogation
d) Arbitration

#149. Which of these includes the elements for establishing a charge of negligence?

a) Breach of reasonable person rule and proximate degree of care
b) Legal duty owed, standard of care, proximate cause, damages
c) Legal duty owed, proximate cause, intervening cause, damages
d) Legal duty owed, willful attempt to cause harm, damages

#150. Which statement is true concerning the premium computation for workers compensation coverage?

a) The premium is established at the start of the policy period and will not change
b) A premium auditor can examine the insured's compensation records at the end of the policy period to resolve the actual premium basis
c) The premium basis for workers compensation coverage varies by the type of industry in which the insured is involved
d) The insured pays a guaranteed premium based on an estimated value of the yearly income received

Practice Exam 1 Answers

#1. **a) Premises and operations.**

All liability losses are covered under the premises and operations hazard, subject to the exclusions and limits of the policy. (pp. 143, 151)

#2. **c) Perils.**

In an insurance policy, perils are the insured against causes of loss. (pp. 24, 40)

#3. **d) Burglary.**

An insurance policy covering the peril of burglary requires visible signs of forced entry or exit from the premises after a loss occurs. (p. 180)

#4. **c) The Sea Side Waterfront Cafe is damaged when flood waters rise and seep into the eatery**

Damage caused by surface water, flood, mudslide, water that backs up from a drain or sewer, or ground surface water that seeps through foundations, basements, windows, or doors is not covered under the basic form. The broad form includes coverage for the peril of water damage. (p. 164)

#5. **d) Errors and omissions.**

In fields other than medical, professional liability is considered errors and omissions insurance. It covers liability resulting from the failure to use due care and the degree of skill expected of an individual in a particular profession. (p. 228)

#6. **b) Additional coverage**

A policy's additional coverage portion provides additional coverage for specific loss expense at no additional premium. (p. 42)

#7. **d) Vicarious liability.**

Under vicarious liability, a policy owner can be held responsible for the acts of other family members or independent contractors hired by the policy owner to perform work. (p. 40)

#8. **a) Accident insurance because it pays medical expenses irrespective of fault.**

Medical payments will pay for the accidental bodily injury of an insured, regardless of fault. It will pay medical expenses of others occupying the insured auto. (p. 102)

#9. **c) To pre-establish the amount of coverage available for property items that are hard to value**

The insured items' value is not determined when the loss occurs but when the policy is written. (p. 42)

#10. **a) Commingling.**

It is illegal for insurance agents to commingle premiums collected from applicants with their personal funds. (p. 30)

#11. **c) Aggregate limit of liability**

The aggregate limit is the maximum coverage limit available during a liability policy's term year, regardless of the number of accidents or claims that may occur. (p. 46)

#12. **d) $25,000**

OBEL (Optional Basic Economic Loss) coverage allows policy owners to purchase an additional $25,000 in coverage. (p. 129)

#13. **a) Comparing different insurance policies**

Accurately comparing insurance policies is not an illegal activity. (p. 13)

#14. **d) Sales.**

The amount of payroll, the hazard of the work, and the employer's prior loss experience are all rating factors. (p. 218)

#15. **c) No more than the per occurrence limit applies, regardless of how many insureds are involved**

The insurance applies separately to each insured. This condition does not increase the insurance provider's liability for any one occurrence. (p. 101)

#16. **d) Insurers would cover any of the above under this form.**

The general property policy form covers other residential and non-residential structures and their contents. Eligible structures include commercial structures, other residential structures, and cooperative associations. (p. 234)

#17. **c) Second injury funds programs.**

Workers compensation statutes require employers to meet capital reserves requirements sufficient to cover any claims that could arise. Employers can meet such requirements through competitive state funds, assigned risk, and self-insurance plans. (p. 213)

#18. **c) It offers coverage for every employee, even those who were terminated in the previous 90 days.**

By definition, an employee insured under the employee dishonesty optional coverage is either currently employed or was terminated during the previous 30 days. (p. 198)

#19. **b) $50,000**

Additional personal injury protection coverage has a maximum limit of $50,000. The APIP will bring the policy owner's total PIP coverage to $100,000. (p. 129)

#20. **d) Reconstruct a timeline of activities leading up to the loss for the insurance provider to use in an investigation.**

The insured must describe when, how, and where the loss or damage occurred. There is no demand for a timeline leading up to the loss. (pp. 196-197)

#21. **c) Principal**

An agent represents the principal, who acts on the entity's behalf in contractual agreements with third parties. (p. 29)

#22. **b) Cancellation.**

Cancellation is the termination of an in-force policy by either the insured or the insurance provider before the expiration date listed in the policy. (p. 44)

#23. **a) None**

Damage by earthquake is specifically excluded from coverage in all homeowners forms. However, coverage may be purchased by endorsement. (p. 83)

#24. **b) Respond to the consumer's complaint.**

The consumer has the right to request the information on the report, the reasons for the declination, and any adverse underwriting decisions. The reporting agency must respond to the consumer's complaint and, if necessary, reinvestigate the report. (pp. 17-18)

#25. **c) $600**

The insurance carrier will cover expenses for which an insured becomes legally liable for loss of use of a vehicle rented or hired without a driver under a written rental contract. If the coverage is obtained, this extension will cover the damaged vehicle's loss of use up to $20 per day to a maximum of $600. (p. 112)

#26. **d) Subrogation.**

When an insured accepts a loss payment from the insurer, they must transfer their rights of recovery to the insurance company. This transfer prevents the policy owner from collecting twice for the same loss. (p. 48)

#27. **b) The insured cannot relinquish ownership of the damaged property to claim a total loss. Still, it must protect damaged property from further loss.**

The insurance carrier can choose how to indemnify the insured. Also, the insured cannot abandon the damaged property to claim a total loss. Most property policies let the insurer repair the damage, replace the damaged property with like kind and quality, or pay the policy's limits and take the insured property as salvage to reduce their loss. (p. 47)

#28. **d) 40 hours per week.**

Every residence employee who works for the same employer must be given coverage if they work less than 40 hours per week. The Workers Compensation – Certain Residence Employees endorsement provides this coverage. (p. 93)

#29. **b) Penalty.**

Bonds are written for a set limit, sometimes called the penalty. If the principal's obligation exceeds the limit, the surety will only be liable for the limit amount. (p. 231)

#30. **a) Self-insured retention.**

In casualty insurance, a retention is the portion of a claim that is not covered by insurance. In property insurance, it is known as a deductible. (pp. 25, 226-228)

#31. **d) Structures rented to a neighbor for use as a private garage**

Under Coverage B, other structures cannot be rented to anyone except a tenant of the main dwelling. However, a garage used for a private garage does not come under this exclusion of rented property. It is covered even if it is rented to someone besides the dwelling's occupant. (p. 60)

#32. **d) Fire or lightning**

Insurers will cover fire and lightning in all policy forms. Answers A, B, and C are exclusions. (pp. 55, 64)

#33. **a) Providing specific details about an occurrence**

In the event of a loss, the insured's duties include the following: notifying the insurance company of the occurrence (how, when, where, and the names and addresses of any injured individuals); prompt written notice of a claim; notifying the insurer of any legal papers received associated with the loss; and cooperating in the investigation of a claim. (pp. 149, 162, 201)

#34. **b) The dwelling needs to be owner-occupied.**

Dwelling policies insure residential exposures with only limited service-type business exposures allowed. The dwelling can be under construction or completed and can be owner- or tenant-occupied. The dwelling policy can insure the dwelling, contents, or both. (p. 54)

#35. **d) Often, any individual occupying a commercial vehicle would be insured under a workers compensation policy.**

Medical payment coverage is not automatically included in commercial auto coverage. Under a workers compensation policy, any individual occupying the vehicle would be covered. (p. 123)

#36. **c) Coverage D**

Coverage D will pay for the loss of use of the insured dwelling when it is rendered uninhabitable due to damage by an insured peril. (p. 183)

#37. **c) A third party breaks an arm when the insured knocks them down.**

The personal injury endorsement covers an invasion of privacy, defamation of character, libel, slander, and false arrest. The policy's personal liability coverage will cover the broken arm. (p. 93)

#38. **a) $3,000**

With additional coverage in the HO policy, grave markers will pay up to $5,000 for grave markers, including mausoleums, for loss resulting from a peril insured against, on, or off the residence premises. (p. 81)

#39. **a) Premiums.**

Retention is a planned assumption of risk. It is the acceptance of responsibility for an insured's loss through deductibles, copayments, or self-insurance. (p. 25)

#40. **b) Water backup and sump discharge or overflow**

The water backup and sump discharge or overflow endorsement will provide up to $5,000 coverage for direct physical loss to the property. The loss must be caused by water or water-borne material that backs up through drains or sewers or overflows or is discharged from a sump, sump pump, or other equipment. (p. 93)

#41. **d) Dwelling policy form**

The dwelling policy form insures residential structures and their contents including individual condominium units. (p. 234)

#42. **b) Sole representative**

The sole representative condition states that the first named insured will act on behalf of all insureds under the policy. (p. 217)

#43. **c) It is an additional coverage**

The fire department service charge is an additional amount of insurance. The builders risk form will include up to $1,000 coverage. (p. 158)

#44. **b) Regulates consumer reports.**

The Fair Credit Reporting Act (FCRA) is a federal law that regulates consumer reports, also known as credit reports or consumer investigative reports. (pp. 17-18)

#45. **a) Truckers coverage form.**

The truckers coverage form was created to handle the unique insurance needs of businesses that use their vehicles to haul goods for others. (pp. 119-122)

#46. **b) Share the risk of loss from terrorist attacks with the federal government.**

The Terrorism Risk Insurance Act of 2002 (TRIA) created a temporary federal program to share the risk of loss from future terrorist attacks with the insurance industry. (pp. 49-50)

#47. **b) The Plan is not allowed to reject any applicant for any reason.**

The applicant must have a valid driver's license and cannot purchase insurance in the standard market to qualify for coverage in the New York Automobile Insurance Plan. (p. 127)

#48. **b) Aleatory**

An insurance contract is an aleatory contract. It requires a relatively small amount of premium for a considerable risk. (p. 31)

#49. **d) $20 per day; $600 maximum**

The physical damage section contains a coverage extension that would cover substitute transportation, up to $20 per day for a maximum of $600, following the theft of a covered auto. (p. 112)

#50. **d) Nothing, sickness is not covered during the first 30 days of the contract**

Loss by illness is not covered if it happens during the first 30 days after the policy is issued. (p. 249)

#51. **a) Turkeys while out in the open**

Covered property includes farm personal property insured on a scheduled basis. It can include property like poultry while out in the open or in any building designated for poultry in the Declarations (excluding turkeys, unless expressly stated). (p. 184)

#52. **b) How parties to the contract must act following a loss.**

The conditions section is an essential part of a policy's structure. Conditions define what each party to the policy must do contractually if a loss occurs. (p. 43)

#53. **b) Ancestry.**

The Fair Credit Reporting Act regulates what information can be collected and how the information can be used. Consumer Reports include written and oral information regarding a consumer's credit, reputation, character, and habits collected by a reporting agency from credit reports, employment records, and other public sources. Ancestry is not a factor evaluated in these reports. (pp. 17-18)

#54. **d) Scheduled personal property endorsement**

Under a scheduled personal property endorsement, scheduled and insured items are covered on a valued basis. (pp. 91-92)

#55. **c) The insurer**

The agent represents the insurance provider, not the insured. (p. 4)

#56. **b) $30,000**

In this scenario, the house is insured for only $60,000 (75% of the minimum requirement of 80%). Therefore, the policy will only cover 75% of the loss, or $30,000. (p. 45)

#57. **a) An employee is caught stealing from the cash register**

Criminal or dishonest acts of any representative or employee are specifically excluded. (p. 181)

#58. **a) Explosion of steam boilers.**

Equipment breakdown coverage protects against loss caused by the sudden and accidental breakdown of the vessel. Business interruption coverage can be attached to the policy by endorsement. (pp. 176-177)

#59. **a) Loss or damage to a locked vault, safe, or cash register**

Under this form, loss or damage to a locked vault, safe, or cash register would be covered. (p. 181)

#60. **d) If it is material and intentional**

A misrepresentation can be considered fraud if it is material and intentional. Fraud would be grounds for voiding a contract. (p. 32)

#61. **b) Unintentional acts arising from operating a farming business**

A farm policy's Coverage I – Personal and Advertising Injury Liability provides coverage for suits arising from the operation of a farming business, provided the specific act is not excluded. (p. 185)

#62. **a) The SIS payment will be reduced dollar-for-dollar by the Social Security benefit payment**

The Social Insurance Supplement (SIS) policy pays a disability benefit in an amount close to what Social Security would pay. If Social Security benefit payments begin, the SIS payment will be reduced dollar-for-dollar by the Social Security benefit payment. (p. 250)

#63. **d) Mobile equipment during transportation to and from the job site**

The contractors equipment floater is an unfiled inland marine coverage form. It insures mobile equipment and contractor's equipment rented, owned, or borrowed by contractors (as opposed to dealers). (p. 172)

#64. **a) 60 days**

Insurers will pay losses within 60 days of receiving proof of loss and agreeing with the insured on the amount payable. (p. 67)

#65. **c) All providers will have the same coverage options and conditions for each plan**

Regarding the standard Medicare Supplement benefits plans, the term "standard" signifies that all providers will have the same coverage options and conditions for every plan. (pp. 259-260)

#66. **b) Private insurers that want to write and service National Flood Insurance policies on a no-risk-bearing basis**

A Write Your Own (WYO) program comprises private insurers that write and service National Flood Insurance policies. These policies are issued on a no-risk-bearing basis through a special agreement with the Federal Insurance Administration. WYO programs retain part of the flood insurance premium to pay for commissions and administrative costs. The remaining premiums, plus investments, are used to cover losses. (p. 233)

#67. **b) Make voluntary payments for the treatment of the worker's injury**

The insured's duties are to notify the insurance company at once, provide immediate medical care required by the law, and furnish the names and addresses of the injured worker and any witnesses. Additional duties include promptly sending any notices or other legal papers, cooperating with the insurer, and not making voluntary payments or assuming any obligations. (p. 216)

#68. **d) The insurance provider pays the mortgagee according to the mortgagee's interest in the property**

If a loss to tangible (real) property occurs, the standard mortgage clause sees that benefits go to the mortgagee and the insured as their interest appears in the policy. (p. 48)

#69. **d) It must be attached by endorsement to a homeowners policy.**

HO policies automatically provide an insurance amount in Coverage B equal to 10% of the amount written in Coverage A. This amount of coverage can be increased by endorsement. (p. 77)

#70. **a) Property damage liability**

Property Damage Liability is the legal liability arising from physical damage to the tangible property of others resulting from the negligence of a policy owner. (p. 100)

#71. **a) Embezzlement.**

Wrongful acts trigger directors and officers liability coverage as opposed to being triggered on an accident or occurrence basis. Wrongful acts include misstatements by directors and officers, breach of duty, and neglect. (p. 228)

#72. **c) Five**

Dwelling policies can insure a property that allows up to five roomers or boarders. (p. 54)

#73. **d) Embezzlement.**

Embezzlement is the criminal act of taking money belonging to someone else. Criminal penalties will be imposed, in addition to revocation of license. (p. 10)

#74. **c) The company's cost for monthly premiums**

The individuals covered under the insurance contract are issued certificates of insurance. The certificate states the following: what is covered in the policy, how to file a claim, how long the coverage will last, and how to convert the policy to an individual policy. (pp. 49, 256)

#75. **c) 25%.**

Under Business Personal Property Limit – Seasonal Increase, the business personal property limit will automatically increase by 25% for seasonal fluctuations unless stated in the Declarations. (p. 196)

#76. **c) Agreed value**

Agreed value works well with items whose value does not fluctuate all that much. When a loss occurs, the policy pays the agreed value as stated on the policy schedule, regardless of the insured item's depreciation or appreciation. (p. 42)

#77. **b) The employer pays for any treatment directly or reimburses the New York State Insurance Fund for treatment expenses.**

Accidents that are not reportable do not impact an employer's premium rates, provided the employer directly pays for any treatment or reimburses the New York State Insurance Fund (NYSIF) for treatment expenses. (p. 219)

#78. **a) Coverage is provided for unlimited medical expenses**

Benefits are paid for a loss of earnings caused by a nonoccupational injury or disease. They will not be paid for any medical expenses. (pp. 219-221)

#79. **c) Guides describing insurer financial integrity**

An insurer's strength and stability are crucial factors in its sustainability. Independent rating services have been formed to publish regular updates on the financial integrity of different insurers. Weiss and Fitch are two of these services, although there are more. (p. 28)

#80. **a) Large pleasure boats.**

Large pleasure boats will not be included in inland marine coverage. They would instead be covered under a boatowners policy, or, if large enough, under a yacht policy. (pp. 169)

#81. **d) Apparent**

Apparent authority (also called perceived authority) is the appearance or assumption of authority based on the principal's actions, words, or deeds or because of circumstances the principal created. (p. 30)

#82. **d) The same as coverage provided on the DP-2 Broad Form.**

Coverages A and B on a DP-3 form are written on an all-risk or open peril basis. The coverage for personal property is written on a specified or named peril basis. (p. 58)

#83. **d) All of these are covered**

Answers A, B, and C are covered items under electronic data processing coverage. (p. 172)

#84. **c) Only if the policyholder does not have commercial auto coverage**

This endorsement can be added to the businessowners policy only if the insured does not have commercial auto insurance. This coverage is excess over any primary insurance coverage on the hired or non-owned auto. (p. 204)

#85. **a) Certificate of Authority**

Before insurance companies can conduct business in New York, they must apply for a license or Certificate of Authority and meet financial capital and surplus requirements. (pp. 8, 27)

#86. **c) Warranty**

In insurance, a warranty is a statement guaranteed to be true. When an applicant applies for insurance, their statements are typically not warranties but representations. Representations are true statements to the best of the applicant's knowledge. (p. 32)

#87. **b) Personal and advertising injury liability**

Personal and advertising injury liability responds to claims caused by the oral or written publication of the material. It is automatically included in the commercial general liability coverage as Coverage B. (pp. 145-146)

#88. **b) $2,500**

Individuals who willfully violate the FCRA enough to demonstrate a general pattern or business practice will be subject to a penalty of up to $2,500. (p. 18)

#89. **b) Permitted incidental occupancies**

A permitted incidental occupancies endorsement protects against liability exposures stemming from an incidental business conducted within a building on the residence premises. (p. 92)

#90. **b) Larger.**

The law of large numbers states that the larger a group becomes, the easier it is to predict losses within that group. Insurance companies use this law to predict certain losses and set appropriate premiums. (p. 26)

#91. **d) A trade, profession, or occupation.**

According to the homeowners ISO forms, "business" means a trade, occupation, or profession engaged in on a full-time, part-time, or occasional basis. (p. 76)

#92. **d) Submitting a hold-harmless agreement with the Motor Vehicle Department.**

Methods of satisfying the financial responsibility law are established by New York state law. (pp. 125-126)

#93. **c) Internal explosion.**

The other three perils are included in the extended coverages that can be added to the basic form for an additional premium. (p. 55)

#94. **b) $1,000 on silverware.**

For a Dwelling Policy, the broad theft coverage limit on silverware is $2,500. (p. 69)

#95. **b) Foreign**

A foreign insurance provider is domiciled in one state and transacts insurance in another. A domestic insurance provider transacts insurance in the domicile state (in this case, Wyoming). An alien insurance provider is domiciled in one country and transacts insurance in another. (p. 28)

#96. **d) Other-than-collision coverage**

Other-than-collision coverage includes losses from contact with animals or birds, hail, windstorm, water or flood, and glass breakage. (p. 99)

#97. **d) Insureds.**

The insureds are individuals covered under a policy, whether named or not. (p. 43)

#98. **c) A house**

Personal property refers to moveable property; real property is non-moveable. (p. 40)

#99. **b) Employees as insureds**

The employees as insureds endorsement provides the insured's employees with additional protection while using a vehicle not hired, owned, or borrowed for the insured business. (p. 124)

#100. **a) Coverage applies only to the extent that the underinsured motorist limits exceed the bodily injury limits the operator of the other vehicle carried**

Underinsured motorist coverage will act as excess coverage over the at fault motorist's bodily injury coverage. (p. 103)

#101. **c) Its goal is to direct patients to providers that offer discount services**

Insureds are treated by providers who agree to discount their fees for services. (pp. 255-256)

#102. **b) Either party can make a written request for an appraisal**

Either party can make a written request for an appraisal if the insured and the insurer cannot reach an agreement. (p. 85)

#103. **a) Its common law defenses against liability suits**

In an elective law, the employer does not have to be subject to the state's workers compensation laws. If the employer chooses not to be subject to these laws, it loses its common law defenses against liability lawsuits. (p. 210)

#104. **c) Norton & Hill Funeral Home**

Expressly excluded from eligibility on a businessowners policy (BOP) are financial institutions, bars and grills, and amusement places. (pp. 190-191)

#105. **d) Transfer of rights and duties under the policy**

Under the transfer of rights and duties under the policy condition, the insured cannot transfer any rights or duties under the policy to any other individual or organization without the insurer's written consent. (pp. 142, 203)

#106. **a) Making derogatory oral statements about another insurance provider's financial condition**

Making written or oral statements indirectly or directly that are maliciously critical or derogatory to another insurer would be an example of defamation. (p. 14)

#107. **c) Per person**

A combined single limit of insurance applies for all property damage and bodily injury losses that arise from a single occurrence. Medical expenses are limited to the per-person limit listed in the Declarations. (p. 46)

#108. **b) The insured's income and net worth at the time of loss.**

The insured must provide all the information relevant to the loss and the property. The insured's income and net worth are not pertinent. (p. 84)

#109. **d) When it is in the business of manufacturing, distributing, furnishing, or serving alcoholic beverages**

Homeowners and general liability policies provide host liquor liability coverage to insureds that entertain employees, guests, or organizations at events where liquor is served. However, those in the business of manufacturing, distributing, selling, furnishing, or serving alcoholic beverages must obtain liquor liability coverage. (p. 229)

#110. **d) Experience modification factor**

A rating bureau develops an experience modification factor. The calculations relate an employer's losses, payroll, and premiums, segregated according to classifications of operations, all as reported to the bureau by the employer's insurance company. (p. 218)

#111. **d) Benefits**

Benefits refer to the money allowances during disability payable to an employee eligible for such benefits, as provided by law. (p. 220)

#112. **c) The coinsurance formula will also apply to total losses.**

In a total loss, the coinsurance clause does not operate, and the policy's face amount is paid. (p. 45)

#113. **d) A self-contained prepackaged policy.**

A businessowners policy (BOP) is similar in structure to the personal lines homeowners policy, except it covers a business exposure for property and liability losses. (p. 190)

#114. **d) Cracks in the foundation.**

The collapse has to be caused by some unexpected, sudden reason. The foundation cracks would take years to result in a collapse, meaning there would be plenty of time to repair the foundation cracks. (pp. 80-81)

#115. **c) Business property while on the residence premises.**

Your contents coverage will cover up to $2,500 for loss of business property on the premises. (p. 78)

#116. **b) 30 days.**

Removal coverage applies for 30 days when the property has been removed to be protected from further damage. (p. 80)

#117. **a) The method of transferring the owner's rights.**

The assignment provision outlines the transfer method of all or a portion of the policy owner's rights under an insurance contract. (pp. 202-203)

#118. **d) It helps insurance carriers refrain from selling policies to applicants who are high risks.**

The Insurance Fraud Prevention Act allows the Superintendent and the Department to utilize their expertise to investigate and uncover insurance fraud, more effectively stop fraudulent activities, and receive assistance from state and federal law enforcement agencies. (pp. 14-15)

#119. **d) Trailer interchange coverage**

Truckers often hire or borrow trailers from others with a written trailer interchange agreement. They need coverage for the trailer in their possession to cover the liability imposed upon them due to the agreement. (pp. 120-121, 123)

#120. **b) License and permit bonds.**

License and permit bonds guarantee the recipients of permits will comply with the ordinances relating to the use of such permits. (p. 232)

#121. **d) An intentional act caused by the insured.**

The employer is not liable for damages resulting from the insured's intentional acts (negligence). (p. 215)

#122. **b) When the auto policy is obtained.**

The limits for uninsured motorist coverage are established when the auto policy is purchased. (p. 103)

#123. **d) Notify the Department within 30 days**

Producers must notify the Department of Financial Services within 30 days of any address change: business, residence, or email. (p. 6)

#124. **b) Performance bonds**

A performance bond will guarantee the principal will complete the contract as agreed. (p. 232)

#125. **b) Coverage E - Personal Liability**

Coverage E – Personal Liability will respond when a lawsuit is brought, or a claim is made, against an insured for damages due to bodily injury (BI) or property damage (PD) caused by an occurrence to which the coverage applies. (p. 86)

#126. **c) Landlord furnishings in an on-premises apartment**

On the HO-5 form, landlord furnishings in an on-premises apartment are insured for up to $2,500. (p. 81)

#127. **a) A residence employee who is injured on the job.**

Under a homeowners policy, Coverage F (Medical Payments) would pay for bodily injury to a residence employee if it arises during employment. (p. 86)

#128. **d) In addition to the limit of liability.**

Supplementary payments are the insurance carrier's claim-related expenses and are made in addition to the limits of liability. (pp. 100, 111, 147)

#129. **c) Allows the insurance producer the right to inspect the insured's premises.**

The inspections and surveys condition allows the insurer to inspect the insured's operations and premises at any reasonable time during the policy period. Inspections and surveys are not mandatory. This condition does not make safety inspections nor guarantees that the conditions are safe or meet safety regulations. (p. 203)

#130. **b) The Jones Act**

The Jones Act provides remedies to injured seamen working on a vessel. It extends the provisions of the Federal Employers Liability Act (FELA). (p. 214)

#131. **c) Coverage C**

Coverage C – Personal Property provides coverage for an insured dwelling's contents if they are damaged by fire. (pp. 60-61, 77-78)

#132. **b) 40**

Single lines of authority will require a minimum of 20 hours of pre-licensing education. Combination licenses will require a minimum of 40 hours. (p. 2)

#133. **c) It is issued to participants of group insurance.**

Before insurers can conduct business in a specific state, they must apply for a state license or Certificate of Authority. (pp. 8, 27)

#134. **b) Automatically.**

Changes made to broaden coverage in a dwelling policy will automatically apply and will not have to be endorsed to the policy if made while the policy is effective or 60 days before it goes into effect. (pp. 67, 90)

#135. **d) 72 hours**

Earthquake coverage provided by endorsement in the HO form considers one or more earthquake shocks occurring within 72 hours as a single earthquake. (p. 91)

#136. **c) Sexual orientation**

It is unfairly discriminatory to ask an applicant for their sexual orientation and use it as a rating factor. (p. 14)

#137. **a) The named insured.**

The terms "you" and "your" used throughout the personal auto policy (PAP) refer to the named insured listed in the Declarations. (p. 98)

#138. **b) Specific coverage.**

One location is insured for specific insurance coverage on the structure or buildings and their contents. (p. 41)

#139. **d) Declarations**

The Declarations provide a policy's who, what, where, and when. This information differs in each contract. (p. 42)

#140. **c) $2,500**

Forgery or alteration coverage in the businessowners policy pays for loss because of forgery or alteration of an insured's promissory note or check. However, the limit is only covered up to $2,500. (p. 194)

#141. **d) It will cover the damage**

The insured's HO liability will pay for damage to the property of others even if the insured is not liable. (pp. 86-87)

#142. **b) The policy owner would be responsible for the amount required as underlying limits in case of a claim**

The amount of coverage required as underlying limits in other insurance policies is treated like a deductible amount to the umbrella for that particular exposure. Therefore, if underlying limits are not maintained, it is the policy owner's responsibility. (pp. 226-228)

#143. **c) An insurance applicant turns in an application to the insurer.**

In insurance, the offer is generally made by the applicant in the form of an application. Acceptance occurs when an insurance company's underwriter approves the application and issues a policy. (p. 30)

#144. **d) The first named insured can cancel the policy at any time by giving written notice to the insurance provider**

Only the first named insured can request any changes in the policy. The first named insured can cancel the policy at any time by giving written notice to the insurance provider. (p. 43)

#145. **a) The Medicare Part A deductible**

Answers B, C, and D are included in a Medigap policy Plan A's basic benefits, except for the Medicare Part A deductible. (p. 260)

#146. **b) Within 100 feet of the described premises.**

In the commercial property policy, business personal property is defined as property located in the insured structure or within 100 feet of that structure. (p. 153)

#147. **b) 30 days**

The Superintendent must be notified within 30 days of any change of business or primary residence address. (p. 6)

#148. **c) Subrogation**

After an insured accepts payment from the insurance provider, they have been indemnified. Insurance policies require the insured to transfer any right of recovery to the insurance provider so that it can seek recovery up to the amount paid as a loss. (p. 48)

#149. **b) Legal duty owed, standard of care, proximate cause, damages**

Negligence is failure to do what a prudent and reasonable individual would do under the same circumstances. The following four elements must be present for negligent liability to exist: legal duty owed, standard of care, proximate cause, damages. (p. 38)

#150. **b) A premium auditor can examine the insured's compensation records at the end of the policy period to resolve the actual premium basis**

Since the initial premium calculation is based on approximated payrolls, a premium auditor can inspect actual payrolls to ensure adequate premiums are being paid. (p. 218)

PRACTICE EXAM: 2

Your preparation is paying off

You are about to take another New York Property and Casualty Insurance Agent/Broker Practice Examination. This exam consists of *150 Questions (plus five to ten non-scored experimental questions)* and is *2 hours and 30 minutes* long. If you do not have enough time to complete this exam right now, it is better to wait until you can fully devote your attention to completing it in the allotted time.

Any skipped questions will be graded as incorrect. The following chart breaks down the number of questions in each chapter and by topic.

Chapter	% of Exam
Insurance Regulation	9%
General Insurance	9%
Property and Casualty Insurance Basics	13%
Dwelling Policy	6%
Homeowners Policy	14%
Auto Insurance	11%
Commercial Package Policy (CPP)	11%
Businessowners Policy	8%
Workers Compensation Insurance	8%
Other Coverages and Options	7%
Accident and Health Insurance	4%
Total	**100%**

To calculate your score, subtract the number of incorrectly answered questions from 150. Take this number and divide it by 150. For example, if you incorrectly answered 45 questions, your score would be 70%, the minimum score needed to pass the exam.

#1. The part of the policy that clarifies the terms that are used throughout the policy is the

a) Definitions.
b) Conditions.
c) Insuring agreement.
d) Declarations.

#2. What legal defense can be used in most states where proportionate damages can be awarded when both the plaintiff and defendant were negligent?

a) Contributory negligence
b) Proximate cause
c) Comparative negligence
d) Relative degree of damage statute

#3. XYZ Corp. has $100,000 of coverage on its building through Insurer A and $50,000 of identical coverage on the same building through Insurer B. Assuming coinsurance will not be an issue when a $24,000 loss occurs and the pro rata method is used, how much will each insurer pay?

a) Insurer A will pay $20,000; Insurer B will pay $4,000
b) Insurer A will pay $12,000; Insurer B will pay $12,000
c) Insurer A will pay $24,000; Insurer B will pay $0
d) Insurer A will pay $16,000; Insurer B will pay $8,000

#4. An insured hit a buffalo and crashed her vehicle into a tree. The total damage to the car is $6,000. How will this loss be covered?

a) $3,000 would be paid under other-than-collision; $3,000 would be paid under collision coverage
b) $6,000 would be paid under collision coverage
c) $6,000 would be paid under other-than-collision coverage
d) This would not be a covered loss

#5. Which of the following is an insurance carrier required to obtain to conduct insurance business within a given state?

a) Producer's certificate
b) Business entity license
c) Insurer's license
d) Certificate of authority

#6. Under a commercial auto policy, the definition of an "auto" does NOT include

a) A semitrailer.
b) Mobile equipment.
c) A land motor vehicle.
d) A trailer.

#7. An insured driving his automobile strikes a large pothole that results in a flat tire. Which personal auto policy coverage will pay for the repair?

a) Comprehensive
b) Collision
c) Transportation expenses
d) The loss is not covered

#8. The liability coverage of the businessowners policy is written on a

a) Policy owners liability coverage form.
b) Aggregate liability coverage form.
c) Homeowners liability coverage form.
d) Businessowners liability coverage form.

#9. A trucking company owns a large fleet of trucks transporting oil across state lines. According to the financial responsibility requirements established by the Motor Carrier Act of 1980, what is the minimum amount of insurance the trucking company must carry on vehicles transporting oil?

a) $500,000
b) $750,000
c) $1 million
d) $5 million

#10. All of the following are conditions usually found in the insurance policy EXCEPT

a) Subrogation.
b) Appraisal.
c) Insuring agreement.
d) Cancellation and nonrenewal.

#11. An insurer with a Certificate of Authority in the state in which it transacts business is a/an

a) Local insurer.
b) Certified insurer.
c) Self-insurer.
d) Authorized insurer.

#12. In a watercraft policy, which of the following will respond to a claim for damages for property damage or bodily injury for which the insured becomes legally liable due to a watercraft accident?

a) Part A
b) Part B
c) Part D
d) Part E

#13. In the commercial general liability policy, Coverage A – Bodily Injury and Property Damage will cover

a) Damage to the insured's product.
b) Losses because of the insured's negligence.
c) Liquor liability.
d) Contractual liability.

#14. Installing a deadbolt lock on the doors of a house is an example of which method of handling risk?

a) Avoidance
b) Transfer
c) Self-insurance
d) Reduction

#15. Under Coverage A in the dwelling policy, which of the following losses would likely NOT be covered?

a) Supplies used to repair the dwelling
b) Theft of a renter's lawnmower used to service the premises
c) Fire damage to building material located on the premises
d) Outdoor personal property of the insured

#16. Any New York producer found guilty of violating insurance licensing laws will be subject to which of the following penalties?

a) Imprisonment for up to one year
b) Automatic license revocation
c) $500 fine for each violation
d) $5,000 fine for each violation

#17. An insurer has published a brochure that inaccurately portrays the advantages of a particular insurance policy. This unfair trade practice is an example of

a) False advertising.
b) Twisting.
c) Defamation.
d) Unfair claims.

#18. After a property loss that is covered under a businessowners policy, if the insurance company and insured cannot agree on the loss amount, what method is used to resolve the issue?

a) Arbitration
b) Adjudication
c) No-fault procedure
d) Appraisal

#19. Which policy comprises the declarations, conditions, endorsements, and other attachments that apply to a single line of insurance?

a) Monoline
b) Insurance
c) Casualty
d) Commercial package

#20. Which one of the following business auto coverage symbols is correctly described?

a) Symbol 9 – non-owned autos only
b) Symbol 1 – owned auto only
c) Symbol 2 – owned autos subject to no-fault
d) Symbol 7 – hired autos only

#21. An insured is admitted to the hospital with a back injury. After checking her disability income policy, she discovers that she will not be eligible for benefits for at least 30 days. This period would indicate that the policy includes a/an

a) Blackout period.
b) Probationary period.
c) Deductible.
d) Elimination period.

#22. What method do insurance providers use to protect themselves against catastrophic losses?

a) Indemnity
b) Pro rata liability
c) Risk management
d) Reinsurance

#23. A nail salon burns to the ground. What type of loss is this to the owner of the salon?

a) Specific
b) Consecutive
c) Direct
d) Consequential

#24. All of the following circumstances would be covered under a professional liability policy EXCEPT

a) A CPA's error that inflated a bid and caused a client to lose a major account.
b) Negligence of an architect who designed an unsafe building.
c) A lawyer's failure to properly defend a client due to their dislike of the client.
d) A physician's failure to render the quality of healthcare that is customary in the medical field.

#25. Under the New York State Disability Benefits Law, which of the following is a type of covered employment?

a) Trade organization employment
b) Services performed for a state agency
c) Maritime employment
d) Casual employment

#26. Which of the following is NOT an indicator that a party to a contract is competent?

a) Comprehension of contract
b) Business profession
c) Legal age
d) Mental proficiency

#27. An insured has an auto liability policy with limits of 25/50/15. The insured caused an accident resulting from her negligence. She is legally liable for bodily injuries of three individuals in the other vehicle as follows: "Person A" $15,000, "Person B" $30,000, and "Person C" $35,000. How much will her insurance provider pay in total for all injuries?

a) $105,000
b) $25,000
c) $30,000
d) $50,000

#28. An insured works outside the home. The insured's brother lives with her and cares for her four children. When the insured's home is badly damaged by fire, the family moves into an apartment while repairs are being done. The largest apartment available in the area has two bedrooms, so the insured's brother has to stay at a hotel. How much will the HO-3 form cover for these additional living expenses?

a) The expense of renting an apartment, and 50% of the expense of the hotel
b) Nothing
c) All of the cost up to the Coverage D limit
d) The expense of renting an apartment, but not the expense of the hotel room

#29. Which of these will NOT be considered unfair discrimination by insurance carriers?

a) Assigning different risk classifications to applicants based on their gender identity
b) Discriminating in coverages and benefits based on the insured's habits and lifestyle
c) Charging applicants with comparable health histories different premiums based on ethnicity
d) Cancelling individual coverage based on the insured's marital status

#30. Under a businessowners policy, which of these risks is eligible for coverage?

a) Automobile dealers
b) Bars or taverns
c) Condominiums
d) Banks

#31. A policy owner's building has an actual cash value (ACV) of $100,000. They have insured the property for $60,000 with a coinsurance clause of 80%. A $20,000 loss occurs. How much will the policy pay?

a) $0
b) $15,000
c) $16,000
d) $20,000

#32. Under Coverage B – Other Structures of a homeowners policy, other structures are covered for what amount?

a) $1,000
b) $10,000
c) 10% of Coverage A
d) 10% of Coverage C

#33. A policy owner was involved in a car accident for which they were at fault. Which coverages would pay for damage to the policy owner's vehicle?

a) Property damage liability coverage
b) Comprehensive coverage
c) Collision
d) Other Than Collision

#34. In a workers compensation policy, the voluntary compensation endorsement stipulates that the insurance company will pay statutory benefits to the insured individual in exchange for

a) The insured individual must use the physician of the insurance company's choosing.
b) The insured individual must pay a deductible before receiving medical care.
c) The insured individual can file only one claim per year.
d) The insured individual must release the employer and the insurance company from further liability.

#35. If the insured owns a Rolex watch valued at $10,000, full coverage can be provided on a homeowners policy by obtaining the

a) Scheduled personal property endorsement.
b) Special limits of liability endorsement.
c) Personal property replacement cost endorsement.
d) Blanket personal property endorsement.

#36. In a participation plan, the policy owner may be eligible for which of the following?

a) An increase in insurance over time
b) Lower premiums
c) Guaranteed dividends
d) A partial premium refund

#37. Who are the parties to a bond?

a) Principal - Obligee - Surety - Obligation
b) Principal - Obligee - Surety
c) Obligee - Surety - Obligation
d) Principal - Obligor

#38. In insurance terms, components refer to

a) The amounts paid out in benefits.
b) The penalties paid for unfair trade practices.
c) The prices charged for policies.
d) The factors that determine rates.

#39. In the liability section of a homeowners policy, additional coverages will pay for all of the following EXCEPT

a) Damage to a third-party property for which the insured is legally liable.
b) Claims expense.
c) Expenses the insured incurs providing first aid for bodily injury to third parties.
d) Damage to the property of others.

#40. Under Coverage C of a homeowners policy, the amount of insurance provided to cover the insured's personal property is

a) 50% of the amount provided as Coverage B.
b) 50% of the amount provided as Coverage A.
c) Equal to the amount provided as Coverage B.
d) Equal to the amount provided as Coverage A.

#41. Which inland marine coverage condition specifies that payment of any claim will not reduce the limit of insurance, except when a total loss occurs on a scheduled item?

a) Reinstatement of limit
b) Legal action against the insurer
c) Privilege to adjust with the owner
d) Transfer of rights of recovery

#42. Which of these individuals would be required to hold a license as an insurance producer?

a) A salaried full-time employee who provides information for group insurance
b) An insurance company director who performs administrative, executive, and managerial duties
c) An insurance service representative who advertises and solicits insurance business
d) A person whose activities are limited to producing insurance advertisements

#43. An insurance agent was born in July of 1977. He obtained his New York insurance license in 2016. When will the agent's license expire?

a) On the agent's birthday every odd-numbered year
b) January 1, every even-numbered year
c) Every year on the license issue date
d) Every two years on the license issue date

#44. The additional living expense coverage in homeowners policies

a) Is automatically paid after any loss to the covered house.
b) Only starts to pay once the family has been out of the house for at least seven days.
c) Is designed to allow the family to stay in the least expensive accommodations available.
d) Is designed to allow the family to maintain its normal standard of living.

#45. What minimum coverage amount should be carried under the HO-2 form on the insured's house purchased three years ago for $75,000, which today has a $100,000 replacement value?

a) $80,000
b) $100,000
c) $60,000
d) $75,000

#46. Which of the following individuals must pass a written exam to be licensed as a life insurance agent?

a) A resident of New York wishing to conduct business in New York
b) A nonresident licensee currently licensed in another state
c) A person seeking to be a representative of a fraternal benefit society as its agent
d) An applicant who has a Chartered Life Underwriter (CLU) designation

#47. Which of these would be considered an uninsured vehicle?

a) A vehicle operated by an insured's family member
b) A vehicle fleeing the scene of a hit-and-run accident
c) A vehicle owned by a self-insurer
d) A government-owned vehicle

#48. Untrue statements unintentionally made by insureds on the application that, if discovered, would alter the underwriting decision of the insurance company are known as

a) Material misrepresentations.
b) Fraudulent statements.
c) Warranties.
d) Common errors.

#49. The transfer of an interest or legal right in an insurance policy is known as

a) Assignment.
b) Abandonment
c) Obligation
d) Legal purpose

#50. Which of the following insures a carrier for liability for loss to cargo while it is being transported in a truck?

a) Motor truck cargo policy - truckers form
b) Motor truck cargo policy - owners form
c) Trip transit policy
d) Truckers coverage form

#51. When an insurance provider refuses to issue a policy based solely on the geographic location of the risk within the state, it is an illegal practice known as

a) Redlining.
b) Churning.
c) Twisting.
d) Collusion.

#52. An insured has a history of cancer in his family. He wants to buy a health insurance policy that covers cancer explicitly. What type of policy is this?

a) Isolated coverage
b) Specified coverage
c) Single protection
d) Unilateral protection

#53. Umbrella policies provide what type of coverage?

a) Excess coverage over an underlying or primary policy
b) Property coverage for those who do not qualify for homeowners insurance
c) Property coverage for the basic perils of wind, fire, and hail
d) Primary coverage for risks that are difficult to insure

#54. When a consumer requests additional information regarding an investigative consumer report, how long does the insurance company or reporting agency have to comply?

a) 10 days
b) 3 days
c) 5 days
d) 7 days

#55. Which of these is the type of property NOT covered by the homeowners policy?

a) Attached structures
b) Land on which the property is located
c) Dwellings
d) Materials and supplies

#56. Which commercial crime coverage will pay for a loss caused by theft of the company's money and securities from an armored vehicle?

a) Outside the premises
b) Forgery or alteration
c) Robbery and safe burglary
d) Inside the premises

#57. An individual who is not named as an insured in a policy's Declarations but is protected by the policy is the

a) First named insured.
b) Additional insured.
c) Policy owner.
d) Named insured.

#58. Which liability coverage must be added by endorsement to the homeowners policy?

a) Bodily injury
b) Property damage liability
c) Medical payments to others
d) Personal injury

#59. Under a personal auto policy's property damage liability coverage, which of the following losses would be covered?

a) The policy owner's vehicle is damaged when it collides with a deer
b) A passenger in the policy owner's vehicle is injured following an accident caused by the policy owner
c) The policy owner damaged a rented garage when they failed to stop in time
d) A temporary substitute vehicle is damaged while the policy owner is driving it

#60. Concerning workers compensation, which of the following is NOT true?

a) The insurance carrier offers benefits
b) The federal government does not regulate benefits
c) Benefits differ from state to state
d) The state government regulates benefits

#61. Commercial inland marine policies would NOT cover which of the following?

a) Bridges and tunnels
b) Property lost because of a military action
c) Commercial property floater risks
d) Loss resulting from weather conditions

#62. Of the following, which is NOT defined as an uninsured motor vehicle in the personal auto policy?

a) A vehicle that is not covered by a bodily injury liability policy
b) A vehicle covered by a bodily injury liability policy, but the coverage limit is less than the minimum required by the financial responsibility law
c) A vehicle owned by a government entity
d) A vehicle in which the owner or driver is unknown

#63. Which of the following entities protects insureds, policy owners, and beneficiaries under insurance policies when insurance providers fail to perform contractual obligations because of financial impairment?

a) Insurance Consumer Protectorate
b) Insurance Solvency Association
c) Consumer Protection Agency
d) Insurance Guaranty Association

#64. In individual health coverage, the insurance provider must cover a newborn from the moment of birth. If additional premium payment is required, how many days should be allowed for payment?

a) 10 calendar days
b) 15 working days
c) 30 days of birth
d) A reasonable period of time

#65. Under the examinations of books and records condition, the insurer can examine and audit the insured's books and records associated with the policy

a) During the policy period and up to five years after the termination of the policy.
b) Only after the policy period.
c) During the policy period and up to three years after the policy's termination.
d) Only during the policy period.

#66. Which type of agent authority is also known as perceived authority?

a) Implied
b) Fiduciary
c) Apparent
d) Express

#67. Which coverage is included in an unendorsed homeowners policy?

a) Medical payments to others
b) Personal property replacement coverage
c) Fungi, wet or dry rot, or bacteria
d) Earthquake

#68. In New York, vandalism and malicious mischief will be covered if the insured's premises have been vacant for no more than

a) 30 consecutive days.
b) 60 consecutive days.
c) 100 consecutive days.
d) 365 consecutive days.

#69. When does uninsured motorist coverage apply?

a) When the insured drives an uninsured vehicle
b) When the insured is legally liable but does not have sufficient coverage
c) When the insured is legally liable
d) When the other party is legally liable but does not have insurance

#70. Under a homeowners policy, which of these would NOT be considered an insured?

a) Residents of the household who are the insured's blood relatives
b) A person under age 21 in the care of but not related to the insured
c) Individuals named in the policy Declarations
d) A divorced spouse residing in another state

#71. Which of the following losses would be fully covered by a homeowners policy?

a) $1,200 pedigreed Alaskan Malamute stolen
b) $24,000 bass boat destroyed in a tornado
c) $5,000 firearm collection stolen
d) $2,000 silver tea set stolen

#72. If a covered loss occurs, the policy that pays first is known as the

a) Pro rata policy.
b) Open peril policy.
c) Primary policy.
d) Excess policy.

#73. An insured with a homeowners policy must be a member of her neighborhood's homeowners association. The association's community house has burned down, and the insured has been assessed $1,200 for her share of the rebuilding cost. How much of the assessment will her HO policy pay?

a) None
b) $500
c) $1,000
d) $1,200

#74. Under businessowners property insurance, how soon after a direct loss does the period of restoration for extra expense coverage begin?

a) Immediately
b) Within 24 hours
c) Within 48 hours
d) Within 72 hours

#75. The voluntary compensation endorsement offers statutory coverage for which employees?

a) Factory workers
b) Police officers
c) Teachers
d) Farmworkers

#76. When a contractor defaults on a performance contract, all of these statements would be true EXCEPT

a) The principal's obligations end.
b) The surety will attempt to seek reimbursement from the contractor for any amounts they pay.
c) The surety can cancel the bond to avoid paying losses and expenses.
d) The obligee can hire another contractor to finish the job and have the surety repay them.

#77. Under a commercial auto insurance policy, what type of coverage will pay for loss or damage to a covered auto resulting from any cause other than collision or overturn?

a) Blanket
b) Loss of use
c) Specified
d) Comprehensive

#78. An owner of a parking garage finished major renovations to the parking garage just before selling it to another company. Three months later, overhead concrete fell onto cars parked on the second-floor level. In the conditions section of the garage coverage policy, which of the following is true?

a) The damage occurred when the concrete fell
b) The renovation contractor is liable
c) The initial owner is liable for the damage
d) The damage occurred when the renovations were completed

#79. Which of the following health insurance provisions is about the insured's duty to provide the insurance carrier with reasonable notice in the event of a loss?

a) Consideration
b) Notice of claim
c) Loss notification
d) Claims initiation

#80. Dwelling coverage includes all of the following EXCEPT

a) The dwelling that is used primarily for residential purposes.
b) Materials on the described location used to repair or alter the dwelling.
c) Building and outdoor equipment used to service the described location.
d) Land on which the dwelling is located.

#81. Compared with other drivers in his age group, a driver has had more minor accidents and traffic violations. Which rating type would most accurately reflect the driver's actual insurance risk?

a) Experience
b) Class
c) Special
d) Schedule

#82. On which of the following is the claims-made trigger based?

a) The date when the claim is first made
b) The total amount of the insured's deductible
c) The place where the injury or damage takes place
d) The date when damage or injury occurs

#83. All of the following are contained in the Declarations of a policy EXCEPT the

a) Limits of insurance.
b) Exclusions.
c) Policy premiums.
d) Name of the insured.

#84. Chad relocated to another state for work. However, he still owns and insures a house in this state but has had no one living in it for three months. He is also storing some clothes and furniture in the house. From an insurance standpoint, Chad's house is

a) Condemned.
b) Under repair.
c) Vacant.
d) Unoccupied.

#85. According to the conditions of a workers compensation policy, the insurance provider can inspect the insured workplace

a) With the consent of the insured.
b) With at least five days' notice.
c) At any time.
d) With at least ten days' notice.

#86. All of the following are special personal property limits under a homeowners policy EXCEPT

a) $500 for business personal property on the insured premises.
b) $1,500 for securities, deeds, accounts, and evidence of debt.
c) $1,500 for trailers not used with watercraft.
d) $2,500 for the theft of firearms.

#87. In New York, all of these employees must be covered by employer's workers compensation insurance EXCEPT

a) Workers of a nonprofit organization.
b) State employees.
c) Full-time domestic workers.
d) Public school aides.

#88. An insured is involved in a boating accident that injures her legs severely enough to confine her to a wheelchair. She works as an airline booking agent, meaning she must sit at a desk all day. What disability benefits would the insured receive?

a) Wheelchair-related costs
b) No benefits
c) Full income benefits for the duration of his disability
d) Partial income benefits for the duration of his disability

#89. The loss ratio compares

a) Losses to interest rates.
b) Premiums to interest rates.
c) Earned premium to company expenses.
d) Earned premium to losses.

#90. An independent adjuster can include which of the following?

a) A firm that acts on behalf of the insurance provider
b) A director, officer, or regular salaried employee of an insurance provider
c) An association or adjustment bureau owned by the insurance providers
d) An attorney at law

#91. A couple bought tickets to a college baseball tournament. At the game, a foul ball flies into the stands hitting the wife in the face and breaking her nose. Which legal defense can bar her from recovering damages for the injury she sustained at the baseball game?

a) Comparative negligence
b) Contributory negligence
c) Defense against negligence
d) Assumption of risk

#92. HO policies limit the amount of property and liability coverage available for Boatowners. How much coverage is provided in the HO policy for damage to watercraft, equipment, accessories, and trailers?

a) $2,000
b) $2,500
c) $1,000
d) $1,500

#93. Another individual alleges that an insured is responsible for damage to their property. The insured notifies their homeowners policy insurance provider who will do which of the following?

a) Defend with the hopes of not paying damages
b) Either defend or pay the claim as it decides
c) Pay the alleged damages
d) Proceed according to the policy owner's request

#94. After the loss of one of a pair of golden candlesticks, the contents coverage on a homeowners policy would pay how much?

a) The replacement cost of the pair
b) The actual cash value of the pair
c) Nothing
d) The difference in the actual cash value as a single and as a pair

#95. Which of these endorsements is used by individual business owners who use company vehicles for personal use instead of buying a personal vehicle?

a) Individual named insured
b) Drive other car
c) Additional insured - lessor
d) Hired autos specified as covered autos you own

#96. In the agent's contract, which type of authority is found?

a) Express
b) Apparent
c) Implied
d) Assumed

#97. The legal liability coverage form protects against damages for which the insured is liable arising from

a) Nuclear event.
b) Work being performed by a contractor.
c) Direct physical damage to the property of others in the insured's care.
d) Earthquake damage.

#98. What type of coverage is Coverage E in a homeowners policy?

a) Personal liability
b) Additional coverage
c) Loss of use
d) Personal property

#99. In both the broad and special form dwelling policies, replacement cost coverage is provided when

a) The amount of insurance on both the dwelling and personal property is at least 80% of its replacement cost when the policy is written.
b) The amount of insurance is at least 90% of the dwelling's replacement cost when the policy is written.
c) The dwelling is insured for 100% of its replacement cost when a loss occurs.
d) The amount of insurance is at least 80% of the dwelling's replacement cost at the time of loss.

#100. Which dwelling coverage would provide coverage to a garage not attached to the primary insured dwelling?

a) Coverage A
b) Coverage B
c) Coverage C
d) Coverage E

#101. Liquor liability insurance is also known as

a) Intoxicants and narcotics insurance.
b) Dram shop insurance.
c) Third-party liability insurance.
d) Errors and omissions insurance.

#102. In the coinsurance clause for Coverage F – Unscheduled Farm Personal Property, what is the required limit of insurance?

a) 75%
b) 80%
c) 85%
d) 90%

#103. The requirement that producers or agents do not commingle insurance monies with their own funds is known as

a) Fiduciary responsibility.
b) Premium accountability.
c) Express authority.
d) Accepted accounting principles.

#104. Valuable papers and records forms cover the reconstruction of all of the following types of records EXCEPT

a) Deeds.
b) Historical records.
c) Prepackaged software.
d) Blueprints.

#105. Under the business auto coverage form, mobile equipment is covered by liability insurance

a) When coverage is written as Symbol 1.
b) When being towed or carried by a covered auto.
c) On an excess basis.
d) When listed on the declarations.

#106. Events in which an individual has both the opportunity of winning or losing are classified as

a) Retained risk.
b) Speculative risk.
c) Insurable.
d) Pure risk.

#107. An insured pays a $100 premium monthly for insurance coverage, yet the insurance company promises to pay $10,000 for a covered loss. What feature of an insurance contract does this describe?

a) Good health
b) Adhesion
c) Conditional
d) Aleatory

#108. The business income coverage form pays for consequential loss of business income when a business has to suspend operations due to a direct loss. Which of the following terms best describes this type of coverage?

a) Time element
b) Claims-made
c) Occurrence
d) Direct damage

#109. All of the following statements are true under the provisions of the Business Income Coverage Form EXCEPT

a) If the insurer and insured cannot agree on the value of the loss, either party can make a written demand for an appraisal.
b) The insured agrees to resume all or part of business operations as quickly as possible.
c) The insured is compensated for payroll that continues after the loss begins.
d) The insured is compensated for the loss from the date of loss to the date of restoration or the policy expiration date, whichever comes first.

#110. The pro rata liability clause is intended to protect the principle of

a) Waiver and estoppel.
b) Indemnity.
c) Subrogation.
d) Insurable interest.

#111. Surplus lines insurance typically involves coverage for which individuals?

a) High-risk individuals
b) Standard-risk individuals
c) Low-risk individuals
d) All of these qualify for surplus lines insurance

#112. States with monopolistic state workers compensation funds

a) Require all employers in their state to obtain workers compensation insurance irrespective of their financial capacity.
b) Sell workers compensation insurance through private insurance companies in the state and receive a kickback for every policy sold annually.
c) Do not allow private insurance companies to be licensed to write workers compensation coverage.
d) Provide workers compensation insurance through managed risk plans.

#113. Which of these can be insured under the garage coverage form?

a) Businesses that use autos to transport the property of others or their own property
b) Every type of organization other than motor carriers and auto businesses
c) Owner-operators who provide their own trucks to haul property for the motor carriers that hire them
d) Auto businesses, like auto repair shops, service stations, and auto dealers

#114. Under a general liability policy, pollution liability coverage protects against which of the following?

a) Bodily injury or property damage resulting from a pollution accident
b) Clean-up costs after acid rain
c) Escape of fluids from an oil or gas well
d) General liability policies do not cover pollution

#115. Employers must keep records of workers compensation claims for all employee illnesses or injuries incurred on the job and preserve those records for at least

a) 5 years.
b) 10 years.
c) 18 years.
d) 20 years.

#116. According to the businessowners policy (BOP) definitions, which of these does NOT mean valuable papers and records?

a) Drawings and maps
b) Inscribed deeds
c) Securities
d) Manuscripts

#117. In health insurance, which of these will vary the length of the grace period?

a) The term of the policy
b) The mode of the premium payment
c) The length of any elimination period
d) The length of time the insured is covered

#118. In 2016, a client's policy lapsed without being renewed. In what year can the insurer destroy the file on this policy?

a) 2017
b) 2018
c) 2022
d) 2026

#119. Which of the following is eligible for a businessowners policy?

a) A convenience store with gas pumps with 60% of gross sales from gasoline sales
b) A mercantile risk with gross sales of $4 million
c) A 6-story office building with less than 100,000 square feet of total area
d) An 8-story office building

#120. When an umbrella policy is broader than underlying insurance, and it pays a loss that is not covered by the underlying policy, it typically only pays

a) The excess over the self-insured retention.
b) The amount stated in the policy under the additional coverage provisions.
c) The amount over and above the underlying policy deductible.
d) A percentage of the loss as described on the declarations page.

#121. What is the minimum age for anyone to be a driver hired by a transportation network company (TNC)?

a) 18
b) 19
c) 21
d) 25

#122. Those in the business of selling mobile equipment and construction equipment should use what type of coverage form?

a) Installation floater
b) Personal property floater
c) Equipment dealers coverage form
d) Contractors equipment floater

#123. Under a homeowners policy, which risk would NOT be eligible for coverage?

a) An individual who owns and lives on a commercial farm
b) An individual who lives in a duplex that they do not own
c) An individual who owns and lives in a duplex
d) An individual who owns and lives in a single-family dwelling that also includes incidental business activities

#124. On the equipment breakdown coverage form, how is property insured?

a) On a replacement cost basis
b) On a valued basis
c) On a stated amount basis
d) On an actual cash value basis

#125. Sonny's construction firm leaves construction machinery and mobile equipment on the job site until the project is finished. Sonny can insure it with a

a) Bailee's customers form.
b) Builders risk form.
c) General property form.
d) Contractors equipment floater.

#126. In this state, which of these losses would NOT be covered by the dwelling policy if the dwelling is vacant for over 30 days?

a) Windstorm
b) Internal explosion
c) Vandalism
d) Fire

#127. The Fair Credit Reporting Act seeks to

a) Ensure consumers receive a copy of investigative consumer reports.
b) Ensure coverage for every applicant.
c) Protect consumers against accumulating obsolete or inaccurate financial or personal information.
d) Protect the insurance provider from adverse selection.

#128. If the premium for a certain insured is increased or decreased for a future time based on that insured's loss experience for a time in the recent past, the policy uses a/an

a) Retrospective rating plan.
b) Experience rating plan.
c) Judgment rating plan.
d) Manual rating plan.

#129. Which of these are the authorities that a producer can hold?

a) Authorized and admitted
b) Primary and secondary
c) Express and implied
d) Apparent and allowed

#130. Under a businessowners policy, the most the insurance provider will pay for a loss is

a) 80% of the loss.
b) 20% of the loss.
c) The limit of insurance after the deductible is paid.
d) The amount of the loss minus the deductible.

#131. According to the Fair Credit Reporting Act, all of these would be considered negative information about a consumer EXCEPT

a) Failure to pay off a loan.
b) Disputes about consumer report information.
c) Tax delinquencies.
d) Late payments.

#132. Under which of these conditions can broad theft coverage be added to a dwelling policy?

a) If permission is given by the department of insurance
b) Broad theft coverage cannot be added to dwelling policies
c) If the policy has been in force for 60 days
d) If the insured is the dwelling's owner-occupant

#133. Negligence refers to

a) An unbroken chain of events that causes bodily injury or property damage to another individual.
b) Conduct that is so hazardous that the person engaging in it will be held entirely responsible for any injury or damage.
c) An intentional act that causes bodily injury or property damage to another individual.
d) Failing to do what a reasonable, prudent individual would do under given circumstances.

#134. In a homeowners policy, first aid costs for others injured on the insured's premises

a) Are paid in addition to the liability limit.
b) Only apply if the insured is legally liable.
c) Also covers injuries to the insured's family members.
d) Are deducted from the liability limit.

#135. A special insurance type that guarantees the faithful performance of a trustee of employee benefit plans is known as

a) Directors and officers insurance.
b) Comprehensive coverage in employee benefit plans.
c) Fiduciary liability insurance.
d) A surety bond.

#136. Where in the policy is the policy period stated?

a) On the policy's conditions page
b) On the policy's definitions page
c) On an endorsement attached to the policy
d) On the policy's declarations page

#137. Under the business property coverage form, which is NOT settled on an actual cash value (ACV) basis?

a) Property of others
b) Manuscripts
c) Works of art or antiques
d) Valuable papers and records

#138. The legal concept requiring workers compensation coverage benefits to be accepted by an injured employee as the only recourse the employee has to settle injury claims is called

a) The unilateral recourse provision.
b) The executive authority provision.
c) The exclusive remedy provision.
d) The omnibus resolution provision.

#139. Which of the following individuals would be eligible for Homeowners Coverage F – Medical Payments in the event of an injury at the insured's premises?

a) The named insured's spouse
b) A guest who was injured at the insured's party five years ago
c) An individual regularly residing with the insured
d) A full-time maid

#140. Which statement is true concerning Coverage C – Medical Payments in the commercial general liability policy?

a) The coverage offers high limits of insurance for bodily injury losses
b) The coverage is viewed as goodwill since payments are made without regard to fault
c) The coverage applies to bodily injury sustained by the named insured
d) The coverage is liability insurance since it only pays if the insured is legally liable

#141. Concerning the business of insurance, a hazard is

a) Any exposure or condition that increases the possibility of loss.
b) The risk taken when performing something dangerous.
c) The tendency of poorer risks to seek insurance more often than better risks.
d) The basic reason for an insured to purchase insurance.

#142. Expenses that a company would not have incurred if the business interruption had not existed are called

a) Additional expenses.
b) All-inclusive expenses.
c) Extra expenses.
d) Continuing expenses.

#143. After signing a contract and beginning the job, a contractor discovers that they cannot finish the job at the agreed-upon price. Which bond would pay in this scenario?

a) Bid
b) Supply
c) Completion
d) None

#144. Which of the following acts committed by a producer would be a sufficient violation to warrant suspension or revocation of the agent's license?

a) Trespassing through a neighbor's yard
b) Public drunkenness
c) Forgery
d) Speeding in an automobile

#145. Workers compensation laws provide the following types of benefits EXCEPT

a) Medical benefits.
b) Rehabilitation benefits.
c) Death benefits.
d) Compensatory benefits.

#146. Which of the following risks is eligible for coverage under a businessowners policy?

a) Automobile dealers
b) Bars or taverns
c) Condominiums
d) Banks

#147. A building covered under commercial property insurance has been vacant for over 60 consecutive days. Which of these statements is NOT true?

a) The insured has no coverage for losses resulting from theft
b) The insured has no coverage for losses resulting from glass breakage
c) Insurers will reduce payment for unnamed perils by 15%
d) Insurers will reduce payment for unnamed perils by 25%

#148. An insured owns a large dog. The first day she must leave the dog home alone to go to work, the insured returns to find her $400 sofa torn apart, her $100 coffee table chewed up, her $50 tablecloth shredded, and a $200 window pane shattered where her dog jumped through. Suppose the insured has personal property coverage under a special form dwelling policy. How much of this loss will the policy pay?

a) $0
b) $200
c) $250
d) $750

#149. The businessowners policy (BOP) liability coverage will pay for all necessary medical expenses of others incurred within what maximum period?

a) 90 days
b) 120 days
c) 1 year
d) 3 years

#150. A professional who wants coverage for liability exposures should obtain what form of liability insurance?

a) Commercial general and professional
b) Directors and officers
c) Fiduciary and employment practices
d) Employee benefits

Practice Exam 2 Answers

#1. **c) Insuring agreement**

The insuring agreement is an insurance policy section containing the insurance provider's promise to pay, the description of coverage, and the covered perils. (p. 42)

#2. **c) Comparative negligence**

Comparative negligence is the allotment of damages when both the plaintiff and the defendant are at fault. Recovery by the plaintiff is reduced or increased depending on the degree of each party's negligence. (p. 39)

#3. **d) Insurer A will pay $16,000; Insurer B will pay $8,000**

Each policy pays its pro rata share of the loss based on each policy's share of the total coverage amount. (p. 46)

#4. **c) $6,000 would be paid under other-than-collision coverage**

The proximate cause of the loss was contact with an animal. The insurer would pay all of the damage under other-than-collision coverage. (p. 99)

#5. **d) Certificate of authority**

Every insurer (domestic, foreign, or alien) must obtain a certificate of authority before conducting insurance business within a given state. (pp. 8, 27)

#6. **b) Mobile equipment**

A land motor vehicle, trailer, or semitrailer intended for use on public roads. "Auto" does not include mobile equipment. (p. 108)

#7. **d) The loss is not covered**

A flat tire resulting from a cause other than vandalism is considered a road hazard. It is expressly excluded from coverage in the policy. (p. 104)

#8. **d) Businessowners liability coverage form.**

The BOP's liability coverage is written on a businessowners liability coverage form. It typically applies to all operations and premises owned or operated by the insured. (p. 199)

#9. **c) $1 million**

The minimum requirement for haulers of oil and specific categories of hazardous waste in interstate commerce is $1 million. (p. 125)

#10. **c) Insuring agreement.**

The insuring agreement furnishes information on the policy's coverages. Conditions specify the legal obligations and duties of the parties to the contract. (pp. 42, 43)

#11. **d) Authorized insurer.**

Insurance companies who meet the state's financial requirements and hold a Certificate of Authority to transact business are considered admitted or authorized. (pp. 8, 27)

#12. **a) Part A**

Part A of a watercraft policy will respond to a claim for damages for property damage or bodily injury for which the insured becomes liable due to a watercraft accident. (pp. 235-236)

#13. **b) Losses because of the insured's negligence.**

A CGL policy's Coverage A protects against bodily injury and property damage sustained by third parties because of the insured's negligence. Answers A, C, and D are exclusions. (pp. 144-145)

#14. **d) Reduction**

Steps taken to prevent losses from transpiring are called risk reduction. (p. 25)

#15. **b) Theft of a renter's lawnmower used to service the premises**

Coverage A on the dwelling insures all attached structures and outdoor personal property or equipment used to service or maintain the premises if not covered elsewhere. (p. 60)

#16. **c) $500 fine for each violation**

Suppose the licensee is found in violation of insurance licensing laws. In that circumstance, the Superintendent can issue a penalty instead of revoking or suspending the person's license: up to $500 for each offense, not exceeding $2,500 aggregate for all offenses. (p. 12)

#17. **a) False advertising**

False advertising is the illegal practice of advertising or circulating deceptive, untrue, or misleading materials. (pp. 13-14)

#18. **d) Appraisal**

The appraisal clause provision permits an insured and insurance carrier that cannot agree on the amount of a loss settlement to each select its own appraiser. The appraisers then choose a disinterested umpire. The umpire settles disagreements between the appraisers. (pp. 66-67, 85, 105)

#19. **a) Monoline**

A monoline policy is a policy that only has one coverage part. (p. 140)

#20. **a) Symbol 9 – non-owned autos only**

Symbol 1 is used for any auto, Symbol 2 is only used for owned autos, and Symbol 7 is only used for specifically described autos. (p. 110)

#21. **d) Elimination period.**

The elimination period refers to the time right after the start of a disability when benefits are not payable. This requirement reduces the cost of providing coverage and eliminates the filing of many claims. (pp. 248, 249)

#22. **d) Reinsurance**

Insurance carriers utilize reinsurance to protect themselves from catastrophic losses. This is a method where the reinsurer indemnifies the ceding insurer for all or part of the losses it sustains related to a policy issued previously. (pp. 28-29)

#23. **c) Direct**

Damage caused by a peril insured against is classified as a direct loss. (p. 40)

#24. **c) A lawyer's failure to properly defend a client due to their dislike of the client.**

A professional liability policy excludes coverage for intentional acts committed by an insured. Intentional breach of duty is not covered. (p. 228)

#25. **a) Trade organization employment**

Services performed for the state and other governmental agencies and services subject to the Federal Railroad and Unemployment Insurance Act are excluded from employment covered under this law. (pp. 219-221)

#26. **b) Business profession**

Competent parties to a contract must be mentally competent, be of legal age, have a clear understanding of the contract, and cannot be under the influence of alcohol or drugs. (p. 31)

#27. **d) $50,000**

The first limit shown is the most the policy will cover for injuries to any individual. The second limit is the most the policy will cover for all injuries if more than one individual is injured in a single accident. The third limit is the most the policy will cover for property damage caused by a single accident. (p. 101)

#28. **c) All of the cost up to the Coverage D limit**

Coverage D pays the expenses to maintain the same lifestyle as before the loss. (p. 79)

#29. **b) Discriminating in coverages and benefits based on the insured's habits and lifestyle**

Discriminating between individuals of the same class with equal life expectancies or due to ethnic group, nationality, or race would be considered unfair discrimination. Insurance providers are also not allowed to cancel individual coverage because of a change in marital status. Discriminating benefits based on the insured's lifestyle and habits (like dangerous hobbies or smoking) is acceptable. (p. 14)

#30. **c) Condominiums**

Insurance Services Office, Inc. (ISO) maintains a list of risks not eligible for a businessowners policy. Auto dealers, financial institutions, and bars and grills are expressly excluded from coverage. (pp. 190-191)

#31. **b) $15,000**

This policy owner only carried 75% of the amount of insurance they had agreed to carry ($60,000 of the agreed $80,000), so the insurance provider will pay only 75% of the loss, or $15,000. If the policy owner had carried the required coverage, the insurer would pay partial losses in full. In the event of a total loss, the insurer would pay the face amount of the policy. If the full amount is not carried, the insurer will divide the amount carried by the coinsurance amount (the amount the policy owner should carry) and multiply it by the loss. (pp. 45, 66, 84)

#32. **c) 10% of Coverage A**

Under Coverage B – Other Structures, a basic amount of insurance equal to 10% of the Coverage A limit is included for other structures. (p. 77)

#33. **c) Collision**

A collision is defined as the upset or impact of a covered vehicle with an object or another vehicle. (p. 99)

#34. **d) The insured individual must release the employer and the insurance company from further liability.**

This endorsement specifies that the insurance carrier will pay statutory benefits to the insured individual in exchange for the injured worker releasing the employer and the insurance carrier from further liability. (p. 217)

#35. **a) Scheduled personal property endorsement.**

The scheduled personal property endorsement covers personal property with high values, such as jewelry, antiques, and furs. (pp. 91-92)

Practice Exam 2 Answers

#36. **d) A partial premium refund.**

The insured qualifies for dividends (partial premium refund) if the experience during the policy term falls within guidelines set forth by the insurance provider at the beginning of the policy term. Dividends are not guaranteed; the account must generate a minimum premium to participate. (p. 218)

#37. **b) Principal - Obligee - Surety**

The principal promises to perform for the obligee; the surety pays for the obligee's loss if the promise is not kept. (pp. 231-232)

#38. **d) The factors that determine rates**

Components determine operating expenses and rates, including loss reserves, loss adjusting expenses, and profits. (p. 38)

#39. **a) Damage to a third-party property for which the insured is legally liable.**

Additional coverages in the homeowners policy pays up to $1,000 per occurrence on a replacement cost basis for damage the insured causes to the property of others. In Section I, this coverage does not apply to the extent a loss is covered for intentional damage to property rented to or owned by a tenant of the insured or arising from a business owned by the insured. (pp. 86-87)

#40. **b) 50% of the amount provided as Coverage A.**

Under the HO forms, Coverage C is provided automatically and is equal to 50% of the amount provided in Coverage A. (pp. 77-78)

#41. **a) Reinstatement of limit**

This condition specifies that payment of any claim will not reduce the limit of insurance, except in case of a total loss on a scheduled item. In this case, the insurer will cancel the specific coverage and refund any unearned premium for the coverage on that item. (p. 170)

#42. **c) An insurance service representative who advertises and solicits insurance business**

A person does not require an insurance producer license if they only advertise without an intent to solicit insurance. (pp. 2-3)

#43. **a) On the agent's birthday every odd-numbered year**

Agent licenses last for two years. The license of every insurance agent born in odd-numbered years will expire on their birthday in odd-numbered years. The license of every insurance agent born in even-numbered years will expire on their birthday in even-numbered years. (p. 5)

#44. **d) Is designed to allow the family to maintain its normal standard of living.**

The family is permitted to maintain its normal standard of living while waiting for its house to be repaired after a covered loss. (p. 62)

#45. **a) $80,000**

At the time of loss, a homeowner must be insured for at least 80% of the replacement cost to collect the total replacement cost of a partial loss. (p. 85)

#46. **a) A resident of New York wishing to conduct business in New York**

Answers B, C, and D can skip taking and passing a written exam in New York. However, a New York resident seeking to act as an agent must take and pass a licensing exam. (pp. 2, 3, 4)

#47. **b) A vehicle fleeing the scene of a hit-and-run accident**

A vehicle not carrying the required liability insurance coverage is deemed uninsured. This definition includes vehicles that flee the scene of a hit-and-run accident. (p. 103)

#48. **a) Material misrepresentations.**

A material misrepresentation is a statement that, if found, would change the insurer's underwriting decision. (p. 32)

#49. **a) Assignment.**

Assignment is transferring a legal right or interest in an insurance policy. In property and casualty insurance, assignments of policies are typically valid only with the insurer's prior written consent. (p. 47)

#50. **a) Motor truck cargo policy - truckers form**

The Motor Truck Cargo Policy – Truckers form is liability insurance, and the owner's form is property coverage. (p. 175)

#51. **a) Redlining.**

Geographic redlining is refusing to serve a specific area solely because of its location or because a volunteer fire department serves it. In New York, redlining is illegal. (p. 36)

#52. **b) Specified coverage**

Specified coverage policies only cover specific medical costs for a particular illness, like cancer, or a field, like dental or prescription drug care. (p. 250)

#53. **a) Excess coverage over an underlying or primary policy**

Umbrella or excess policies are used when an insured is required or chooses to purchase limits higher than what is offered in the primary or underlying policy. (pp. 226-228)

#54. **c) 5 days**

Consumers must be advised that they can request additional information about their investigative consumer reports. The insurance provider or reporting agency has five days to provide the consumer with this information. (p. 18)

#55. **b) Land on which the property is located**

Homeowners policies do not cover land on which the property is located. (pp. 60, 83)

#56. **a) Outside the premises**

Outside the premises (theft, disappearance, and destruction) covers a company's money and securities if an outside loss occurs. (p. 181)

#57. **b) Additional insured.**

An additional insured is typically added by endorsement. Additional insureds are not named in the Declarations but are protected by the policy. (p. 44)

#58. **d) Personal injury**

Personal injury only applies if added by endorsement, and the policy owner pays an additional premium. (p. 93)

#59. **c) The policy owner damaged a rented garage when they failed to stop in time**

Insurers would cover damage to a non-owned building or structure under a personal auto policy's property damage liability coverage. (pp. 100-102)

#60. **a) The insurance carrier offers benefits**

Workers compensation benefits are regulated by the state government, which differs from state to state. (pp. 210-214)

#61. **b) Property lost because of a military action**

According to the Nationwide Marine Insurance Definition, inland marine policies cover instruments of transportation and communication and movable property. Losses caused by military actions or war are excluded. (p. 169)

#62. **c) A vehicle owned by a government entity**

Vehicles owned by the government are excluded explicitly as uninsured. (p. 103)

#63. **d) Insurance Guaranty Association**

Guaranty Associations protect insureds, policy owners, and beneficiaries under life and health insurance policies, annuity contracts, and supplemental contracts from insurers that suffer financial impairment. (p. 9)

#64. **c) 30 days of birth**

The insured must inform the insurance company of a newly born dependent, and if additional payment is required, pay within 30 days. (p. 257)

#65. **c) During the policy period and up to three years after the policy's termination.**

The insurance provider can examine the books and records at any time during the policy period and at least once every three years. (pp. 7-8)

#66. **c) Apparent**

Apparent authority, also called perceived authority, is the appearance or the assumption of authority based on the words, actions, or deeds of the principal or because of circumstances the principal created. (p. 30)

#67. **a) Medical payments to others**

Medical payment to others is automatically included in Section II of all unendorsed HO policies. (p. 86)

#68. **a) 30 consecutive days.**

In New York, vandalism and malicious mischief coverage will not apply if a covered property has been vacant for more than 30 consecutive days (not the 60 days specified in generic ISO forms). (p. 70)

#69. **d) When the other party is legally liable but does not have insurance**

Uninsured motorist coverage only applies if the other driver is at fault but does not have coverage. (p. 103)

#70. **d) A divorced spouse residing in another state**

Insureds are the named insured and their spouse if they reside in the same household. Insureds also include individuals related to the named insured by blood or marriage. (p. 75)

#71. **d) $2,000 silver tea set stolen**

Tea sets are covered with a special limit of $2,500 for theft. Boats are covered for no more than $1,500 for any peril. If stolen, the firearm collection is covered for no more than $2,500. The dog would not be covered. (p. 70)

#72. **c) Primary policy.**

In the event of a covered loss, the primary policy is the one that pays first. This policy covers the first layer of loss in a layered insurance program. (p. 46)

#73. **c) $1,000**

As an additional coverage, homeowners policies will cover up to $1,000 of a loss assessment. (p. 80)

#74. **a) Immediately**

In a BOP, the period of restoration for extra expense coverage starts immediately after a direct loss. (p. 198)

#75. **d) Farmworkers**

This endorsement added to a workers compensation policy provides statutory coverage for employees who do not fall under a state's workers compensation act, like farmworkers. (p. 217)

#76. **c) The surety can cancel the bond to avoid paying losses and expenses.**

The performance bond is a guarantee by the surety that if the contractor (principal) does not perform as promised, the surety will pay the obligee any losses. The surety will then attempt to make the principal repay them. (p. 232)

#77. **d) Comprehensive**

Comprehensive coverage pays for loss or damage to a covered auto arising from any cause besides collision or overturn. (p. 112)

#78. **a) The damage occurred when the concrete fell**

Under a garage coverage policy's conditions, the loss takes place at the time of the incident, not when the faulty work was completed. (p. 117)

#79. **b) Notice of claim**

The notice of claim provision spells out the insured's duty to provide the insurer with reasonable notice in the event of a loss. (pp. 244-245)

#80. **d) Land on which the dwelling is located.**

Under a dwelling policy, the land is not covered, and nothing that happens to the land would be considered a covered loss by the insurer. (p. 60)

#81. **a) Experience**

In experience rating, the insured's past loss experience determines the final premium. Experience rating is superimposed on a class-rating system. It adjusts the insured's premium either up or down. This adjustment will depend on how much the insured's experience deviates from the average experience of the class. (p. 38)

#82. **a) The date when the claim is first made**

The claims-made trigger is based on the date the claim is first made. (p. 150)

#83. **b) Exclusions.**

The exclusions section includes causes of exposure, loss, conditions, etc., listed in the policy for which insurers will not pay insurance benefits. (p. 43)

#84. **d) Unoccupied.**

Unoccupancy is any insured structure or building in which no one has been working or living within the required period, but the structure contains contents. A house is unoccupied if the policy owner goes on vacation for two weeks. (p. 47)

#85. **c) At any time.**

The insurance provider can inspect the insured workplace at any time. (p. 217)

#86. **a) $500 for business personal property on the insured premises.**

A special limit covered under a homeowners policy is $2,500 for business personal property on the insured premises. (p. 78)

#87. **d) Public school aides.**

Public school aides are excluded from the required workers compensation insurance coverage. The employer's workers compensation insurance must cover the other types of employees in answers A, B, and C. (p. 39)

#88. **b) No benefits**

An individual must be unable to perform their occupation to be eligible for disability income benefits. While the insured is confined to a wheelchair, her injuries do not hinder her from sitting at a desk for long periods. The insured does not qualify to receive disability income. (pp. 247-248)

#89. **d) Earned premium to losses.**

The loss ratio compares the premium incomes to losses, including claims paid and claim-related expenses. (p. 36)

#90. **a) A firm that acts on behalf of the insurance provider**

An independent adjuster is any individual, firm, corporation, or association who, for a commission, acts on behalf of an insurer to investigate and adjust claims. (p. 4)

#91. **d) Assumption of risk**

When an individual recognizes and understands the danger involved in an activity and voluntarily decides to encounter it, this assumption of risk can bar recovery for injury caused by negligence. (p. 39)

#92. **d) $1,500**

Only $1,500 of coverage is provided in the HO policy for damage to watercraft, equipment, accessories, and trailers. If additional coverage is required, a separate Boatowners policy can be purchased. (p. 78)

#93. **b) Either defend or pay the claim as it decides**

The insurance provider will decide whether to pay or defend. (p. 89)

#94. **d) The difference in the actual cash value as a single and as a pair**

Under the pair or set clause, insurers can restore the set to its value before the loss. It could also pay the difference between the property's actual cash value before and after the loss. (p. 66)

#95. **a) Individual named insured**

This endorsement is used by individual business owners who use company vehicles for personal use instead of purchasing a personal vehicle. (p. 38)

#96. **a) Express**

The authority a principal intends to grant an agent through the agent's contract is called express authority. It is the authority that is written into the contract. (p. 29)

#97. **c) Direct physical damage to the property of others in the insured's care.**

The legal liability coverage form covers direct physical loss to the property of others in the insured's care, custody, and control. (pp. 161-162)

#98. **a) Personal liability**

Coverage E is personal liability coverage in homeowners policies. (p. 86)

#99. **d) The amount of insurance is at least 80% of the dwelling's replacement cost at the time of loss.**

It is always a requirement on property forms that provide replacement cost coverage that insurance on the dwelling be at least 80% of its replacement cost when the time of loss occurred. (pp. 41, 66)

#100. **b) Coverage B**

Coverage B in a dwelling policy covers other structures not attached to the primary dwelling except by fence, utility line, or something similar. (p. 60)

#101. **b) Dram shop insurance.**

Liquor liability is also called dram shop liability. It refers to the exposure that restaurants, bars, and other similar establishments encounter because they manufacture, sell, distribute, or serve alcoholic beverages. (p. 225)

#102. **b) 80%**

Coverage F (Unscheduled Farm Personal Property) insures farm personal property on a blanket basis. It is subject to an 80% coinsurance clause. (p. 194)

#103. **a) Fiduciary responsibility.**

When an individual collects funds on behalf of another person or entity engaged in an insurance transaction, that individual receives the funds in a fiduciary capacity. (p. 10)

#104. **c) Prepackaged software.**

Valuable papers and records are printed, written, or inscribed documents, manuscripts or historical records, books, abstracts, deeds, films, blueprints, drawings, maps, or mortgages. (p. 174)

#105. **b) When being towed or carried by a covered auto.**

Liability coverage is automatically provided on mobile equipment while being towed or carried by a vehicle insured as a covered auto. There is a business auto endorsement that provides auto coverage to mobile equipment for an additional premium. (p. 109)

#106. **b) Speculative risk.**

Speculative risks are not insurable since they involve the chance of gain or loss. (p. 24)

#107. **d) Aleatory**

In an aleatory contract, unequal amounts are exchanged between payments and benefits. In this example, the insured receives a significant benefit for a small price. (p. 31)

#108. **a) Time element**

These coverage forms are also known as time element forms due to the direct relation of the time a business cannot operate to the amount of the loss. (pp. 158-160)

#109. **d) The insured is compensated for the loss from the date of loss to the date of restoration or the policy expiration date, whichever comes first.**

Business income will pay beyond the policy's expiration date. It will pay until the business has resumed or the coverage limits are depleted. (pp. 158-160)

#110. **b) Indemnity.**

If more than one policy is in force on the same property while covering the same perils, this is concurrent coverage. In insurance, following a loss, the insured is restored to their condition before the loss (indemnified). Each policy will pay a percentage of a loss directly related to the amount of coverage it provides compared to the total amount of insurance. (pp. 32, 46)

#111. **a) High-risk individuals**

Surplus lines typically involve insurance for high-risk individuals. It is written by non-admitted insurers specializing in offering insurance to the high-risk market. (pp. 27, 230-231)

#112. **c) Do not allow private insurance companies to be licensed to write workers compensation coverage.**

Under the monopolistic state fund program, no private insurer can market competitive programs in the state. In these states, workers compensation is available to every employer, but employers liability may or may not be offered. (p. 210)

#113. **d) Auto businesses, like auto repair shops, service stations, and auto dealers**

The garage coverage form is used for businesses with the autos of others in their custody, care, or control. Such businesses include auto repair and service garages, auto dealerships, and businesses that park vehicles for others. (pp. 114-119)

#114. **a) Bodily injury or property damage resulting from a pollution accident**

This coverage is only written on a claims-made basis. Insurers can also write the coverage as a separate policy or an endorsement. It provides two types of coverage: bodily injury or property damage liability resulting from a pollution accident and clean-up costs mandated by a government entity. (pp. 229-230)

#115. **c) 18 years**

When a covered employer has a workers compensation claim, they must keep records of all employee illnesses or injuries incurred on the job and maintain those records for at least 18 years. (p. 212)

#116. **c) Securities**

Valuable papers and records include inscribed, printed, or written documents, manuscripts, and records, including deeds, abstracts, books, drawings, films, mortgages, or maps. The term does not mean money or securities. (p. 174)

#117. **b) The mode of the premium payment**

The grace period is seven days on a policy with a weekly premium mode, ten days with a monthly premium mode, and 31 days on other premium modes. (p. 244)

#118. **c) 2022**

Insurers must keep policy records for six years after the policy is no longer in effect or until the filing of a review of the record, whichever is longer. (p. 7)

#119. **c) A 6-story office building with less than 100,000 square feet of total area**

The maximum eligibility requirements for a BOP are six stories high, 100,000 square feet for the office building, 25,000 square feet of mercantile space in the apartment building, and at least $3 million in gross sales. (pp. 190-191)

#120. **a) The excess over the self-insured retention.**

Once a liability claim is filed for recovery of damage or injury, the primary policy pays up to the policy limits, after which the umbrella policy will apply. If there is no primary underlying insurance, the excess policy will apply after the insured pays the self-insured retention. (pp. 226-228)

#121. **b) 19**

In New York, the minimum age for a TNC driver is age 19. (p. 126)

#122. **c) Equipment dealers coverage form**

An equipment dealer's coverage form covers a dealer's stock in trade consisting mainly of construction equipment and mobile agricultural equipment. It also covers the property of others in the dealer's custody, care, or control. It excludes coverage for autos, motorcycles, watercraft, and aircraft. (pp. 172-173)

#123. **a) An individual who owns and lives on a commercial farm**

Risks that contain any farming exposures are not eligible for homeowners insurance. (p. 75)

#124. **a) On a replacement cost basis**

The property is insured on a replacement cost basis on the equipment breakdown coverage form. (p. 176)

#125. **d) Contractors equipment floater**

The contractors equipment floater insures equipment left unattended on a job site until the project is completed. (p. 172)

#126. **c) Vandalism**

In New York, there is no vandalism and malicious mischief (VMM) coverage if the insured's location has been vacant for more than 30 consecutive days. (p. 70)

#127. **c) Protect consumers against accumulating obsolete or inaccurate financial or personal information.**

The Federal Trade Commission administers the Fair Credit Reporting Act (FCRA). The law was designed to protect consumers against the accumulation and circulation of obsolete or inaccurate information and to ensure that consumer reporting agencies are fair and equitable in how they treat consumers. (pp. 17-18)

#128. **b) Experience rating plan.**

Experience rating plans adjust the premium charges based on the individual insured's claims history, positive or negative. (p. 38)

#129. **c) Express and implied**

The powers and authorities that a producer holds are express and implied. Apparent authority is the assumption of, or the appearance of, authority based on the words, principal's actions, or deeds or because of events the principal created. (pp. 29-30)

#130. **c) The limit of insurance after the deductible is paid.**

For losses covered under a businessowners policy, the insured has to pay a deductible, after which the insurance provider will pay up to the limit of insurance. (p. 196)

#131. **b) Disputes about consumer report information.**

As defined by the FCRA, negative information includes information regarding a customer's late payments, delinquencies, insolvency, or any other form of default. Customer disputes are not negative information and must be included in consumer reports. (p. 58)

#132. **d) If the insured is the dwelling's owner-occupant**

Broad theft coverage can be added as an endorsement to a dwelling policy if the insured is the dwelling's owner-occupant. (pp. 69-70)

#133. **d) Failing to do what a reasonable, prudent individual would do under given circumstances.**

Negligence is the failure to use care that a reasonable, prudent person would have in a similar situation or circumstance. (pp. 38-39)

#134. **a) Are paid in addition to the liability limit.**

The homeowners policy will pay expenses the insured incurs to render first aid for bodily injury to third parties injured on the insured's premises. (p. 87)

#135. **c) Fiduciary liability insurance.**

Fiduciary liability insurance covers an employee benefit plan against bad acts of the plan's fiduciaries or trustees. (pp. 228-229)

#136. **d) On the policy's declarations page**

The policy period is stated on the policy's declarations page. (p. 44)

#137. **d) Valuable papers and records**

Valuable papers and records are valued according to the cost of blank materials used for reproducing the records and the labor to copy the records. (pp. 174-175)

#138. **c) The exclusive remedy provision.**

Workers compensation is considered the exclusive remedy for all injury claims against employers. (p. 210)

#139. **d) A full-time maid**

Medical payments on the HO policy cover costs incurred for up to three years after the accident. Coverage does not apply to any insured or a regular resident of the premises, except residence employees not covered by workers compensation. (p. 86)

#140. **b) The coverage is viewed as goodwill since payments are made without regard to fault**

Coverage C – Medical Payments will provide necessary medical, surgical, ambulance, hospital, nursing, or funeral expenses for injuries to third parties. Payments are paid without regard to the negligence or fault of the insured. (p. 162)

#141. **a) Any exposure or condition that increases the possibility of loss.**

A hazard is any circumstance that increases the likelihood of a loss. (p. 24)

#142. **c) Extra expenses.**

Extra expenses are expenses that an organization would not have incurred if the business interruption had not happened. (pp. 160-161)

#143. **d) None**

Bid bonds guarantee a contractor will enter a contract at the price bid if selected. A supply bond guarantees supplies are delivered according to a supply contract. Completion bonds guarantee money borrowed will be spent to complete the job free of liens and encumbrances. No bond protects the contractor from faulty bids or cost overruns. (p. 232)

#144. **c) Forgery**

Forging another individual's name or committing a felony would result in license revocation or suspension. Answers A, B, and D are not criminal activities. (pp. 11-12)

#145. **d) Compensatory benefits**

Awards for pain and suffering are not compensated under workers compensation. (p. 212)

#146. **c) Condominiums**

The Insurance Services Office (ISO) manages a list of risks not eligible for consideration for a BOP. Bars and grills, auto dealers, and financial institutions are expressly excluded from coverage. (pp. 190-191)

#147. **d) Insurers will reduce payment for unnamed perils by 25%**

Suppose the building has been vacant for more than 60 consecutive days before the loss. In that instance, the insurer will not pay for damage caused by vandalism, glass breakage, sprinkler leakage, water damage, theft, or attempted theft. When any other peril causes the loss, the insurance company will reduce the amount they would have paid by 15%. (p. 155)

#148. **a) $0**

Under the special form dwelling policy, damage that domestic animals cause is excluded. (p. 61)

#149. **c) 1 year**

Medical payments coverage of a businessowners policy (BOP) will pay the medical, dental, hospital, and funeral services incurred within one year from the date of an accident. The person must suffer bodily injury by accident on or near the insured's premises or due to the insured's operations. (p. 199)

#150. **a) Commercial general and professional**

Commercial general liability (CGL) excludes professional liability, and professional liability does not insure premises liability. (pp. 142, 228)

FINAL EXAM

This last test will ensure you are ready to pass the licensing exam

You are about to take a New York Property and Casualty Insurance Agent/Broker Final Practice Exam. This exam consists of *150 Questions (plus five to ten non-scored experimental questions)* and is *2 hours and 30 minutes* long. If you do not have enough time to complete this exam right now, it is better to wait until you can fully devote your attention to completing it in the allotted time.

If you score well answering the Final Exam, you can be reasonably certain that you have the knowledge necessary to perform well on the actual test.

Any skipped questions will be graded as incorrect. The following chart breaks down the number of questions in each chapter and by topic.

Chapter	% of Exam
Insurance Regulation	9%
General Insurance	9%
Property and Casualty Insurance Basics	13%
Dwelling Policy	6%
Homeowners Policy	14%
Auto Insurance	11%
Commercial Package Policy (CPP)	11%
Businessowners Policy	8%
Workers Compensation Insurance	8%
Other Coverages and Options	7%
Accident and Health Insurance	4%
Total	**100%**

To calculate your score, subtract the number of incorrectly answered questions from 150. Take this number and divide by 150. For example, if you incorrectly answered 45 questions, your score would be 70%, the minimum score needed to pass the exam.

#1. An agent in another state wants to be licensed in New York. The other state gives the same privileges to New York agents wishing to be licensed in that state as it does its agents. New York, therefore, extends the privileges of its agents to the prospective agent of the other state. What is this called?

a) Equality
b) Fair exchange
c) Equanimity
d) Reciprocity

#2. Which of these is the federal body that regulates truckers traveling across state lines?

a) Federal Motor Carrier Safety Administration
b) Motor Carriers Commerce Agency
c) Truckers and Trade Commission
d) Federal Trade Commission

#3. When a policy does not offer a replacement or continuation at its expiration date, it is considered a

a) Nonrenewal.
b) Suspension.
c) Cessation.
d) Cancellation.

#4. Under a dwelling policy, which of these is NOT a factor in determining a loss?

a) The amount required to repair or replace the property
b) The amount negotiated by the insured
c) The policy limit
d) The amount reflecting the insured's interest in the property when the loss occurs

#5. Which of these is NOT a consideration when paying an inland marine claim?

a) The actual cash value (ACV) on the date of loss
b) The cost to repair or restore the property
c) The market value when the property was initially purchased
d) The cost to replace the property

#6. Regarding insurance, which is an example of a producer's fiduciary responsibility?

a) Promptly forwarding premiums to the insurance carrier
b) Helping insureds file claims
c) Performing reviews of the insured's coverage
d) Offering additional coverage to insureds

#7. Under the broad theft endorsement in a dwelling policy, which of the following would be covered?

a) A camera the insured has brought on vacation
b) A pedigreed show dog
c) Fabric and patterns in a clothing designer's home studio
d) An antique car

#8. Most major medical plans have high maximum limits and cover medical expenses in and out of the hospital. The term used to describe this is

a) General.
b) Preferred.
c) Eligible.
d) Comprehensive.

#9. An employee drives a company car but does not own a vehicle himself. What endorsement could be added to the company vehicle policy that would cover the employee when he drives someone else's car for personal use?

a) Drive other car coverage
b) Bobtail coverage
c) Rental car coverage
d) Personal injury protection

#10. Which of the following could be covered by a homeowners policy?

a) Property of a tenant not related to the insured
b) An oriental rug in an on-premises apartment
c) Birds, fish, and animals
d) A sports car parked in an attached garage

#11. The New York Superintendent is responsible for ensuring that each entity transacting insurance in this state remains solvent. Insurance carriers must file a statement with the Superintendent

a) Semiannually on or before January and June 1.
b) Every two years, by the renewal date.
c) Annually on or before March 1.
d) Biannually on or before April 1.

#12. Which of these is eligible for a businessowners policy?

a) A convenience store with gasoline pumps earning 60% of gross sales from gas sales
b) A retail business with gross sales of $10 million
c) A 5-story office building with less than 100,000 square feet
d) An 8-story office building

#13. Under the homeowners (HO) policy, how much coverage is provided for theft or unauthorized credit card use?

a) $100
b) $500
c) $1,000
d) $5,000

#14. Which of these losses would NOT be covered by the homeowners policy?

a) A $550 utility trailer blown away by a tornado
b) A stolen silver tea set valued at $2,000
c) A $800 outboard motor destroyed by hail
d) A coin collection worth $500 lost in a fire

#15. The business personal property coverage form covers all of these EXCEPT

a) Furniture and fixtures.
b) Machinery that is not permanently installed.
c) Stock.
d) Automobiles held for sale.

#16. Who is issued a certificate of insurance in a group policy?

a) The healthcare provider
b) The insurer
c) The employer
d) Those covered under the insurance policy

#17. Who is NOT an employee in a commercial general liability (CGL) policy?

a) Temporary worker
b) Leased worker
c) Full-time worker
d) Part-time worker

#18. Only some losses are insurable, and specific requirements must be satisfied before a risk is a proper subject for insurance. These requirements include all of these EXCEPT

a) The loss can be intentional.
b) The loss must not be catastrophic.
c) There must be a sufficient number of homogeneous exposure units to make losses reasonably predictable.
d) The loss produced by the risk must be definite.

#19. All of these are essential elements of a commercial package policy (CPP) EXCEPT

a) Policy conditions.
b) Valuations and settlement provisions.
c) Interline endorsements.
d) The declarations page.

#20. Under the dwelling policy, within how many years of a loss can insureds bring a suit against an insurance company?

a) 2 years
b) 3 years
c) 5 years
d) 7 years

#21. Phoenix trucking company recently acquired Elite manufacturing company. Phoenix wants to transport the new company's freight using its trucking division. The company also intends to continue hauling freight for the clients it has served for many years. Regarding coverage, which of the following is true?

a) The company must choose between being a common or contract carrier and a private carrier
b) The truckers coverage form is needed
c) A truckers coverage form and the business auto coverage form are required
d) Motor carrier coverage is required

#22. According to the BOP Section I, which is NOT a condition to be satisfied for the policy terms to apply to mortgage holders?

a) If the insurer denies the claim, the mortgage holder may still take steps to receive loss payment
b) The mortgage holder has the right to receive a loss payment
c) The insurer will pay covered losses or damage to each mortgage holder shown in the Declarations
d) The mortgage holder must petition the state insurance department for named status

#23. Which statement concerning workers compensation is NOT TRUE in New York State?

a) If a work-related injury or illness causes an employee's death, a death benefit is paid to a survivor
b) Workers compensation provides coverage for nonwork-related injuries and illnesses so long as the employee was employed at the time of death
c) Medical benefits are provided for work-related injuries
d) Insurers will only provide lost wages and benefits for covered work-related injuries or illnesses

#24. Which farm coverage form will cover farm fences, except for the field and pasture fences?

a) Coverage A
b) Coverage B
c) Coverage E
d) Coverage G

#25. Under a businessowners policy, the inspections and surveys condition stipulates all of the following EXCEPT

a) The insurance provider cannot inspect the insured's property and operations.
b) The insurance provider does not make safety inspections for the insured.
c) The insurance provider does not guarantee safe or healthful conditions.
d) The insurance provider does not guarantee the insured is satisfying all required safety regulations.

#26. Two applicants are in the same risk and age class. However, they are charged different premium rates for their insurance policies because of an insignificant factor. What is this called?

a) Misrepresentation
b) Adverse selection
c) Discrimination
d) Law of large numbers

#27. Which of these would NOT be covered by medical payments to others in Section II of the homeowners policy?

a) A policy owner allows the neighborhood kids to play flag football in their yard; one child is injured
b) A policy owner cuts their leg while whacking weeds in their backyard with their neighbor's weed whacker
c) A policy owner's child's nanny falls while walking down the home's steps
d) A policy owner is walking their neighbor's dog, and it bites someone

#28. Terminating an insurance contract with the premium charge being adjusted proportionately to the exact time the protection has been in force is considered a

a) Pro rata cancellation.
b) Refund cancellation.
c) Short-rate cancellation.
d) Flat rate cancellation.

#29. Which of the following describes a unique characteristic of investigative consumer reports compared to consumer reports?

a) The customer does not know this action
b) The customer's friends, associates, and neighbors provide the report's data
c) They provide additional information from an outside source about a particular risk
d) They provide information about a customer's character and reputation

#30. Which individual would not have an insurable interest in the insured property?

a) Homeowner's spouse
b) Mortgage company
c) Neighbor
d) Homeowner

#31. In which of the following types of property valuation will the policy pay the total value as stated on the policy schedule, irrespective of the insured property's depreciation or appreciation?

a) Market value
b) Agreed value
c) Replacement cost
d) Stated amount

#32. Which of the following is used in the formula to calculate a property's actual cash value (ACV)?

a) Stated value
b) Fair market value
c) Agreed value
d) Replacement cost

#33. The risk of loss can be classified as

a) High risk and low risk.
b) Pure risk and speculative risk.
c) Certain risk and uncertain risk.
d) Named risk and un-named risk.

#34. In the businessowners policy, the pollutant cleanup and removal coverage has a limit of

a) $2,500 during any 12-month period.
b) $5,000 during any 6-month period.
c) $20,000 during any 6-month period.
d) $10,000 during any 12-month period.

#35. Which of these is defined as a covered cause of loss in businessowners property coverage?

a) Smoke from agricultural smudging
b) Pollution
c) Leakage from fire-extinguishing equipment
d) Rain

#36. To be eligible for coverage under the National Flood Insurance Program (NFIP), an insured must live in which of the following communities?

a) One that is surrounded by water
b) One that has met the minimum population requirements
c) One that gets flooded at least annually
d) One that has met the minimum floodplain management guidelines

#37. All of the following are causes for the Superintendent to suspend or impose conditions on the continuation of an agent's license EXCEPT

a) Conviction of dishonest or fraudulent practices.
b) The applicant has been proven to be a poor personal credit risk.
c) Demonstrated untrustworthiness or incompetence to act under the license.
d) Acquiring a license through fraud.

#38. Which policy condition in the homeowners policy states that insurance applies separately to each insured?

a) Payment of claim
b) Severability of insurance
c) Appraisal
d) Limit of liability

#39. When other insurance is issued on the same basis as a commercial property policy, the insurance carrier must cover

a) The loss on an excess basis.
b) The loss on a primary basis.
c) A share of the loss.
d) All of the loss.

#40. In equipment breakdown coverage, every accident would be considered a single accident if it occurs

a) At all insured locations simultaneously and from the same cause.
b) At the same location within 24 hours.
c) At the same location within 48 hours.
d) At a single location simultaneously and from the same cause.

#41. The section of the policy that establishes the duties, rules of conduct, and obligations of the parties is known as the

a) Insuring clause.
b) Conditions.
c) Exclusions.
d) Declarations.

#42. Which of these is NOT one of the four primary elements in establishing negligence?

a) Legal duty
b) Standard of care
c) Proof of carelessness
d) Proximate cause

#43. Which of these provisions stipulates that the insured protects the damaged property from additional damage, cooperates with the insurer in settling the loss, and submits signed proof of loss to the insurer within a specified period?

a) Loss settlement
b) Proof of loss
c) Duties after loss
d) Legal action

#44. Which term describes withholding material information critical to an underwriting decision?

a) Leading
b) Breach of warranty
c) Concealment
d) Withholding

#45. Under a CGL policy, Coverage B (Personal and Advertising Injury) will cover

a) The failure of goods to conform to advertised quality or performance.
b) Written or oral publication of material the insured knows is false.
c) An offense committed by an insured whose business is advertising.
d) Unintentional injury to others caused when marketing the insured's product.

#46. An insured has a standard HO-4 policy with a $30,000 coverage limit for personal property. While traveling, a hotel fire destroys clothing and luggage with a replacement value of $10,000 and jewelry with a replacement value of $10,000. Disregarding any deductible and assuming a 20% depreciation has occurred in both properties, what amount is the insurance provider obligated to pay?

a) $16,000
b) $20,000
c) $30,000
d) $11,000

#47. When only one party in an insurance contract makes a legally enforceable promise, what kind of contract is it?

a) A legal (but unethical) contract
b) Unilateral
c) Adhesion
d) Conditional

#48. Which of these symbols is available to an insured with a vehicle subject to no-fault coverage?

a) Symbol 5
b) Symbol 6
c) Symbol 7
d) Symbol 9

#49. All of these are optional coverages that may be attached to the HO-3 policy EXCEPT

a) Personal property replacement cost.
b) Dwelling replacement cost.
c) Home business coverage.
d) Earthquake coverage.

#50. Which of the following describes the concept of contributory negligence?

a) The voluntary assumption of exposure to risk
b) Any negligence by the injured party can bar recovery
c) The period in which an insured must file a claim
d) Negligence is apportioned between both parties in an accident

#51. Workers compensation laws provide all of the following benefits EXCEPT

a) Death benefits.
b) Compensatory benefits.
c) Medical benefits.
d) Rehabilitation benefits.

#52. To qualify for a certificate of authority, every individual, association, firm, corporation, or joint-stock company must meet all of these requirements EXCEPT

a) If a mutual company, provide statements of at least three incorporators, the necessary amount and number of actual applications for insurance, and proof of the required initial surplus in cash or investments.
b) The entity must be part of the New York Labor Union.
c) The entity must comply with all applicable New York insurance laws and provisions.
d) If a stock company, the amount of capital and surplus required by law must be paid in cash or investments.

#53. The removal coverage included in the broad form dwelling policy will insure property that is temporarily removed from the premises to protect it from damage for how long?

a) 5 days
b) 15 days
c) 30 days
d) 60 days

#54. A passenger in a friend's vehicle is injured while getting into the car. Which statement would apply if the driver and the passenger had medical payments coverage under a personal auto policy (PAP)?

a) The driver's policy would be primary
b) The driver's policy will act in excess of the passenger's policy
c) The passenger's policy would be primary
d) Both policies will share equally in the loss

#55. Section I of the homeowners insurance policy must include

a) Liability coverage.
b) Immediate coverage.
c) Negligence coverage.
d) Property coverage.

#56. An insured has Inside the Premises – Robbery or Safe Burglary of Other Property commercial crime coverage. What special per occurrence limit applies to damage or loss to precious metals, precious and semiprecious stones, pearls, furs, manuscripts, drawings, or records?

a) $1,000
b) $5,000
c) $10,000
d) $25,000

#57. NY Insurance Law requires an excess lines broker to demonstrate that at least three licensed insurance providers that write the specific type of insurance have

a) Requested a current rate plan quote from the ELANY.
b) Declined to insure the specific risk.
c) Prepared specialized rate quotes for the given risk.
d) Reviewed the risk analysis statement for coverage.

#58. Which commercial crime form would cover a loss that did not necessarily occur during the policy period but was revealed during the policy period?

a) Discovery form
b) Retro form
c) Reporting form
d) Loss sustained form

#59. Which claim does NOT fall under the liability coverage in Section II of the HO policy?

a) A visitor slips on some ice, causing her to be injured when falling down the patio steps
b) The named insured borrows a friend's coat which is damaged at a later time
c) The named insured's 9-year-old daughter throws a rock and strikes a neighbor's child, breaking his eyeglasses and cutting his face
d) The named insured's dog bites the neighbor, tearing her clothes and causing her to receive treatment from a doctor

#60. If an insured has an umbrella liability policy in addition to their personal auto policy, which would be the underlying policy?

a) Excess policy
b) General liability policy
c) Auto policy
d) Umbrella policy

#61. An insured suffers a windstorm loss where the insured's driveway is blocked by two of the insured's trees and two of the neighbor's trees. The total removal amount adds up to three trees at $300 per tree and one tree at $600. How much will the homeowners insurer pay for the loss?

a) $1,500
b) $1,400
c) $1,000
d) $900

#62. Which of the following additional perils is covered under both the basic form and broad form dwelling policies?

a) Internal explosion
b) Falling objects
c) Weight of ice, snow, or sleet
d) Freezing of plumbing, heating, or air conditioning systems

#63. The towing and labor costs endorsement provides what basic limit for expenses incurred at the place a vehicle is disabled?

a) $25
b) $50
c) $75
d) $100

#64. When an insured has an own occupation plan, what is the maximum amount of time an insured can collect benefits on their current job?

a) One year
b) Two years
c) Three years
d) For the duration of the contract

#65. Which of these is INCORRECT regarding the conditions found in a workers compensation policy?

a) The insured's rights and duties cannot be transferred to anyone else without the insurance provider's written consent
b) The first named insured will act on behalf of every insured under the policy
c) The insurance provider can inspect the workplace after giving the insured five days' notice
d) If the policy period is longer than one year and 16 days, every policy provision will apply as though a new policy was issued on each anniversary date

#66. A person applies for a life policy. Two years ago, he sustained a head injury from an auto accident. He cannot remember details of his past, but he is otherwise competent. This individual was also hospitalized for drug abuse; however, he does not remember this when applying for a life policy. The insurance company issues the policy and learns of his history one year later. What will more than likely happen?

a) The insurer will void the policy
b) The insurance carrier will sue the insured for committing fraud
c) Since the insured is no longer a drug user, his policy will not be impacted
d) The policy will not be impacted

#67. Which of these must be included in every Medicare supplement plan?

a) Plan C coinsurance
b) Plan A
c) Foreign travel provisions
d) Outpatient drugs

#68. A commercial liability umbrella policy's deductible is called

a) The SIR.
b) The PIL.
c) The CGL.
d) The CPP.

#69. A contractor who builds custom houses has never filed a claim on his business insurance policy. His agent learns that his policy is written using a scheduled rating. Which is most likely if the contractor changes to an experience rating policy?

a) Coinsurance will be necessary
b) Premiums will go down
c) Premiums will go up
d) Premiums will be unchanged

#70. The provision that prevents the insured from bringing a lawsuit against the insurance company for at least 60 days after proof of loss is known as

a) Notice of claim.
b) Incontestability.
c) Legal actions.
d) Time limit on certain defenses.

#71. The Superintendent can refuse to renew a license if a licensee receives more than 10% of the aggregate commissions from controlled business for how many months?

a) 12
b) 15
c) 18
d) 24

#72. An insurance producer who, by contract, is bound to write insurance for only one company is considered a/an

a) Independent producer.
b) Captive agent.
c) Solicitor.
d) Broker.

#73. A premium discount describes when an insured owes a total standard premium more than

a) $5,000.
b) $10,000.
c) $15,000.
d) $1,000.

#74. An insured owns a building valued at $400,000. To comply with the insurance policy's 80% coinsurance provision, what amount is sufficient for the owner to insure the property?

a) 80% of the property's replacement cost or more
b) 100% of the market value
c) $400,000
d) $32,000

#75. When a covered auto is involved in an auto accident in another state, what happens to the limits of liability in a personal auto policy (PAP)?

a) They do not change
b) They do not apply
c) They adjust to at least the minimum limits of the other state
d) They decrease based on the state's law

#76. When doing business in this state, an insurer formed under another state's laws is considered what type of insurer?

a) Alien
b) Non-admitted
c) Foreign
d) Domestic

#77. For each excess lines policy or policy renewal procured from an unauthorized insurance carrier, producers must file which of the following?

a) An affidavit
b) A disclosure
c) A certificate of coverage
d) A binder

#78. An insurance contract must comprise all of these to be considered legally binding EXCEPT

a) Consideration.
b) Competent parties.
c) Beneficiary's consent.
d) Offer and acceptance.

#79. Which of these is covered under the physical damage coverage of a personal auto policy?

a) A covered auto seized and destroyed by a government authority
b) A cellular phone in a locked car
c) Custom furnishings or equipment in a van or pickup exceeding the coverage of $1,500
d) Sound reproduction equipment permanently installed in the covered auto

#80. Which statement is NOT true concerning a personal umbrella liability policy?

a) It provides an agency with errors and omissions coverage
b) It can cover certain exposures not provided under the primary layer
c) It can require the payment of a self-insured retention
d) It provides excess liability coverage over underlying personal liability

#81. Which of these is a cancellation procedure in which the premium returned to the policy owner is NOT directly proportional to the number of days remaining in the policy period?

a) Flat rate
b) Proportional
c) Short rate
d) Pro rata

#82. The authority granted to a producer through the agent's contract is known as

a) Absolute authority.
b) Express authority.
c) Apparent authority.
d) Implied authority.

#83. Events or conditions that increase the odds of an insured loss occurring are called

a) Hazards.
b) Exposures.
c) Risks.
d) Perils.

#84. An insured's business is damaged due to a fire and is forced to close the business for repairs temporarily. Because of the closure, the insured lost income. This type of loss is known as

a) Special.
b) Additional.
c) Consequential.
d) Direct.

#85. An insured has a liability policy establishing the amount for all claims resulting from a single incident at $50,000. What type of limit of liability does the insured's policy have?

a) Aggregate
b) Split
c) Per occurrence
d) Per person

#86. The Employee Theft crime policy form contains a coverage extension that applies to any employee temporarily outside the coverage territory for up to

a) 30 days.
b) 60 days.
c) 90 days.
d) 120 days.

#87. The occurrence form trigger is based on

a) The number of claims made in the policy period.
b) The date when damage or injury occurs.
c) The place where the damage or injury occurs.
d) The amount of the insured's deductible.

#88. For which of these reasons can a temporary license be issued?

a) To solicit new business
b) To negotiate new insurance contracts
c) To deliver temporary help to a licensed producer
d) To provide service to the existing business

#89. A homeowner sells their house to a coworker. The coworker wants to maintain the homeowner's current in-force policy. Which of the following is most likely under the assignment provision?

a) The policy will need to be canceled
b) The homeowner should allow the coworker to take over the premium payments
c) The coworker will have to apply for coinsurance from another insurer
d) The homeowner must obtain written consent from the insurance provider before the policy can be reassigned

#90. Who represents the insured during the investigation of a claim?

a) Agent
b) Public adjuster
c) Broker
d) Independent adjuster

#91. An insured added the scheduled personal property endorsement to their homeowners policy to protect musical instruments. When the insured buys a new musical instrument, when must the insurance carrier be reported for the musical instrument to be covered?

a) Within 10 days
b) Within 20 days
c) Within 30 days
d) Within 90 days

#92. An insured has a personal property replacement cost endorsement under their homeowners policy. When an antique chair and an expensive painting are stolen from the insured's home, what will the insured receive on the claim under that endorsement?

a) 70% of the replacement cost
b) 80% of the replacement cost
c) 100% of the actual cash value
d) Nothing

#93. Under Coverage B – Other Structures of the homeowners policy, what coverage amount is available for a detached garage?

a) No coverage
b) 10% of Coverage A
c) 20% of Coverage A
d) A flat amount listed in the policy Declarations

#94. Paid Family Leave (PFL) currently guarantees how many weeks of paid time off?

a) 4 weeks
b) 6 weeks
c) 12 weeks
d) 20 weeks

#95. Which report will provide the underwriter with information about an insurance applicant's credit?

a) Agent's report
b) Any federal report
c) Consumer report
d) Inspection report

#96. A 2-year policy has a value of $2,000. The policy has been effective for one year. What is the policy's earned premium?

a) $250
b) $500
c) $1,000
d) $1,500

#97. The extra expense coverage form provides

a) Additional money for an insured whose accounts receivable records were damaged.
b) Extra money to pay for property damage losses at a covered location.
c) Payment for unanticipated expenses an insured can incur while the business is shut down after a property damage loss.
d) Coverage that permits the insured to continue in business without interruption after a loss of property damage.

#98. Which of these is NOT a justifiable reason for the Superintendent to suspend, revoke, or refuse to renew a license?

a) A licensee made a material misstatement in the license application
b) A licensee demonstrated untrustworthiness or incompetence to act in such a capacity
c) A licensee does not sell enough policies to meet their financial goals
d) A licensee violated a provision of the New York Insurance Code

#99. Which insurance providers must be members of the New York Property Insurance Underwriting Association?

a) Insurance carriers authorized to write fire and extended coverage insurance
b) Commercial lines insurers
c) All authorized insurers in this state
d) Surplus lines insurers

#100. An insured's home is damaged by a fire and is deemed uninhabitable. Consequently, the insured must rent an apartment until repairs are completed. A dwelling insurance policy will cover the expense of the rental apartment. The insured has which type of broad or special form coverage?

a) Coverage E – Additional Living Expense
b) Coverage A – Dwelling
c) Coverage B – Other Structures
d) Coverage D – Fair Rental Value

#101. Replacement cost refers to

a) The property's market value of like kind and quality.
b) Full replacement of property with like kind and quality, minus an allowance for depreciation and physical deterioration.
c) Payment of the full policy limits if a total loss occurs.
d) Full replacement of property at its current cost, new and without a reduction for depreciation.

#102. A commercial property special form covers property in transit up to

a) $5,000.
b) ACV.
c) $500.
d) Full replacement cost.

#103. All of these are covered perils under the broad form dwelling policy EXCEPT

a) Theft.
b) Fire.
c) Lightning.
d) Collapse.

#104. When an individual is using an auto with the belief that they are entitled to do so, under a personal auto policy (PAP), subrogation rights will apply to all coverages EXCEPT

a) No-fault medical payments.
b) Liability.
c) Physical damage.
d) Uninsured motorist.

#105. Intentionally concealing or misrepresenting a material fact to induce an insurer to make a contract is called

a) Avoidance.
b) Misrepresentation.
c) Concealment.
d) Fraud.

#106. Which of these statements regarding flood and earthquake perils coverage is true?

a) Flood and earthquake coverage is available in every policy
b) Flood and earthquake coverage is available only through government insurance
c) Flood insurance is typically provided in property policies, but earthquake coverage is available by endorsement only
d) Both flood and earthquake are excluded perils in every property policy

#107. The valuable papers and records coverage form covers the reconstruction of the following types of records EXCEPT

a) Historical records.
b) Prepackaged software.
c) Blueprints.
d) Deeds.

#108. How often must a producer licensed in New York renew their insurance license?

a) Every even-numbered year
b) Every odd-numbered year
c) Every birthday
d) Every two years

#109. What are the two prominent sections of a commercial crime policy?

a) Occurrence and claims made
b) Commercial entities and government entities
c) Discovery form and loss sustained form
d) Property and liability

#110. In the HO policy's loss payment condition, insurers must pay losses within how many days of receiving proof of loss?

a) 30 days
b) 60 days
c) 90 days
d) 120 days

#111. All of the following are exclusions to benefits under the New York State Disability Benefits Law EXCEPT

a) A disability commencing before the employee became eligible.
b) A disability because of an act of war.
c) Up to 26 weeks of benefits during 52 consecutive calendar weeks of one period of disability.
d) Any period of disability during which an employee is not under the care of a physician.

#112. How long does a New York licensee have to deliver the information requested by the Superintendent?

a) 10 days
b) 15 days
c) 25 days
d) 30 days

#113. Participating insurance policies can do which of the following?

a) Provide group coverage
b) Pay dividends to the stockholder
c) Require 80% participation
d) Pay dividends to the policy owner

#114. What is the limit payable on any business property away from the premises under Coverage C of a farm policy?

a) $1,000
b) $100
c) $250
d) $500

#115. An insured bake shop is sued because its marketing specifies that the products of another bakery might not be safe. Which coverage of a commercial general liability (CGL) policy will defend the lawsuit?

a) Personal and advertising injury liability
b) Premises and operations
c) Product liability
d) Completed operations

#116. What policy condition states that if a policy is broadened with no additional premium, the expanded coverage will automatically apply to all policies of the same type?

a) Limit of insurance clause
b) Liberalization clause
c) Maximum indemnity clause
d) Loss control clause

#117. A businessowners policy (BOP) is most similar to which of the following?

a) Auto
b) Umbrella
c) Cargo
d) Homeowners

#118. When a Transportation Network Company arranges a ride for a customer, which of the following vehicles would be used?

a) A driver's own vehicle
b) A taxi
c) A limousine
d) A company vehicle

#119. An insurance policy is not drawn up through negotiations, and an insured does not have much to say about its provisions. This contract characteristic describes

a) Adhesion.
b) Unilateral.
c) Conditional.
d) Personal.

#120. Which of these perils is covered by the HO-2 and HO-3?

a) War
b) Sudden and accidental rupture of a heating system
c) Loss due to power interruption that occurs off the premises
d) Flood

#121. Under the dwelling policy, if an insurance provider decides to repair or replace lost or damaged property, it must inform the insured within how many days of receiving proof of loss?

a) 10 days
b) 30 days
c) 45 days
d) 60 days

#122. In insurance transactions, fiduciary responsibility refers to

a) Being liable for payment of claims.
b) Commingling premiums with the agent's personal funds.
c) Handling insurance carrier funds in a trust capacity.
d) Maintaining a good credit record.

#123. The amount an insurance company will pay under Coverage D (Loss of Use) depends on

a) If a dwelling is owner-occupied or rented out.
b) The length of time a dwelling is uninhabitable.
c) The amount of coverage on a dwelling.
d) How long the dwelling has been occupied.

#124. Which of the following describes the amount of loss assessment coverage included under the HO policy's liability coverage section?

a) Up to $5,000 aggregate for the policy period
b) Up to $1,000 per occurrence
c) Up to $2,500 per occurrence
d) Up to $10,000 aggregate for the policy period

#125. All of these are factual statements regarding a commercial general liability (CGL) policy's supplementary payments EXCEPT

a) They pay pre-judgment and post-judgment interest.
b) They pay all reasonable costs incurred by the insured in helping to investigate or defend a claim.
c) They pay defense costs even after reaching the aggregate limit.
d) They pay all expenses incurred by the insurance provider.

#126. What type of information is found in a policy's insuring agreement?

a) Insurance carrier's address
b) Renewal dates
c) Location of premises
d) Policy limits

#127. What type of bond guarantees that a construction contractor will enter the contract at a designated price?

a) Maintenance bond
b) Bid bond
c) Performance bond
d) Payment bond

#128. A dwelling policy had been in effect for 60 days when the insurance provider discovered fraud. Before the cancellation date, the insurance provider must provide a notice of

a) 14 days.
b) 21 days.
c) 30 days.
d) 45 days.

#129. All of these statements describe the concept of strict liability EXCEPT

a) Claimants might need to prove that a product defect resulted in an injury.
b) It is imposed irrespective of fault.
c) It is applied in product liability cases.
d) It is imposed on defendants involved in hazardous activities.

#130. The purpose of a personal auto policy's miscellaneous type vehicle endorsement is

a) To extend coverage to motorized vehicles rented for recreation.
b) To broaden the definition of a covered auto to include various motorized vehicles.
c) To limit coverage to various motorized vehicles only.
d) To cover hit-and-run accidents.

#131. Which statement regarding insurable risks is NOT correct?

a) Insurable risks must involve a loss that is definite regarding time, cause, place, and amount
b) Insureds cannot be randomly chosen
c) Insurance cannot be mandatory
d) The insurable risk must be statistically predictable

#132. An automobile owned by multiple individuals who are not spouses or residing in the same household can be insured under a personal auto policy (PAP) if

a) Separate policies are written for each person involved.
b) A joint ownership coverage endorsement is added to the PAP.
c) A miscellaneous-type vehicle endorsement is added to the PAP.
d) An extended ownership endorsement is added to the PAP.

#133. What is the advantage of an experience rating?

a) It allows employers with high claims experience to obtain group coverage
b) It allows employees with low claims experience to become exempt from group premiums
c) It helps employers with high claims experience to obtain insurance
d) It helps employers with low claims experience to get lower premiums

#134. Under businessowners property insurance, how soon after a direct loss does the period of restoration for business income coverage begin?

a) 12 hours
b) 24 hours
c) 36 hours
d) 72 hours

#135. Supplementary payments on a commercial general liability (CGL) policy provide all of the following EXCEPT

a) $100 in gasoline costs by the insured driving a witness to and from court.
b) Pre-judgment and post-judgment interest.
c) The cost of bonds to release attachment.
d) Up to $500 per day for lost earnings and $2,000 for the cost of bail bonds.

#136. A deli owner has a businessowners liability policy. The liability policy covered medical expenses when a customer slipped and hurt herself at the deli counter. However, the customer is now suing the business owner because she contends there was no caution sign warning her about the wet floor. What is the insurance provider bound to do?

a) Provide legal aid to the customer suing the policy owner
b) Nothing; they have paid the claim and their responsibility ends there
c) Pay to defend the policy owner in the suit because liability coverage includes a duty-to-defend provision
d) Automatically renew the owner's policy, but they will have nothing to do with the suit

#137. When an insurance carrier intends to nonrenew a dwelling policy, it must alert the insured of the nonrenewal at least how many days before the effective date?

a) 15 days
b) 30 days
c) 45 days
d) 60 days

#138. What is the maximum period an insurance company would pay benefits according to an additional monthly benefit rider?

a) For the duration of the contract or the disability, depending on which ends first
b) One month
c) One year
d) Two years

#139. Which of the following is the cost to replace damaged property with more modern and less expensive construction or equipment?

a) Market value
b) Actual cash value
c) Replacement cost
d) Functional replacement cost

#140. Personal property coverage under the homeowners policy would cover

a) The insured's camera if it is stolen while on vacation.
b) A neighbor's fence if it is damaged by the insured.
c) Property moved to a newly acquired residence after 60 days.
d) A pet the insured is temporarily keeping for a neighbor.

#141. All of the following are marketing arrangements used by insurers EXCEPT

a) Direct Response Marketing System.
b) Independent Agency System.
c) Reinsurance System.
d) General Agency System.

#142. Which of these is NOT a prerequisite for an insurance license in New York?

a) Completing a pre-licensing education course
b) Be a state resident on the application date
c) Pass the licensing examination
d) Be at least 21 years old

#143. An insurer sells an insurance policy over the phone in response to a television ad. Which of these describes this action?

a) Independent agency marketing
b) Illegal
c) Insurance telemarketing
d) Direct response marketing

#144. When an individual has been found liable for a civil penalty in a hearing, that ruling may be entered as a judgment and enforced after

a) 45 days.
b) 60 days.
c) 90 days.
d) 120 days.

#145. What type of compensatory damages will pay for disfigurement and pain and suffering?

a) Normal
b) General
c) Special (specific)
d) Tort

#146. Proximate cause refers to

a) The reason for filing a lawsuit.
b) Negligence that causes an injury.
c) Injury that leads to monetary compensation.
d) The defendant's duty to act.

#147. After issuing a policy, an insurer discovers that the policy owner has concealed information on the application. The insurer wants to cancel the policy and give back the money the policy owner has paid. This scenario is an example of

a) Contestability.
b) Renewal.
c) Rescission.
d) Refund.

#148. Which services are associated with AM Best and Standard & Poor's?

a) Investigating violations of The Fair Credit Reporting Act
b) Providing employment histories for investigative consumer reports
c) Storing medical information collected by insurance carriers
d) Rating the financial strength of insurance carriers

#149. A medical insurance plan where the health care provider is paid a regular fixed amount for delivering care to the insured and does not receive additional amounts of compensation dependent upon the procedure performed is known as a/an

a) Fee-for-service plan.
b) Prepaid plan.
c) Indemnity plan.
d) Reimbursement plan.

#150. Which professional liability form provides coverage for liability arising from errors or mistakes in rendering medical services?

a) Druggist
b) Directors and officers
c) Errors and omissions
d) Physicians, surgeons, and dentists malpractice

Final Exam Answers

#1. d) Reciprocity

Reciprocity occurs when the state in which the individual resides grants the same privilege to residents of New York. (p. 5)

#2. a) Federal Motor Carrier Safety Administration

The Federal Motor Carrier Safety Administration (FMCSA) is the federal body that regulates interstate truckers. (p. 124)

#3. a) Nonrenewal.

When an insurance policy does not offer a continuation or replacement at expiration, it is deemed a nonrenewal. (p. 44)

#4. b) The amount negotiated by the insured

The value of a loss is determined according to the following: the property's actual cash value, the policy limit, the amount required to repair or replace the property, or the amount reflective of the insured's interest in the property. (p. 66)

#5. c) The market value when the property was initially purchased

Inland marine policies will pay actual cash value (ACV), but the insurance provider reserves the right to repair or replace instead. The insured property's value when new is not considered. (p. 169)

#6. a) Promptly forwarding premiums to the insurance carrier

An agent acts in a fiduciary capacity, based on confidence and trust, when handling their customers' financial affairs and insurer funds, including premiums. (pp. 10, 30)

#7. a) A camera the insured has brought on vacation

Under the broad theft endorsement, all of these examples, except the camera, are types of property expressly excluded from coverage. (pp. 69-70)

#8. c) Eligible.

Eligible plans are major medical plans with high maximum limits that cover medical expenses both in and out of the hospital. (p. 254)

#9. a) Drive other car coverage

A drive other car endorsement covers these situations when added to a business auto policy. It provides coverage for the employees named in the endorsement and their spouses when they drive another vehicle for personal use. (p. 124)

#10. b) An oriental rug in an on-premises apartment

Homeowners contents coverage does not apply to cars, animals, or the property of individuals who pay to reside at the policy owner's house. It does provide up to $2,500 for a loss of the landlord's furnishings in an on-premises apartment. (p. 81)

#11. c) Annually on or before March 1.

Every entity must file a statement with the Superintendent annually on or before March 1. (p. 8)

#12. c) A 5-story office building with less than 100,000 square feet

Office buildings up to six stories high and up to 100,000 square feet meet the maximum eligibility requirements for a businessowners policy. (p. 191)

#13. **b) $500**

$500 is provided automatically for theft or unauthorized use of a credit card and can be increased by endorsement. (p. 80)

#14. **d) A coin collection worth $500 lost in a fire**

The HO policy will pay up to $2,500 for silverware by theft, $1,500 for boats, motors, and trailers, $1,500 for loss of trailers not used with boats, but no more than $200 for coins. (p. 78)

#15. **d) Automobiles held for sale.**

Automobiles held for sale are among the exclusions in the business personal property form. Answers A, B, and C are covered types of property under BPP coverage. (p. 153)

#16. **d) Those covered under the insurance policy**

The individuals covered under the insurance policy are issued certificates of insurance. The certificate specifies what the policy covers, how to file a claim, how long the coverage will last, and how to convert the policy to an individual policy. (p. 256)

#17. **a) Temporary worker**

A temporary worker is not considered an employee in a CGL policy. (p. 143)

#18. **a) The loss can be intentional.**

To insure an intentional loss would be against public policy. (p. 25)

#19. **b) Valuations and settlement provisions.**

Regardless of how the policy is written, it will include the following essential elements: a declarations page, conditions, interline endorsements, and coverage parts. (pp. 140-141)

#20. **a) 2 years**

When an insured wants to bring a lawsuit against an insurance provider, the insured must comply with all policy conditions and initiate action against the insurer within two years of the loss. (p. 67)

#21. **d) Motor carrier coverage is required**

The motor carrier coverage form can cover anyone who transports goods. Since the truckers coverage form does not cover private carriers, the motor carrier coverage will cover private and common or contract carriers. (pp. 109, 119, 122)

#22. **d) The mortgage holder must petition the state insurance department for named status**

The insurance provider will pay covered losses or damage to each mortgage holder. The mortgage holder has the right to receive a loss payment. When the insurer denies the claim due to the insured's act or because the insured failed to comply with the policy terms, the mortgage holder still has the right to receive a loss payment. (p. 197)

#23. **b) Workers compensation provides coverage for nonwork-related injuries and illnesses so long as the employee was employed at the time of death**

The injury or illness must be related to the employee's job for benefits to be paid. (pp. 210-213)

#24. **d) Coverage G**

Fences, except pasture and field fences, are considered other farm structures. They are covered by Coverage G – Other Farm Structures. (pp. 184-185)

#25. **a) The insurance provider cannot inspect the insured's property and operations.**

The inspection and survey condition will allow the insurance provider to inspect the property and operations. These inspections are essential in deciding the insurability of the insured's property and operations, in making loss control recommendations, and in setting proper insurance rates. (p. 203)

#26. **c) Discrimination**

Allowing individuals of the same class to be charged a different rate for the same insurance is the unfair trade practice known as discrimination. (p. 14)

#27. **b) A policy owner cuts their leg while whacking weeds in their backyard with their neighbor's weed whacker**

Medical payments to others will cover invitees, residence employees not covered by workers compensation, and injury to others caused by animals in a policy owner's control. If policy owners hurt themselves, they need accident and health insurance for their injuries. (p. 86)

#28. **a) Pro rata cancellation.**

Terminating a bond or insurance contract with the premium charge being adjusted in proportion to the precise time the protection has been in force is considered a pro rata cancellation. (p. 45)

#29. **b) The customer's friends, associates, and neighbors provide the report's data**

Both consumer and investigative consumer reports provide additional information from an outside source about a customer's character and reputation, and both reports are used under the Fair Credit Reporting Act. The primary difference is that the information for investigative consumer reports is obtained through an investigation and interviews with the consumer's friends, associates, and neighbors. (p. 18)

#30. **c) Neighbor**

A neighbor does not have a financial interest in the insured property. (p. 36)

#31. **b) Agreed value**

Agreed value is a property policy with a provision agreed upon by the insurance company and insured regarding the amount of coverage representing a fair valuation for the property when the insurance is written. When a loss occurs, the policy pays the agreed value as stated on the policy schedule, irrespective of the insured property's depreciation or appreciation. (p. 42)

#32. **d) Replacement cost**

The actual cash value (ACV) valuation method reinforces the principle of indemnity because it recognizes the reduction of property value as it ages. Depreciation is subtracted from the current replacement cost to calculate ACV. (p. 41)

#33. **b) Pure risk and speculative risk.**

Pure risks involve the possibility or probability of loss with no chance for gain. Pure risks are typically insurable. Speculative risks involve uncertainty regarding whether the outcome will be a gain or loss. Speculative risks are generally uninsurable. (p. 24)

#34. **d) $10,000 during any 12-month period.**

In the BOP, the policy limit is $10,000 during any 12-month period if the release resulted from a covered loss during the policy period. (p. 194)

#35. **c) Leakage from fire-extinguishing equipment**

Only leakage for fire-extinguishing equipment is defined as a covered loss. The other causes are specifically excluded from coverage. (p. 198)

#36. **d) One that has met the minimum floodplain management guidelines**

To be eligible for the flood program, an insured must live in a community that has satisfied the minimum floodplain management guidelines. (pp. 232-234)

#37. **b) The applicant has been proven to be a poor personal credit risk.**

A producer's poor personal credit status is not grounds for license revocation or suspension. Answers A, C, and D may be grounds for a producer's license revocation, suspension, or nonrenewal. (pp. 11-12)

#38. **b) Severability of insurance**

The severability of insurance indicates that the insurance applies separately to each insured. This condition does not increase the insurance provider's liability for any one occurrence. (p. 89)

#39. **c) A share of the loss.**

The commercial property other insurance provision specifies that the insurance provider will be responsible for only a proportional share of an insured loss. This stipulation occurs when the insured has other insurance issued according to the terms and conditions. (p. 167)

#40. **d) At a single location simultaneously and from the same cause.**

If an accident causes other accidents, the insurer will treat all related accidents like one accident. All accidents occurring at a single location with the same cause will be viewed as one accident. (pp. 175-178)

#41. **b) Conditions.**

The conditions are the section of an insurance policy that establishes the obligations and duties of the insurance provider and the insured. (p. 43)

#42. **c) Proof of carelessness**

It must be proven that the defendant had a legal duty to act or not to act, and they must have used a standard of care that breached this legal duty. Actual damage or injury must have been suffered by the party seeking recovery. (p. 38)

#43. **c) Duties after loss**

The duties after loss provision will require that the insured protects the damaged property from further damage, cooperates with the insurer in settling the loss, and submits signed proof of loss to the insurer within a specified period. (pp. 47, 65)

#44. **c) Concealment**

Concealment happens when an individual withholds a material fact critical to making a decision. In insurance, this involves withholding information that would be essential for making underwriting decisions. (p. 32)

#45. **d) Unintentional injury to others caused when marketing the insured's product.**

Personal and advertising injury coverage does not apply to professional advertisers or intentional injury. It does not guarantee the product will perform as advertised. (pp. 145-146)

#46. **a) $16,000**

This loss would be settled on an actual cash value (ACV) basis: $20,000 total for the loss minus $4,000 for depreciation. The limitation on losing jewelry applies to the peril of theft only. (p. 41)

#47. **b) Unilateral**

In unilateral contracts, only one of the parties to the contract is legally bound to do anything. (p. 31)

#48. **a) Symbol 5**

Symbol 5 covers owned autos subject to no-fault coverage. (p. 110)

#49. **b) Dwelling replacement cost.**

The HO-3 provides replacement cost coverage for losses to the dwelling without endorsement or optional coverage being added. (pp. 91-93)

#50. **b) Any negligence by the injured party can bar recovery**

In states with contributory negligence laws, the defendant must be 100% at fault for an accident. The claimant must be free of fault if the claimant is to be successful in collecting damages. (p. 39)

#51. **b) Compensatory benefits.**

Awards for pain and suffering are not paid under workers compensation. (p. 212)

#52. **b) The entity must be part of the New York Labor Union.**

To qualify for a certificate of authority, all individuals, firms, corporations, associations, or joint-stock companies must meet all the above requirements except for membership in the state Labor Union. (p. 8)

#53. **c) 30 days**

Removal coverage is provided for 30 days in the broad and special form, as long as that endangerment by a covered peril made the removal necessary. (pp. 62, 63)

#54. **a) The driver's policy would be primary**

Medical payments coverage pays all necessary medical and funeral expenses incurred and services provided to the insured or passengers in the insured's car, regardless of fault. (pp. 102-103)

#55. **d) Property coverage.**

Section I of the homeowners form must include property coverage. Section II must include personal liability coverage. (p. 76)

#56. **b) $5,000**

A special limit of $5,000 per occurrence applies to loss or damage to precious metals, precious and semiprecious stones, pearls, furs, drawings, manuscripts, or records. (p. 181)

#57. **b) Declined to insure the specific risk.**

Before the excess lines broker can place the risk with an eligible excess lines insurer, they must comply with New York Insurance Law, Section 2118. Typically, the excess lines broker must demonstrate that three licensed insurers writing the same specific type of insurance have declined to write the risk. (pp. 230-231)

#58. **a) Discovery form**

The discovery form is used for losses discovered during the policy period. These losses might not have happened during the policy period. The discovery form is one of the conditions in the crime general provisions forms, which contain conditions and exclusions that apply to all crime forms. The discovery period usually is one year. (p. 179)

#59. **b) The named insured borrows a friend's coat which is damaged at a later time**

Damage to the property of others in the insured's care, custody, or control is expressly excluded. (p. 88)

#60. **c) Auto policy**

The underlying policy is the primary liability policy. In this scenario, it is the insured's personal auto policy. (pp. 46, 226-227)

#61. **c) $1,000**

It is essential to pay special attention to coverages that have a maximum amount of coverage and an additional sublimit for one particular item. The most the policy will pay for this loss is $1,000. (p. 80)

#62. **a) Internal explosion**

An internal explosion is covered under both the basic form and broad form dwelling policies. (pp. 55, 56, 59)

#63. **a) $25**

This endorsement provides a basic limit of $25 for towing and labor charges incurred at the place a vehicle is disabled. Higher limits are available for an added premium. (p. 107)

#64. **b) Two years**

With an own occupation plan, if the insured cannot perform their current job for up to two years, disability benefits will be issued. Benefits are paid, even if the insured can perform a similar position during those two years. After that, if the insured can perform another job using similar skills, the insurer will not pay benefits. (p. 248)

#65. **c) The insurance provider can inspect the workplace after giving the insured five days' notice**

The insurance carrier can inspect the workplace at any time without giving notice. (p. 217)

#66. **d) The policy will not be impacted**

When an insurance company discovers that an applicant has committed fraud, it can void the contract, provided the discovery occurs within the first two years of the policy's effective date. In this particular example, the applicant did not commit intentional fraud. (p. 32)

#67. **b) Plan A**

To standardize the coverage provided under Medicare supplement policies, the NAIC has developed standard Medicare Supplement benefit plans, which are identified with the letters A through N. Plan A's benefits are considered core benefits and must be included in the other types. (p. 260)

#68. **a) The SIR.**

The self-insured retention (SIR) is an initial part of a loss the insured pays before the umbrella pays if no other policy covers the loss. (pp. 45, 226-228)

#69. **b) Premiums will go down**

In an experience rating, the insured's prior claims experience determines the premium. It is unlikely the rest of the industry will have zero claims. A contractor with no claims will likely pay a lower premium than a company with a scheduled rating policy. (pp. 37-38)

#70. **c) Legal actions.**

This mandatory provision requires that an insured can only initiate legal action to collect benefits 60 days after proof of loss is filed with the insurance company. This provision provides the insurer time to evaluate the claim. (p. 245)

#71. **a) 12**

An insurance license is not meant to generate commissions on personal insurance needs or those of business associates, family members, etc. The Insurance Code limits the amount of controlled business a producer can write. (p. 10)

#72. **b) Captive agent.**

A captive/exclusive agent has agreed, by contract, to produce insurance business only for that insurer. (p. 28)

#73. **a) $5,000.**

A premium discount is applied when an insured owes more than $5,000 in total standard premium. (p. 218)

#74. **a) 80% of the property's replacement cost or more**

The coinsurance clause stipulates that in consideration of a reduced rate, the insured agrees to maintain a specific minimum amount of insurance on the insured property. Insurance is designed to pay the replacement cost minus depreciation if a covered loss occurs. (p. 85)

#75. **c) They adjust to at least the minimum limits of the other state**

According to the out-of-state coverage provision in the PAP, if the state or province has a financial responsibility law requiring limits of liability higher than those shown in the Declarations, the insured's policy will provide the higher specified limits. (pp. 101-102)

#76. **c) Foreign**

A foreign insurance company is formed under the laws of another state. A non-admitted or unauthorized insurance company is an insurer that has not applied for or has applied and been denied a Certificate of Authority and cannot transact insurance. (p. 28)

#77. **a) An affidavit**

Pursuant to insurance law, excess lines brokers must file an affidavit for every excess lines policy or policy renewal procured from an unauthorized insurance carrier. (p. 231)

#78. **c) Beneficiary's consent.**

The four essential elements of a legal contract are offer and acceptance, consideration, legal purpose, and competent parties. (pp. 30-31)

#79. **d) Sound reproduction equipment permanently installed in the covered auto**

Sound reproduction equipment is covered if installed by the manufacturer or installed later where the manufacturer would have installed the equipment. (pp. 104, 113)

#80. **a) It provides an agency with errors and omissions coverage**

A personal umbrella policy covers the personal exposure of the insured. Errors and omissions coverage is only provided in a professional liability policy. (pp. 226-228)

#81. **c) Short rate**

Short-rate cancellation is a procedure in which the premium returned to the policy owner is not directly proportional to the number of remaining days in the policy period. (p. 45)

#82. **b) Express authority.**

Express powers are written into the contract between the insurance company and the producer. (p. 29)

#83. **a) Hazards.**

Hazards are conditions or situations that increase the probability of an insured loss occurring. (p. 24)

#84. **c) Consequential.**

Consequential loss, also called indirect loss, is a second financial loss caused by a covered direct loss. (p. 41)

#85. **c) Per occurrence**

Per occurrence sets the amount for all claims that arise from a single incident at a certain number. (p. 46)

#86. **c) 90 days.**

This coverage contains an extension that applies to any employee temporarily outside the coverage territory for up to 90 days. (p. 180)

#87. **b) The date when damage or injury occurs.**

The occurrence form is triggered by the date when damage or injury occurs. It covers claims made at any time for injuries arising during the policy period. (p. 46)

#88. **d) To provide service to the existing business**

Licensees can only use a temporary license to service existing insurance business, not to solicit, negotiate, or procure new business. (p. 5)

#89. **d) The homeowner must obtain written consent from the insurance provider before the policy can be reassigned**

Assignments of policies in property and casualty insurance are generally valid only with the prior written consent of the insurance carrier. (p. 47)

#90. **b) Public adjuster**

A public adjuster is any individual, association, firm, or corporation who, for a commission, acts on the insured's behalf in negotiating a settlement of a claim for damage or loss to property. (p. 5)

#91. **c) Within 30 days**

The new property must be reported to the insurer within 30 days of acquisition. The insured could be required to pay the added premium from that date. (pp. 91-92)

#92. **d) Nothing**

The personal property replacement cost endorsement excludes property like antiques and art. (p. 92)

#93. **b) 10% of Coverage A**

Coverage B – Other Structures will cover other separate structures at the same location, like detached garages and other outbuildings. The basic amount of insurance is 10% of the Coverage A limit. (p. 77)

#94. **c) 12 weeks**

Paid Family Leave (PFL) guarantees 12 weeks of paid time off. (p. 221)

#95. **c) Consumer report**

Consumer reports contain written or oral information about a consumer's character, credit, reputation, or habits collected by a reporting agency from credit reports, employment records, and other public sources. (p. 18)

#96. **c) $1,000**

The earned premium of this policy is $1,000. $2,000 divided by two years equals a $1,000 earned yearly premium. Because the policy has been in effect for one year, the earned premium is $1,000. (pp. 44-45)

#97. **d) Coverage that permits the insured to continue in business without interruption after a loss of property damage.**

Extra expense coverage is for money spent to minimize a business interruption after a direct property loss. (pp. 160-161)

#98. **c) A licensee does not sell enough policies to meet their financial goals**

A licensee not selling enough policies to meet their financial goals may cause the insurance carrier to not reappoint the producer. The Superintendent and the Department of Financial Services are not concerned with such issues. (pp. 11-12)

#99. **a) Insurance carriers authorized to write fire and extended coverage insurance**

All authorized insurers who sell fire and extended coverage insurance, including insurance carriers covering such perils in homeowners and commercial multiple peril package policies, must be and remain a member of the New York Property Insurance Underwriting Association as a condition of its authority. (pp. 238-239)

#100. **a) Coverage E – Additional Living Expense**

Coverage E is a broad or special form under the dwelling policy that covers additional living expenses while the insured's dwelling is undergoing repairs. (p. 62)

#101. **d) Full replacement of property at its current cost, new and without a reduction for depreciation.**

Replacement cost policies do not consider depreciation if the appropriate amount of insurance is maintained. Policies that provide replacement cost coverage mandate that the amount of insurance written be 80% or more of the property's replacement cost at the time of loss. (pp. 41, 66, 84-85)

#102. **a) $5,000.**

A commercial property special form will cover property in transit up to $5,000. Policy owners can add this extension of coverage to the special form. It is additional insurance (in addition to the coverage limit), and coinsurance will not apply. (p. 166)

#103. **a) Theft.**

Theft is not a named peril in the broad form dwelling policy. (pp. 57-58)

#104. **c) Physical damage.**

Subrogation rights will not apply to physical damage coverage when the damage resulted from an individual using the auto with a reasonable belief that they were entitled to do so. (pp. 105, 106)

#105. **d) Fraud.**

Fraud is the intentional concealment or misrepresentation of a material fact used to induce another party to make or refrain from making a contract or deceiving or cheating a party. (p. 32)

#106. **d) Both flood and earthquake are excluded perils in every property policy**

Flood and earthquake are both excluded perils in all property policies. However, coverage for both or either one can usually be purchased separately for an additional premium (by endorsement). (pp. 64, 83, 91)

#107. **b) Prepackaged software.**

Coverage for reconstructing prepackaged software is expressly excluded. (p. 174)

#108. **d) Every two years**

An insurance producer's license expires every two years. Licensees born in odd-numbered years must renew their licenses by their birthdays in odd-numbered years. In contrast, licensees born in even-numbered years must renew their licenses by their birthdays in even-numbered years. (p. 5)

#109. **b) Commercial entities and government entities**

The crime program offers policies in two major sections: commercial and government entities. For each section, the insured can choose a form with different coverage triggers, a discovery form, or a loss sustained form. (p. 178)

#110. **b) 60 days**

According to the homeowners policy, insurers will pay all losses within 60 days of receiving proof of loss according to the loss payment condition. (p. 85)

#111. **c) Up to 26 weeks of benefits during 52 consecutive calendar weeks of one period of disability.**

The New York Disability Benefits Law is nonoccupational. It provides disability income benefits for nonoccupational injuries or diseases preventing employees from earning a living. The law only provides income benefits and does not provide medical or other benefits. The Workers Compensation Board of New York administers this law. (pp. 219-221)

#112. **b) 15 days**

A licensee in NY must submit the requested information to the Superintendent within 15 days. (p. 8)

#113. **d) Pay dividends to the policy owner**

Participating insurance policies will pay dividends to the policy owner based on actual mortality cost, interest earned, and standard costs. (p. 26)

#114. **d) $500**

Business property away from the premises is covered for up to $500 under Coverage C of a farm policy. (p. 183)

#115. **a) Personal and advertising injury liability**

Personal injury and advertising injury liability in a CGL policy covers suits arising from slander and libel. (pp. 143, 145-146)

#116. **b) Liberalization clause**

The liberalization clause states that if a policy is broadened with no added premium, the expanded coverage will automatically apply to every policy of the same type. (pp. 48, 67, 90)

#117. **d) Homeowners**

The businessowners policy (BOP) is most similar in structure to the personal lines homeowners policy. Both require the policy to provide property and liability insurance in a single policy. (p. 191)

#118. **a) A driver's own vehicle**

A prearranged ride does not include using a taxi, a vanpool van, or a limousine for transportation. (p. 126)

#119. **a) Adhesion.**

Only the insurance company prepares a contract of adhesion; the insured's option is to accept or reject the policy as it is written. (p. 31)

#120. **b) Sudden and accidental rupture of a heating system**

Off-premises power failure, flood, and war are excluded from all dwelling and homeowners policies. (pp. 64, 83-84)

#121. **b) 30 days**

The insurance provider has 30 days to notify the insured that it has chosen to repair or replace the covered property. (p. 67)

#122. **c) Handling insurance carrier funds in a trust capacity.**

A producer's fiduciary responsibility includes handling insurance company funds in a trust capacity. (pp. 10, 30)

#123. **c) The amount of coverage on a dwelling.**

Loss of use is typically limited to a percentage of the overall dwelling or personal property coverage (when using the HO-4 and HO-6 forms). (pp. 61, 79)

#124. **b) Up to $1,000 per occurrence**

Section II – Loss Assessment Coverage of the HO policy applies to assessments against the insured by a condominium association or other cooperative body of property owners. Coverage is limited to $1,000, but an increased limit of coverage is available by endorsement. (p. 87)

#125. **c) They pay defense costs even after reaching the aggregate limit.**

Once the aggregate has been reached, the insurance provider will not be responsible for paying further claims. In other words, the insurance provider no longer pays to defend. (p. 147)

#126. **b) Renewal dates**

An Insuring Agreement sets forth the obligation of the insurer to provide the insurance coverages as specified in the policy. The insuring agreement lists effective and renewal dates, the parties to the contract, the description of coverage provided, and perils. Answers A, C, and D are found in the Declarations. (p. 42)

#127. **b) Bid bond**

The obligee typically requires a bid bond when construction projects are granted based on the lowest bid. This type of bond promises that if the contractor is awarded the contract, they will accept it. (p. 232)

#128. **c) 30 days.**

The insurance company can cancel a dwelling policy anytime for fraud. An advance notice of 30 days is required before the proposed cancellation. (p. 68)

#129. **d) It is imposed on defendants involved in hazardous activities.**

Strict liability is generally applied in product liability cases. The business is liable for defective products, irrespective of fault or negligence. (p. 40)

#130. **b) To broaden the definition of a covered auto to include various motorized vehicles.**

A PAP's miscellaneous type vehicle endorsement expands the definition of a covered auto. This expanded definition includes motorized vehicles like motor homes, motorcycles, dune buggies, golf carts, and other similar vehicles. (p. 107)

#131. **b) Insureds cannot be randomly chosen**

Granting insurance cannot be mandatory. Randomly choosing insureds will help the insurance carrier to have a reasonable proportion of good risks to poor risks. Answers A, C, and D are true. (p. 25)

#132. **b) A joint ownership coverage endorsement is added to the PAP.**

The joint ownership coverage endorsement provides coverage for individuals residing in the same household besides spouses or other family members. (p. 107)

#133. **d) It helps employers with low claims experience to get lower premiums**

Group health is subject to experience rating, where the group's experience determines the premiums. Experience rating assists employers with low claims experience because they obtain lower premiums. (pp. 38, 256-257)

#134. **d) 72 hours**

Under business income coverage, the period of restoration starts 72 hours after the direct loss or immediately for extra expense coverage. It ends when the property has been repaired or business operations are resumed. (p. 159)

#135. **d) Up to $500 per day for lost earnings and $2,000 for the cost of bail bonds.**

Supplementary payments in the CGL policy will only cover $250 for lost earnings and $250 for the cost of bonds. (p. 147)

#136. **c) Pay to defend the policy owner in the suit because liability coverage includes a duty-to-defend provision**

Liability coverage includes a promise to defend the insured in any suit involving the type of liability insured under the coverage. (p. 201)

#137. **c) 45 days**

When an insurer decides not to renew a dwelling policy, as allowed by New York law, such an insurer must notify the insured at least 45 days before the policy's expiration date. (p. 68)

#138. **c) One year**

The additional monthly benefit rider stipulates that the insurance provider will pay benefits comparable to what Social Security would pay. After a year, the insurer ends the benefit and assumes that Social Security will begin benefit payments. (p. 250)

#139. **d) Functional replacement cost**

Functional replacement cost is replacing the damaged property with more modern and less expensive construction or equipment. (p. 42)

#140. **a) The insured's camera if it is stolen while on vacation.**

Coverage C under the HO policy is provided on a worldwide basis. (pp. 77-79)

#141. **c) Reinsurance System.**

Reinsurance is a method used by insurance companies to protect against catastrophic losses. Answers A, B, and D are marketing arrangements. (pp. 28-29)

#142. **d) Be at least 21 years old**

The Insurance Code states that the minimum age for obtaining an insurance license is 18. (p. 2)

#143. **d) Direct response marketing**

A direct response marketing system virtually bypasses the insurance producer. Business is conducted through the mail, over the phone, or online. This approach is a perfectly legal approach to selling insurance. It is optional for the insured to sign any documents for coverage to go into effect. (p. 28)

#144. **d) 120 days.**

Once it has been determined that an individual is liable for a civil penalty, that determination can be entered 120 days later as a judgment and enforced without court proceedings. (p. 11)

#145. **b) General**

General compensatory damages are intangible elements that cannot be expressly measured in dollars. (pp. 39-40)

#146. **b) Negligence that causes an injury.**

Proximate cause is the reasonably foreseeable act or event that causes injury or damage. Negligence can often be the proximate cause of the damage; without it, the accident would not have occurred. (pp. 38-39)

#147. **c) Rescission.**

Rescission is when a company wants to cancel a policy and returns funds paid. (p. 32)

#148. **d) Rating the financial strength of insurance carriers**

Reports generated by AM Best and Standard & Poor's help prospective consumers judge the financial security of various insurance carriers. (p. 28)

#149. **b) Prepaid plan.**

Under a prepaid plan, the health care providers are paid for services in advance. Payment is made whether or not any services are delivered. The amount paid to the provider is based on the expected annual cost determined by the provider. (p. 250)

#150. **d) Physicians, surgeons, and dentists malpractice**

The physicians, surgeons, and dentists malpractice form covers liability arising from malpractice, error, or mistakes made in rendering or failing to render professional medical services. (p. 228)

INDEX

"Write Your Own" vs. Direct, 233
"You," "Your," and "We", 76

A

Abandonment, 47
Absolute Liability, 40
Accidental Discharge or Overflow of Water or Steam, 57
Accounts Receivable, 171
Actual Cash Value (ACV), 41, 84
Actual Loss or Damage, 39
Additional Coverages, 86
Additional Insureds, 44
Additional Monthly Benefit (AMB), 250
Additional or Supplementary Coverage, 43
Additionally (Newly) Acquired Property, 172
Adjusters, 4
Admitted vs. Non-Admitted Insurers, 27
Adverse Selection, 25
Affidavit, 231
Affordable Care Act, 263
Agents, 4
Agents and General Rules of Agency, 29
Aggregate Limit, 46
Agreed Value, 42
Agreement (Offer and Acceptance), 30
Aiding an Unauthorized Insurer, 12
Aircraft, 56
Aleatory Contract, 31
Alien Insurer, 28
Amendment of Policy Provisions - New York, 106
An Organization Other Than a Partnership, Joint Venture, or LLC, 148
Any Occupation, 248
Any Provider vs. Limited Choice of Providers, 251
Apparent Authority, 30
Appeal rights, 265
Appointment of Agent, 9
Appraisal, 66, 85
Appropriateness of Recommended Purchase or Replacement, 262
Assignment, 47, 90
Assumed Names, 6
Assumption of Risk, 39
Authority and Powers of Agents, 29
Auto, 108, 144
Auto ID Cards, 126
Auto Medical Payments Coverage, 123
Auto Symbols Used with Business Auto Coverage Form, 110
Average Weekly Wage, 220
Avoidance, 24

B

Bailee Insurance, 169
Banking Premises, 179
Bankruptcy of an Insured, 89
Basic Dwelling Form DP-1, 55
Basic Extended Reporting Period, 150
Basic Form, 163
Basic Hospital, Basic Medical, Basic Surgical, 251
Basic Total Disability Plan, 249
Basic Types of Construction, 41
Benchmark Plans, 268
Benefit Period, 249
Benefit Schedule vs. Usual, Customary, and Reasonable Charges, 251
Bid Bonds, 232
Binding Authority, 127
Blanket Insurance, 41
Boating Equipment, 235
Bodily Injury, 75, 98, 142
Bodily Injury Only, 132
Breakage of Glass, 58, 63
Broad Form, 164
Broad Form (DP-2), 57
Broad Theft Coverage, 69
Brokers, 4
Builders Risk, 157
Building Additions and Alterations, 81
Building and Personal Property Form, 153
Burglary, 180
Business, 76
Business Auto, 110
  Section I – Covered Autos, 110
  Section II – Liability Coverage, 111
  Section III – Physical Damage Coverage, 112
  Section IV – Conditions, 113
Business Entities, 5
Business Income, 158
Business Interruption, 160
Business Liability, 88, 199
Business Personal Property (BPP) Coverage, 153
Businessowners Policy (BOP), 190

C

Cancellation, 44, 68
Cancellation and Nonrenewal, 90, 133
Carrier, 220
Causes of Loss (Perils), 40
Causes of Loss Forms, 163
Cease and Desist Order, 11
Certificate of Authority, 8
Certificate of Coverage, 256
Certificate of Insurance, 49
Change of Address, 6
Change of Beneficiary, 245
Change of Occupation, 245
Characteristics of Group Insurance, 256
Characteristics of Group Plans, 68
Characteristics of Insurance Contracts, 31
Chief Information Security Officer (CISO), 16

Choice of Repair Shop, 134
Civil Authority, 159
Claim Information, 151
Claims Expense, 86
Claims Procedures, 244
Claims Reporting Requirements, 212
Claims-Made, 149
Class Rating, 37
Coastal Market Assistance Program (C-MAP), 238
Coinsurance, 45
Coinsurance Penalties, 45
Collapse, 58, 63, 80
Collision, 99
Collision Coverage and Other Than Collision Coverage, 99
Combined Single, 46
Commercial Articles, 172
Commercial Auto, 107
Commercial Auto Coverage Forms, 109
Commercial Carrier Regulations, 124
Commercial Crime, 178
Commercial Floater, 170
Commercial General Liability (CGL) Coverage Forms, 142
Commercial Inland Marine, 169
Commercial Property, 152
Commercial Property Conditions, 166
Commissions and Compensation, 10
Common Policy Provisions, 43
Company Regulation, 8
Comparative Negligence, 39
Compensatory Damages, 40
Competent Parties, 31
Components, 38
Comprehensive Motor Vehicle Insurance Reparations Act (PIP), 127
Compulsory vs. Elective, 210
Computer Fraud, 182
Concealment, 32
Concealment or Fraud, 65
Conditional Contract, 31, 32
Conditions, 43
Conditions Form, 169
Condominium (Commercial) Unit-Owners, 157
Condominium Associations, 156
Conformity with State Statutes, 246
Consequential Losses, 41
Consideration, 30
Consideration Clause, 247
Consultants, 4

Consumer Privacy Regulation, 15
Consumer Reports, 18
Continuing Education, 6
Contract of Adhesion, 31
Contractors Equipment Floater, 172
Contracts, 30
Contributory Negligence, 39
Controlled Business, 10
Coordination with Social Insurance and Workers Compensation Benefits, 249
Copayments, 255
Core Benefits, 260
Cost-sharing under Group Health Plans, 265
Coverage for Children of the Insured, 265
Coverage Forms – Perils Insured Against, 55
Coverage Territory, 143
Coverage Trigger, 150
Covered Autos, 108
Covered Entity, 16
Covered Injuries, 211
Covered Watercraft, 235
Credit Card, Electronic Funds Transfer Card or Access Device, Counterfeit Money and Forgery, 80
Customer's Auto, 117
Cyber Liability and Data Breach, 230
Cyber Regulation, 16
Cybersecurity Event, 16
Cybersecurity Program, 16

D

Damage by Burglars, 57
Damage to the Property of Others, 87
Death, 67, 90
Debris Removal, 62, 79
Declarations, 42
Deductible, 65
Deductibles, 45
Defamation of an Insurer, 14
Defenses Against Negligence, 39
Definitions, 42
Dependent Child Age Limit, 257
Direct Loss, 40
Directors and Officers Liability, 228
Disability, 220
Disability Income and Related Insurance, 247
Disciplinary Actions, 11
Disclosure (No Guaranty Fund), 231

Disclosure of Producer Compensation, 15
Disclosure Statement, 262
Discover or Discovered, 179
Discovery, 178
Discovery and Loss Sustained Forms, 178
Domestic Insurer, 27
Drive Other Car - Broadened Coverage for Named Individuals, 124
Duties After an Occurrence, 89
Duties After Loss, 47, 65
Duties In the Event of an Accident, Claim, or Suit, 162
Duties of an Injured Person – Coverage F (Medical Payments to Others), 89
Duty to Defend, 48
Dwelling Under Construction, 68

E

Earned Premium, 44
Earth Movement, 64
Earthquake, 91, 167
Electronic Data Processing, 172
Elements of a Legal Contract, 30
Elements of Insurable Risks, 25
Elimination Period, 249
Emergency Care, 265
Employee, 143, 179, 220
Employee Theft, 180
Employees as Insureds, 124
Employer, 220
Employer Penalties, 267
Employment Covered, 210, 220
Employment Practices Liability, 229
Endorsement for Motor Carrier Policies of Insurance for Public Liability, 125
Endorsements, 43
Entire Contract; Changes, 244
Environmental Liability, 229
Equipment Breakdown Coverage Form, 175
Equipment Dealers, 172
Errors and Omissions, 228
Essential benefits, 264
Essential Health Benefits, 265
Estimation of Claims, 68
Estimation of Claims (NY), 85
Estoppel, 33
Examination of Books and Records, 7
Excess (Follow Form), 226
Excess Lines, 230
Exchanges, 266
Exclusions, 43

Exclusive Remedy, 210
Exemption from Licensing, 3
Expected or Intended Injury, 88
Expense-Incurred Basis, 246
Experience Modification Factor, 218
Experience Rating, 38
Experience Rating vs. Community Rating, 256
Explosion, 56
Export List, 231
Exposure, 24
Express Authority, 29
Extended Business Income, 159
Extended Coverage Perils, 55
Extended Reporting Period - Claims-Made Form, 150
Extended Reporting Period (ERP), 150
Extra Expense, 160

F

Fair Credit Reporting Act, 17
Falling Objects, 57
False Advertising, 13
False Statements Including 1033 Waiver, 18
Family Member, 98
Farm Coverage, 182
Farm Liability Coverage Form, 185
Farm Property Coverage Form, 183
Federal Employers Liability Act (FELA), 213
Federal Patient Protection and Affordable Care Act (PPACA), 263
Federal Regulation, 17
Federal Workers Compensation Laws, 213
Fee-for-Service Basis vs. Prepaid Basis, 250
Fiduciary, 30
Fiduciary Liability, 228
Fiduciary Responsibility, 10
Filed Form, 170
Financial Status (Independent Rating Services), 28
Fire Department Service Charge, 63, 80
Fire Legal Liability, 144
Fire or Lightning and Internal Explosion, 55
First Aid to Others, 87
First Named Insured, 44
First Named Insured Provisions, 47
Flat-Rate Cancellation, 44
Flood Coverage, 168
Flood Definition, 234

Foreign Coverage Endorsement, 217
Foreign Insurers, 28
Forgery or Alteration, 181
Fraternal Benefit Society, 26
Fraud, 18, 32
Fraud Prevention Plans and Special Investigations Units, 14
Freezing, 58
Function, 36
Functional Replacement Cost, 42
Funds, 179
Funds Transfer Fraud, 182

G

Garage, 114
  Section I – Covered Autos, 114
  Section II – Liability Coverage, 115
  Section III – Garagekeepers, 117
  Section IV – Physical Damage, 118
  Section V – Garage Conditions, 119
General Damages, 40
General Liability, 142
Geographic Redlining, 36
Glass or Safety Glazing Material, 81
Governmental Action, 64
Grace Period, 244
Grave Markers, 81
Group Contract, 256
Group Health and Blanket Insurance, 256
Group Underwriting Requirements, 69
Guaranteed Issue, 259, 265
Guaranteed Renewability, 265
Guaranteed Renewable, 247
Guaranty Association, 9

H

Hazards, 24
Health Maintenance Organizations (HMOs), 254
Health Status (No Discrimination), 264
Hearings, 11
HIPAA Requirements, 258
Hired Auto and Non-owned Auto Liability, 124, 204
HO-8 (Modified Coverage Form), 93
Home Business, 92
Home State, 2
Homogeneous, 24

Hospital Services and Emergency Care, 255

I

Identity Fraud Expense, 91
Identity Theft, 182
Illegal Occupation, 246
Illness, 249
Immunity, 14
Implied authority, 29
Improvements, Alterations, and Additions, 62
Inability to Perform Duties, 248
Income Benefits (Monthly Indemnity), 249
Indemnity, 32
Indemnity Plan Features, 256
Independent Adjuster, 4
Independent and Subcontractors, 211
Individual (Sole Proprietor), 147
Individual Disability Income Insurance, 248
Individual Health Insurance Policy General Provisions, 244
Individual Mandate, 267
Individual Named Insured, 124
Information System, 16
Injury, 249
Inside the premises (Robbery or Safe Burglary of Other Property), 181
Inside the Premises (Theft of Money and Securities), 181
Installations Floater, 173
Insurable Interest, 36
Insurable Interest and Limit of Insurance, 65
Insurance, 24
Insurance Frauds Bureau, 14
Insurance Frauds Prevention Act, 14
Insurance Information and Enforcement System (IIES) Notification to DMV, 127
Insurance Risk Score (Credit Scoring), 37
Insurance Services Office (ISO), viii
Insured, 43, 75
Insured Contract, 109, 151, 202
Insured Duties After a Loss, 84
Insured Location, 75
Insured Perils, 92
Insured Product, 202
Insureds – Named, First, Additional, 43
Insureds vs. Subscribers and Participants, 251

Insurer Provisions, 48
Insurer's Option to Repair or Replace, 67
Insurers, 26
Insuring Agreement, 42, 100
Insuring Clause, 247
Intentional Loss, 64
Internal Explosion, 56
Intervening Cause, 39
Intoxicants and Narcotics, 246
Investigative Consumer Reports, 18

J

Jewelers Block, 173
Job Classification – Payroll and Rates, 218
Joint Ownership Coverage, 107
Judgment rating, 37

L

Labor and Materials Bonds, 232
Landlord's Furnishings, 81
Law of Agency, 29
Law of Large Numbers, 26
Law or Ordinance, 81
Lawns, Trees, Shrubs, and Plants, 58
Laws, 125
Leased Worker, 143
Legal Actions, 245
Legal Concepts and Interpretations Affecting Contracts, 32
Legal Duty, 38
Legal Liability, 161
Legal Purpose, 31
Lessor - Additional Insured and Loss Payee, 123
Liability Coverage, 108
Liberalization, 48, 67
Liberalization Clause, 90
License and Permit Bonds, 232
License Display, 10
Licensee Regulation, 10
Licensing, 2
Licensing Examination Exemptions, 2
Licensing Requirements, 230
Lifetime and Annual Limits, 265
Limit of Liability, 89
Limited Choice of Providers, 255
Limited Liability Company (LLC), 148
Limited Service Area, 255
Limits of Liability, 46
Limits of Liability and Other Insurance, 103

Liquor Liability, 229
Lloyd's Associations, 27
Loss, 24
Loss Assessment, 80
Loss Assessment Coverage, 87
Loss Costs, 38
Loss Payable Clause, 49, 85
Loss Payment, 67, 85
Loss Ratio, 36
Loss Settlement, 66, 84
Loss Settlement Options, 48
Loss Sustained, 179
Loss to a Pair or Set, 66
Loss Valuation, 41

M

Maintenance and Duration, 5
Major Medical Insurance (Indemnity Plans), 253
Mandatory Coverage, 132
Mandatory Inspection Requirements for Private Passenger Automobiles, 133
Market Value, 42
Marketing (Distribution) Systems, 28
Medical Expense Insurance, 251
Medical Expenses, 199
Medical Plan Concepts, 250
Medicare Supplements, 259
Merit Rating, 38
Metal Levels, 266
Methods of Handling Risk, 24
Midi Tail, 151
Mini Tail, 151
Miscellaneous Hospital Expenses, 252
Miscellaneous Type Vehicles, 107
Misrepresentation, 13
Misstatement of Age, 245
Mobile Equipment, 108, 123, 143
Modified Comparative Negligence, 39
Money, 179
Money Orders and Counterfeit Paper Currency, 182
Monopolistic vs. Competitive, 210
Moral Hazards, 24
Morale Hazards, 24
Mortgage Holders Clause, 85
Motor Carrier, 122
Motor Truck Cargo Forms, 175
Motor Vehicle Accident Indemnification Corporation Act, 129
Motor Vehicle Liability, 87
Multi-Factor Authentication, 16
Mutual Companies, 26

N

Named Insured, 44
Named Nonowner, 107
Named Peril, 40
National Association of Registered Agents and Brokers (NARAB) Reform Act, 50
National Flood Insurance Program (NFIP), 232
Nationwide Marine Definition, 169
Neglect, 64
Negligence, 38
Negotiate, 2
New York Automobile Insurance Plan (Assigned Risk), 127
New York Credit Card Coverage, 82
New York Mandated Benefits and Offers (Individual/Group), 257
New York Motor Vehicle Financial Responsibility Law, 125
New York Property Insurance Underwriting Association, 238
New York Regulations and Required Provisions, 261
New York State Disability Benefits Law, 219
New York State Insurance Fund, 219
New York Workers Compensation Law, 210
Newborn Child Coverage, 257
Newly Acquired Auto, 99
No Benefit to the Bailee, 49
Noncancelable, 247
Non-Owned Autos, 104
Non-Owned Watercraft, 235
Nonpublic Information, 16
Nonrenewal, 44, 68
Nonresident, 5
Nonstacking, 132
Notice Regarding Replacement, 262
Nuclear Hazard, 64, 67
Numbers, Dollars, Days, and Dates, 19

O

OBEL (Optional Basic Economic Loss), 129
Obligee, 232
Occupational Disease, 211
Occupational vs. Nonoccupational Coverage, 250
Occupying, 100
Occurrence, 142, 149, 179
Occurrence vs. Claims Made, 149
Open Enrollment, 259

Open Peril, 40
Operations, 159
Optional Limits – Transportation Expenses, 104
Ordinance or Law, 46, 63, 64
Ordinance or Law Coverage, 168
Other Coverages, 62
Other Insurance, 45
Other Insurance – Coverage E (Personal Liability), 90
Other Insurance and Service Agreement, 85
Other Insurance in this Insurer, 245
Other Policies - Watercraft, 235
Other Property, 179
Other Structures, 62
Other-Than-Collision, 99
Out of State Coverage, 101
Outboard Motor, 235
Outside the Premises (Theft of Money and Securities), 181
Own Occupation, 248
Owners and Contractors Protective Liability (OCP), 152

P

Paid Family Leave, 221
P
Partial Premium Refund, 218
Participation (Dividend) Plans, 218
Partnership or Joint Venture, 147
Payment of Claim – Coverage F (Medical Payments to Others), 89
Penetration Testing, 16
Per Occurrence (Accident), 46
Per Person, 46
Per Project, Per Location, 46
Performance Bonds, 232
Perils, 24
Period of Restoration, 159
Permitted Compensation Arrangements, 262
Personal Auto Policy, 98
Personal Contract, 31
Personal Injury – New York, 93
Personal Property – Replacement Cost, 92
Personal Property of Others, 153
Personal Use of Non-owned Auto Endorsements, 123
Personal Watercraft, 235
Physical Damage Coverage, 108
Physical Hazards, 24
Plants, Shrubs, Trees, and Lawns, 63
Point of Service (POS) Plans, 255

Policy Extensions for Disabled Children, 257
Policy Period, 44, 90
Policy Structure, 42
Policy Territory, 44
Power Failure, 64
Pre-Existing Conditions, 265
Preferred Provider Organizations (PPOs), 255
Premises, 179
Premises and Operations, 143, 151
Premium Computation, 218
Premium Discount, 218
Prepaid Basis, 255
Preventive Benefits, 265
Preventive Care Services, 254
Primary and Excess, 46
Primary Care Physician (PCP), 255
Primary Care Physician Referral, 256
Primary Care Physician vs. Referral (Specialty) Physician, 255
Principal, 231
Principles and Concepts, 36
Privacy Protection, 259
Private Carriers, 119
Private Passenger Type, 120
Private vs. Government Insurers, 27
Pro Rata, 46
Producer, 2
Producer Compensation Transparency, 15
Products and Completed Operations, 143, 151
Professional Liability, 228
Professionalism, 30
Property Damage, 76, 98, 143
Property Removed, 63, 80
Protected Health Information (PHI), 259
Protective Safeguards, 168
Provisions Affecting Cost to Insureds, 253, 254
Proximate Cause, 38
Proximate Cause of Loss, 40
Public Adjuster, 5
Punitive Damages, 40
Pure Comparative Negligence, 39
Pure Risk, 24

Q

Qualifying for Disability Benefits, 247

R

Rates, 37

Reasonable Repairs, 63, 80
Rebating, 14
Recovered Property, 67
Recurrent Disability, 249
Reduction, 25
Referral (Specialty) Physician, 255
Refuse to Issue a License, 3
Reinstatement, 244
Reinsurance, 28
Relation of Earnings to Insurance, 246
Renewability, 259, 263
Renewability Clause, 247
Renewal, 5
Rental Value and Additional Living Expense, 62
Rental Vehicle Coverage - New York, 107
Replacement, 262
Replacement Cost, 41, 85
Reporting, 10
Reporting of Actions, 6
Representations and Misrepresentations, 32
Required Limits of Liability, 125
Required Proof of Insurance, 125
Required Provisions, 244
Rescission, 32
Residence Employee, 76
Residence Premises, 76
Residential Condominium Building Association Policy, 234
Responsibilities to the Applicant and Insured, 30
Resumption of Operations, 159
Retention, 25
Retroactive Date, 150
Retrospective Rating, 38
Right to Examine (Free Look), 247
Riot or Civil Commotion, 56
Risk, 24
Risk Management Key Terms, 24
Risk Purchasing Group, 29
Risk Retention Group (RRG), 29
Robbery, 180

S

Safe Burglary, 180
Salvage, 48
Schedule Rating, 37
Scheduled Personal Property, 91
Section 1034: Civil Penalties and Injunctions, 19
Securities, 179
Self-Insured Employers and Employer Groups, 219
Self-Insured Retention (SIR), 45, 226

Sell, 2
Severability of Insurance, 89
Sharing, 25
Sharing Commissions, 10
Signs, 174
Single Contract (Package), 140
Single Coverage (Monoline), 140
Smoke, 56
Social Insurance Supplement (SIS), 250
Solicit, 2
Solvency, 8
Special Damages, 40
Special Form, 165
Special Form (DP-3), 58
Special Provisions – New York, 91
Specific Conditions – New York, 67
Specific Insurance, 41
Specified Coverages vs. Comprehensive Care, 250
Speculative Risk, 24
Split Limits, 46, 101
Spoilage, 167
Standard Mortgage Clause, 48
Standard of Care, 38
Standardized Medicare Supplement Plans, 260
Standards for Marketing, 261
State Fund, 220
State Regulation, 6
Stated Amount, 42
Statute of Limitations, 39
Stock Companies, 26
Strict Liability, 40
Sublimit, 46
Subrogation, 48, 90
Sudden and Accidental Bulging, Burning, Cracking or Tearing Apart, 57
Sudden and Accidental Damage from Artificially Generated Electrical Current, 58
Suit Against the Insurer, 67, 90
Superintendent's General Duties and Powers, 6
Supplemental Spousal Liability, 134
Supplementary Payments, 100, 147
Supplementary Uninsured and Underinsured Motorist Coverage, 132
Surety, 232
Surety Bonds, 231
Suspension, 159
Suspension, Revocation, and Nonrenewal, 11

T

Tangible Property, 179
Temporary, 5
Temporary Worker, 143
Termination of Agent Appointment, 9
Termination Responsibilities of Producer, 10
Terrorism, 49
Terrorism Risk Insurance Act of 2002, 49
Terrorism Risk Insurance Program Reauthorization Act of 2015, 50
The Jones Act, 214
The Motor Carrier Act of 1980, 125
Theft, 180
Third-Party Provisions, 48
Time Element Coverage, 159
Time Limit on Certain Defenses, 244
Total Cost Form, 231
Total Disability, 249
Towing and Labor Costs, 107
Trailer, 99
Trailer Interchange Coverage, 123
Transfer, 25
Transportation Network Companies (Ride-Sharing), 126
Trees, Shrubs, and Other Plants, 80
Trigger, 150
Truckers, 119
Truckers Coverage Form, 119
Trust, 148
Types of Bonds, 232
Types of Insurers, 26
Types of Licensees, 4
Types of Plan Sponsors, 68

U

U.S. Longshore and Harbor Workers Compensation Act, 213
Umbrella (Stand-Alone), 226
Umbrella and Excess Liability, 226
Underlying Policy (Primary Liability Policy), 226
Underwriting, 36
Unfair and Prohibited Practices, 13
Unfair Claims Settlement Practices, 9
Unfair Discrimination, 14
Unfiled Form, 170
Unilateral Contract, 31
Uninsured and Underinsured Motorist, 131
Uninsured Motorist (UM), 103
Unlawful Insurance Fraud, 18
Unoccupancy, 47
Unpaid Premium, 246
Utmost Good Faith, 32

V

Vacancy, 47
Valuable Papers and Records, 174
Vandalism or Malicious Mischief (VMM), 56
Vehicles, 56
Vicarious Liability, 40
Volcanic Eruption, 56
Volcanic Eruption Period, 85
Volcanic Eruptions, 67
Voluntary Compensation, 217
Volunteer Firefighters and Ambulance Workers Endorsements, 217

W

Wages, 220
Waiver, 33
Waiver of Premium, 249
Waiver of Subrogation, 217
Waiver or Change of Policy Provisions, 90
War, 64
Warranties, 32
Water Back-Up and Sump Discharge or Overflow – New York, 93
Water Damage, 64
Watercraft Liability, 87
Watercraft Trailer, 235
Weight of Snow, Sleet, or Ice, 57
Who is an Insured, 100
Windstorm or Hail, 56
Workers Compensation – Residence Employees – New York, 93
Workers Compensation and Employers Liability Insurance, 214
Workers Compensation Laws, 210
Worldwide Coverage, 62

Y

You and Your, 98
Your Covered Auto, 98
Your Product, 143
Your Work, 143

A NOTE FROM LELAND

What did you think of *New York Property and Casualty Insurance License Exam Prep*?

First of all, thank you for purchasing this study guide. I know you could have picked any resource to help prepare for your Property and Casualty exam, but you chose this book, and I am incredibly grateful.

I hope that it added value and provided the confidence to pass the exam on your first attempt. If you feel this book adequately prepared you and helped you pass the exam, I'd like to hear from you. I hope you can take some time to post a review on Amazon and include a screenshot of your passing score. Your feedback and support will help this author improve this book and his writing craft for future projects.

Thank you again, and I wish you all the best in your future success!

Leland Chant

Made in United States
North Haven, CT
27 January 2025